MAY 1 1 2012

Murder Made in Italy

Trentino-Alto Adige

Friuli-Venezia Guilia

Valle d'Aosta

Lombardy

Veneto

Piedmont

Emilia-Romagna

Liguria

Marche

Tuscany

Umbria

Lazio

Abruzzo

Molise

Campania

Puglia

Basilicata

Sardinia

Calabria

Sicily

Murder Made in Italy

Homicide, Media, and
Contemporary Italian Culture

ELLEN NERENBERG

INDIANA UNIVERSITY PRESS
Bloomington & Indianapolis

This book is a publication of

Indiana University Press
601 North Morton Street
Bloomington, Indiana
47404-3797 USA

iupress.indiana.edu

Telephone orders 800-842-6796
Fax orders 812-855-7931

Manufactured in the United States
of America

Cataloging information is available
from the Library of Congress.
ISBN 978-0-253-35625-3 cloth
ISBN 978-0-253-22309-8 paper

1 2 3 4 5 16 15 14 13 12

For my tireless companions of the mind,
Elizabeth Jones and Anthony Valerio

Vengeance is practiced. . . . Real murders take place as part of it, but also (insofar as they can be distinguished) cultural murders, murders of minds, emotions, and intelligence.

LUCE IRIGARAY, "WOMEN, THE SACRED, AND MONEY"

Periodically, some trial, and not necessarily fictitious like the one in Camus's *The Outsider,* comes to remind you that the Law is always prepared to lend you a spare brain in order to condemn you without remorse, and that, like Corneille, it depicts you as you should be, not as you are.

ROLAND BARTHES, *MYTHOLOGIES*

CONTENTS

PREFACE

In some ways, *Murder Made in Italy* is two books in one. One of these—not the "first" in terms of priority—is a narrative destined for an audience of readers who are interested in media studies, crime studies, and studies in popular culture and whose interest in contemporary Italy is not necessarily characterized by great familiarity with Italian culture or the Italian justice system. The other book—but not the "second"—seeks to contribute to an evolving discussion in contemporary Italian cultural studies staged largely among scholars of Italian studies. All readers, I imagine, will read parts of the narrative. At the same time, I doubt all readers will turn to the notes. Neither of the books stands independent from the other, and my goal has been to bridge, not to shore up, the differences between them. Achieving the required balance between the two texts has constituted one of my toughest challenges as a scholar and one that has brought some of the most satisfying rewards.

In her study on sex, gender, and science published in 2000, *Sexing the Body*, Anne Fausto-Sterling made shrewd choices concerning how much of her technical discussion to leave in the text and what to present in the extensive and finely detailed notes. I have adopted a similar strategy. In the main, Fausto-Sterling's choices concerned the sort and amount of scientific discourse to maintain in the text. The decisions I made, on the other hand, concerned the presence of critical theory and theoreticians and how much to rely on readers' knowledge of, say, Italian regional geography, anthropology, and cultural history. I hope to have made wise choices between the sometimes competing needs of different readerships.

Given the nature of the academy, one's progress and success (tenure, retention, promotion) depend on advancing academic arguments and furthering knowledge on a subject, sometimes within a very narrow subfield. One consequence of this is scholarship that is not accessible to the "lay" reader. In fact, one sometimes hears opinions about how making scholarly research "accessible" amounts to diluting it or, said with less politesse, "dumbing it down." Even worse than saying that the book or essay is accessible is to assert that it is not research at all, but is, instead, journalism.

Yet, writing for a wider audience is an admirable goal. A colleague who works at the intersection of sexuality and textuality in medieval studies has repeatedly—and, to my mind, wisely—told me that one of the goals she sets for herself is to be able, at all times, to explain her research to her mother. I discovered that her mother, like my own, was a highly educated professional woman *d'un certain âge*. I am an Italianist, though my family is not Italian even at its farthest reaches, and my mother does not speak Italian. Remarkably nondenominational in her tastes and reading practices, my mother is the gamest, most fearless reader I know. Trained as a scientist and armed with curiosity and a wish for empirical evidence, she straddles the "humanistic divide," reading widely in history and literature. Her respect for interdisciplinary research is exemplary. I have been considering the thoughts of colleagues in Italian studies for the past twenty years, and, as a result, it has not been difficult to understand the shape *Murder Made in Italy* should take in their regard. It is for this reason that, as I sought to synthesize the "two books" that compose this study, my thoughts have gone in the direction of my mother's universal qualities as a reader.

A word about translations and stylistic conventions in the pages that follow. When Italian appears in the body of the text, an English translation will usually follow in close proximity. In cases where a citation from an Italian source is offered in English only, the original Italian will be found in the notes. For Italian films released in the United States, the italicized English title will follow the Italian in parentheses. If the Italian film in question was never released or distributed in the U.S., my own English translation of the title follows the Italian in parentheses but is not italicized or capitalized. Well-known films that have never featured translated titles (e.g., *La Dolce Vita*) will remain untranslated. Translations for books follow the same conventions.

ACKNOWLEDGMENTS

This book has been in the making for close to ten years, and many colleagues and students, both here and abroad, have offered help and advice along the way. I am sure those I name below do not constitute an exhaustive list.

I am grateful to the trustees of Wesleyan University for the continued support of my research in the form of regular sabbaticals. At Wesleyan I am indebted to the tireless staff of Olin Library's Interlibrary Loan office as well as to the Catharine and Thomas McMahon Fund for its support of my scholarship. Thanks are also owed to the Woodrow Wilson Foundation. At Indiana University Press, special thanks go to Jane Behnken, Angela Burton, and Sarah Wyatt Swanson.

Some of my research was conducted at the archives of the RAI, Italy's state television and radio network. Among those I would like to thank at the RAI Teche in Rome are Dottoressa Antonella Rita Roscilli, Dottoressa Francesca Cadin, and Andrea Persio. At the RAI Teche in Turin, thanks go to Dottoressa Susanna Gianandrea. My thanks also go out to Dottore Patrizio Rossano, of the Associazione TV e Minori in Rome. I extend my gratitude to Professors Stefano Baia Curioni and Antonio Calabrò at Bocconi University in Milan and to the students of their course, "Pubblica Opinione." Thanks to filmmaker Guido Chiesa for providing me with a copy of his documentary about the Novi Ligure murders and the eruption of xenophobia that followed, *Sono stati loro: 48 ore a Novi Ligure*.

Several colleagues have provided great insight into—and explanation of—the Italian justice system, criminal law procedure, and, in general, Italian law and order. These include Andrea Alberti and Roberto

Passini, attorneys at law; the Honorable Emilio Gironi; Ret. Col. Luciano Garofano, formerly of the Reparto investigazioni scientifiche; and Vittoria Calvi. For precise elucidation of police procedure, special thanks to Paola Madonna of Interpol.

A collection of colleagues deserves acknowledgment and thanks. These include Nadja Aksamija, Michael Armstrong-Roche, Giorgio Bertellini, Norma Bouchard, Suzanne Branciforte, Simona Ceci, Mark Chu, Christina Crosby, Andrew Curran, Jane Edwards, Ruth Glynn, B. Antonio Gonzàlez, Lina Insana, Natasha Korda, Marcia Landy, Typhaine Leservot, Stefania Lucamante, Nicoletta Marini-Maio, Sean McCann, Giuseppina Mecchia, Laurie Nussdorfer, Jill Morawski, John Paoletti, Christopher Parslow, Robin Pickering-Iazzi, Laura Rascaroli, Michael Roberts, Silvia Ross, David Schorr, and Daniela Viale. I am deeply grateful to Keala Jewell for the subtlety of her reading and her powerful critique. I owe a similar debt to Rebecca West. My thanks to Claire Potter for her rigorous interrogation of my thoughts on "moral panic." Among my students, I give special thanks to Benjamin Fels, Class of 2006. I also thank Erin Teske, Wesleyan Class of 2007, and Erin McCarthy, Class of 2010, for their help in preparing the manuscript. Massive thanks to Wesleyan's Allynn Wilkinson and John Wareham for technical support.

I owe tremendous, heartfelt thanks to my *corazzieri,* a special honor guard composed of Ruth Ben-Ghiat, Giancarlo Lombardi, and Jacqueline Reich. Their constructive criticism has made me work harder and enjoy it more. I am unable to fully express my gratitude for their intellectual generosity.

For their kindness and material goodwill, the Calvi-Zambon family in Milan, the Calvi-Fausti family in Bergamo, and the Annunizato-Madonna family in Rome. Stateside, no one could have been more supportive of this project than my family, those near and far. My mother, Elizabeth Jones Nerenberg Wilkinson, has offered support of titanic proportions, for which I thank her.

In memory of Carolyn Demcy, I offer special thanks: Angelo del fango, I wish you could have read this cover to cover.

It is to Anthony, who helped at every step and whose acumen I could not have done without, that I dedicate this book, every word on every page.

Murder Made in Italy

INTRODUCTION

Making a Killing in Contemporary Italy

THIS BOOK IS ABOUT MURDER—that is, three prominent murder cases in contemporary Italy. Part 1 examines the serial double homicides of couples in flagrante delicto that took place in Florence between 1975 and 1984 and were attributed to the "Monster," allegedly Pietro Pacciani, who was tried for these crimes in 1994.[1] Controversy surrounded the trial and the setting aside of his conviction: although Pacciani's alleged coconspirators were prosecuted, the murders remain unsolved. At the center of Part 2 lies the 2001 double homicide of Susy Cassini and her son, Gianluca De Nardo, in the small northern Italian town of Novi Ligure, for which Cassini's daughter, Erika, and Erika's boyfriend, Mauro "Omar" Fàvaro, were tried and convicted. Finally, Part 3 focuses on the case against Annamaria Franzoni, accused and convicted of the 2002 murder of her son, Samuele, in their Cogne home in the Valle D'Aosta, Italy's remote northwestern region adjacent to France. Signing a way toward further and future research, the epilogue presents a discussion of the case against U.S. citizen Amanda Knox for the murder of Meredith Kercher, her British roommate in Perugia, where they were both students of Italian. This case challenges the regional and national character of murder in Italy confirmed in each of the three parts.

Murder Made in Italy places these killings in the larger cultural, social, and political context of contemporary Italy, exploring the ways in which the issues each homicide raised were represented in both fictional and nonfictional narratives: press coverage, novels, short stories, television news broadcasts, talk shows, and film. The frenzied attention that surrounded each murder was fed by—and fed into—the recent expansion of the Italian mass media buoyed by Italian prime minister

Silvio Berlusconi's domination of it and by the increasing popularity of the true-crime story and other popular literary and film genres.[2] The enormous fascination these murders elicited presents an important index of changes in Italy and Italian culture in recent decades. Despite Italy's relatively low murder rate, these killings illuminate a widespread perception of Italian lawlessness and, more subtly, an anxious awareness of cultural change. Each of the murders became an occasion for moral panic, highlighting transformations in contemporary Italian culture and society, including challenges to the conventional Italian family, the myth of Italy as *il bel Paese,* notions of Italian cultural autonomy from "foreign" influences, a plummeting birthrate, ramped-up violence among Italian youth, and public safety generally. Significantly, none of these stories was set in the south, commonly considered the location of Italian lawlessness and violence. Rather, these homicides took place in those parts of the country that are typically regarded as orderly and law-abiding. At their core lay symbols that threatened the traditional Italian way of life—sexual predators, abusive and incompetent officials, feral children, foreign migrants, and predatory tourists.

To offer the thickest description possible of each case, *Murder Made in Italy* works between historical analysis of the event, the law, and cultural expressions, primarily contemporary Italian films and novels.[3] A brief look at one of these films, Roberto Benigni's *Il Mostro* (*The Monster,* 1994), the comic actor's send-up of the 1990s serial murder craze in Italy, offers an example of this book's method and approach.[4]

Il Mostro opens with a long shot of an apartment complex on a residential street. The low lighting is natural: it is night, with street lamps the only light source. A shrill scream pierces the street's quiet and signals a series of fast-paced changes. Natural sound gives way to the jolly sound track, Evan Lurie's rollicking and lighthearted circus theme, recalling some of the melodies Nino Rota composed for Federico Fellini's films, particularly *La Strada* and *Amarcord.* The long shot of the apartment house's exterior is then replaced by an interior medium shot that shows only the top half of elevator doors as they open and close repeatedly— some object beneath our line of vision is clearly obstructing them. As the opening credits begin to roll, the camera tracks back to show a body on the elevator floor: one of the inert female figure's legs sticking out from

FIGURE 0.1. *Il Mostro* (*The Monster*) (Roberto Benigni, 1994).

the elevator prevents the doors from closing. The other leg, splayed out on the elevator floor, sports a black stocking that has been ripped away. The dead woman's head lies outside the frame. (See Figure 0.1.) The message is clear. Violence has happened, deadly sexual violence against an anonymous woman.

The quick series of changes in camera distance, sound, and framing continues as it switches from live action to animation. Forging a sound bridge to the next scene, the circus-like music plays on, now accompanying an animated cityscape where buildings loom off-kilter, like something out of a grotesque, albeit comical, Expressionist painting. Down the side street comes a shadow. No menacing killer out of an Otto Dix painting appears. Rather, the shadow belongs to a dog—an English bull terrier if the patch on the eye is any indication—that begins comically and indiscriminately to eat everything in sight. Objects both animate and inanimate flee the strangely calm creature: a snail, a flower, a car, an umbrella, a cat that resembles Jerry of the Hanna-Barbera *Tom and Jerry* cartoon series. The message here, too, is clear: mistaken identity has produced unfounded, albeit comic terror, which has, in turn, produced a level of hysteria that obscures the source of disquiet.

The penultimate sequence of this opening returns to live action and cinematic realism that borders on the documentary. A continuous aerial shot shows apartment buildings in an unnamed city. The red-tiled roofs and the Italian voiceover locate the action somewhere in Italy, but in no more precise a locale than the apartment complex in the establishing shot. A police inspector (Michel Blanc) narrates the crimes of a serial rapist-murderer as the editing intercuts a crime scene with images of a press conference taking place inside police headquarters. Concluding, the inspector states that the murderer is *"un tipo comune, qualunque. Dietro quella maschera di banalità c'è un violentatore. C'è un vizioso . . . dietro quella maschera per bene . . . c'è un mostro"* (a normal man, any man. Behind that mask of normality lies a rapist. Behind that mask of respectability lies . . . a monster).[5]

The film's setup is nearly complete. A quick cut takes us from inside police headquarters to a nighttime garden party. A man, shot from behind, fusses over a flowering shrub. Behind him we see mannequins staged next to electric hedge trimmers and lawn mowers. Their stiff limbs recall the lifeless cadaver visible on the elevator floor from seconds before and add to a strange, highly artificial landscaping diorama. The man turns—it is Loris, the character played by Roberto Benigni—and the camera centers him in the frame. He is an image of balance, at the center of his universe—and ours, for as long as we watch this film. As before, the message is clear. Masks, deception, and public terror will play key roles, and Benigni's character will be at the clownish center of it all.

For decades before winning the 1998 Academy Award for best actor for his role in *La vita è bella* (*Life Is Beautiful*), Benigni had made his career in stand-up comedy and as a comic actor in films he both wrote and directed. Benigni's early work depends on the actor's recognizable Tuscan quotient or, as Italian film historian Lino Miccichè has termed it, his *effervescenza toscana*, or Tuscan effervescence.[6] This is especially so in a role like Cioni Mario in Giuseppe Bertolucci's *Berlinguer ti voglio bene* (*I Love You, Berlinguer*, 1977).[7] In this film, Benigni's unmistakable regional accent, combined with the film's setting in Prato, the neighboring town to the north of Florence, underscores the pro-Communist political context particular to Tuscany in the mid-1970s. In *Johnny Stecchino* (1991), which Benigni wrote and directed, the actor stars as Dante, whose marked and identifiable Tuscan speech sharply distinguishes him from Johnny Stecchino, his lookalike and a dangerous Sicilian mafioso.[8] *Johnny Stecchino* broke all box-office records in Italy, remaining the most commercially successful film in Italian cinematic history until Benigni's follow-up, *Il Mostro*.[9]

This film about a Tuscan ignoramus mistaken for a serial killer struck a familiar chord throughout Italy, where the media had made a killing turning Pietro Pacciani, the presumed "Monster" of Florence, into a household name. Although critical reception was only lukewarm, *Il Mostro* nevertheless enjoyed enormous commercial success.[10] Also significant was the timing of the film's release. Like many of his other films, Benigni scheduled the movie's premier for October, the month of his birthday (he was born October 27, 1952).[11] However, in the case of *Il Mostro,* an October 1994 release meant that the film premiered one month before the court was to hand down its verdict in the case against Pietro Pacciani.

The plot of Benigni's film is both the same as and different from the serial sex murders imputed to "Il Mostro di Firenze," or the "Monster" of Florence, and the state's case against Pacciani. The way *Il Mostro* satirizes public hysteria, the obsession with psychological profiling, and general police incompetence all echo aspects of the actual case. The film's lead investigator (Blanc) is obsessed with Americanized types of FBI profiling. He is a thinly disguised satirization of Inspector Ruggero Perugini, the actual case investigator, who had trained at the FBI's Behavioral Science Unit in Quantico before he was assigned to Florence's "Anti-Monster Squad." At the same time, *Il Mostro* pulls away from direct comparison with the "Monster" case. The near-absence of recognizable locales, for example, undermines the comparison with the actual serial murders committed on the bucolic outskirts of Florence. Geographically speaking, although Benigni's broad Tuscan accent could be said to help locate the film regionally within Italy, *Il Mostro* offers very few such definite markers.[12] Benigni's film was shot almost entirely on set. Its few exterior sequences show not the famously beautiful Florentine periphery but a forgettable condominium complex in an equally undistinguished exurban setting.

Yet if the film's setting is only distantly and doubtfully Tuscan, Benigni's bumbling Loris, the mistaken killer, slyly recalls certain characteristics of Pacciani, the accused. *Il Mostro* suggests that the ungainly Loris could no more have successfully orchestrated the film's serial crimes than Pacciani, the farmer from Mercatale (located some 25 kilometers south of Florence), could have acted as the sole perpetrator of the "Monster's" murders. In this regard, the inept Loris corresponds to the oafish and seemingly near-illiterate Pacciani. The "Monster's" series of complex crimes required tremendous organizational skill and patience and more than a little intellect. Consequently, those maintaining Pacciani's innocence insisted on his inability to carry out such an elaborate scheme. At the conclusion of *Il Mostro,* when Loris unwittingly leads the police to the actual homicidal mastermind, Benigni makes it clear that it is luck, not skill—certainly not newfangled forensic techniques imported from the United States—that allows the forces of law and order to solve the case.

Although Benigni's film clearly draws from the actual case against Pacciani, the relation of the actual three murder cases examined here to their corresponding literary and cinematic depictions is not a matter of equivalency. Before analyzing how these murders found expression in various cultural forms, each part of this study begins with a detailed history of the renowned murder in question. The chapters that follow these fact-based narratives examine the cultural issues that emerge from the murders, studying their representations in various cultural texts— chiefly contemporary Italian novels and films—but also in a wide array of related nonfictional narratives such as newspapers, court proceedings, self-help manuals, and memoirs. Attentive to the social and cultural contexts in which specific murders are embedded, *Murder Made in Italy* studies approximations—such as Benigni's film, for example—that produce the cultural significance of murder in contemporary Italy.[13]

Murder, unlike some other crimes, offers a relatively simple story to tell. White-collar crimes, on the other hand, such as corruption and financial malfeasance, often demand an understanding of complex points of law that complicate their retelling.[14] Despite similarities between murders in, say, Rome, Italy, and Rome, New York, murder is a crime that is tried and judged locally. Excluding relatively rare types of murder designated as war crimes and crimes against humanity, murders are tried in the jurisdictions in which they were committed. As the title of this introduction—"Making a Killing"—suggests, it is extremely important to emphasize the socially constructed nature of these murders, that is, the aspects of the various cases that make them uniquely Italian despite their apparent universalities.

Four key concepts serve as guides for the interpretation of the three murders *Murder Made in Italy* probes: moral panic; media spectacle; *cronaca,* or true crime; and the body.

MORAL PANIC

The concept of moral panic helps explain phenomena believed to erode a society's social fabric. Moral panic is the result of the media's fierce attention to the perceived threats to existing social practices, customs, and mores posed by specific social groups. A broad array of social concerns have produced various types of "panics," ranging from juvenile crime, child abuse, and drug cultures to anorexia, xenophobia, and, more recently, social networking Internet sites and the possibilities they offer to a variety of social predators. The socially deviant behavior of a particular group or an individual believed to represent a group excites media commentary of all stripes. Such heightened attention enables forces of social order (e.g., politicians, law enforcement agents, legislators) to call for reform, often followed by legislation intended to prohibit further deviancy.[15]

Moral panic would be impossible to achieve without the fuel and vehicle for contagion that the media provides. The interlacing of event, journalistic reportage, and legal consequence shows the intersection of the law and the media, where one field comes into contact with and therefore shapes and conditions the other. *Murder Made in Italy* focuses on these conjoined and mutually informing fields, asking questions about the ways the law and the media represent each specific case and the violence that underlies it.

Each of the case studies I examine reveals different facets of moral panic. The Pacciani affair, the event narrative that anchors part 1, was predicated on unacceptable sexual and social practices, including Satanism.[16] The slaying of couples in the Florentine hinterland also called up panic over the danger of "stranger killings," as serial murder is also sometimes called. Strangers return as a theme in the second case I study, the Novi Ligure double homicide of 2001. Xenophobia fueled the moral panic that grew in response to this case. Bursting from her home to report the murders of her mother and younger brother at the hands of intruders, Erika De Nardo claimed that "the Albanians did it."[17] Her false denunciation radiated through the media like a seismic shock wave, receiving wide coverage. The killers of Susy Cassini and Gianluca De Nardo did indeed come to stand for a social group, but not for Albanian immigrants or even the problem of Italian immigration in general. Rather, Erika De Nardo and her boyfriend Mauro "Omar" Fàvaro came to symbolize disaffected and delinquent youth at risk of becoming perpetrators or victims—or both—of violence.

Erika De Nardo was not the only murderer, however, to invoke "stranger danger," the rhyming caution so many parents in Anglophone countries drum into their children to put them on their guard against abduction and abuse. In January 2002, like De Nardo, Annamaria Franzoni, the convicted killer in the third case, claimed that an intruder had violated the sanctity of her home and murdered a family member. Rather than a xenophobic alarm raised to cover a daughter's murder of her mother, however, the Cogne affair, according to the state's accusation and conviction of Franzoni, featured a mother who killed her child and lucidly set out to cover up her actions. What the Novi Ligure and Cogne cases reveal is the threat to the family posed from within its structure, not from outside.[18]

The Amanda Knox case reprises various aspects of these different panics. Xenophobia erupted against Knox in the form of anti-Americanism and against the two black African men implicated, first Diya "Patrick" Lumumba and then Rudy Guede. The murdered body of Meredith Kercher, found in her bedroom with her throat slashed, recalled the terror of home invasion. Allegations surfaced that a sex game gone too far may have played a role in the murder, bringing with them commentary on the sexual aggression and prurience of one more demonized female criminal offender, the American college student Amanda Knox. In addition, the media landscape of the Knox case is located to the far side of the "digital divide" separating the investigations and trials of Pietro Pacciani, Erika De Nardo and Omar Fàvaro, and Annamaria Franzoni. The "viral" aspects of the circulation of information about the Knox case separate it from the "murders made in Italy" that serve as my chief focus. While all of the cases contain attributes of being a "judicial media circus," as Daniel Soulez-Larivière describes it, they are worlds—and mediascapes—apart.[19] Attending to the kind of media, the breadth of the media's reach, and the cultural and historical context in which that media system is embedded is crucial.

MURDER, MEDIA, SPECTACLE

The murders I explore are not political murders like, for example, the assassination of either John F. or Robert Kennedy or Martin Luther King Jr. in the United States; Mohandas or Indira Gandhi in India; Yitzhak Rabin in Israel; Benazir Bhutto in Pakistan; Aldo Moro in Italy; or any of the others in the sad litany of slain political and religious leaders either associated with the state or profoundly enmeshed in social policy.[20] The "Monster" case is often woven into the tapestry of the *misteri d'Italia*, or Italy's mysteries, as the series of unresolved crimes—largely but not exclusively unexplained murders that are considered as allegories of the state—are referred to. The double homicide in Novi Ligure and the murder of Samuele Lorenzi in Cogne, however, are not mysteries of this type.[21] Yet the shift in focus to less overtly political murders does not strip them of political significance and ideological meaning.[22] Rather, these three murders reveal ideological operations of different dimensions. Moreover, despite their smaller stature, each of the murders explored here achieved notoriety of spectacular proportions, with the media transforming each case into a "judicial media circus."[23]

Television was not, of course, the only medium "making a killing" or contributing to the spectacle of these murder cases. While print journalism and radio broadcasts still played a role in the dissemination of information, developments in electronic media, especially Internet access and cell-phone technology, all participated in the narration and re-narration of the murders and their investigations and trials. It is important to note that at the time of these trials, use of the Internet in Italy was increasing but by no means constituted a "digital revolution" for a variety of reasons, including its limited availability, Italy's notoriously shaky telephone connectivity, and low awareness among the majority of Italians.[24] In the Novi Ligure case, for example, the use of cell phones among Italian youth became a hot-button topic of concern. As in the United States, young adults circumvented parental control via cell-phone communication and text messaging. The abbreviation SMS (short messaging system), for the application made available by both cell-phone and Internet technology, came to signify "*Se mamma sapesse*" (should Mom suspect) and became a symptom of the aggressive and promiscuous behavior Erika De Nardo displayed only among her contemporaries.[25] Moreover, advances in Internet technology enabled the rapid circulation of information freed of the burden of fact checking. More significant than this, however, Internet discussions about the murders in Novi Ligure—for both those who actively posted to the discussions and those who passively read the comments—created a virtual community in which regional proximity was not required.[26] Technological advances in telecommunications also affected the third murder case. Jurist Enzo Tardino noted in his account of the "Little" Samuele case in Cogne, that "for the first time in the judicial history of the nation (the conditions in which) the preliminary investigations . . . were followed live in their entirety by the media."[27] As mentioned, what distinguishes the context of the Knox case is the mediascape in which is it set. For example, cell phones and the information they provide (time and, often, location) were instrumental in the investigation of Kercher's murder and played a key role in the state's theory of the crime, that is, that Amanda Knox and her boyfriend, Raffaele Sollecito, had staged a burglary to cover up their involvement in the murder. Circulation of information concerning the investigation and the trial had "gone viral," providing a global audience with daily footage and commentary in the form of blogs and Internet chats.

CRONACA, OR TRUE CRIME: MURDER, REAL AND REPRESENTED

In the opening "chapter," "In Vespa" ("On a Vespa"), of *Caro diario,* director Nanni Moretti's three-part 1993 film, Moretti plays himself as the protagonist and samples offerings of Rome's movie theaters during the slow summer months.[28] The selections are uninviting: monotonous Italian films, drab pornography, or imported slasher movies. Moretti first chooses a talky Italian film, a self-conscious parody of his own 1978 outing *Ecce bombo,* and then a slasher film. The camera follows the director into the theater as he watches *Henry: Portrait of a Serial Killer,* John McNaughton's cult splatter flick from 1990. Appalled but also fascinated by its badness, Moretti devotes entire pages in his diary, the structuring device for the film's three chapters, to reproducing the favorable reviews that led him to McNaughton's movie. One of "In Vespa's" most successful scenes stages Moretti's fantasy visit to a film critic's house. The critic lies whimpering in bed while Moretti sits beside him, reading aloud the critic's incomprehensible reviews like some sort of diabolical bedtime story.

Structurally, the scene performs an important function. Just as Moretti collects hatchet-job film reviews, he also gathers clippings of other newsworthy events to include in his diary for reflection.[29] Taking a reverse tack to Benigni's in *Il Mostro,* "In Vespa" transforms from fantasy to quasi-documentary, literally from one sequence to the next. From the fantasy of the critic's bedroom, we cut to an altogether different scene. Positioned over the director's shoulder, the camera shows Moretti's hands in close-up as they sift through newspaper clippings.[30] Unlike the preceding sequence, the focus here is on the newspapers themselves, not the filmmaker. The clippings are, in fact, *cronaca,* or crime reports, from the newspapers *Il manifesto, Il corriere della sera,* and other Italian dailies that tell the story of the violent death of cultural critic, filmmaker, and author Pier Paolo Pasolini in 1975. By juxtaposing these two scenes of radically different styles, Moretti calls attention to the differences between them—the first a director's revenge fantasy against a film critic who glorified the cinematic representation of serial killing, the second the factual retelling of a murder that still haunts Italy today—forcing their comparison by the obvious montage and the rapid cut that separates them and, in a sense, creating a hybrid montage of fantasy and reality.

Moretti's diary entries mirror this hybridity. The diary is filled with all manner of entries, ranging from brief reflections and sketches to fantasies and ideas for films. His Vespa, which furnishes the title for this chapter of the film, underscores the diary's hybrid form. Moretti's scooter zips between these two modes of representation—between reality and fantasy—and the many tracking shots emphasize the organic union of Rome's cinematic spaces, which contrasts with the staccato editing.[31]

Like Moretti's and Benigni's films, *cronaca,* too, is a hybrid genre combining different modes of representation. Contemporary Italian fictional representations of murder constitute a rich and growing subfield that has enjoyed much critical attention in the last decade.[32] The various fictional and nonfictional narratives I study help map the social and cultural terrain in Italy in the last twenty-five years, a period that could be characterized generally as an atmosphere of lawlessness, of which the Tangentopoli corruption scandals of the 1990s offer but one (extended) scenario.[33]

But first, it is important to understand that in Italy, crime is considered to be largely, if not solely, a regional problem that chiefly afflicts the southern reaches of the peninsula. While this has been true historically, as evidenced by the fact that the majority of murders in Italy are associated with crime organizations located south of Rome and in the islands of Sicily and Sardinia, the murders discussed here invert the notion that delinquency is rooted in the *mezzogiorno,* as Italy south of Rome is called.[34] A drawing by noted cartoonist Forattini published in *La Repubblica* in September 1990 offers an example. The drawing shows the most southern quadrant of Italy, Campania and south, inverted, with a danger sign reading "*Attenzione! State entrando nella zona dove si ammazzano i bambini!*" (Attention! You are now entering the zone where they kill children!). (See Figure 0.2.) The caption refers to the notorious killing in that time period of two children by the Camorra, the organized crime syndicate centered in the region of Campania and its capital, Naples.[35]

What makes the cases I probe so fascinating is that they all take place north of Rome, indeed in Florence and points north. This work

FIGURE 0.2. "Attenzione! State entrando nella zona dove si ammazzano i bambini!" (Attention! You are now entering the zone where they kill children!) Drawing by Forattini (*La Repubblica* in September 1990).

challenges notions of southern Italian criminality and, by extension, northern Italian public safety. In truth, one might post a sign outside the Valle D'Aosta, the location of the Cogne murder, or Piedmont, where the Novi Ligure slayings took place, to announce *those* areas as "zone(s) of child-killers." However, Gianluca De Nardo and Samuele Lorenzi were not killed in the crossfire of warring southern Italian gangs. They were killed in the putatively safe havens of their northern homes, a sort of double violation of perceived notions of the geography of delinquency and the domestic sphere. Yet, while these murders help us reimagine Italian geography, they also invite us to imagine an Italy that is much less regionally disparate than previously considered.[36]

Significantly, the contemporary Italian *giallo,* or detective story, also challenges received wisdom of geography, particularly regionality. This genre portrays widespread delinquency, especially in Italy's central and

northern regions.[37] The reconfiguration of Italian contours of criminality that takes place in contemporary fiction corresponds, in many
ways, to the sort of "virtual" proximity to crime that increasingly rapid
and widespread telecommunications is making possible. The Knox case
makes this particularly apparent, especially, perhaps, by the role played
by the Web pages Knox had designed for herself on the social networking
sites MySpace and Facebook.

The notoriety of Italy's various organized criminal organizations,
from the Mafia to the Camorra, has principally accounted for the perception that the murder rate in the country is high.[38] Acknowledging
the caveat that comparative data on crimes committed in distinct countries has not been historically entirely reliable, the crime rate in Italy in
general and the murder rate specifically is low in comparison to other
nation-states worldwide and specifically within Europe.[39] Comparative
statistics gathered and presented by the British Home Office in 1997 put
Italy's murder rate at 1.61 in 100,000, virtually the equivalent of France's
(1.60), slightly higher than Germany's (1.40) and the UK's (1.49), but
distinctly lower than Spain's (2.60) and Finland's (2.76).[40] Since World
War II, the gap in murder rates in Italy and other European countries
has narrowed. In the last decade, per-capita murder rates in Italy have
fallen to a 500-year low.[41] When murders carried out by the organized
crime syndicates long associated with Italy are pieced out from other
kinds of homicides, this rate declines still further.[42]

Yet social and symbolic articulations such as Italian crime novels
do not register the public perception of such safety and lawfulness in
Italy. Indeed, an interest in event narratives may constitute eroded faith
in the democratic rule of law. Such erosion could account for the ways
the fictional narratives considered here sketch and traverse the parameters of the law, contesting any binary that insists on strict distinctions
between what takes place "inside" legal institutions and what happens
outside of them.

The shifting geography of delinquency compares to a general lack
of definition concerning the shape and contours of crime narrative. In
Italian literature, the category encompasses several forms, including the
poliziesco (the police procedural), the *giallo* or noir (the detective/mur-
der mystery), and *cronaca*.[43] The Italian publishing market has drawn

no specific distinctions between these three literary genres. The critical reception of this genre has steadily increased over the last twenty-five years, as has its market share.[44]

Cronaca, or "true crime," actually operates on the principle of an ambiguity of form. True crime tends to blur genres, bringing together such incongruent forms as memoir, detective story, biography, and so forth.[45] In North American bookstores, true-crime books are often located next to sociology books, making true crime "the nonfictional counterpart—and theory of—fictional narratives about crime and criminality," as Annalee Newitz notes.[46] Truman Capote's *In Cold Blood* is a classic in this genre. Published in 1966, it explores the 1959 murder of the Clutter family in Holcomb, Kansas. In formal terms, Capote's work has been described as the "non-fiction novel," collapsing the distinctions that typically separate these two genres.[47]

Along these lines, I explore a mix of fictional narrative and nonfiction. Part 1, for example, examines publications written about the "Monster" murders from a variety of sources, including writings by jurists, journalists, and novelists.[48] Likewise, part 2 explores a nonfiction work about the De Nardo–Fàvaro killings written by a novelist as well as explorations of teenage privacy, one of the key issues in the case, in various literary genres. This opens wide a best-selling genre in Italy that includes parenting manuals and self-help books, to which, incidentally, the category of true crime might also belong. True-crime treatments of serial killers, for example, constitute, according to Mary Jean DeMarr, "books (that) both horrify and reassure us" and, significantly, teach us either how to live our lives to avoid encountering serial killers, as far-fetched as that seems, or what to do if in fact we are ever in the clutches of a serial killer.[49] Part 3 also joins varied texts, bringing together memoirs, journalism, and exposé to reveal the many issues raised by the Franzoni case, including contemporary maternity, the spectacle of public mourning, the general safety of children in Italy, and the childhood witness of violence.[50]

MURDER AND THE BODY: POSTMODERN POSTMORTEM

The body of the deceased has irrefutable material power in a murder case. Its power is no less potent in fictional representations of murder or, for that matter, in critical theory. As Mark Seltzer (who has worked more exhaustively on the subject of the representation of serial murder than any other critic) has observed, "Murder is where bodies and history cross."[51] Murder fundamentally records the effects of violence inflicted upon the body, and in the process it unmakes the body.[52] In this way, murder disengages the body from its privileged place and status as a critical instrument. It is for this reason that the study of murder cannot be limited to the canonical sites of its investigation. It needs the kind of approach I have been describing, one that brings together a variety of critical discourses to explore less canonical narrative forms, asking how this union produces cultural meaning.

The body, the last of the four key principles that organize *Murder Made in Italy,* embraces multiple forms. Alive or dead, sexed and gendered, child or adult, classed and nationalized, maternal or filial, the body marks the convergence of subordination to so many social norms and their contestations. Murder undoes the body.[53] The body's privacy is destroyed by murder, which demands redress from a state, which makes public the quest for justice.

Its life extinguished, the body becomes the most powerful marker of the abject, as proposed by Julia Kristeva and elaborated upon by Elizabeth Grosz, Barbara Creed, and others.[54] For Kristeva, the abject is an experience of limits and boundaries. Given its aim to distinguish one thing from another (pure from impure, inside from outside, and so forth), the abject indicates a process of identity formation, which Kristeva links to the social subject's pre-linguistic connection to the maternal.[55] Signs of defilement associated with the abject are often indistinct: the means of containment of blood, viscera, excrement, and so forth often give way, and their collapse or erosion results in blurred boundaries. Attempts to determine fixed boundaries mirror the powerful fantasy of stable identity. Consequently, signs of the abject are themselves often signs of flux and flow that is "out of place."[56] In its verbal form, the abject describes expulsion, the abjection of that which must be expelled (e.g., feces, the untouchable, the soul).

The murders and the issues they generate cluster around what is unacceptable and that which is abjected, or, expelled, from the social norm. *Murder Made in Italy,* taking a cue from the blurred boundaries of the abject, explores cultural forms—the slasher and horror film, pulp novels, Italian fiction of the so-called cannibals of the 1990s—similarly abjected from the canon of high cultural expression in Italy. Murder has probably always been considered unacceptable, one reason for its largely homogenous treatment by different cultures. Expulsion from society—exile—for the crime of murder has been a motif in cultural representations of the crime since, for example, the *Oedipus*. Surely since Freud's exploration of Oedipus's murder of his father Laius and its cultural echoes, murder has functioned symptomatically: it is the colophon, or the indicator, pointing to some other, deferred meaning. Thus "killing the father," for example, has signified killing the state, the government, the existing social order, history.

No fathers are killed in this study, only children, siblings, mothers, and lovers. Nor do I focus on the "grand narratives" of the type of allegorical murders of state I described. The murders I explore, nevertheless, are powerful indicators of boundaries, transgression, and ideology, which is understood in a "minor" register.[57] The murder cases in Florence, Novi Ligure, and Cogne in the chapters that follow highlight anxieties about the erosion of putatively stable social values. *Murder Made in Italy* explores these unacceptable acts and the cultural forms they take.

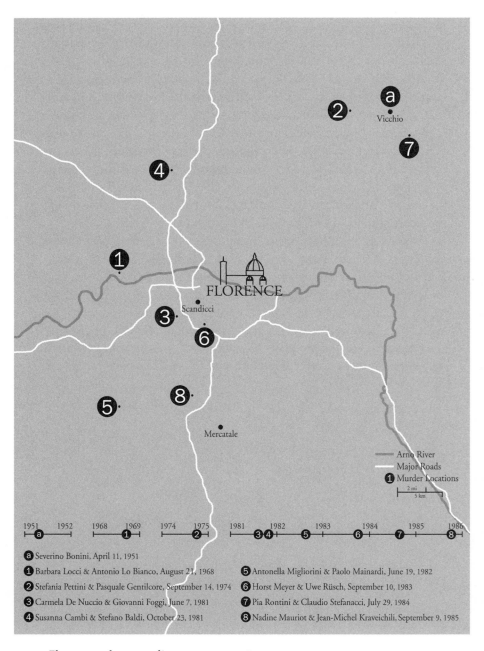

MAP 1. Florence and surrounding areas, 1974–1985.

PART ONE

Serial Killing

INTRODUCTION

Extemplo Libyae magnas it *Fama* per urbes:
Fama malum quo velocius ullum;
Mobilitate viget, virisque acquirit eundo;
Parva metu primo; mox sese attollit in auras,
Ingrediturque solo, et caput inter nubila condit.

Monstrum, horrendum ingens;
 cui quot sunt corpore plumae
Tot vigiles oculi subter, mirabile dictu,
Tot linguae, totidem ora sonant, tot subrigit aures.

—VIRGIL, *THE AENEID* IV, LL. 219–230 (MY ITALICS)

Straightway *Rumor* flies through Libya's great cities,
Rumor, swiftest of all the evils in the world
She thrives on speed, stronger for every stride,
Slight with fear at first, soon soaring into the air
She treads the ground and hides her head in the clouds.

A monster, horrific, huge
and under every feather on her body—what a marvel—
an eye that never sleeps and as many tongues as eyes
and as many raucous mouths and ears pricked up for news.
and for every plume a sharp eye, for every opinion a biting tongue.
Everywhere its voices sound, to everything
its ears are open.) (MY ITALICS)

⤳

With his description of rumor in *The Aeneid*, the classical Roman poet Virgil offers an image that emphasizes rumor's rapid spread and at the same time calls attention to the underpinning element of monstrosity. With its feathers like so many monstrous eyes, rumor is able to spread its wings and take flight. Long before the swiftness afforded by air travel—not to mention the advent of telecommunications—Virgil's image insists on rumor's speedy transport and transmission. Although it clearly travels, rumor appears to be omnipresent: since its voice is "everywhere," it appears somehow "already" at its destination before it arrives.

Pietro Pacciani, the first man to stand trial for the serial murders attributed to the "Monster," was convicted of murder in 1952, and the ways in which the news of that crime revisited his 1994 trial also recalls Virgil's spread of rumor, this time aided by the speed and capacities for saturation that characterize contemporary media.[1] In this way, the nearly forty-year span between Pacciani's 1952 conviction and his 1994 trial provides the opportunity to discuss the seismic shifts in the terrain occupied by the media in contemporary Italy.[2] Thus, I will draw attention to the proliferation of privately owned television channels and to the explosion of global telecommunications enabled by the development of the Internet.

The "Monster" narratives mark a period of transition in contemporary Italian society on several counts. This transition is visible both in the management and circulation of information and in its registration with government agencies; in criminological methodologies; in the powers of the police and the judiciary; and, finally, in an understanding of cultural identity shaped by regional location within Italy. For the ways this transition depends upon and exploits the "looping of information" and the "radical entanglement between forms of eroticized violence and mass technologies of registration, identification, and repudiation," serial murder offers a point of departure for examining murder's relation to media.[3]

Returning in time and tenor to Virgil's rapid and monstrous rumor, we note its multiform, protean character. Like the collage of monstrous characteristics, the construction of the public discourse of serial killers in Italy—where they are commonly referred to as "monsters"—bears a similarly constructed aspect.[4] Like Mary Shelley's Frankenstein, these monsters are stitched together from anthropology, folkways, literature, cinema, and (as the narrative of the case of the "Monster" illustrates) legal narrative. This suturing indicates other blurred distinctions between what is "real" and what is "represented," between fiction and nonfiction, between legal and illegal, professional and amateur, and a host of other oppositions.

Like the construction of monstrosity, the murders attributed to the "Monster" and the trials that followed feature a contamination of form, hovering somewhere in the transom between rumor and reality. Hearkening back to a spread of rumor, Manlio Cancogni notes that "like most Italians, what I know about the case of the Monster of Florence is based on hearsay."[5] The shifts between these varying registers reveal slippages between seemingly clear divisions of the real and the represented.

Examining the slippage between genres enacts the type of genealogical project that French philosopher of history Michel Foucault explored. As Foucault described it, adopting a genealogical approach means "operat(ing) on a field of entangled and confused parchments, on documents that have been scratched over and recopied many times."[6] In this part of *Murder Made in Italy,* comprising chapters 1, 2, and 3, the "parchments" vary. The examination of the murders ascribed to the "Monster," the subject of chapter 1, probes true-crime investigations of the murders, including television programs and broadcasts and accounts in print media. Yet nonfiction is not the only genre to illustrate the crimes and the sense of moral panic that unfolded from them: a ballad dating to the 1950s and performed by one of the region's last *cantastorie*—the Tuscan version of the griot, the fabled storyteller of some African cultures—offers useful insight into the "Monster's" crimes and Pietro Pacciani's 1994 trial. Chapter 2 examines the representation of serial killers in contemporary Italian prose fiction, while chapter 3 focuses on serial killer, detection, and police incompetence in the films of the "master of horror," Dario Argento.

The spectacle of these crimes underscores the dangers and pleasures of looking, the central matter that links the "Monster" narrative with its representation in assorted genres. Vision, sight, and looking constituted a chief concern in the investigation of the "Monster's" murders, which relied in part on evidence supplied by some of the nocturnal voyeurs active in the countryside outside Florence. Sight and vision, for example, are emphasized in the announcement posted everywhere in and around Florence in the 1983–1984 biennial that cautioned young couples against seeking the privacy of wooded areas. The poster showed two eyes staring out with a caption that reads, "*Occhio ragazzi: Non nascondetevi. C'è il Mostro.*" (Watch out, kids. Don't seek cover. The Monster is out there.)[7] Looking and seeing, moreover, enjoy elevated attention in the detective novel, where they serve as the capital metaphor for understanding, a point Andrea Pinketts makes particularly clear in his novels.[8] Vision holds obvious importance for cinema, never more so than in the repeated display of the dangers of "hurtable" sight thematic in Argento's films of the horror/slasher genre: as Argento's cinema works to underscore the vulnerability of sight, paradoxically, because of their perceived extreme violence, his films are subject to considerable censorship.[9] This juridical response intends, quite literally, to protect the commonweal's vision by keeping such violent displays out of public view.

ONE

The "Monster" of Florence

Serial Murders and Investigation

IN THE ELEVEN-YEAR PERIOD from September 1974 to September 1985, seven couples were killed in Florence and the surrounding countryside. Once the seriality of the murders was established, panic and hysteria ensued. The victims were Stefania Pettini and Pasquale Gentilcore, murdered the night of September 14, 1974, in a rural lane in Borgo San Lorenzo; Carmela De Nuccio and Giovanni Foggi, whose bodies were discovered on June 7, 1981, near Scandicci; Susanna Cambi and Stefano Baldi, found on October 23 of the same year, in a park near Calenzano; Antonella Migliorini and Paolo Mainardi, murdered the night of June 19, 1982, on a country road near Montespertoli; Horst Meyer and Uwe Rüsch, whose bodies were discovered on September 10, 1983, in Galluzzo; Pia Rontini and Claudio Stefanacci, killed the night of July 29, 1984, in the woods near Vicchio di Mugello; and Nadine Mauriot and Jean-Michel Kraveichili, found murdered on September 9, 1985, in the woods near San Casciano.

The "monster event" in Florence generates two stories that, although by now inextricably connected by historical circumstance, must be considered as discrete narratives. The first story unfolds from the series of seven double homicides.[1] The second concerns the investigation of the crimes, in particular the investigation of Pietro Pacciani, an agricultural worker who had been in and out of prison for violent crimes and who became the state's prime "monstrous" suspect. Although very few people doubt that the fourteen grisly homicides constitute a series, dispute erupted surrounding the killer's identity.

The "Monster's" crimes have excited a great deal of speculation about the identity of the perpetrator (or perpetrators) and possible motivations for the murders. The controversy that emerged concerned whether the crimes could likely have been done by one individual and whether more than one actor was involved. While many unsolved aspects of the murders exist, to say, as Douglas Preston does at the outset of the 2008 exposé *The Monster of Florence* (written with journalist Mario Spezi), that "despite the longest manhunt in modern Italian history, the Monster of Florence has never been found" and that "in the year 2000 the case was still unsolved, the Monster presumably still on the loose" is an exaggeration.[2]

If one believes in the theory of a lone killer, then it is true that no such individual has been brought to justice for the homicides. Pietro Pacciani, a farmer from Mercatale, was convicted for the murders in 1994, but his conviction was overturned two years later on the basis of poor evidence. At that point, the handling of the case descended into chaos. It was widely believed that Pacciani was the killer, and the public outcry was so great that the Supreme Court quickly scheduled a second trial. Meanwhile, on the day before Pacciani was released in 1996, two of his *compagni di merenda,* or picnicking pals—Mario Vanni and Gianfranco Lotti—were arrested. The state's new theory was that these two men were part of a rural gang of voyeurs that was responsible for the serial murders. Two years later, they were convicted of conspiracy in the serial murders. That same year, Pacciani died at home of cardiac arrest brought on by an overdose of heart medication. In 2001, it mounted a third theory that a doctor, who had died in 1985, was the center of a group of wealthy Satanists that killed at his bidding and brought him body parts as human fetishes. However, after an extensive investigation, no arrest was made. Although the last of the murders took place in 1984, the state has still not solved the mystery; many believe that Pacciani was the killer, but the state has not proved any of the three theories—lone serial killer, gang of voyeurs-turned-murderers, or Satanic group seeking fetishes—conclusively.

The bodies in the serial homicides outside Florence act as a colophon, or an indicator, of the abject. A frequent presence in horror films,

among other cultural expressions, the abject pressures boundaries between discrete spheres of order and disorder, between inside and outside,
between the imaginary and the symbolic.[3] Used as coordinates for map-
ping the murders, the victims' abject bodies trace an open circle around
greater Florence. Those who subscribe to the more esoteric theory of
the murders—the gang of Satanists as the perpetrators—point to the
geographical locations of the murders as support for their theory. The
seven murder sites form a rough sickle shape constellated around Florence and opening to the east. (See Map 1.) To the proponents of this
theory, the open-jawed map inscribed around Florence appears "unfinished" or somehow incomplete, awaiting the final sacrifice to "close" the
sacrilegious circle.[4] The sexed and nationalized bodies of the murdered
visitors threatened the city's cachet as a destination, long celebrated by
non-Italian participants on the Grand Tour.[5] Further, the rough circle
inscribed by the victims' bodies reveals a city that can be breached. The
city seems assailable, its abilities to defend itself (and its residents and
visitors) from menaces threatening from outside the city impaired. The
imperfect circle created by the linked murder sites marks the arrival of
a criminal problem of the magnitude of serial killing, once associated
with metropolitan centers in foreign lands, to Italian soil, setting upon
Italian cities and outlying areas that had previously been considered
secure, even bucolic.[6]

The murders shared significant traits that helped draw them together in a series and, consequently, shape the view that a serial killer
had murdered "by numbers," as serial killing is sometimes known.[7] The
victims died from gunshot wounds, they died out of doors in remote
areas, they died in their cars, they died in a condition of partial undress,
they died at either the beginning or the end of sexual activity, and they
died in a state of complete surprise. In each case, the couple was killed
with a .22 caliber Beretta handgun that fired a Winchester Long Rifle
series H bullet, and in a significant number of cases, each victim was
also stabbed. In a significant number of cases, the car's glove compart-
ment was left open and the female victim's purse, which was left at the
scene, had been searched. All the DNA evidence recovered at the scene
from semen or blood belonged to one of the victims and thus could not
be attributed to the killer. In a significant number of cases, the flesh of

the female victim's pubic area had been sheared off with what looked like a hunting knife or some kind of surgical instrument.[8] As well, in a significant number of cases, the female victim's left breast had been removed, using what was apparently a similar instrument.

The police did not immediately link the first two double murders, which took place in 1974 and 1981, respectively. In Spezi's narrative, a young journalist on staff at the Florentine daily *La Nazione* was credited with recalling the Borgo San Lorenzo murders seven years earlier.[9] Once ballistic analysis certified that the same weapon had been used in both crimes, "the idea that a crazed voyeur had committed the crimes became the preferred theory."[10]

One year later, after two more couples had been murdered, a carabiniere stationed in Florence remembered a double murder from 1968 that had occurred near Signa, some 15 kilometers west of Florence. A couple, surprised during a sexual encounter in their car, had been shot to death at close range. One fact different from all subsequent homicides ascribed to the "Monster" was that the car contained an additional passenger, a 6-year-old boy, Natalino Mele, the female victim's son. The victim's husband, Stefano Mele, confessed to the crime, which he committed, he said, out of his injured honor: Barbara had taken many lovers since their marriage. He said that he had thrown the pistol away after the crime. This assertion later proved significant in efforts to track the killer. Mele was sentenced to sixteen years in prison for the double murder. As Carlo Lucarelli, author of detective stories and host of the popular television series *Blu Notte,* explains, the case had been closed; therefore, the case file should not have contained any evidence. Nevertheless, the file housed bullet casings that demonstrated the weapon used in 1968 in Signa to murder Barbara Locci and Antonio Lo Bianco was used subsequently in the crimes attributed to the "Monster." But the incongruities between the evidence and Stefano Mele's story did not stop there. When he was unable to allocute to the crime, Mele's story was revealed as false. The fact came to light that another Sardinian man, Francesco Vinci, another of Locci's lovers, had given Mele the gun with the instructions that Mele should kill his wife for her betrayal of Vinci. Vinci told Mele that if he failed to act accordingly, he would expose Mele's homosexual activities.[11]

We arrive at the theories proposing a gang as the murderer. Proponents of the *pista sarda,* the so-called Sardinian trail, theorized that a known group of criminals comprising Sardinian immigrants, the *anonima sarda* (band of criminals), was the "Monster." This group had been responsible for high-profile kidnappings in Tuscany in the 1970s, and investigators pointed to the criminality of the group and the perceived prurience of the sexual proclivities of its members (e.g., voyeurism, homosexuality, group sex). The chief proponents of the *pista sarda* are Preston and Spezi, who believe they know who committed the "Monster's" murders. A second theory, the *pista perugina,* the Perugia trail, argues that a group of wealthy Satanists murdered couples in order to obtain fetishes from the bodies of the female victims for Black Masses. This trail leads to Dr. Francesco Narducci, the scion of a wealthy Umbrian family, who supposedly safeguarded these trophies. (Narducci lived in Perugia, thus the name for this "trail.") However, Narducci died in 1985, and no member of the supposed Satanist group has been arrested. Inspector Michele Giuttari, the chief of Florence's Squadra mobile (Criminal Investigations) from 1995 to 2003 and the director of GIDES, the Gruppo investigativo dei delitti seriali (Serial Crimes Investigation Squad), is the chief proponent of group-of-Satanists theory, or *pista perugina.*[12]

The groups at the terminal points of both trails differ in a great many respects: in terms of motive, geographic location, socioeconomic class, and ethnic subculture. What they share is their status as a group, making plausible the theory of *mandanti* (masterminds), those who sent the murderers toward specific victims and may (or may not) have hired the murderers.[13] But the motive each group could have had in commissioning the crimes differs substantially. The band of delinquents at the end of the *pista sarda* had varied motives, some of which concerned *omertà,* or honor killings. The leaders of the Satanic group believed to lie at the endpoint of the *pista perugina* were thought to have commissioned the killings in order to secure the human fetishes for Satanic worship.

Yet not everyone believed that a group was responsible for the series of homicides. The bodies of the serially murdered point also to the developments in information and forensic technology brought to bear on the investigation of the "Monster's" crimes. In the opinion of Francesco De Fazio, a forensic anthropologist who headed an institute for criminal investigation in Modena, the "Monster's" acts were carried out *rigorosamente da solo* (rigorously on his own).[14] In collaboration with De Fazio and his team and profilers at the FBI, Deputy Chief of Police Ruggero Perugini began assembling a computer-assisted screening, or profiling, program. Perugini had been named the head of the Squadra Anti-Mostro (SAM, the Anti-Monster Team) in 1985. To the position of director of the joint task force of local and national police Perugini brought an arsenal of sophisticated forensic tools that he had been introduced to at the FBI's Behavioral Science Unit in Quantico. Perugini trained his team of *acchiappamostri* (monster snatchers) in the latest techniques for the collection of forensic data and its analysis, especially in sophisticated computer programming aimed at "reconstruct(ing) the personality of the killer by individuating physical characteristics, race, presumed age, profession, social status, sexual tendencies, IQ, education, religion, and so forth."[15]

But the use of FBI software was marred from the start. For reasons not explained, and contrary to the advice of the FBI, one of the limiting principles for the profile included subjects who had been in prison. The list did not include any names of individuals who had not served time in jail. The profile also posited limits to age and time frame as well: the parameters for the perpetrator's age were set at 30 and 60 years of age, and the time frame ended in 1989. The first screening produced sixty names. This list was reduced to twenty-six suspects for reasons that have not been established. Francesco Ferri, who presided over the appellate section of the Court of Assizes where Pacciani was absolved, later wrote that Pacciani's name probably should never have appeared on the list of suspects.[16] Despite the fact that he was 64 years old at the time and thus outside the criteria Perugini had set, the computerized analysis identified him as the chief suspect. Pacciani, who had earlier been convicted and done time for murdering his fiancée's lover, had been out of prison for a number of years before the series of murders began in 1974 and for eighteen months after it was believed to have concluded in 1985. How could a serial killer with the compulsion to "murder by numbers" have displayed such restraint?

A second screening again produced Pacciani's name among a field of eighty-two others.[17] Ferri supposes that Pacciani emerged as the prime suspect because his name appeared on both lists. An *avviso di garanzia,* or the notice that the state considers an individual a person of considerable interest in a crime, was issued to Pacciani on June 11, 1990, while he was still serving a sentence for the sexual abuse of his daughters, informing him that he would be investigated for possession of firearms, presumably the .22 Beretta used in the "Monster's" crimes. Seventeen months later, on October 29, 1991, a second *avviso di garanzia* was issued, this time for the murders themselves. In January 1993, Pacciani was taken into custody.

Although the logarithms used in the screenings should not have produced Pacciani's name, the less-scientific—perhaps "old school"—investigative technique of canvassing a suspect's neighbors revealed little surprise that Pacciani had become a suspect in the "Monster's" crimes. But however awful a person he was—and his repeated physical abuse of his wife and sexual abuse of his daughters supply ample evidence for his monstrousness—the state's case against Pacciani for the series of murders attributed to the "Monster" was riddled with gaps, some that were not so serious, others that assailed the integral logic of the prosecution.

The bleed between the categories of the real and the imagined troubled the Pacciani case and characterizes the relationship of actual serial violence to its representation. Real and material issues vexing to the Pacciani affair include some of the following questions: Where was the murder weapon? The *maxiperquisizione* (search and seizure) of Pacciani's property, which was legendarily long and thorough, did not produce the Beretta used in the crimes. Pacciani would have had to have foreseen that his property would be searched and to have hidden the revolver before the start of his jail sentence for sexual abuse, a time frame when he had not yet been accused of being the serial killer; the police were not convinced of this possibility. The handle of a revolver, wrapped in rags, was recovered in a building on Pacciani's property, but its origin mystified investigators. If Pacciani was a sexual deviant who abused his daughters, why was the display of sexual violence in the serial murders not greater, including signs of rape? No one claimed that Pacciani was brilliant: could he have engineered a series of crimes as sophisticated and organized as these? Did the slip of paper with *coppia* (couple) and a license plate number written on it found at Pacciani's point to a wider circuit of voyeurs who traded information along with pornography, and is it possible this circle was involved? Who wrote and sent a letter to the carabinieri implicating Pacciani? Could it have been his own daughters as retribution for the abuse they sustained, a *vendetta in famiglia* (a family vendetta)? The search of his property had yielded no evidence directly connected to the serial killings. However, police found a blank notebook that had been manufactured in Germany and was unavailable in Italy and theorized that it could have belonged to Horst Meyer or Uwe Rüsch, the male tourists killed in Galluzzo in 1983.

The small yet troubling trail of paper and rags unearthed during the investigation of the 1980s serial crimes hearkened back to other rags that really confounded the case against Pacciani. His indictment for the murder of ragman (*cenciaiolo*) Severino Bonini in 1951 functions as a pivot between sporadically connected registers, swimming between fact and amalgamated fictions, many of them spurious. We might draw these bits of paper and rags into proximity with the divers "parchments," as Michel Foucault has described the varied documents employed in discursive analysis of political and social control, here functioning almost like posters advertising the circus, in this case, the "mediatic judicial circus" that characterized both temporal moments in the "Monster event."[18]

On April 11, 1951, in Tassinaia, in the Mugello area outside of Florence, Pacciani had stabbed to death traveling salesman Severino Bonini, whom he discovered in flagrante delicto with Pacciani's fiancée, Miranda Bugli. The case was heard in Florence's Court of Assizes in late December, and the sentence was handed down in early January 1952. The case entered popular culture almost at once when the popular performer Giubba, one of Tuscany's last *cantastorie,* turned the event into a ballad. Giubba sang the story of Bonini's murder in twenty quatrains during the summer of 1952 at fairs and other public gatherings throughout the Florentine hinterland.[19] Thus, rural residents who could not read the accounts in the pages of Florence's daily newspaper, *La Nazione,* or did not own a radio could still learn the story of Pietro, Miranda, and Severino. The ballad was also published as a broadsheet by Florence's Vallechi Press, so city dwellers who might not attend the fairs of the suburban periphery also had access to Giubba's opinion-making ballad.

Delitto a Tassinaia di Vicchio

"Delitto a Tassinaia di Vic-
chio sorprende la fidanzata
con l'amante uccide il rivale a
colpi di coltello."

"Crime at Tassinaia in Vicchio, (he) surprises his fiancée with her lover; and stabs
the rival to death."

1. Un grande tragico fatto è
avvenuto nel Comune Vic-
chio di Mugello un giovanotto
iniquo e fello che a sentirlo ne
desta pietà.

A great tragedy has occurred
in the town of Vicchio in
the Mugello, by a youth so
wicked and bad that hearing
of it arouses compassion.

2. Tal Pier Pacciani ha ven-
tisei anni che a parlarne il
sangue si ghiaccia lui sta a
Paterno poder detto l'Aiaccia
oh sentite tutto quello che fa.

This Pier Pacciani is twenty-
six, and to speak of it makes
the blood run cold; he lives at
Paterno in a farm called Aia-
cia; oh, listen to what he does.

3. La ragazza si chiama Mi-
randa che è l'amante di Pier e
ne dà la prova lei sta a Villore
detto Casanova su il colle vi-
cino a Maiol.

The girl is called Miranda
and she is Pier's lover and
shows it; she lives in Villore,
called Casanova, on a hill
near Maiol.

4. A quattordici anni la pas-
torella una sua avventura
nel bosco in lei niente c'era
nascosto prematura donna
rendeva lei già.

At fourteen years this young
shepherdess had her own
adventure in the woods, and
she hid nothing, for she was
already older than her years.

5. Da tanto tempo lui la
conosceva così tanto si era in-
namorato che da breve si era
fidanzato le alla giovane disse
così.

For some time he knew that
he was so in love with her
that they were soon prom-
ised, and so he said to her:

6. *"Io ti amo così pazzamente ed anche tu mi vorrai contraccambiare quel che fu non ne voglio parlare all'avvenire pensaci tu."*

"I love you so wildly (like) you want me to; I don't want to talk about the past, I'll leave you to plan the future."

7. *E per breve trascorse l'amore e da qui il fatto avviene ritroso lui divenne così tanto geloso interi giorni la stava abbadar.*

And their love was short-lived and the deed now turns wayward; he became so jealous that he hung around her days on end.

8. *L'undici aprile un sol di primavera tal Severino venditore ambulante di cenci e pelle da case tante e tante anche da Casanova come il solito passò.*

April 11th and a spring sun. This Severino, traveling ragman often passes many houses, including the one at Casanova.

9. *I familiari della Miranda son le tredici lo invitano a pranzare, dopo pranzo via volle andare a Poggiosecco si deve recar.*

At one p.m. the family of Miranda invite him to eat, and after lunch he wanted to leave, for he had to get to Poggiosecco.

10. *La sedicenne Miranda pastorella il suo gregge nel bosco a pascolare lui nel passar la volle chiamare sbuca la macchia e le va vicin.*

The sixteen-year-old shepherdess Miranda takes her fold to the woods to graze, and in passing he calls out to her, starts through the thicket and draws near.

11. *Accanto a lei si mette seduto per abbracciarla ne dà di piglio e non sapeva che lì c'è un nascondiglio il Pacciani che stava a sentir.*

He sits down next to her and moves to embrace her; he didn't realize that through a peephole Pacciani was watching.

12. *A questo punto Bonino Severino non riesce a esser tanto audace fa un tentativo e riesce capace e la donzella alla gioia si dà.*

Here Severino Bonino isn't so bold. He makes a move and succeeds, and the young girl gives herself over.

13. *Il fidanzato che più non resiste inferocito sorte dal cespuglio e vol far strage proprio nel mescuglio disse "ambedue vi voglio ammazzar."*

The fiancé can stand it no longer he emerges enraged from the bush and, wanting a bloodbath, says to them both "I want to kill you."

14. *Col coltello a serra manico il sanguinario come fé Caino questo squilibrato paccianino diciannove colpi su lui vibrò.*

With a serrated blade, in a bloodbath like Cain's, this unhinged Pacciani delivers nineteen blows.

15. *Così lasciava il Bonino straziato che di salto la ragazza afferrava lei con questo suo udir si salvava dice Pierino presto ci sposerem.*

Thus he leaves Bonino in pieces and, bounding toward the girl, he grabs her; she with these words saves herself: Pierino, soon we will be wed.

16. *Lui rispose se sposi saremo s'immutava e la volle abbracciare giura a nessuno di non rivelare quel che è stato e nessuno lo sa.*

If we will be married, he said, altering his mood and embracing her, swear to no one will you tell what has happened here and no one will know.

17. *Lui tornava dopo mezzanotte a caricarselo con le gambe al collo come può fare la volpe a un pollo trecento metri così lo trascinò.*

He returned after midnight and took his burden, its legs around his neck, like the fox with a chicken, and in this way dragged the dead Bonino three hundred meters.

18. *La mattina a Vicchio era*
il mercato lui tranquillo come
a mene frego in una bottega
di un certo Pellegro molti lo
videro bere e giocar.

The next day was market day
in Vicchio, and he as carefree
as Riley; many saw him drink
and play cards in Pellegro's
place.

19. *Ma purtroppo la cosa*
s'inoltrava per Bonini ognuno
era allarmato a Tassinaia
viene ritrovato tra le foglie
nascosto così.

But alas the deed developed
and all were worried about
Bonini; and he was found
hidden in the thicket at
Tassinaia.

20. *Giovanotti all'amore voi*
fate è bene che ognuno abbia
la fidanzata, ma se sapete che
è donna depravata come il
Pacciani non dovete far.

You young folk, if you make
love, it's good that every guy
have his girl, but if you know
she's depraved, don't do like
Pacciani did.[20]

Giubba's ballad rehearses each element of the crime, immortalizing it in the process. It publicizes Bugli's aborted pregnancy at age fourteen, two years before the time of the murder. On the fateful day of the crime, Bonini was invited to lunch, where Bugli caught his eye. He followed her as she took her flock of sheep to graze and then tried to make the most of a promising situation. However, as we read in quatrain 7, Pacciani "*divenne tanto geloso (e) interi giorni la stava abbadar*" (became so jealous (that) he hung around her days on end) and, true to his reputation for jealousy, shadowed Bugli's movements.

Through an opening in the bushes, Pacciani watched as Bonini uncovered one breast and as Bugli "*alla gioia si dà*" (gave herself to pleasure), as quatrain 12 says. Seized by a jealous rage, he crashed through the thicket "*inferocito,*" as described in quatrain 13, and set on Bonini with his serrated knife, stabbing him nineteen times. When questioned about his prior conviction for murder while on the witness stand during his 1994 trial, Pacciani denied any accusation that he had gone in "armed" pursuit of Bugli and Bonini. Rather, he said, he seized the knife that all Tuscan farmers carry with them. At this point, Giubba describes

Bugli's reaction as a quick-witted one intended to save herself from Bonini's fate. *"Pierino, presto ci sposerem"* (soon we will be wed), she says to dissuade him in quatrain 15. The two decided to say nothing, robbed the dead man, and left him. Pacciani returned that evening and, as Giubba represents in quatrain 17, like the fox with a dead hen draped Bonini's legs about his neck and dragged him 300 meters deeper into the thicket. Stupidly, Pacciani spent the money the following day, just as news of Bonini's absence became public.

In this ballad, Giubba, predictably, perhaps, vilified the teenaged Bugli, making *her* the reason for Pacciani's fall from grace and good standing. In quatrain 4, she is described as *"prematura donna,"* to whom Pacciani (in quatrain 6) entrusts the planning of their future. In quatrain 15, Giubba dwells on the near-deceit of a Bugli who wishes to save herself—*"lei con questo suo udir si salvava"*—playing on Pacciani's helpless passion for her by saying they would soon be wed. Miranda, who was deemed *"depravata,"* as the last lines of the ballad attest, was the root and reason for the downfall of a stupid but otherwise harmless young man. Miranda testified at trial that she had called out to Pacciani, but before he had attacked Bonini.

The *pubblico ministero* successfully convinced the court that Bugli had known that Pacciani was witnessing the events and cried out to him that Bonini was raping her. The murder thus became a *crime passionelle*. While the court believed that Pacciani had become explicably drawn into a homicidal rage, it did not find Bugli's claim of rape credible. It is probable that the opprobrium of Miranda's abortion at age fourteen acted as an unofficial conditioning factor. The court sentenced both Pacciani and Bugli in 1952: Pacciani was found guilty of *omicidio colposo* (manslaughter) and *furto aggravato* (aggravated theft), and Bugli was later convicted of being an accessory to murder. She was sentenced to ten years, he to eighteen years and ten months, though he was paroled in 1964 for good behavior.

La Nazione, the paper that had covered the 1951 case, began to incorporate details from the earlier case into its coverage of the investigation of Pacciani for the murders attributed to the "Monster."[21] The image of Pacciani's homicidal rage was revisited, and Giubba's ballad resurrected. The excision of the left breast of several of the female serial homicide victims was adduced as the somatization of Pacciani's witness of Bugli's exposed left breast in the copse in Tassinaia. The proximity of Tassinaia to the 1974 murders in Vicchio was mentioned. Pacciani's abuse of his daughters, his interest in pornography, his penchant for voyeurism, the unsubstantiated testimony of a witness who claimed to have seen Pacciani in the vicinity of the Scopeti murders—all spilled out of the court building and into the public eye. Coverage of the investigation of the serial murders and Pacciani's 1994 trial collapsed the 1951 murder with the 1974–1985 series, effacing the time that had passed between them.

Both of Pacciani's trials were media spectacles; however, they occupied different mediascapes. I have referred to Virgil's presentation of Rumor in the *Aeneid*, pointing to the ways in which it might still describe the circulation of half-truths and speculation. One could also employ the sort of geological analogy Umberto Eco has used to describe the phases of development in Italian television, that is, the major shifts between the "Paleolithic" and "Neolithic" ages. Eco christened the era of state-monopolized television from 1954 to the mid-1970s *paleotelevisione,* or "Paleo-television", with the period of privatization that followed *neotelevisione.*[22] The "Monster" narrative actually spans three, not two, different phases of development in the circulation and consumption of information in Italy and documents the ways in which the shifts are not complete or how vestiges of a previous practice may remain.[23] Since Pacciani's trial for the murder of Severino Bonini precedes the first, experimental stage of television (1954), the first phase of the "Monster" narrative could be described as corresponding to the Stone or Pleistocene Age of twentieth-century media. Print media of the time, although well beyond this initial stage, nevertheless presented mixed indications of circulation and consumption.[24] On the other hand, Giubba, his ballad's popularity, and the venues in which he performed suggest the sort of oral transmission of information that could be said to relate to television's beginnings.[25]

The second phase of the "Monster" narrative, which corresponds to the eleven-year period of the serial murders (1974 to 1985) and their investigation, corresponds to television moving into its "Neolithic" age, to continue with Eco's geological periodization, in which the privatization of television reordered the relationship between spectator and broad-

caster.[26] But despite the modernization, and poised against the privatization of Italian television and the expansion in broadcast networks that
was the consequence, Mario Spezi, who had made his career in *cronaca*
at *La Nazione*, describes the sensation of lagging well behind the times.
He notes how the serial murders seemed to catch the forces of law and
order as well as the press unaware. For Spezi, the press, the police, and
the carabinieri were all *impreparati* (unprepared) for the emergence of a
serial killer in Florence.[27] The unpreparedness of *cronaca* reporters and
law enforcement agents suggests not only a lack of experience with serial
murder but also, and perhaps more importantly, an absence of information circulating about them.[28]

The probe of the *guardoni* in this period as part of the investigation
of the serial homicides also unearths some Paleolithic aspects as regards
the dissemination and circulation of information. The mechanisms for
the exchange of information among the *guardoni* rely on oral transmission. The account of one of the *guardoni,* Fabbri, and his interrogation point up the absence of any technological developments (even the
telephone) that might have facilitated rapid exchange of information.
Fabbri confirmed that he and others relied on the oral transmission
of information concerning the location of couples that could be seen
engaged in sex. A restaurant called the Taverna del Diavolo functioned
as a rallying point "where the Indiani would gather to do business and
swap information before going out for the evening."[29] The passing of information orally or, literally, from one hand to another in a group where
all the members know one another seems to link to an earlier age when
information was distributed and opinions formed by way of the kind of
performance that a *cantastorie* such as Giubba specialized in.

The third phase of the "Monster" narrative corresponds to Pacciani's
1994 trial. In January of that year, Pacciani was informed he would
stand trial for the eight double homicides attributed to the "Monster."
Three months later, in April, the trial began. As Spezi was positioned as
the figure pivoting between a Neo- and a Paleolithic age, so does Pacciani emerge as a character clashing with the dawn of the digital age of
telecommunications.[30] Courtroom footage of Pacciani shows an oafish,
vulgar man from a bygone era. In describing the various appearances of
Pacciani and his picnicking pals Lotti and Vanni, Roberta Petrelluzzi,

host of the multipart episode "Storia infinita del Mostro di Firenze" ("Infinite Story of the Monster of Florence") for the television program *Un giorno in pretura*, called them all "*contadini vecchio stampo*" (old-fashioned farmers).[31]

Pacciani's thick Tuscan accent is conspicuous in the 1994 trial footage. More than locate him regionally, Pacciani's oral testimony implies he is beyond the reach of mass media's homogenizing effects on spoken Italian. In 1963, some thirty years before Pacciani's trial for the "Monster's" murders, Tullio De Mauro had charted the rise of *italiano popolare,* popular Italian, that is, the standardization of spoken Italian brought about by broadcast media (radio and the relatively recent phenomenon of television) and sound cinema. The *italiano popolare* consisted of "the varieties of colloquial spoken Italian for informal everyday use that were gradually supplanting the use of dialects in different parts of the country."[32] This is not to suggest that a Tuscan accent constitutes a dialect. On the contrary, given the literary bases for standard written Italian, one could argue that there was very little, or even no, difference between "Tuscan" and "Italian."[33] Yet Pacciani's deeply accented, regionally inflected speech shows how the standardization that De Mauro had predicted, and that prevails in the courtroom, itself the locus of (juridical and constitutional) codification, did not come to pass.[34]

Despite the circumstantial nature of the evidence against him, despite the fact that one of the witnesses against him later was convicted of conspiracy in the crimes, despite the absence of a murder weapon or a confession, despite the absence of a psychiatric evaluation, Pacciani was found guilty on November 1, 1994, for each pair of murders save the Lo Bianco–Locci murder of 1968. He was given seven life sentences.

Nearly a year later, Michele Giuttari, the recently appointed head of the Florentine Squadra mobile, began a systematic review of all the evidence associated with the homicides and the Pacciani trial as the case made its way through the mandatory appellate phase. It was at this point that he noticed the absence of follow-up on the *supertestimoni,* the chief witnesses that helped establish the presence of accomplices and challenged the notion of a lone killer. This next phase became known as the *inchiesta bis,* or the second helping of the inquiry. Pacciani's appeal was heard by the appeals part of the Court of Assizes in January of 1996. One month later, Mario Vanni, one of Pacciani's "picnicking pals," was arrested for his suspected role in the 1985 homicides of the French tourists, Mauriot and Karaveichili. The following day, on February 13, 1996, the court absolved Pacciani of the crimes and annulled the sentence handed down by the lower court. However, in December 1996, on a technicality, the Court of Cassation vacated the decision of the Court of Appeals with a *rinvia,* remanding it to a lower court for further consideration.

In the intervening months, two other companions were given notice that they were suspects in the case: Giancarlo Lotti and Giovanni Faggi. The trials were severed, and it was ruled that Pacciani would stand accused once more of the crimes ascribed to the "Monster," this time for conspiracy to commit murder but not as the sole author of the crimes, thus avoiding double jeopardy. The trial date was set for October 1998, but in February of that year, the carabinieri found the lifeless body of Pietro Pacciani in his home. He had died from a major cardiac arrest, the result of a contraindicated combination of medications. The story of the "Monster" of Firenze did not end with Pacciani's death. The day after Pacciani's body was found, the district attorney for Florence asked that his *compagni* be found guilty for the series of double homicides. Vanni and Lotti were convicted in 1998.

THE "MONSTER" AND MORAL PANIC

Moral panic is the consequence of intense scrutiny by the media of the perceived threats from specific social groups to existing or accepted social practices, customs, and mores. In the dynamic of moral panic, the behaviors of the suspect group are believed to erode existing social and cultural structures and to therefore require social censure and juridical redress. Distribution of information plays a crucial role in the development of a sense of urgency, emergency, and crisis.

The "Monster" narrative highlighted three subcultures that contributed to the public's perception of impending moral panic: first, voyeurs engaged in a putatively deviant sexual practice; second, a possible group of Satanists whose members were thought to rank high in the social hierarchy; and, third, a group of Sardinians transplanted to Tuscany whose deviance extended to criminal delinquency and, allegedly, sexual practice. Each of these groups received intense scrutiny in the press and on television news. In different ways, public fears about each of these groups put pressure on the disciplinary and judicial systems to produce some kind of action that would allay the public's fears.

The first group to raise alarm consisted of a ring of *guardoni* (voyeurs) that was active in the countryside outside of Florence. The *guardoni* provided the investigation with key pieces of information (as well as disinformation) that led to the first arrest for the crimes ascribed to the "Monster." After ballistic analysis and comparisons of the crime scenes linked the 1974 and June 1981 murders, the reaction was one of disbelief, carrying over even to the existence of such familiar activities as the nocturnal pursuits of the Peeping Toms in remotely located areas around Florence. As Lucarelli said of the voyeurs on an episode of *Blu Notte*, "There are a lot of them and everyone knows about it but it seems as though they wake up to the fact only at this point."[35] These men were sometimes referred to locally as "Indiani" because of their "tribal attitude" regarding the areas they trawled.[36] Lucarelli adds that among the voyeurs there are the *Insospettabili,* high-ranking social figures who are "well-known . . . esteemed professionals."[37]A secondary market of extortion existed to shake down the luminaries who, mindful of their social status, were prepared to pay a price to ensure their anonymity.[38]

One of the voyeurs who did not hold an exalted social position was Enzo Spalletti, an ambulance driver arrested in June 1981 and charged with the two double homicides that had taken place by that date. The morning following the De Nuccio–Foggi murders in Scandicci, Spalletti revealed specific details to his wife about the state of Carmela De Nuccio's body, particularly its mutilation. Since these details had not been made public, Spalletti came under suspicion. In addition, the couple had been murdered on Spalletti's "tribal" land. He was arrested on June 15, 1981. When the bodies of Susanna Cambi and Stefano Baldi were found on October 23, 1981, and were considered to be two more victims in the "Monster's" series, Spalletti was released from custody.

Engaging in sex in public areas in and around Florence did not elicit the social censure it might have in other locations where serial killings have occurred. The standard example of this is found in the serial murders of prostitutes in London in the late 1880s attributed to Jack the

Ripper. As Judith Walkowitz has documented in her classic study *The City of Dreadful Delight,* the moral panic that emerged from the prostitutes' slayings located the blame with the prostitutes themselves.[39] The frightened and morally outraged citizens of London determined that the prostitutes themselves created the dangerous circumstances to which they fell victim by engaging in sexual acts for hire.

But this aspect of moral panic does not hold for the "Monster" narrative, where response to sex in public venues was more varied. For example, there appears to be no evidence that anyone believed that the young couples, seized in their "moment of joy (and) of affirmation of their youth," as the mayor of San Casciano, Pietro Roselli, expressed it, had created the circumstances that contributed to their untimely deaths.[40] They were simply enjoying the beauties and privacy of the less-crowded Tuscan countryside, long a destination for both tourists and natives. As concerns the voyeurs and their activities, although Spalletti's wife was reportedly mortified by her husband's nocturnal pastime, there is also no evidence of real censure of the *guardoni:* the ring of *guardoni* that operated in the Florentine hinterland was both known and tolerated.[41] Self-censorship may account for the absence of sweeps of the "tribes" conducted by the police or a significant number of arrests. Nothing of this kind appears to be part of this phase of the "Monster" narrative.

As a result of the "Monster" hysteria, the voyeurs had less to look at: given the prudence that followed from the October 23, 1981, slayings, the traffic of couples in the outlying areas of Florence diminished. Spezi and Preston observe that "the countryside at night was utterly deserted."[42] As a result, areas at the periphery of the city in the hills that rose immediately from the Arno, such as those around San Miniato and Piazzale Michelangelo, "were packed with cars, bumper to bumper, the windows plastered with newspapers or towels, young lovers inside."[43] Such amorous activity continued as the "Monster" case remained unsolved, and in the summer of 1984 the remote roads on the Florentine periphery that had been used as lovers' lanes were empty. A civil servant's suggestion that the city establish "villages of love" that would provide safe places of consort for the city's youth incited consternation.[44] Some Florentines believed that if safe havens were founded and maintained by the city, "Florence might as well open whorehouses."[45] Yet Florence was no

stranger to whorehouses, even in its relatively recent history: the Merlin
Law, enacted thirty years earlier, had called for disbandment of the *case
chiuse,* as the brothels were known.[46]

Issues pertaining to sex and freedom of sexual expression characterize the second group of actors that contributed to the dynamic of
moral panic in the "Monster" affair, the band of delinquent Sardinians
that the *pista sarda* pointed to. If the series of murders attributed to the
"Monster" included the murders of Barbara Locci and Antonio LoBi-
anco in 1968, then the sexual proclivities of the agents in this group
were germane to the motives of the crimes. Although the "Monster's"
weapon was used in the 1968 double murder, it is an outlying data point
in the series. In the main, however, the gang at the end of the "Sardinian trail" appear to have been vilified for their practices and considered
deviant, which contributed to the xenophobic reception of the Sardinians in Tuscany in the 1960s, 1970s, and 1980s. Most of these internal
immigrants, like other groups on the move within the peninsula, sought
more work than was available in southern Italy or the islands (Sicily
and Sardinia).[47]

The use of the .22 Beretta makes including the 1968 murders logical
and led investigators to consider a circle of sex partners that included
Barbara Locci's husband, Stefano Mele; Salvatore Vinci, a family tenant
with whom Locci had an affair; and Francesco Vinci, Salvatore's brother,
also Barbara's lover. After his confession, as mentioned above, Mele alone
was convicted of the murder of his wife and her lover. Barbara Locci,
whom Spezi describes as "slinky and sloe-eyed," appears to have moved
freely from one partner to the next, providing a link between Mele and
the Vincis that accords with the notion of the "traffic" in women that
solidifies male relationships.[48] According to Spezi and Preston, Salvatore
Vinci's sexual practices were assorted: group sex ranging from ménages
à trois to foursomes to orgies; voyeurism; homosexual activities on his
own and in group situations; and the use of sex toys and aids.[49] Salvatore
appeared unembarrassed by the public disclosure of his sexual activities. For example, in 1988, while he was on trial in Cagliari for the 1961
murder of his wife Barbarina, Vinci discussed with the press corps his
views on "such themes as sexual freedom."[50]

Barbara Locci moved back and forth among the men in the Sardinian band, like the proverbial traveling signifier that affects the meaning

of each signified it becomes associated with, but she was not the only roving agent. Freedom of movement is crucial to the logic behind the *pista sarda* theory, which insists on a similar freedom of movement for the Beretta. According to the theory, which Spezi and Preston endorsed, the weapon was passed from one Vinci to another until it found Antonio. Although following the Sardinian trail offered no precise match in terms of the geography or time frame of the killings, it did show that Francesco Vinci was in the vicinity of San Lorenzo in 1974, when the Borgo San Lorenzo murders took place, and was near Montespertoli in 1982, when Migliorini and Mainardi were killed.

In addition to freedom of movement, the logic behind the *pista sarda* theory relies on putatively Sardinian characteristics, most of them the sort of stereotypes that contributed to the xenophobic response of the Tuscans. For example, after moving to Tuscany from Sardinia, Francesco Vinci worked in a "classic Sardinian business: kidnapping for ransom."[51] However, as Preston and Spezi describe, the Vinci brothers distinguished themselves from their fellow Sardinian immigrants by being "self-assured, adaptable, and surprisingly sophisticated."[52] Perhaps the most significant feature of the "Sardinianness" of the Vincis that bears on the logic of the theory concerns certain ethnic traits and undiluted and unmodified cultural practices that the Sardinians appear to have carried to the "continent."

The two most significant include the transplanted Sardinians' diffidence with regard to organized social institutions, especially law enforcement agencies, and the continuation of the practice of *balentia*. Derived from the profoundly patriarchal Barbagian code, the practice of *balentia,* similar to other pseudo-familial organizations such as the Mafia in Sicily and the Camorra in Campania, condoned an outlaw sense of justice.[53] The movement of the murder weapon from Salvatore Vinci to, say, Antonio, the theory posits, was accomplished by a theft that had not been listed as a missing household item, even though Salvatore had reported a breaking and entering to the local outpost of the carabinieri. Preston and Spezi attribute this to his "Sardinianness," with Spezi reasoning that "this fine fellow, a Sardinian" would not report a stolen firearm out of a "deep and ancient suspicion of authority."[54]

A setting aside of the ethnocentric reasoning that potentially mobilizes the *pista sarda* must not come at the expense of recognizing the historic delinquency of some Sardinian immigrants in Tuscany in the 1970s. Juridical responses to the presence of Sardinians in Tuscany ranged from very specific (the arrests of Salvatore and Francesco Vinci, for example) to the more general. For example, the local *procuratore della repubblica*, Pier Luigi Vigna (one of the lead prosecutors in the "Monster" affair, incidentally), successfully curtailed the kidnappings of wealthy residents of Tuscany by freezing the financial assets of victims.[55]

Although sexual deviance is also an issue of note for the *pista perugina,* the group at the end of the path leading to the third subculture that fostered conditions of moral panic, it differed from the case presented by the Sardinians. The Sardinians constituted a group that was transplanted from their indigenous island locale and lived as bicultural immigrants working largely in the agrarian sector. They were known for their delinquency and for their limited knowledge of the Italian language.[56] At the end of the Perugia trail was a patrician class of landed aristocracy whose wealth and power facilitated the successful camouflaging of their tracks. The sexual deviancy of this group is subordinated to the practice that truly would have eroded social mores and elicited a panicked response: Satanism.

The last of the double murders, the victims of which were the French tourists Mauriot and Karaveichili, marks the most "Satanic" or "esoteric" of the crimes attributed to the "Monster." As Spezi has pointed out, the 1985 Scopeti murders differ from the others in the series in at least two regards, both concerning the fear of discovery.[57] In the crime scenes of the first fourteen murders, no great attention was paid to hiding the cadavers, something amply attested to by the crime scene photos, which were visible in such true crime journals as *Cronaca vera* and in the still photos used for montage in television broadcasts. However, after Nadine Mauriot was murdered, her body was brought back inside the tent that she and Karaveichili had been occupying and covered by a sleeping bag, according to those present at the crime scene. Presumably both actions made the inert body appear less like that of a murder victim. Moreover, Karaveichili's body had been dragged from the site. Both details, in Spezi's view, indicated an interest in delaying discovery of the bodies.[58]

But other details, allegedly of a Satanic nature, distinguish this double murder from the others. The location of the murder in San Casciano is not far from a deconsecrated church where, it was rumored, Black Masses, usually blasphemous inversions of the Catholic Mass, were celebrated. In keeping with such a motif were the interpretations of various symbols and stagings thought to relate to the murders. An "esoteric" reading of the double homicide highlighted a mass of stones nearby that were arranged in a semicircle and bore signs of obvious organization. Within this semicircle, or open-jawed rectangle, an inverted wooden cross was found. As Irene Pivetti intoned on the episode of *Giallo 1* dedicated to the "Monster's" crimes, this homicide in particular pointed to "a powerful international sect" of Satanists.[59]

The Italian branch of the sect allegedly centered in Perugia, and the *pista perguina* led to Dr. Francesco Narducci, who had died in mysterious circumstances in October 1985, a month after the last double homicide attributed to the "Monster." Rumors that Narducci was the "Monster" circulated during his life, fueled perhaps by his profession. The profile established by law enforcement agencies for the killer predicted that the killer was a doctor or a butcher or was involved in some trade that required handling tools with precision and some knowledge of anatomy, though not necessarily human anatomy (not unlike the suppositions about Jack the Ripper).[60] The unusual circumstances of Narducci's death and the exhumation of his body in 2002, seven years after his burial, also contributed to rumors of his relation to the "Monster."[61] Narducci's death had been ruled a boating accident. However, the autopsy performed after the exhumation revealed what a carabiniere who was present at the retrieval of Narducci's body had observed but had been forbidden by his superior to report: signs of strangulation and, consequently, homicide. The chief proponent of the theory that the *pista perugina* leads to a powerful group of Satanists engaged in a conspiracy to cover sixteen murders is Michele Giuttari. The animosity between those who expound the validity of the *pista sarda* and those who endorse instead the *pista perugina* aside, my aim is to recognize the key roles Giuttari and Giuliano Mignini, Perugia's *pubblico ministero,* played in the juridical response to the perceived moral threat of Satanism.

Following the identification of a social menace and its intense scrutiny by the media, forces of social order call for reform. Legislation in response to the panic often follows. As Angela McRobbie explains, the dynamic of moral panic reveals "the social conditions of consent . . . necessary for the construction of a society more focused toward law and order."[62] Whether or not a group of Satan worshippers existed that sought to secure its members' anonymity and safeguard their positions of power within Florentine and Umbrian society is not the issue so much as the very public disciplining of members of the police force and judiciary (namely, Giuttari and Mignini, who also served as the prosecutor in the murder trial of Amanda Knox).[63]

It is significant that a personage as august as Count Niccolò Neri Capponi, of noble Florentine lineage, should have written a letter to the *Atlantic Monthly* disparaging the Italian judiciary in response to its publication of Douglas Preston's article on the "Monster" case in July 2006. The judiciary, a branch of the Italian civil service, was "a state within a state," whose largest contingent is made of individuals who are themselves "corrupt (and) *affiliated with the former communist party.*"[64] In his first term (1994–1995), Silvio Berlusconi had sought to limit the powers of a judiciary he argued was bloated and unruly even as that branch of government was distinguishing itself in unraveling corruption in the Tangentopoli scandal about public works speculation and corruption among public officials. To be sure, criticism of the judiciary could hail from any location on the political spectrum, but the affiliations of those who have decried the Italian judiciary in the last fifteen years seem fairly clear.[65]

Given the direction of their investigation, Mignini and Giuttari both came under attack. Significantly, "the social conditions of consent" that McRobbie and Thornton discuss include more than the power of prominent private citizens but also the power of representatives of the press. In a civil suit, Mario Spezi accused Giuttari of violating his civil rights and of impugning the reputations of "upper-middle-class professionals" and "seemingly upstanding persons" with his attempts to reveal a Satanic sect.[66] Mignini was accused of illegally using wiretaps in the collection of evidence and was indicted for abuse of office. Preston recounts his "glee" at seeing Giuttari indicted for falsifying evidence.[67] Since Preston and Spezi held Giuttari responsible for the accusation against them for obstruction of justice, glee might be a reasonable response, but the upbraiding and disciplining Giuttari and Mignini received underscores the theme of the incompetence of agents of law enforcement, one reason amateur detectives recur in both literature and cinema that give artistic and cultural expression to serial killing. Perhaps peninsular Italians also share that most Sardinian of qualities that Preston and Spezi locate in Salvatore Vinci, a "deep and ancient suspicion of authority."[68]

In addition to its urban trappings, serial killing was also not considered an Italian crime—that is, a crime that Italians commit. Despite the fact that Tuscany had at least one serial killer in its annals—Carlo Grandi, who killed four children in Incisa Valdarno in the period 1873 to 1875—Italians disavow serial killing and identify it as an American phenomenon. This disavowal is patent in contemporary Italian prose fiction. In the face of such alienating phenomena, it must have been reassuring to suppose that the killer was a single individual with a criminal record that included a murder who lived so close to the first murder in the series. This is the profile Pietro Pacciani presented.

One of the most interesting features of the serial murders in Florence concerns its nonurban character: murder, if not under the Tuscan sun, then by the light of its moon. Serial killing has been considered quintessentially urban, a crime that speaks to the ills of urban living. Underscoring the feeling of disbelief that characterized the reception of the "Monster's" crimes, Lucarelli reminds his *Blu Notte* viewers that the murders took place in "a place where you would never think such things happen. The Tuscan countryside."[69] As Spezi observed, Florence's adjacency to the countryside provided Florentines with easy access and a more organic relationship with the nearby suburban areas. Metropolitan anonymity, it was believed, enhanced the conditions that made serial murder possible.

Yet the etiology of the "Monster's" crimes shows not the spread of violence from the urban center to the periphery but rather the opposite: an origin on the periphery. If crimes such as the "Monster's" begin outside the city, what does that mean for the city itself?[70] Will a plague of violence enter the city from the hinterland in a move contra Boccaccio, whose prudent narrators of *The Decameron* leave the center of Florence, which was afflicted by the Black Plague in the fourteenth century, for a *locus amoenus* in the hills of nearby Fiesole? Will contagion of the sort present in American films such as Don Siegel's *Invasion of the Body Snatchers* (1956, remade by Philip Kaufman in 1978), where zombie aliens infiltrate a small city, chart a course for the contagion of serial murder in Florence? Or would a film such as George Romero's *Night of the Living Dead* (1968), where zombies stay fairly contained in the countryside, describe the course? On the other hand, does the movement of the zombies toward commerce (in the form of a shopping mall), in Romero's 1978 *Dawn of the Dead*—entitled *Zombi* in Italy— signal a movement toward urban life? Perhaps references to *Invasion of the Body Snatchers* and Romero's pentology (there are five films in the *Dead* series) are apt: Dario Argento's films are routinely brought into comparison with horror directors worldwide, including Romero and Don Siegel (1956) and Philip Kaufman (the 1978 remake of *Invasion of the Body Snatchers*). Significantly, would Florence as a destination see a fall-off in tourist trade from the fear of a diminished security?

AFTERLIFE: LE MONSTRE, C'EST NOUS

If there is a zombie attached to the story of the serial murders committed in Florence in the years 1974 to 1985, it is the "Monster" narrative itself, which refuses to die. Like the Undead, it resurges time and again into public discourse, the subject of various inquiries. Like so many postmodern expressions, interpretations, and theories, the "Monster" affair has no ending.[71] Fueled by a small industry of publications, public perception of the seven serially executed murders in Florence from 1974 to 1985 holds that the crimes remain unsolved. As Gianni Vattimo and Giorgio Agamben have detailed, justice, too, is in some sort of unshriven state.[72] Like Jacques Derrida before them, they indicate the aporia, or the null, at the center of justice.[73] Perhaps the "Monster" case could have been solved had it not been fouled at almost every level of the Italian justice system and had the modes of representation not created the monster of rumor that affected the judicial sentence and investigation.

Representations of the "Monster" of Florence have taken many forms. In addition to news broadcasts, televised programs on Italy's

RAI network include the episodes of *Blu notte* I have already described as well as *La cronaca in diretta* (Crime reporting live); *I fatti vostri* (The facts are yours); *Chi l'ha visto?* (Have you seen this man? Italy's version of *America's Most Wanted*); *Un giorno in pretura* (A day in court), which broadcast Pacciani's trial and, therefore, seemed more like "100 giorni in pretura," or 100 days in court, and was aptly given the second title *Storia infinita del Mostro di Firenze* ("The Infinite Story of the Monster of Florence"); *La vita in diretta* (Life, live); and *Porta a porta* (Door to door).[74] Foreign broadcasts included services from the UK, Australia, Japan, and the United States, including a 2007 installment of *Dateline* (NBC). Filmed versions of the "Monster" narrative include *Il mostro di Firenze* (*The Monster of Florence*), directed by Cesare Ferrario (1986); *Firenze: L'assassino è ancora tra di noi* (The Killer is among us), directed by Camillo Teti (1986), noteworthy for the difficulties during filming that included civic outrage on the part of Florentines; Antonio Grimaldi's television series *Il mostro di Firenze* (2009), made for Fox Crime television in Italy; and, presumably, *The Monster of Florence*, a film based on Preston and Spezi's book, starring George Clooney as Douglas Preston, scheduled for tentative release in 2013.

Writing about the "Monster" has taken on many forms, both fiction and nonfiction and, as in the case of Preston and Spezi's volume, something in between. Nonfictional coverage of the "Monster" case includes, in chronological order, Spezi's work from 1986, criminal attorney and author Nino Filastò's thoughtful *Pacciani innocente* (Pacciani innocent, 1994), forensic profiler Ruggero Perugini's *Un uomo abbastanza normale* (A normal enough man, 1994), Giuseppe Alessandri's shameless *La leggenda del Vampa: La storia del Mostro di Firenze?* (The Legend of the Vampa: History of the Monster of Florence?, 1995), jurist Francesco Ferri's *Il caso Pacciani* (The Pacciani case, 1996), Lucarelli and Giuttari's *Compagni di sangue* (*Blood Companions*, 1996), and Giuttari's *Il mostro di Firenze: anatomia di un'indagine* (The Monster of Florence: Anatomy of an investigation, 2006).

Fictional representations include seasoned Italian mystery writer Laura Grimaldi's *Il sospetto* (*Suspicion*); Pierre-Jean Rémy's 1986 novel *Una Ville Immortelle* (*An Immortal City*), which won the Grand Prix du roman de L'Académie française; and British mystery writer Magdalen

Nabb's *The Monster of Florence,* a book featuring her fictional Inspector Guarnaccia (Verlag, 1996). This list excludes novels "inspired" by the "Monster" crimes, which would feature works such as *Hannibal* by Thomas Harris (1999), in which the demented title character works as a curator in Florence; and the series of novels by Michele Giuttari featuring Chief Superintendent Michele Ferrara, *Scarabeo* and *Loggia degli Innocenti* (The Loggia of the innocent) (both published by Rizzoli in 2005).

Like magistrates Giancarlo De Cataldo and Gianrico Carofiglio, Giuttari distinguishes between his activities in law enforcement and his work as a novelist. Not everyone acknowledges his ability to do so. San Casciano mayor Roselli has said that "Giutarri (*sic*) must make up his mind whether he is a policeman or a novelist."[75] Giancarlo De Cataldo's wildly popular 2002 novel *Romanzo criminale* (*Crime Novel*) must no more be confused with an intention to present a factual representation of the Banda della Magliana, the Roman crime syndicate, than should Carofiglio's series of novels about the cases Bari defense attorney Guido Guerrieri advocates (e.g., *Testimone inconsapevole* (*Involuntary Witness*), *Ad occhi chiusi* (*With Eyes Closed*), *Ragionevoli dubbi* (*Reasonable Doubts*)). The same distinction holds for author and TV host Carlo Lucarelli, who, apart from his forays into true crime, saves his imagination (which is, to be sure, inspired by facts and the contemporary reality of daily life in Italy) for his novels.

Like other exemplars of the true crime genre, Preston and Spezi's book lies somewhere between fact and fiction, in some ways duplicating some of the troubled path taken by the investigation into the serial murders in Florence. When they are each interrogated by the police for obstruction in the case, and, in Spezi's case, when he is arrested, the coauthors of *The Monster of Florence* go down the rabbit hole, becoming themselves characters in the "Monster" narrative. Spezi and Preston's book is everywhere characterized by aspirations of fiction. Preston identifies himself immediately as a "journalist and writer of murder mysteries" who moved to Italy "to write a murder mystery set at the time of the Florentine flood."[76] We might compare this with Giuttari's aim in his nonfictional monograph on the case, where he writes that "unlike paperback *gialli,* scene-stopping revelations do not propel a true investigation; rather, it builds by inching forward in those small steps that come out of a daily routine that is evidently flat and boring."[77]

Since the infiltration of a host of literary devices is constitutive of the true crime genre, there is no foul or harm in Spezi and Preston enlisting them in the creation of their text, save, perhaps, that their stated purpose is "to find out the truth."[78] Perhaps they should no more be held responsible for this assertion than Umberto Eco, who used the literary device of the "found" manuscript as the basis for his hugely successful 1980s novel *The Name of the Rose,* or Truman Capote, who presented the massacre of the Clutter family as a nonfiction novel. Yet the dust jacket of Preston and Spezi's stresses the book's truth claim, not its fictionalization: "The Monster of Florence—A True Story." Moreover, it should be noted that Spezi appears to take pride in his literary abilities. In the 2006 civil suit he filed against Michele Giuttari for infractions of *segreto istruttorio,* or judicial seal, he "deliver(ed) an uppercut to Giuttari's soft underbelly—his literary talent."[79] More than deploying literary devices in the interest of making their nonfiction book more readable, however, their own investigations of the "Monster's" crimes appear to be catalyzed by literary aspirations. While contemplating possible killers, for example, Spezi suggests that Preston "look at it as Philip Marlowe might."[80]

Citing Raymond Chandler's legendary private detective is revealing for several reasons. First, although Chandler's books are popular in Italy, recourse to an American model is significant for the way it recalls the "Monster's" displacement onto non-Italian provenance and the disbelief in and subsequent repeated disavowal of the presence of a serial killer in Florence. The tensions between notions of "old" and "new" world are also repeated as generational tensions. Mario Spezi and Douglas Preston offer a case in point. Preston describes arranging an initial meeting with Spezi, who had been described to him as "a legendary Tuscan crime reporter" and whom he describes as "a journalist of the old school, dry, witty, cynical."[81]

"Old school" also describes the attitude toward the civic role of the press. The "Monster" narrative in which Preston and Spezi participate illustrates an understanding of the civic duties and responsibilities of the press that might also be described as "old school." During the search of his house in November 2004, Spezi called ANSA, the Italian national news agency, and mobilized his colleagues' outrage about the dangers such a search posed to freedom of the press. Preston's February 2006 police interrogation raised similar alarms in Italy as well as in the United States, where, as he notes, news stories about his predicament "went out on the AP wire, and news items appeared on CNN and ABC News."[82] As a final accolade, "On November 3, 2006, Spezi was awarded the most coveted journalistic prize in Italy for *Dolci colline di sangue* (Sweet hills of blood) and named Writer of the Year for Press."[83]

The antagonism between Spezi and Preston on the one side and Giuttari (and Lucarelli) on the other constitutes more than envy of market share, for real and material consequences have resulted for both camps as a result of their division over the underlying theory of the serial murders. Whether the "Monster" was a unique agent or several different actors distinguishes the two prevailing theories about and approaches to the case and contributes heavily to the division between the "Pacciani *innocentisti*," as those who believed in his innocence described themselves, and the "Pacciani *colpevolisti*," who posited his guilt. In this regard, the Spezi-Preston collaboration, which endorses a lone killer, stands in contrast to the joint effort of Lucarelli and Giuttari, whose theory of the crime argues for the possibility of more than one murderer.

To tell the story of a killer who is either completely innocent or completely guilty is a simple matter. Yet the "Monster" narrative is not. Who committed the crimes? Ballistic analysis established a unique feature of each bullet fired from the Beretta that killed all the victims, which, in turn, argued for linking the murders and treating them as serial crimes. However, Giuttari, when tasked by Pier Luigi Vigna with reexamining all of the court documents, uncovered a witness's deposition that established—for him, at least—that the last two double murders of 1984 and 1985 were not committed by a "lone gunman": eyewitness testimony demonstrated that the killer did not act alone. The judicial sentence of the lower court similarly determined the difference of especially the last murder.

In reality, the two theories—one of the single killer and the other of multiple offenders—need not contradict each other and appear to have cohabitated peaceably for a period of time in the public sphere of television, print media, and law enforcement. Spezi, for example, appeared on one of Lucarelli's February 2003 *Blu Notte* episodes, where he made several compelling observations about the "Monster's" crimes that seem to have been accepted respectfully.

Yet relations between coauthors Preston and Spezi and Giuttari and (by extension) his coauthor Lucarelli became strained, possibly by the competition for the market share of their differing accounts of the "Monster" crimes in both print and broadcast forums. According to Spezi and Preston, "Spezi's appearance on *Chi l'ha visto?* did have one definitive effect. It seemed to inspire Chief Inspector Giuttari's undying hatred."[84] In their view, this putative hatred drove Lucarelli's coauthor to engineer Preston and Spezi's legal woes: the two searches of Spezi's home (November 2004 and January 2005) and his April 2006 arrest, interrogation, and detention as well as Preston's February 2006 interrogation. Spezi's arrest and incarceration bracket the April 2006 publication date of his *Dolci colline di sangue,* which was published by Sonzogno. Preston and Spezi's account appeared four months after Giuttari's monograph, *Il mostro: anatomia di un'indagine,* had been released by Rizzoli. Since both Sonzogno and Rizzoli come under the management of RCS MediaGroup (others in the group include Adelphi, Bompiani, and BUR), who, one might ask, is making a killing?

The hold of the "Monster" of Florence's narrative on the Italian public imagination has been strengthened by cultural expressions and legal or mediatic investigations. Indeed, the "Monster of Florence" was nourished in the collective imagination in the way of all monsters: it was fed an admixture of "real" reportage and cultural representation. By word of mouth—or, as in the case of Giubba the troubadour, oral performance—the tale allowed rumor (as well as occasional and groundless notions of conspiracy) to prosper.

TWO

Monstrous Murder

Serial Killers and Detectives in
Contemporary Italian Fiction

*Non ci sono altri casi. Gliel'ho già detto una volta cosa penso
della sua teoria del serial killer . . . guarda un po', lo vede?
Anche la parola . . . è americana e qua siamo in Italia e non in
America. Da noi si chiamano mostri e sono quelli che tirano i
sassi sulle autostrade o quei calabresi che hanno massacrato
quella bambina per farle un esorcismo, perché la credevano
indemoniata . . . altro che serial killer. A Modena, poi, in Emilia!*

(There are no other cases. I already told you once what I think
about your theory of a "serial killer." Don't you see? Even the
word is American and we're in Italy here, not the U.S. Here we
call them *monsters* and they're like those people who throw rocks
onto the highways from the overpasses or those Calabrese guys
who killed that little girl because they thought she was possessed
by the devil. A serial killer? In *Modena*, yet, in Emilia!)

—LANZARINI, *VOX POPULI*[1]

SERIAL MURDERER, DISTRICT ATTORNEY Lanzarini adamantly informs
a police detective in Carlo Lucarelli's novel *Lupo mannaro* (Werewolf),
is an American phenomenon; it is not European and it is decidedly not
Italian. In fact, serial murder is a concept so alien in Italy that no word

exists in Italian to denote a serial murderer.[2] "In Italy," Lanzarini says, "we call them *monsters*."[3] Something perceived to be as foreign as the serial occurrence of ritualized murder requires no process that would familiarize the concept linguistically and therefore make the inconceivable cognitively comprehensible. Calling serial murderers "monsters" accomplishes an important linguistic, not to mention psychical, operation. It transposes the unthinkable onto the irrational, Gothic, and fantastic terrain where monsters dwell. This sets the phenomenon at a safer distance for an eventual contemplation that will diminish the "monsters" as the stuff of folklore, dreams, nightmares, and artistic artifacts.

While he is not wrong, Lanzarini is not exactly right, either. Like the fictitious district attorney, the Italian press, as the preceding chapter demonstrates, favors the designation "monster," frequently using it in reportage about the various incidences of serial murder in Italy.[4] Nearly all of the twenty-four murderers identified as "serial killers" were described as "monstrous" in the press. Geographically distributed throughout the peninsula, they become a frightful, frightening legion: "the Monster of Genoa," "the Monster of Valpolcevra," "the Monster of Aosta," "the Monster of Norma," the "Monster of Foligno," and "the Monster of Verona," to mention just a few. Perhaps the most celebrated case in Italy is that of Pietro Pacciani, the alleged "Monster" believed responsible for the seven serial double murders on the Florentine perimeter from 1974 to 1985.[5]

When the fictitious Lanzarini scoffs at the possibility of a serial killer in removed, pastoral Modena, he recalls the dynamic of disavowal that characterized the initial phases of the investigation of crimes attributed to the "Monster." Lanzarini's disbelief that an urban plague such as serial murder could spread to nonurban Italian locales links to the anxiety over the defamiliarization of Italian geography as experienced from within the national ranks. The contemporary Italian literary *giallo* generally worries the distinction between urban center and periphery.[6] Through their fictional representations of serial killers in Emilia Romagna and greater Milan of the 1990s, Lucarelli and Andrea Pinketts demonstrate an evolving notion of the interconnections between urban centers and the spread, or rather contagion, of social woes once believed to be restricted to urban life. Such interconnection is mirrored by the accelerating developments in telecommunications in the mid-1990s, the period largely under consideration in this part of the book, drawing distinct locales into ever-greater proximity, albeit mediated and virtual.[7] The murders that convicted serial killer Donato Bilancia committed on trains running between Monte Carlo and Genoa in 1998 are, in this regard, particularly suggestive.[8] No longer limited to urban centers or even the urban periphery, these murders were committed in the "nowhere" made possible by train travel.[9] Clearly, no causal relation exists between the literary representations published in the mid-1990s and Bilancia's 1998 homicides. Rather, Lucarelli, Pinketts, and other *giallisti* of the 1990s documented the phenomenon of increasing urban sprawl.

The train on which Donato Bilancia committed murder joins two discrete urban locales. Its to-and-fro movement sketches a similar linguistic linking characteristic of the perception of serial murder in Italy. For while the popular press favors and publicizes the *monstrous* aspect of these killers, experts (among whose ranks the fabricated Lanzarini should number, incidentally) usually call such criminals *pluriomicidi* or *pluriassassini*. These words are compounds that indicate not the serial aspect of this kind of murder so much as its multiplicity; consequently, the compound terms disallow a relationship between one homicide and another wherein murder occurs at regular intervals.[10]

As Lanzarini reminds us, "serial killer" is an American term, not to mention an American obsession.[11] Of their undeniable presence in the United States, and the infinite stories they generate, James Kincaid has asked a series of helpful questions. "What are we doing . . . with serial killers? Why do we construct them as we do? What do they represent for us? What stories do they allow us to circulate? What conditions of knowing do they generate? What needs do they bring into being and then serve? What cultural itches do they scratch?"[12]

My question, particularized for the Italian situation, concerns the need to *disavow* the presence of serial killing in Italy, a need that Lucarelli and, I believe, writers like him exploit in their "pulp" fiction of violence. To recast Kincaid's question: What are we doing *without* serial killers? How can we live without them? Or, as Edward Ingebretsen has asked about serial killers in the U.S. context, what narratives of safety and innocence are projected as a result of the outrage and hysteria produced by serial killing in Italy?[13] If, as philosopher Giorgio Agamben believes, we have become denizens of a global culture, it is a commodity culture that knows no national boundaries.[14] As denizens, how can we escape the violence so pervasive in the other geographical outposts that consume this culture?

Parallel to the increased relays between disparate sites for the production of culture made possible by developments in global communication, the markets for literature in translation and for cinema have increased without any apparent regard for the need to explain cultural differences. In this vein, we might consider, for example, the kind of cultural morphing Elaine Chang studies in the intersection of "Japanese" and "Italian" ethnic identities put into question by the Teenage Mutant Ninja Turtles.[15] The literature of horror writers such Clive Barker and Stephen King and the work of filmmakers like such as Argento, David Cronenberg, David Lynch, and Quentin Tarantino go to nearly immediate release in other countries, Italy among them.[16]

Clearly, Lucarelli, Argento, and other Italian practitioners trafficking in splatter pulp aim at an ironic representation of the bucolic Italy of yore. With no remnants of the Enlightenment-era utopia Arcadia, the Italy discursively created by a faction of contemporary cultural practitioners is one in which serial killers and other transcultural and multinationally commodified monsters frolic. Recognized materially by the wake of victims real serial killers leave behind them or produced phantasmatically by, among others, the discursive industries of pornography and fashion, the monsters I inspect here fetishize skin, and by extension, the body politic, training on its assailable places and violating them.

The narrative of the "Monster" of Florence, as noted in the preceding chapter, serves as a template in numerous ways. First, as the most notorious instance of serial murder in Italy, the double homicides committed around Florence between the years of 1974 and 1985, seriously challenge the claim that serial murder is not an Italian phenomenon. Second, we notice the serial nature of the case and the meaning that unfolds from it. Third, we attend to the topography, noting the relation that the discrete murders have to the series and to the nearby city of Florence. Significantly, this is not a Jack the Ripper–style urban nightmare, for all the murders occur in places that, if not exactly the hinterland, are at least locales removed from urban centers.[17] Finally, we note the posture of the law and its officers. These cultural representations underscore the ways the law failed to explain, resolve, and contain the Pacciani case.

"COSÌ È LA LEGGE UN CAZZO!" TAKING A BITE AT / THE BITE OUT OF THE LAW

"A serial killer in Emilia Romagna! In Lambrusco country?"[18]

No one believes that the succession of wrongful deaths of young, female drug addicts constitutes the work of a serial killer. No one, that is, save Inspector Romeo, who suspects that one killer is responsible for the corpses of the young women with slashed throats and cadavers that exhibit human bite marks. In a way, Prosecutor Lanzarini is right once again: no series of murders has occurred in Modena proper. But Romeo and his unit identify the Via Emilia, the region's principal traffic corridor. It is lined with the shanty towns of *extracomunitari,* as noncitizens of the European Union present in Italy are called, and it provides the main conduit through the region for the traffic in women and narcotics. As one of Romeo's men observes, "In effect you can see this region as one huge city that stretches from Reggio to Cattolica . . . a kind of Los Angeles with several million inhabitants and Via Emilia as an enormous surface 'on the road.'"[19] His statement exemplifies the sort of defamiliarization of terrain described in the introduction and chapter 1, and in some respects, it captures the dynamic of the process of symbolic coding and deterritorialization.

The roving killer, affluent engineer Mario Velasco, does not elude the police for long. Lucarelli contrasts the killer and Romeo, the detective on his trail. Wealthy, married with two children, an exemplar of the managerial class in Silvio Berlusconi's Italy, Velasco lacks affect almost entirely, like the "monstrous" Adolf Eichmann, whom Hannah Arendt described during his trial in Jerusalem for his crimes against humanity. For Arendt, Eichmann appeared "terribly and terrifyingly normal."[20] Apart from the nefarious murders, Velasco operates within, or even according to, the letter of the law. For example, far from fleeing law enforcement and its agents, he presents himself with his attorney at the precinct house to inquire into the charges brought against him. Assured that he is no longer under suspicion, he continues with the business of his daily life, even surprising Romeo and Grazia, the inspector's sidekick at the office—and, more recently, in bed—as they surveil him illegally. Opposed to this picture of deadly calm we have Romeo, a certifiable wreck. Recently diagnosed with *insonnia familiare letale,* a chronic and, it seems, ultimately terminal form of insomnia, Romeo suffers throughout the novel from sleeplessness and the side effects of medication to counteract it.[21]

The contrast in character not only anticipates Romeo's demise, it structurally guarantees the failure of his inquest. He has no official command to continue the investigation, nor can he link any of the evidence— that is, the length of the belt used to strangle the victims, the eyewitness's account of the license plate, or even the size of incisors in the dental cast—to his prime suspect. Ever imperturbable, Velasco realizes that Romeo and Grazia have finally grasped the only possible link between him and the murders: Monica Pasini, a young woman reported missing in 1987, whose remains, Romeo is convinced, are hidden on the engineer's property. A brief and illicit inspection of Velasco's house verifies what the architectural plans expose: the cellar, location of the architecturally repressed, can be the only hiding place for the human remains.

After days of wakefulness and stakeout outside Velasco's apartment house, sleep finally overcomes Romeo. Waking quickly in his car, he discovers his error and, in a succession of quick maneuvers, rushes the engineer and his abode. This impulsive act reveals nothing extraordinary except the cellar floor that the engineer has only just completed paving over with cement. The novel's climax and quick denouement ushers in the police department's official sanction of Romeo for pursuing a private, law-abiding citizen without cause and authority, which results in his suspension from the force and compelled early retirement. The stripping of Romeo's authority for presumed ineptitude recalls in some respects the ways Michele Giuttari, the former director of GIDES (Gruppo investigativo dei delitti seriali, Serial Crimes Investigation Squad) and a lead inspector on the case of the "Monster" of Florence, was disciplined for his alleged abuse of office.

Romeo's public censure and subsequent dismissal are not the only examples of the ways *Lupo mannaro* works to rebuke organs of law, law enforcement, and social regulation. Early on, Romeo loses a material witness, Emir Ben Abid, a Senegalese immigrant who had seen a black Mercedes at the most recent murder. Ben Abid has successfully provided the police with a partial license plate number, proving Velasco's ownership of the car and placing him at the murder. Notwithstanding such valuable corroboration, however, the *extracomunitario* is quickly processed for deportation. "*Così è la legge, dottore*" (That's the law, boss), one of his officers tells him. When Romeo, who cannot overlook the ways in which several levels of police bureaucracy accommodate Velasco, explodes "*Così è la legge un cazzo!*" (That's the law, my ass!), he illustrates the inadequacy of the law and the inefficacy of legal investigation.[22] The killer observes rules, and the novel leaves him free to roam the interregional arteries to kill again. Romeo, by contrast, although a member of the police force, performs his role outside legal purview and is punished for it.

In *Lupo mannaro,* the piercing of the victims' skin signals the vulnerability of *social* tissue, something the law cannot even protect, much less embody or reinforce.[23] Killing for pleasure is no longer extraordinary or limited to the subjectivity of an individual such as a Freikorps soldier who would kill with the impunity his "armored body" afforded.[24] Rather, a more pervasive subjectivity of violence, imposed from without like a "social substitute skin," has replaced it.[25] As Julia Kristeva elaborated in *The Powers of Horror,* the skin contains the "abject"—that which the body will expel and, given the social subject's consequent revulsion of it, which functions vitally in the dynamic of horror.[26] No dam, the skin is hymenal, permeable, penetrable, able to be ruptured, able to heal but whose scar, as Freud says, will endlessly serve as the trace of the wound. And crime itself is abject, Kristeva reminds us: "Any crime, because it draws attention to the frailty of the law, is abject. Premeditated crime, cunning murder, hypocritical revenge are even more so because they heighten the display of such frailty."[27] The monstrous also points to the other key condition of abjectivity, the notion of excess in whose economy the violence of the recent cannibal fiction in Italy functions.[28] Representations of serial killers may contribute to the system of disavowal I described with regard to the reception of the "Monster" case in Florence. A nation as wary as Italy of segmentation of the body—at least inasmuch as organ donation demonstrates this tendency—would find alarming, indeed, the abundance of shredded, pierced, flayed, and damaged skin situated at the intersection of serial killing and the monstrous.[29]

Skin and its perforation fascinates Romeo and Velasco equally, although in different ways. Romeo defends his station within the *organ* of the law, against Velasco's impinging and external force. Thus, Velasco's position resembles the formulation of the serial killer as the menacing "Other" who "fulfill(s) a critical social function in defining conventional morality and behavior by providing a *ne plus ultra* against which normal society readily finds common ground."[30]

Drawn to the bite marks exhibited on one of the cadavers during the coroner's inquest, Romeo sees "the bluish signs of the teeth on the girl's legs, the violet holes that dig into her skin in a tight, deep, perfectly circular crown. And I see them on her buttocks, numerous and dark, when the doctor grabs her by the arm with a soft, flat crack to turn her on the marble tabletop, something that surprises me."[31]

Although Velasco understands his impulse to kill, a rationale for the compulsion to bite his victims eludes him. Killing the young women, he coolly tells the inspector when he informally confesses to the crimes, "makes me feel better. . . . It's a way of eliminating stress and in a manager's job . . . you accumulate a lot of it."[32] On the other hand, he tells Romeo during their colloquy that "the only thing I don't know is why I bite them."[33] Lucarelli hints at vampirism by referring to Velasco's skin, which Romeo finds "strange." Like the milky, preternaturally youthful skin of a nocturnal vampire, the engineer's skin is "smooth and rosy, almost without wrinkles, taut like that of a child."[34] Thus, framing the biting as vampiric (and not lycanthropic, as the title *Lupo mannaro*— Werewolf—might suggest), Lucarelli permits one monster to bleed, as it were, into another. That the bites are located not only on the victim's throat, the mythic and familiar point of the vampire's entry, but also on the legs and buttocks illustrates just how formidable is this method of assault; it needs no orifice to violate or rape: skin is everywhere and therefore everywhere violable.

BODY OF CRIME, EMBODIED LAW AND ORDER

Grazia Negro, Inspector Romeo's sidekick from *Lupo mannaro,* centers Lucarelli's *Almost Blue.* In this novel, Negro acts as a young specialist attached to the national UACS (l'Unità per l'Analisi dei Crimini Violenti), the actual behavioral science unit headed by the forensic expert in the "Monster" case, Ruggero Perugini.[35] Grazia's superior, Vittorio Poletto, has deployed her to Bologna to catch the Iguana, a serial killer targeting students at the university. These are not the conditions of the hinterland trysts in which the "Monster's" victims were attacked and killed. Given that, as Vittorio estimates, some 200,000 students live and study in Bologna, the cause for alarm is genuine. Vittorio and Grazia encounter the same skepticism Lanzarini displayed in *Lupo mannaro*. As though Vittorio has learned the lessons Romeo could not, he avoids using English to name the serial killer, preferring instead *"assassino seriale,"* a literal translation of the English. Notwithstanding Vittorio's lexical care, however, the police chief reminds him, in language identical to Lanzarini's, "We're not in America here, we're in Italy."[36] More than from her male counterparts on the Bologna police force or from the father figure Poletto plays, Grazia receives help from Simone, a young blind man who rarely leaves the house and prefers to eavesdrop on cell-phone and CB conversations he intercepts with his police scanner.

Simone exemplifies one of those for whom developments in telecommunications were thought to provide greater access to the public sphere. Citizens who, like Simone, are challenged in ways that might isolate them from social discourse—the infirm, the less mobile, the blind, and so forth—can, nevertheless, contribute and participate in activities as varied as commerce or social networking.[37] But Simone's technophilia substitutes for actual engagement: he infinitely prefers the controlled atmosphere of his room and the bodyless and therefore anonymous voices he picks up with his apparatuses.[38] Like the blind soothsayer Tiresias "seeing" Oedipus's murderous act, Simone—ever an astute listener—develops concern about the "green" voice of the Internet chat participant that is eventually identified as the wanted killer.[39]

Much more soothing to Simone's finely tuned ear is Grazia's "blue" voice that he picks up on his audio scanner, and Simone subsequently contacts Grazia with his information about the voice he has associated with the killer. "Almost blue" describes both Grazia's voice and the cool jazz of Chet Baker—and, after him, Elvis Costello—singing the song of the same name. Lucarelli exerts himself to establish Grazia's female presence. Her disembodied voice is one of the devices he uses.[40]

It would be tempting to link this to Kaja Silverman's thoughts about the disembodied female presence in cinema, but in fact *Almost Blue* strips embodiment from many of its characters irrespective of gender. The Iguana's voice takes on more importance than the body that he tries to hide or make invisible. It is the murderer's voice that betrays him in ways his shaved head never could in a city like Bologna, where so many university students in the 1990s adopted similar *punk a bestia* (skinhead) dress and wore headphones for personal stereo systems. Further, the effect of Vittorio's numerous telephonic interventions from great distances is to constantly underscore his absence, making him seem all the more God-like.

Although her voice helps establish her female presence, Grazia, by contrast, is almost relentlessly embodied in the text. Lucarelli persists in giving Grazia her body with all its "grace" (as her name suggests) and in all its female reproductive glory. Descriptions of Grazia's menstruation appear from her first entrance and continue until her eventual meeting with Simone. When she and Vittorio present their theories about a serial killer to the Bologna police force and magistrates, the imminent cramps signaling her menstrual period rumble like a constant thought, furnishing Grazia with a strong sense of body. At the very moment in the presentation that she projects images of the Iguana's annihilation of his victim's bodies, the relation of menstruation to reproduction serves literally to enliven her.

Vittorio later describes the killer's work as the attempt to create a mask to shield his naked and vulnerable inner being.[41] As he remarks, "This is why he kills. More than this, this is why he rips people apart, he pulverizes, he destroys them. He annihilates them. He strips them nude and he strips himself nude and takes on their appearance, as if he was putting on a second skin."[42] Ripping the flesh away from his victims, the Iguana commits the "ontological offense" that Adriana Cavarero explores in her recent work on the victims of trauma, violence, and war, *Horrorism: Naming Contemporary Violence*.[43] Glossing Hannah Arendt, Cavarero notes how murder constitutes the "killing of uniqueness," something the Iguana's destruction of his victims' flesh ensures.

Adopting a second skin relates to the motif of shredded skin that threads through this chapter and, in this instance, sharply recalls

Thomas Harris's fictional portrayals of serial killers. Given the careful removal of the skins of his victims, Jame Gumb in *The Silence of the Lambs* (1989), for example, is known to law enforcement officials as Buffalo Bill.[44] But more than to this villain, Lucarelli's Iguana owes a debt to the first novel in Harris's Hannibal Lecter trilogy, *Red Dragon* (1981). Here, the killer, Frances Dolarhyde, also seeks a second skin, something he tries to achieve through extensive tattooing. He hopes the inscribed ink will at least bring him visual resemblance to his obsession, the paintings of the Great Red Dragon by early-nineteenth-century English poet and artist William Blake.[45] The Iguana's attempts with paint, however, lack the permanent inscription of Dolarhyde's tattoos. Lucarelli's serial killer might be altogether less indelible than Harris's.

Apart from the reference to serial killers in the annals of popular Anglo-American literature, within Lucarelli's narrative the dragon has a different provenance and signifies almost any lizard or reptile. The Iguana, whose name is Alessio Crotti, complained to the priests at his orphanage of being terrified of "a dragon covered in scales that leapt up on his chest *and tried to eat his face.*"[46] When Grazia learns that Crotti escaped from a deadly fire in a hospital for the criminally insane, she is struck by his emergence from the fire and begins to call him the Iguana, even though Vittorio reminds her that salamanders are the lizards that mythology and folktales have associated with fires.

Lucarelli's Iguana of *Almost Blue,* in his monstrousness, recalls Anna Maria Ortese's 1965 novel *L'Iguana.*[47] Comparing figurations of the monstrous illustrates the profound difference between these two iguanas. Whereas in her discursive formation of monstrosity Ortese aspires to invite the abject subject out of isolation into circulation and, perhaps, into a fluid state of becoming, Lucarelli's narrative rigidifies Crotti's incurable monstrousness.[48] Though the altered state of mental illness might offer radical possibility for some cultural critics, schizophrenia of the sort that afflicts Lucarelli's Iguana will not lead to greater ontological prospects. The serial murderer will be tracked and will die by his own hand at the brink of capture. Law and order will be restored, ironically, by Simone and Grazia, both of whom are themselves marginalized by the patriarchy of the justice system that Lucarelli's novel makes crystal clear.

As a female police officer, and consequently already a liminal figure, Grazia need not reject police protocol as her former superior, Romeo, does in *Lupo mannaro*.[49] Her liminality is reinforced by her "special agent" status on the national forensic investigative unit, which requires her to collaborate with various counterparts throughout Italy, and by her regionality. As Grazia tells an officer who challenges her expertise with such an unusual phenomenon as serial killing, "My name isn't Callaghan, it's Negro. And I'm from Nardò, outside Lecce."[50] She is, in other words, from the southern hinterland, not the likeliest of places, she implies, to find a crack homicide detective.

Lucarelli comments on the uncomfortable presence of women on the police force by allowing one of Grazia's male counterparts to remark, "I know you female police officers . . . always pissed off and ready to prove that they're better than men . . . and for Christ's sake, dress a little bit like a woman!"[51] Lucarelli's Grazia seems virtually invincible. Her determination to remain on the case distinguishes her from, say, Silvia della Monica, the female magistrate involved in the investigation of the "Monster's" crimes, who resigned following her receipt of an anonymous letter containing fragments of the excised breast of Nadine Mauriot, the French tourist found murdered in Scopeti in September 1985.

Grazia denies any claim of overweening ambition, saying, "I'll never become chief of detectives because I don't hold a college degree," even assuring her male colleague that "I'd even dress like a woman if I could figure out where the fuck to carry my gun."[52] Grazia is undermined by her male colleagues. No matter how great his admiration, Vittorio blanches when informed that Grazia has her period. In his frequent phone calls and messages, Vittorio repeatedly calls her "*bambina*." For Vittorio, this is an obvious endearment, but it nevertheless inscribes her subordinate position.[53]

Grazia only occasionally wears women's clothing, and, like the Iguana hunting a skin that fits, she seeks some sort of comfort zone within the police force. Another element linking the two characters is the discomfort each feels "in" their skin. In Grazia's case, this is created by the frequently referred-to menstrual cramps always hovering close by. Similarly, the Iguana believes that "sometimes there's something moving underneath my skin like an animal."[54]

Grazia dresses appropriately for work, typically wearing trousers, combat boots, and a leather bomber jacket.[55] The first time Simone meets her, he immediately notices Grazia's unusual scent. Like many of the blind, Simone has a refined sense of smell and tries to discern the uncommon odor that trails Grazia into the rarified air of his room: "Her smell isn't great. It's like old smoke that her jacket has absorbed, sharp like sweat and a little sweet, like blood, like his mother's smell on certain days."[56] Lucarelli could have stopped there, on a time-honored misogynistic note, but what Simone really discerns is the metallic note of, and smell of the lubricant for, Grazia's gun.

Almost Blue never separates Grazia from her pistol. Grazia has accumulated considerable expertise aimed at making police work more about science, less about force and firearms. Her skills, including the scientific gathering of physical evidence and its analysis, as well as her extensive familiarity with computer software programs intended to make crime fighting more precise, should result in a more gender-neutral police force. But the technologies applied to warfare have not necessarily reduced gender as an element of difference in the military any more than the applied technology of the Internet has made for a participatory democracy with a broader base.[57] Simone's great reluctance to become involved in the police investigation speaks eloquently to this point.

Skin, skinning, and even another insomniac investigator also appear in Eraldo Baldini's *Bambine*. In Ravenna, it is journalist and insomniac Carlo Bertelli who comes closest to establishing the identikit, the profile of the killer using methods developed by the Federal Bureau of Investigation's Behavioral Science Unit. As in Lucarelli's *Lupo mannaro*, the murderer, suspected of the abduction, rape, bludgeoning, and scalping of little girls, is not apprehended. Seriality builds in two ways in this novel: the accumulation of the victims' bodies and the growing number of losses sustained by the protagonist. The killer, probably a neurosurgeon from Ferrara—though Baldini categorically denies the reader any presentation of him—makes his gruesome way from one young victim to the next. Although Bertelli personally knows none of the casualties, their accumulation in a series implicates his own series of losses: sleep, his youth, the pristine Ravenna he knew, his marriage, his father, his best friend Luca. Just as Lucarelli had occasion to do in *Lupo mannaro*,

Baldini refers overtly to the Florentine case. Citing the removal of body parts (the left breast and the pubic flesh) in the murders attributed to the "Monster" of Florence, Baldini draws our attention to the scalping of the beautiful "*bambine.*"

What does the skinning of these young victims suggest? The scalps appear as ghastly trophies for the killer's hapless go-between in crime, the wanderer Salvo Gremmi, who pastes them on the heads of dolls, so remarkable for their inanimation, which accompany him on his rounds of Ravenna. Gremmi's three-wheeled motorized cart is the first thing Carlo spies at the beginning of the novel, where his gaze is drawn to "those things. Those fetishes, it occurred to me. Dolls and dollies of discolored plastic, perhaps gathered from some dump, or from along the banks of one of the many canals in the area, where the current often leaves refuse. I saw . . . their hair wave in the breeze. They seemed . . . like tiny, nude, macabre trophies."[58]

Baldini underscores what is at once quintessentially abject and feminized.[59] Richard Tithecott, observing the close link with the abject, reminds us that "the motivation of serial killers is frequently explained in terms of the need to expel: to expel the feminine, to expel the homosexual."[60] Gremmi himself, who is merely the serial killer's factotum, would feel little need to render abject the container for the elusive, veiled truth.[61] Like some masochistic counterpart, Gremmi *retrieves* what the killer feels the "need to expel," reclaiming the dolls from the ash heap of "things thrown out." These jettisoned dolls, once the toys of projection (of maternity? sorority? friendship?) of, it is likely, little girls, are as dead and discarded, as feminized and abject, as the victims whose hair ghoulishly adorns their heads.[62]

These pretty dolls, fetishes once more, reappear as the fashion models of Andrea Pinketts's beautiful, complex *Il senso della frase* (A way with words). All three of Pinketts's novels—*Lazzaro, vieni fuori* (Lazarus, come forth), *Il vizio dell'agnello* (The lamb's sin), and especially *Il senso della frase*—exhibit traits of the monstrous and feature a legal apparatus that is unable to account for or resolve it. Set in and around Milan in the 1990s, these novels stage the antics and ruminations of amateur detective Lazzaro Sant'Andrea.[63] Milan, home to domestic and international fashion titans, produces series upon series, series of series.

In Pinketts's text, one series is embedded within and implicates another. First, taken together, his books constitute a series for junior detective Lazzaro, for we see him practice his detective skills and improve them through repetition. Second, each book concerns a series of crimes, serial murder more often than not.

Monsters appear in extreme shapes and sizes in Pinketts's novels. Wherever Lazzaro happens to stray—within or outside nocturnal Milan, his primary beat—he encounters the grotesque: the abnormally tiny (midgets—principally in *Il vizio dell'agnello*), the abnormally huge (giants, in *Lazzaro, vieni fuori* and *Il senso della frase*), and characters sporting all manner of noticeable disfigurements. The grotesque players pave the way for the series of monstrous crimes that occur in each of the three novels: a succession of dead children in *Lazzaro, vieni fuori*; a train of poisoned homeless people throughout Milan in *Il vizio dell'agnello*; and a sequence of murders in *Il senso della frase* that at first seem unrelated but ultimately serve to reshape our notion of series and serial murder.

Like Lucarelli's and Baldini's novels, *Il senso della frase* displays scarce respect for the law or the faith that standard legal or police practice will unravel intricate cases like those presented by serial murder. Lazzaro baldly states his mistrust and dismissal of the law: of the serial murderer, Lazzaro says, "I don't want to denounce (him to authorities). I want to punish him"[64] In *Il senso della frase,* Lazzaro's considerable *senso della frase,* his way with words, leads him to the case of the vanished pathological liar, Nicky.

Nicky the liar, who claims to be the daughter of Joan Collins and an Italian painter, has disappeared from the Milan club circuit, and Lazzaro misses her. Although Lucarelli proposed the engineer Velasco as an exemplar of Italy in the age of Berlusconi, Milan offers a more convincing backdrop for this than Modena. Milan, the locus of Berlusconi's media empire and political headquarters of Bettino Craxi, is also the epicenter of the Tangentopoli (Bribe City) scandal that began in 1992.[65] Not a beautiful woman, Nicky admirably passed as the most desirable woman in the White Bear, a gathering place for members of Milan's international fashion industry. The walls of the White Bear, located in Via Vincenzo Monti, are papered with the composites of the clientele.

As a poet, Lazzaro says, Monti was never a marvel. Yet the street that bears his name "is the street in which life and death ideally conjoin. Life is represented by the bars in which the American models, starved for cappuccinos and the covers of fashion magazines, park themselves. Death is found in the somberness of Via Vincenzo Monti."[66]

The meeting of life and death in Via Vincenzo Monti is replicated by the joining of "Eros and Thanatos," both of which are represented by the fashion industry mavens that frequent the bars in the area. In the White Bear, as Lazzaro observes, the walls were "papered with the composites of the models, male and female. *A human tapestry*. Photos from the past and the present. . . . *The composites were like the shellacked photos on headstones*. A death certificate."[67]

Although Nicky could never land a modeling job with her unorthodox looks, she has her "book" made and her head shots distributed. Lazzaro repeatedly refers to her resemblance to a "prehistoric bird," with her "hooked nose." In a novel where women adopt the identities of others with confusing fluidity, Nicky's nose is her distinguishing attribute. It also leads to her untimely end. Searching for the absent Nicky leads Lazzaro through a series of series in a Milan that grows in unfamiliarity as the Christmas holiday draws near. Sisters pretend to be each other, cousins pretend to be sisters, women of no relation pretend to be sisters, a sequence of goon Santa Clauses is on the loose, disreputable porn stars surprisingly become good Samaritans, and on and on. Lazzaro's way with words—the *"senso della frase"* of the novel's title—ultimately leads him to Olegario Bizzi, a monster in the making.[68]

Although Milan seems to produce nothing but serials, reproductions, and simulacra, a phenomenon Pinketts makes all the more clear with the backdrop of the fashion industry's objectification of the body, serial murder itself is once again relegated to the provinces, this time to Bizzi's town of Mona, near Vicenza. Bizzi's wife Amelia, long dead, and Nicky are the banal casualties of sadomasochism. Their untimely ends have also primed Olegario's homicidal pump, for now he has developed a taste for murder and relishes killing Barbaro Zanotto, the homeless man he ritually crucifies.

Pinketts draws Mona and Milan, the warehouse and the White Bear bar in Via Vincenzo Monti, into proximity as he narrates Bizzi's wall of photomontage in his Mona lair. The geographical collapse, a frequent device of the Italian literary *giallo* I have been describing here, mirrors the proximity into which fashion, the grotesque, and photography are drawn. The photographic evidence on the walls detailing an endless succession of human deformity and mutilation explicitly corresponds to the other wall in Via Vincenzo Monti. Bizzi's display of a photographic series of a different stripe offers the same spectatorial fascination and fetishization. At the novel's climax, Bizzi switches on the light and all Lazzaro can see are "gigantic photographs. The photos showed different subjects, subjects reduced to objects for the most part. There were blindfolds, whips, chains, forceps. It would have been a scene of the most banal sadomasochistic stuff if not for the subjects. Every type of deformity was present, from the most innocuous to the most shocking."[69] Lazzaro takes in the detailed montage of the victims of torture and, eventually, murder at the hands of Bizzi.[70]

Pinketts's Via Vincenzo Monti recalls Lucarelli's use of the Via Emilia in *Lupo mannaro*. Both thoroughfares have urban origins that stretch far into and across outlying areas.[71] The Via Emilia permits Bologna's urban unruliness to stretch into the pastoral area of "Lambrusco country." For Pinketts, Via Vincenzo Monti slices across Milan's extraurban areas, joining Bizzi's fetishized violence in the Po hinterland and the fashion industry's fetishization of the body in the center of Milan. Lazzaro observes that the Via Vincenzo Monti, at its erotic provenance in Milan, is the place where the fashion industry enacts its *symbolic* murder of the models, objectifying the body through endless photographs to the point where the models' composites "were like the shellacked photos on headstones."[72]

A set of exchanges takes place at Via Vincenzo Monti's figurative terminus in Mona: Thanatos replaces Eros, repetition cedes to seriality of the sort that characterizes ritual murder, and the restitution of the body achieves a chilling, singular effect. In place of Milan's fragmentation and subsequent fetishization of body parts by way of the close photographic focus that contributes to the "disciplinary apparatus of fashion" photography, Mona reinstates the body entire.[73] Can it be accidental that *mona* means, in dialect, "pussy" (a relationship Pinketts elsewhere ironizes) and that synecdoche and segmentation take place as well on another level entirely? The fetishization of the part transforms into the fetishization of the complete, colossal (the photos are "*in gigantografie*," wall-size prints), *monstrous* whole. The welter of deformities Bizzi's warehouse wall chronicles discloses what drew Nicky's murderer to her: her nonstandardly beautiful "hooked nose." Equal in its attractive power is the skin of one of Bizzi's victims, which is like *polpa rossa* (red pulp), an image that strikes Lazzaro powerfully.[74]

The skin of the deformed model marks the confluence of "pulp" and "fiction."[75] As the iconoclastic mid-twentieth-century Italian author and critic Curzio Malaparte wrote, "One's skin is the only thing that counts now. The only certain, tangible, undeniable thing is one's skin. It's the only thing we possess, the only thing that's our own. . . . Everything is made of human skin. Men no longer fight for honor, freedom, and justice. They fight for their skins. Their loathsome skins."[76] What draws all these texts together, what establishes a series among them, and what fits them under the rubric of pulp fiction is the fetishization of skin and of the body, whether in the commodity structure of the fashion industry or the economy of the monstrous, trained as it is on the abject (Malaparte's "repellent skin"), the Gothic, and the unspeakable.

Like Nanni Moretti in *Caro Diario,* as I discussed in the introduction, Italy and Italians are repelled and at the same time fascinated by serial killers.[77] In the variegated style of Moretti's film, they disregard the boundaries of fantasy and *cronaca,* fashioning a complex, blurry vision of serial murder that dismisses it as "monstrous." Availing the construction of the monstrous in Italy, the skin-mongering serial killers in the print of newspapers and novels travel freely between the competing realms of representation and experience, history and fiction. However much the nation, with its bulwark of language, folklore, and fantasy, would care to pave over their existence, by running together, say, the graphemes *pluri* and *omicida,* these serial killers emerge, as if from the interstices between Lanzarini's iterated "serial killer," to puncture, slash, and eat away at the delicate skin of the body politic.

THREE

"Penile" Procedure

Law and Order in Dario Argento's Cinema

Go to Italy. It's a peaceful country. Nothing ever happens there.

—DARIO ARGENTO, *L'UCCELLO DALLE PIUME DI CRISTALLO*

SOCIALLY SYMBOLIC PRACTICES IN ITALY representing serial murder
span a variety of genres, including examples that are literary, such as the
texts explored in the preceding chapter, as well as cinematic, the primary
focus of this chapter, which addresses specifically the films of Dario
Argento. My aim is not to make the fictional and cinematic narratives
equivalent to the investigation of the serial sex murders in and around
Florence attributed to the "Monster." Rather, my interest lies in the way
murders that are real and those that are represented are interwoven.
Consequently, the cinema of Dario Argento in some instances links explicitly to the "Monster's" murders. At the same time, Argento's cinema
also reveals the broader context of the representation of serial violence in
contemporary Italy, the very context in which the "Monster's" murders
are embedded. The film that garners the most attention in this chapter,
La Sindrome di Stendhal (*The Stendhal Syndrome*, 1996), enters into an
obvious dialogue with the "Monster" narrative.

At the conclusion of the preceding chapter, only when amateur detective Lazzaro Sant'Andrea switches on the light does he see (and real-

ize) the magnitude of Olegario's crimes: it is no accident that the photographic evidence is offered in the form of *gigantografie*, or wall-sized blow-ups.[1] The sense of sight has obvious and crucial importance for the film spectator, for the discovery of homicide, and especially for police detective Anna Manni in Argento's *La Sindrome di Stendhal*. The eye as the locus of recognition and realization is often, in the director's oeuvre, the site of tremendous vulnerability. Although, as stated, equivalency is not my intention, visual witness and spying played a key role in the "Monster" narratives. This is attested to by the role played in the investigation by the *guardoni*, the voyeurs roaming the Tuscan countryside in search of sexual activity to view covertly, who were at first considered suspects and then believed to be witnesses to the "Monster's" crimes.

The serial murders in Pinketts's novels play out not in a Tuscan setting, but in cosmopolitan Milan, hub of the international fashion world to which photography is central. This foreign presence links Milan and the surrounding hinterland to Tuscany, where disbelief that serial murder could take place in the pastoral Florentine periphery became a blanket rejection of the "Italianness" of the double homicides, considered the likely work of a foreigner. As Francesco Ferri, president of the Court of Assizes in which Pacciani's sentence was overturned, observed, cases of *Lustmord* "had been identified in the Germanic and Anglo-Saxon contexts, (but) never in a Latin one."[2]

As Dario Argento's corpus of films testifies, violence like that attributed to the Monster was not completely absent from the Italian imaginary, however much it was displaced, disavowed and, in the case of cinema, censored. Argento's films point to violence indigenous to Italian locales. Like other fictional and cinematic narratives featuring amateur detectives, Argento's films highlight police incompetence, another key element in the "Monster" narratives. Consequently, the director's films also help configure and represent state authority and gender norms.

∽

Since the release of his first film, *L'uccello dalle piume di cristallo* (*The Bird with the Crystal Plumage*, 1970), Dario Argento has distinguished himself as a practitioner of films in the interrelated genres of the Italian film noir, the *giallo*, the slasher film, and the horror film. Rather

than observe strict distinctions between these genres, some critics allow the term *filone* to stand as an umbrella category. A *filone* is a thick
braid of varied film "fibers," as it were, rather than a codifiable genre.
The term is useful for the way it captures how many of these films, and
Dario Argento's films in particular, work between and among varied
popular film types.[3] The term *filone* instead of *school* is useful for the
way it spans varied cinematic genres as well as locations of production.
As Mary Wood has observed, "Horror film-makers refuse to regard
themselves as an 'Italian School' and there is constant creative contact,
particularly with American directors such as Tobe Hooper, Wes Craven,
Sam Raimi, Aaron Lipstadt, David Cronenberg, and Roger Corman."[4]
Wood also notes that technical staff responsible for a film's overall design, for example, assistant directors and camera operators, tend to move
from one horror production to another, furthering the *filone*'s hybrid
character.[5] Argento's Italian predecessors in the *filone* of horror include
Antonio Margheriti, Lucio Fulci, Mario Bava, and Riccardo Freda—the
so-called step-brothers of neorealism, for the way they contrast with the
reigning school that dominated critical camps.[6]

Argento's films weave in and out of the various strands of this *filone*.
Films from the first part of his career tend to be considered representative of the *giallo,* or murder mystery, trend. In addition to *L'uccello
dalle piume di cristallo, Quattro mosche di velluto grigio (Four Flies on
Grey Velvet,* 1971) and *Profondo rosso (Deep Red)*, Argento's popular and
highly praised film of 1975, might all be located at the intersection of
film noir and the *giallo.*[7] However, with the 1977 film *Suspiria*, the first
in the Triologia delle madri (the Mothers' Trilogy, which also includes
Inferno [1980] and *La terza madre [Mother of Tears,* 2007]), Argento
veered more in the direction of supernatural horror. In addition to the
Mothers' Trilogy, films that could be considered in this league include
Tenebre (Tenebrae/Unsane, 1982), *Trauma* (1993), and Argento's remake
of *Il fantasma dell'opera (The Phantom of the Opera,* 1998). As in the
novels of Carlo Lucarelli and Andrea Pinketts that are discussed in the
preceding chapter, in these films monstrous figures tend to bleed together and blur generic distinction so that, for example, a film might be
a *giallo* but the catalyst for its serial killer may be supernatural. Argento
finds codification similarly rigid and sometimes specious. When an in-

terviewer observed a distinction between Argento's naturalistic thrillers and supernatural horror films, the filmmaker replied, "I think that's an artificial distinction: I don't see a great difference between them. The realistic pictures are not very realistic, even though they're about psychopaths rather than witches."[8]

One element binding Argento's different films is the phenomenon of serial murder. The pathology of serial murder is rooted in the killer's unsettled relation to heteronormativity and to social behavior that is organized "properly" and according to gender.[9] Several canonical cinematic examples can be found in Hitchcock's *Psycho* (1960), Brian De Palma's *Dressed to Kill* (1980), and Jonathan Demme's *The Silence of the Lambs* (1991). Argento's oeuvre includes many female protagonists, which establishes many opportunities for policing them to make sure they fill their "proper" roles. Films featuring a female protagonist include the Asia Tetrology, as I call the four films in which Argento's daughter, Asia Argento, stars: *Trauma, La Sindrome di Stendhal* (1996), *Il fantasma dell'opera,* and *La terza madre.* Other films with female leads include *Suspiria, Inferno, Phenomena,* and *Opera* (1987).

Argento's films illustrate in multiple settings the failure of standard methods of police investigation, recalling how the Florence press corps and law enforcement agencies were flummoxed by the extreme novelty of the "Monster's" serial murders and were caught *impreparati,* to use veteran crime journalist and author Mario Spezi's description.[10] Additionally, in Argento's cinema, agents of the police are routinely depicted as imbeciles unable to solve violent crimes. The fact that murder in Argento's films is often serial in nature, and therefore repeated and frequent, affords the police ample opportunity to demonstrate their incompetence. In Argento's corpus, striking tensions between gendered subjectivities deeply etch the process of detection and the resolution of the mystery, parapsychological or otherwise, making for the substitution of "penile" for "penal" in the title of this chapter.

The amateur detectives in the corpus of Argento's films, including, for example, *L'uccello dalle piume di cristallo, Profondo rosso, Non ho sonno (Sleepless,* 2001), and *Il cartaio (The Card Player,* 2004), clearly illustrate police incompetence. Agents of the police in Argento's films, especially detectives who should know better, are not just dim-witted but far stupider than any viewer, and certainly inferior to the film's amateur detective. Importantly, they are abysmal semioticians: the police fail to decipher signs and their significance even if, literally, they stare them straight in the face.

"HURTABLE" VISION AND POLICE INCOMPETENCE

Through the representation of violence, horror films assault the sense of vision. As if in warning that looks can kill, the annals of horror overflow with images of damage to sight and to the eyes. The films of Dario Argento are no exception. Before examining the interlocking motifs of detection, seriality, looking, and the price exacted for seeing in several examples from Argento's oeuvre, I offer a few remarks about the pleasures and dangers of the cinematic gaze.

Horror films exploit a concept that Carol Clover has called "hurtable vision." Films in this genre lay siege to the eyes, placing them "under attack (where they are) punctured, burned, gouged out, and blinded by light, by everything from hypodermic needles and hot coffee to 'blip-verts,'" highly condensed and rapid television commericals, all of which "underlines . . . vision on the defense."[11] Studying the sensory reception to cinema, Vivian Sobchak aligns the vulnerability of vision with the defenselessness of the flesh, which is everywhere assailed in a genre that celebrates its shredding, piercing, or slashing. "It is the flesh through which vision is accomplished," for "this is vision embodied—a material activity that not only sees but can be seen, that makes vision itself visible."[12] In his marginal notes to the *Psycho* screenplay at the point where Janet Leigh meets Mother while showering, Alfred Hitchcock wrote, "An impression of a knife slashing, as if tearing at the very screen, ripping the film."[13] Hitchcock's comments suggest not only wounding the victim within the film's diegesis but also breaking free from the celluloid to wound the audience. Scholars have observed that in early cinema there was a related anxiety that the medium of film itself was believed to have the potential to "hurt" the spectator.[14] While this anxiety is perceived as more literal in the earlier eras of cinema, remnants of it remain, for example, in the form of censorship and the legislation deriving from it that is meant to preserve and protect vision by removing potential offenses from sight.

Although such suturing of vision and sight seems densely theoretical, or at least a dense theoretical concern, it nonetheless has real consequences, juridically speaking, for the freedom of expression in the form of state censorship. In this chapter, I begin with an exploration of "hurtable vision" in Argento's cinema, move to examine the significance of sight to detectives and detection in several key Argento films, and conclude by contemplating the censorship of violence in Argento's films.

Wounded sight and vision is an established topos, or motif, in Dario Argento's films. The eye itself in Argento's work is, to use Clover's language, "under siege." The consequences of witnessing violence and the trauma of wounded vision is so common a trope in Argento's work that Fabio Maiello entitled his 1996 collection of interviews with Argento *L'occhio che uccide* (the assassinating eye). It happens that this is also the title in Italian for Michael Powell's prototypic slasher film, *Peeping Tom* (1960). This creates a circuit of references from Powell to Argento, but a second reference emerges as well. *L'occhio che uccide* loops from the role by peeping Toms played in the "Monster" of Florence case to the pleasures and dangers of looking in Argento's cinema.

Attacks on the eyes in Argento's *Opera* (1987) variously illustrate manifestations of "hurtable vision."[15] This film, about a mysterious series of murders accompanying the staging of Giuseppe Verdi's opera *Macbeth*, opens with an extreme close-up of a watchful, nonhuman eye in which we see the reflection of a theater while listening to an operatic baritone sing his part of a duet from the opera. This is literally a bird's-eye view, a recurring image throughout the film. The sumptuous velvet draping the auditorium's boxes is seen as reflected in the eye of a raven used in the post-apocalyptic production of *Macbeth* staged at Parma's Teatro Regio, the setting for the film. Betty (Cristina Marsillach), the company's young soprano understudy, is making her operatic debut as Lady Macbeth. Although she tries to banish the superstitious canard (or, perhaps, *corbeau*, or raven), that this Verdi opera in particular invites bad luck, a series of accidents and murders nevertheless confirms this fear.[16]

The scene of the first murder sets the tone and the killer's modus operandi: the victims will be anyone of significance to the young singer. In homage to Stanley Kubrick's *A Clockwork Orange* (1971), Betty will be forced to witness the violent ends of her loved ones. Like Alex in Kubrick's film, Betty is immobilized with her eyes propped open; her assailant uses homemade instruments made from a slim strip of wood and nails, so that if she closes her eyes, she risks puncturing her own pupils [17] (See Figure 3.1.) As it is, simply enduring the presence of the torture instruments grazes her eyebrows; this is the source of the blood trickling down her face. (A kinder version of this torture returns in Argento's *La terza madre.* Temporarily paralyzed by the alchemist whose help she has enlisted, the character Sarah has her eyes forcibly propped open so that she can be shown methods for defense against the witches who have Rome in their thrall.) In *Opera,* the villain's victims quickly meet gruesome ends: the stage manager at the Teatro Regio; the Opera's *costumière*; Betty's friend, Myra (played by Daria Nicolodi, Argento's former domestic partner and a veteran ensemble player in his work); and the director of *Macbeth,* whom, in a parodic poke at himself, Argento portrays as a director of horror films rather than a director of Italian opera classics.[18]

Betty's torture may privilege the eye as the locus of the potential wound, but the demises of two of the serial killer's victims certify the eye's vulnerability.[19] Myra's death, for example, offers an object lesson on "hurtable vision." Daring to look through the peephole in the door to Betty's apartment to see if the person outside is in fact the officer he claims to be and not the serial killer, Myra is shot through the eye. The ravens, whose memory for trespasses against them surpasses that of even the elephant (at least according to their handler), settle their score with the serial killer, who has decimated their flock. Tipping his hat to *The Birds* (1963) and Hitchcock, Argento has the ravens swarm the killer in his seat at a performance of *Macbeth,* gouging out an eye.

The eyes are thematic in Argento's 1996 film *La Sindrome di Stendhal* in a different way. The chief problem for Roman policewoman Anna Manni (Asia Argento) is that she sees too much and too well. Manni tracks a serial rapist through several of Italy's *città d'arte,* a designation by the Ministero di turismo e spettacolo (Ministry of Tourism and Performance) that indicates noteworthy stops on a pilgrimage of Italy's artistic patrimony. When she visits the Uffizi Gallery in Florence, Anna is overcome by her proximity to sublime art and succumbs to the Stend-

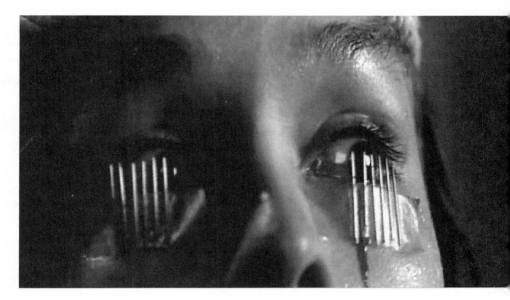

FIGURE 3.1. *Opera* (Dario Argento, 1987).

hal syndrome that lends its name to the film, a psychosomatic illness in which those who view great beauty are overcome with symptoms of shortness of breath, dizziness, and confusion. Disoriented by onset of the malaise, Anna loses her bearings and becomes a victim of the rapist herself. Her rape and the onset of the Stendhal syndrome begin to transform Anna's personality, which Argento visually codes by presenting Anna first as feminine and demure, then as butch, and finally as an almost parodically feminine persona. When the rapist attacks her in a second episode while she is on furlough in Viterbo, rather than apprehend him when she gets the upper hand like the law-abiding agent of the police force that she is, Anna kills him and disposes of the body, dumping it into the rapids nearby. More profound characterological changes commence, and after killing a young suitor, her boyfriend, and her psychologist, Anna is finally taken into custody at the film's conclusion. Order is restored, but not without revealing some of the chinks in its armor.

The setting for the episode of Anna's second rape is an abandoned culvert outside Viterbo. Chained to a mattress where her assailant Alfredo will once again repeatedly rape her, Anna is forced to train her

FIGURE 3.2. *La Sindrome di Stendhal* (The Stendhal Syndrome)
(Dario Argento, 1996).

gaze on the childish, though scary, graffiti cartoons that thickly cover
the walls. This culvert, Alfredo tells her, is a former shooting gallery.
Although junkies originally found its seclusion attractive, even they
have abandoned it because the place has become too frightening. The
addicts did their hallucinogenic best to capture and represent the stuff
of their opiatic nightmares on the walls of the culvert.[20] One image in
particular takes on significance as it comes to life, peels itself off the wall,
and lunges menacingly toward a petrified Anna. The humor of a life-size
Pikachu Pokemon with an unmistakable erection vanishes as the figure
comes to life.[21] (See Figure 3.2.) Its indistinct form and lurching gait are
the stuff boogeymen and monsters are made of. The spooky figure with
an enormous erection terrifies us and reminds us that penetration is
the sine qua non of rape. It is no wonder that this figure increases the
nightmare of Anna's repeated rape and galvanizes the principles underpinning the Stendhal syndrome.

The "Stendhal syndrome" is a twentieth-century name for a concept
that originated in the early nineteenth century. As the French writer
Stendhal (a pseudonym for Henri-Marie Beyle) stood in a Florence

church in 1817, he gazed up at Giotto's frescoes and became literally overwhelmed: his head reeled, he staggered. As he wrote in his diary,

> I was in a sort of ecstasy, from the idea of being in Florence.... Absorbed in the contemplation of sublime beauty, I reached the point where one encounters celestial sensations. . . . Everything spoke so vividly to my soul. Ah, if only I could forget. I had palpitations of the heart.... Life was drained from me. I walked with the fear of falling.[22]

The syndrome, so christened by Florentine psychiatrist Graziella Magherini in the 1970s, is a well-documented phenomenon: the onset of the syndrome was so common at the Uffizi that certain rooms were designated within the august structure as fainting chambers to accommodate tourists who had succumbed to "cold sweat, nausea, anxiety, hallucinations, severe depression, and personality changes."[23]

It appears that Argento and his longtime writing partner, Franco Ferrini, drew substantially from Magherini's case histories. In one of those cases, "Franz," a "mature" tourist from Bavaria, becomes preoccupied with the *dentro* (interior) of the painting, which constitutes the provenance of his malaise. As Magherini describes, Franz presented a psychic portrait in which "sensations of pleasure and pain are mingled, he is consumed by a strange curiosity to know what is 'behind, inside, and not in front.' The word 'inside' recurs in his memories of the onset (of the syndrome) with unusual frequency: inside the painting, inside of himself."[24]

Argento's *Sindrome di Stendhal* was not the first feature film in the 1990s to make explicit reference to the homicides attributed to the "Monster" of Florence.[25] As I mentioned in the introduction, *Il Mostro,* cowritten by, directed by, and starring Roberto Benigni, was released in October 1994, one month before the court delivered its guilty verdict for Pietro Pacciani. Both filmmakers underscore the inability of law enforcement to track, apprehend, and convict a serial rapist and murderer, Benigni in the mode of parody and Argento within the slasher genre. Benigni openly parodies actual members of the team assembled to track the "Monster." For example, the character of the officious "expert" who instructs the policewoman Jessica (Nicoletta Braschi) about the maniac's psychological profile clearly refers to FBI-trained police inspector Ruggero Perugini, chief of Florence's Squadra Anti-Mostro. In *Il Mostro,* a scantily clad Jessica sashays through the apartment of the petty thief Loris (Benigni), whom she mistakenly thinks is a serial rapist and murderer, in the hope of luring him into a "monstrous" act so that she can apprehend him. *Il Mostro* ends with the arrest of the real assassin (Loris's tutor for Chinese) and a happy union for Loris and Jessica. Argento, on the other hand, tells a darker tale; his policewoman plunges into homicide herself and is last seen being subdued by a phalanx of armed police officers.

While obviously and substantially different, the films share two significant traits: they were both produced and released near the time of significant judicial events in the "Monster" case and they both visualized an unrecognizable Florence. When Benigni's film was released in October 1994, Pietro Pacciani's case had been in its trial phase for six months. Benigni's goal in the film was to establish an explicit likeness with the actual "Monster" event. Likewise, *La Sindrome di Stendhal* was shot in Florence in the summer of 1995, following Pacciani's conviction of the previous November and before vacation of his sentence in 1996, when two others—Mario Vanni and Gianfranco Lotti—were accused of conspiracy to commit the murders attributed to the "Monster."[26] Michele Anselmi wrote in *L'Unità* in January 1996 that it "took nearly three years (for Argento) to finish the ambitious project."[27] While Argento describes being drawn into the project through reading Magherini's collection of case histories (*La Sindrome Stendhal,* 1989), he already had the "Monster's" crimes in mind at that time.[28]

In addition, both *Il Mostro* and *La Sindrome di Stendhal* labor to defamiliarize a visualized Florence. Benigni's film is shot almost entirely on sets, save for the exteriors of a warren of depersonalized condominiums on the outskirts of a nameless Tuscan city.[29] Argento's film studiously detaches Florence from its *città d'arte* status as a tourist destination, making it instead a city of rape and murder.

SEEING AND DECODING

Seeing and decoding clues, the work of detection (not to mention of semiotics and cinema studies), perform key functions in the Argento films named above. Argento often embeds clues in an obviously "artistic" structure that serves to frame knowledge, detection, and resolution. Two examples from his earliest films make this impulse clear.[30] Like *La Sindrome di Stendhal*, *L'uccello dalle piume di cristallo* is also set in the art world. The primal scene of the murder takes place in a gallery in Rome and is framed by the gallery's twin set of double doors. This scene signifies misunderstanding and frustration, of seeing something but not believing it, and, importantly, seeing something but not trusting yourself to testify about it. Above all, the scene is about the difficulty of expressing what you believe you have witnessed.

Sam Dalmas (Tony Musante), an American journalist in Rome (doubtless a reference to Raymond Chandler's noir private detective John Dalmas), has been drawn to a gallery of modern art owned by Monica and Alberto Raineri, which in the film occupies an illuminated spot on the darkened streetscape. Positioned outside the brightly lit gallery, Sam sees two figures, one dressed in black, the other in white, struggling inside. Like these polarized color values, the sequence alternates between seeing and hearing, separating sight from sound, a technique Argento reproduced in later films, notably *Profondo rosso*.[31] The black-gloved hand of the assailant—a sign that would become associated with Argento's *giallo* films—presses the entry button, and Sam is able to enter the first set of double doors. However, he remains here, powerless, for the balance of the sequence.[32] Sam is literally caught in the space in between.

Allowed to see but not to hear, Sam is denied thorough and conclusive knowledge of the assault. (In fact, Inspector Morosini is so convinced that Sam has repressed what he has seen and that it is only a matter of time before the memory will surface that he takes Sam's passport away, ensuring that he will stay in Rome.) As Sam paces in the transparent space between the gallery's locked inner and outer doors, the camera pans the gallery to show a smooth, unified vista. (See Figure 3.3.) Such contained seamlessness is reinforced by the regularity of the gallery's architectural organization, where the shallow steps form clean vertical breaks in the horizontal planes of the ground floor and the mezzanine. In fact, Argento aimed at a "geometric" presentation of the space in terms of both mise-en-scène and camera movements.[33] In opposition to this controlled and orderly setting are the unsteady, handheld shots of

FIGURE 3.3. *L'uccello dalle piume di cristallo* (The Bird with the Crystal Plumage)
(Dario Argento, 1970).

the attack inside the gallery and the ragged breath that only the viewer
can hear.

Crosscutting between the interior and the exterior emphasizes the
split between sight and sound. Since he cannot grasp the meaning of
what he has seen, Sam's testimony is incomplete. His understanding
and therefore the resolution of the crime is constantly deferred. We
see Sam, as the film's amateur detective and protagonist, triumph over
the void of interpretation to arrive at the solution: she dunnit. In other
words, the "woman in white"—a visual reference to the title of Wilkie
Collins's classic gothic tale from 1859—struggling in the gallery, who
Sam believes is the victim, is actually the murderer. As Argento said in
an interview, it was almost too simple to guarantee this error in reasoning: costuming was all that was required to ensure that Sam, and, with
him, the viewer, would believe the villain was the figure in black.[34] While
Sam's quest enables him, like Oedipus, to move beyond incomprehen-
sion into cognition, the police, on the other hand, remain firmly rooted
in their ignorance.

The disbelief that a woman is the murderer, even when her crime has been witnessed, is similarly framed in *Profondo rosso,* the second early example of the way Argento frames knowledge visually in the context of painting. Like *L'uccello dalle piume di cristallo,* this film features an amateur detective, a clever but "lay" reader of the signs of the crime. Like Sam, jazz pianist Marc Daly (David Hemmings) must overcome his submerged memory to uncover the identity of the assassin who killed Helga the psychic with a hatchet while Marc watched from the street.[35] Like Sam, Marc has seen and forgotten an important clue embedded within a captivating artistic context, this time not an example of art's powers of distraction, but something within the actual frame of a work of art itself, a trompe l'oeil painting in the apartment of the victim. The face of the killer, played to screeching, yet elegant, perfection by an aged Clara Calamai, "hides," as it were, within the reflected image of a painting. At the film's climax, Marc remembers the "true" painting from the murder scene at the film's beginning. Successfully interpreting this clue, he is able to defend against the killer's attack, save himself, kill her, and solve the crime.

Argento puts forward the amateur detective motif in several other films, but before examining *La Sindrome di Stendhal* in more detail, I will mention one other, the psychological thriller *Trauma* (1992), the first film in the Asia Tetrology. *Trauma* pays homage to Brian De Palma's *Carrie* (1976) in the way it instrumentalizes the adolescent female body and maneuvers the maternal body in antagonistic response. To shore up this correspondence, Argento cast Piper Laurie, who reprises her role as Carrie's deranged mother, this time as Adriana Petrescu, a Rumanian medium whose reliable contact with the spirit world, a presence named Nicholas, has provided her with security among the bourgeois spiritualism set. Aura (Asia Argento) is a troubled 16-year-old already institutionalized for anorexia at the film's beginning. She has been orphaned by the attack of a crazed killer who has killed her parents and several townspeople. From a tangle of bushes, Aura watches as the killer brandishes her parents' decapitated heads, like Perseus with the Medusa.[36] This, at least, is what the audience, like Aura, believes it has seen.

The link between the killings in the series is the fact that each of the victims worked at Saint Bartholomew's hospital. We are not really surprised when Adriana appears again as the killer and reveals the reason for her murderous rampage. As Adriana labored hard in the delivery room in Saint Bart's some years earlier, a rogue electrical storm descended, creating a power outage at the precise moment that her labor was concluding. The doctors botched something in the dark, killing Adriana's newborn son, Nicholas. To cover their error, the staff drugged the hysterical mother and then administered unnecessary electroshock therapy, after which Adriana is never the same.

The release of *Trauma* in 1993 coincided with an explosion of critical theorizations of trauma. This academic work is relevant to the topic of horror in general and to Argento's cinematic corpus in particular. In *Trauma Culture: The Politics of Terror and Loss in Media and Literature,* Ann Kaplan traces the historical lineage of trauma theory from Freud to deconstruction and beyond. Departing from Freud's study of visceral trauma, Kaplan sketches the itinerary of detachment, arriving at trauma theorists' concern for ontological trauma. Trauma theorists "associate trauma not with the effects of triggered associations but with the ontologically unbearable nature of the event itself."[37] What is valuable in this exploration is the decision of whether to question the framing of trauma in terms of the specific (associations triggered by specific incidents) or in terms of the generalizable, a concern of greater ontological moment for a greater number of subjects.

Trauma is a frequent guest in horror cinema. While Argento's film *Trauma* foregrounds the physical trauma of birth (and the psychological trauma of stillbirth), the circumstances are still fairly specific—the storm causing the power outage produces a fairly unique set of consequences. Aura's anorexia, on the other hand, displays evidence of a more generalized perception of preexisting traumatic conditions. Seen in this way, her anorexia is the precursor for the "ontologically unbearable event" of rape that Argento explores in his next film. What makes an event "ontologically unbearable" is the unpredictability of who will become its next victim.[38] Cavarero's point about "horrorism" in a post–September 11 universe concerns the factor of chance in choosing or designating victims. Anyone, at any time, may fall victim to assault. It strikes me that such a description aptly characterizes the circumstances of rape, particularly the circumstances of the genocidal rape that took place in the context of the war in Bosnia and Herzegovina, which began in March 1992 and lasted until November 1995, coinciding with Argento's production.[39]

As visual reminder of the relay between visual witness and horror, *La Sindrome di Stendhal*, like *Trauma*, features a motif of the Medusa as a symbol of an excess of knowledge. Moreover, *La Sindrome di Stendhal* reprises the pattern of a young female character (again played by Asia Argento) who *already* carries the burden of some psychological trauma. Anna's marked transformation from detective to sociopath makes *La Sindrome di Stendhal* the most troubling representation of police work in the Argentian corpus.

This transformation accomplishes four tasks. First, by focusing on the figure of the female detective Anna (Asia Argento), *La Sindrome di Stendhal* moves the question of the police and their incompetence from subtext to text. Second, Argento obviously emphasizes Anna's dilemma as a female police officer by having her raped not once but repeatedly, transforming her from rape victim to sexual aggressor and from police officer to criminal.[40] The shifts in Anna's gender styles from femme to butch to the masquerade of ultra-femme is a secondary theme that relates to the more significant question of the social ordering of gender, a transformation that mirrors her principal conversion from police officer to criminal. The third task Argento accomplishes with Anna's transformation is a repositioning of the police from their previous spot in the background to full view, or from the background to the foreground. Finally, the film gives the police a previously denied subjectivity, including the contrary, yet related, aspects of power and vulnerability.

LA SINDROME DI STENDHAL:
DISTURBING ITALIAN LANDSCAPES

In addition to unseating firm and bounded notions of gender, *La Sindrome di Stendhal* similarly queers space and place, making the familiar unrecognizable.[41] Although Argento's strategy recalls the notions of deterritorialization of French philosophers Gilles Deleuze and Félix Guattari, I am not suggesting that the fit is perfect or that Argento somehow apes the dynamic of deterritorialization, which concerns the symbolic coding and recoding of terrain.[42] Deleuze and Guattari elaborate their theory in *Anti-Oedipus*: meaning codes first are inscribed on the surface of the earth (territorialization). Then they are appropriated by a patriarch, whereupon the meaning is "recoded" and "deterritorialized." After the initial recoding, the patriarch appropriates the sign in order to "reterritorialize" it. But the coding does not remain the patriarch's to enact when he wishes. Rather, the material flows within capitalism reassign the power of coding to the body of capital, the more recent social machine.[43] As capital flows freely and transnationally, the power of coding attaches to a symbolic frame that is less "national" in character. Deleuze and Guattari's conceptualization is useful, I find, for exploring the motif of tourism in Argento's *La Sindrome di Stendhal*, given the fact that the film is titled for one of Europe's best-known early tourists and takes place principally in Florence, birthplace of mercantile capitalism. Further, the concept of defamiliarized landscape tallies with the reordered criminal geography explored in the contemporary Italian crime fiction I considered in the preceding chapter, not to mention the destabilizing effects of the serial murders attributed to the "Monster" of Florence.[44]

La Sindrome di Stendhal renders tourism's effects on Italy, specifically Florence, visual and thematic. From the film's first frames, Argento shows a Florence beset by tourists. Concerning the dampening effect that a series of violent crimes might have on the tourist industry in Italy, it is worth recalling the anxieties during the "Monster" event in the period 1974 to 1985 about damage that might be done to the status of Florence as a destination city.[45] Michele Giuttari, head of Florence's Squadra mobile and a chief investigator of the crimes ascribed to the "Monster," has stated of Florence that "the tourists who come to this city think of it as all art and beauty—palazzos, the Ponte Vecchio, churches, museums—but there is a history of brutality as well as beauty. In the 1970s and 1980s there were terrible crimes, cases of extreme sexual violence, women murdered and mutilated. It was as ferocious and brutal as anything I dealt with in the South."[46] In what must be the only point of agreement between Giuttari and Mario Spezi, given their history of animosity and legal entanglement, the latter, a weathered crime reporter from the Florentine daily *La Nazione,* observed that "Florence is a nasty city and always has been."[47] This was not the "dream" of Italy being purveyed globally that resulted in couples from distant lands making Florence their wedding destination, exemplified in *La Sindrome di Stendhal* by the brief shot in the opening "travelogue" of the Asian couple being showered with rice.[48] (See Figure 3.4.) Since Argento's travelogue reproduces the kind of errant progress through an unknown city that a tourist might make, it is impossible to determine in this brief shot whether the couple is outside a church or, say, the Palazzo Vecchio, where many foreigners engage in civil marriage ceremonies.[49]

From its beginning, *La Sindrome di Stendhal* repeatedly ruptures the logic of urban spatial relations in Florence and in so doing recreates the sort of urban exploration a tourist or *flâneur* would do. *Errance* of this sort is typical of Argento in general, for, as he has said, "From the beginning I never thought I was imprisoned in the city. . . . For me jumping from one city to another, all the while maintaining a continuity of storyline, was very normal."[50] From its establishing shots of Anna striding decisively over the Ponte Vecchio, *La Sindrome di Stendhal* studiously seeks to disorient the viewer, or at least any viewer familiar with Florence, by presenting a geographically discontinuous and unrecognizable city.[51] Anna poorly follows the maps in the guidebooks she totes in her purse alongside her pistol; she could have done a better job of reaching

FIGURE 3.4. *La Sindrome di Stendhal* (The Stendhal Syndrome) (Dario Argento, 1996).

the entrance to the Uffizi Gallery in Piazza della Signoria from the Ponte Vecchio. Her wide detour takes her by the statue of a stern Dante outside Santa Croce and then up Via dei Calzaiuoli toward Piazza della Signoria. While this route affords Argento a quick nod to Stendhal at the film's opening, this is not the quickest and most direct path to take from the Ponte Vecchio to the Uffizi by a policewoman who has received a phone call telling her she will find the rapist she is hunting at the gallery that morning. Her stride indicates determination, her route something else. Anna's itinerary is like the dislocated cinematic space in both *Profondo rosso* and *Quattro mosche di velluto grigio*. In the latter film, as Argento observed, "Someone is walking along a street in Milan and then walks down a staircase in Turin, but no one noticed."[52] In *Profondo rosso*, Argento notes, "You've got Perugia, Rome, Turin, a slice of Milan. You can't tell."[53]

But you can tell. What is more, it is clear from the relocation of shooting from the United States to Italy that exterior spaces are not as equally interchangeable as Argento maintains. *La Sindrome di Stendhal* changed locations, moving from the American Southwest to the cities and outlying areas of Tuscany and Lazio in a maneuver that was heralded as the director's "return" to filmmaking in Italy following experiences abroad.[54] Argento had originally planned to shoot in Phoenix, Arizona, with Bridget Fonda starring as Anna. However, the director says he immediately realized "that I couldn't make a film about art in Phoenix. It was really impossible. . . . You cannot be disturbed, not to mention faint, by the sight of a skyscraper or a bridge, no matter how magnificent. A bridge and a skyscraper cannot substitute for Raffaello. Looking at Raffaello is like getting stabbed in the heart."[55] Filming in Italy solved this dilemma. The film nonetheless goes to tremendous effort to make familiar spaces and places—the appropriate settings for the shock that seeing Raffaello produces—unidentifiable.

The central concern of *La Sindrome di Stendhal* is the extraordinary, unexpected, and unwanted penetration that accompanies rape. Significantly, this unwanted and illegal action extends to the Italian landscape, which is portrayed as similarly "raped." The culvert near Viterbo is the visual reminder of Tangentopoli, or "Bribe City," as the corruption scandal of the 1990s was called in English, a scandal that involved pervasive speculation in public works projects such as highways, deep tunnels, and water treatment systems. Several scenes featuring a civil engineer poring over maps in an attempt to trace the water's course make explicit reference to the maze of redirected water systems affected by Tangentopoli. The scandal erupted when evidence came to light of negligence in the construction of public works projects that resulted in the deaths of numerous Italians throughout the peninsula, some victims of poorly designed highways, others of mudslides or floods attributable to flaws in the planning of dams and reservoirs. By the time the magistrates' investigation of the corruption scandal concluded in April 1998, 2,970 cases of political corruption had been associated with this particular scandal. Of this number, only 566 had been ruled on. In these cases, judges had ruled guilty in 460 cases, not guilty in 106. However, in some cases, the not-guilty verdicts were rendered because the law of statutes, which requires cases to be heard within a finite period of time, had expired. As historian Paul Ginsborg has observed, similar political corruption scandals erupted in Germany and France at the same time, making corruption seem like "a structural part of modern European democracy."[56] Reference to Tangentopoli actually performs a structural function in the film's plot: so long as the police are unable to find Alfredo's body, the deranged Anna has an alibi for the crimes that she commits.[57]

OFF THE WALL: PENETRATING
PAINTING, DISLOCATING GENDER

Anna's transformation from detective to delinquent underpins a question often posed of the horror-film genre: does it work to destabilize patriarchal "law and order," or does it reify it? I would argue that, for Argento's film, the answer is yes as well as no to both questions.

Some critics of the slasher genre argue that it affords resistant viewing strategies and possibilities for realigning spectatorial sympathies.[58] The viewing public for the slasher genre, which is mostly male, does not identify with the sadism of the torturer killer solely but also, significantly, with the heroic and often adolescent female who thwarts the killer; the figure that Carol Clover refers to as the "Final Girl."[59] The "Final Girl" survives in some of the films of the practitioners I named at the beginning of this chapter. She prevails, for example, in Tobe Hooper's classic *Texas Chainsaw Massacre* (1974) and in its remake (2003); in John Carpenter's *Halloween* (1978); and in Wes Craven's parody *Scream* (1996) and the others that followed (e.g., *Scream 2, Scream 3, I Still Know What You Did Last Summer*, etc.).

Like the "Final Girl," Anna survives in *La Sindrome di Stendhal* but pays a high price. Configured around the act of rape, this film significantly destabilizes gender norms through a series of strategies intended to visually disorient the spectator. At the level of plot, Argento's film traces the transformation of the protagonist from law-enforcer to criminal, a motif reinforced visually as it tracks the parallel development of the protagonist from femme to butch to an ultrafeminine persona bordering on masquerade.

The disturbed spatial relations of the city of Florence and the "raped" landscape of Italy after the corrupt construction practices that Tangentopoli uncovered correspond to the way the film makes interior spaces within the built environment unrecognizable and unfamiliar. Such disturbance of interiors allows for a reading of the way the film erodes heteronormativity (at least to a degree) and routinized social gender norms. Argento's film allows its protagonist to be inside and outside a work of art simultaneously—his portrayal of the manifestation of the Stendhal syndrome. The impossibility of this location, at once inside and outside, provides a different location, or subject position, in the dynamic process of gendering. When, for example, the film's protagonist observes that the young French professor's name, "Marie," is "a girl's name," he replies, "In France it's not so exact; (Marie) can be one or the other." In Argento's film, gender, like this French name, can be one thing *and* another.

The way Argento defamiliarizes geographical space is matched by the alienating presentation of familiar, indeed, famous, interior spaces, such as the galleries within Florence's Uffizi. As Anna makes her way through the various Uffizi galleries, she is often crowded out of the way by tourists. In the sequence running up to Anna's first major hallucination, which takes place in the Uffizi, she frequently shares the frame with non-Italian tourists, who crowd her out of the way.[60] For example, the German couple admiring the view of the Arno from a window is oblivious to having elbowed Anna out of their way. An Asian tourist taking a

FIGURE 3.5. *La Sindrome di Stendhal* (The Stendhal Syndrome)
(Dario Argento, 1996).

photograph in Room 7 literally displaces Anna from the camera's frame.
(See Figure 3.5.) Finally, while the black tourists admiring a painting
in the Botticelli Room could be Italian, they round out the group of
Anna's fellow museum visitors who are "different" from her, in this case,
racially, though not necessarily nationally.[61]

Anna has not been in the Uffizi long before Argento reveals her
alterity. In Room 7, with Piero della Francesca's twin portraits of the
Duke and Duchess of Urbino behind her, Anna stands before Paolo
Uccello's *Battle of San Romano*. Before piercing the surface of art in her
hallucinations, she first penetrates the silence of the painting. As she
stands before the Uccello canvas, we see Anna "hearing" the scene and
we hear the sounds of her auditory hallucination: the whinnying of the
bucking horse, excited voices speaking in Italian. In her hallucination,
after she slices through the silence of art, Anna penetrates the barrier
of its surface.

In addition to describing the modus operandi of Anna's hallucinations, forced penetration is also the juridical prerequisite of rape. As
Alfredo will render her powerless during the attacks that penetrate her,

Anna will experience helplessness in the face of the absorptive powers of art, whose surface she herself hallucinogenically penetrates. We have an initial glimpse of Anna's desire to pierce the surface of art as she stands before Botticelli's *La Primavera*. Her image is reflected by the protective glass, and Anna reaches out to touch beyond its transparency to the canvas depicting the idyllic transformation of a female figure subdued by force. The superimposition of her reflection clearly links Anna and the nymph Chloris, who, first seized by Zephyr and then transformed into Flora, triumphs over the pastoral scene as the central figure of the painting. In the thrall of art, Anna's police intuition begins to fail her. Curiously, neither the alarm she has activated nor the thematization of kidnapping and force alert her to the coming danger she herself will experience.[62]

If the alarm does not suffice, Caravaggio's 1598 painting of the death mask of the Medusa, on display in the adjacent room, Anna's next stop on her trip through the museum, should signal the perils of reflection, not to mention the tenuousness of female power, whether established in myth or juridically ordained by a police officer's badge. The image recalls the scene from *Trauma* in which Aura sees the killer wield her parents' decapitated heads as Perseus does the Medusa's. The brief appearance of Caravaggio's *Medusa* may constitute an oblique reference to the film's producers—Medusa Film—but there is greater resonance. If the figure of Medusa can be read as an allegory of castration, then yet another symbolic castration occurs as we realize at the end of the sequence, with her, that the pistol in her open bag has gone missing.[63]

Anna's journey through the symptoms of the Stendahl syndrome begins with her hallucination in Room 16 of the Uffizi. This should be the Map Room (in fact, large maps cover the walls), but it is a hallucinogenic, impossible Map Room, at least inasmuch as the logic of the Uffizi is concerned. A tall blond man who stands parallel to the vertical border of a map is Alfredo, who witnesses Anna's fainting spell and steals the pistol from her purse in the ensuing confusion. Then, with the maps as background, Anna stands before Breughel's *Landscape with the Fall of Icarus*, which, like the Uccello and Caravaggio canvases she has already seen, comes to life. Although they remain stationary, the painting's figures begin emitting sounds.

Computer graphics carry us, with the hallucinating Anna, deep within the painting, toward its vanishing point where the sea meets the sky.[64] The waking Anna collapses in the gallery and falls, rupturing the vertical unity of the visual frame. The rupture finds a corresponding visual fissure within the hallucination itself, as Anna pierces not only the dimension of surface of the canvas, but also that of the painted image of the ocean's surface. Simultaneous with her fall, Anna's chin hits what looks like a baptismal font positioned in the center of the room. The force of the fall suggests she might have sustained greater hurt, but she merely splits her lip, calling attention to another opening in a surface, this time the skin.

The real start of the Breughel hallucination, however, might come somewhat earlier. The presence of so many frames within the museum—not only of the works of art but also the windowpanes and the doorways, and Anna's spatial relation to them—suggests that there are many different ways to frame what is made audible and visible. Part of Anna's hallucination might comprise standing in the presence of the Breughel painting at all. Since *Landscape with the Fall of Icarus,* painted in 1558, is part of the permanent collection of Brussel's Museé Royaux de Beaux Arts de Belgique, Anna cannot simultaneously stand before it and continue to be in the Uffizi.[65] Yet Argento clearly aims at filmic continuity, for when she regains her consciousness, she is surrounded by the concerned expressions of some of the same faces she saw in the rooms of the Uffizi she had already visited. Although Breughel's painting is a transitory element in the mise-en-scène, something telegraphed by the ornamental (and temporary) easel on which it is displayed, Argento must have chosen it to do more than simply establish an impossible presence. What is it about *Landscape with the Fall of Icarus* that makes it the proving ground in the film for the malaise known as the Stendhal syndrome?[66]

Argento was aware of stripping works of art from their "proper" contexts in this film. His preparation for *La Sindrome di Stendhal* consisted of a trip in which "I went all over Europe visiting the great museums just so I could have a truer, deeper sensation of this famous syndrome."[67] His inclusion of displaced artworks in the film is therefore deliberate. In the case of the Breughel painting, a number of elements link the Icarus of myth to Argento's film. Mythological origin holds that Icarus was the son of Daedalus, the architect of King Minos's Labyrinth, where the Minotaur was confined. The Labyrinth is deadly to nearly all those who try to divine its secrets save for Daedalus, its creator, and Theseus, who, with the help of Ariadne's ball of string, successfully navigates the maze and slays the beast. So that he and Icarus might escape Crete, Daedalus crafts wings made of feathers and wax. The flight gives Icarus an aerial view and, consequently, a unique perspective. However, his youthful exuberance—flying too close to the heat of the sun—costs him his life. Perspective and risk bring the myth into proximity with Argento's film: no bird with the crystal plumage this time, but wings made of wax and feathers. No literal bird's-eye view, as in *Opera*, but a perspective from on high. The constructed character of the wings, along with rapid travel— in the case of Icarus plummeting to the ocean, too rapid—also recalls another constructed avian from the classical age: Virgil's monstrous, winged Rumor, whose importance to the "Monster" spectacle in Florence I outlined in chapter 1.

Argento confirms the alignment of Icarus and Anna in *La Sindrome di Stendhal*. Like the eponymous figure of Breughel's painting, Anna lands on the ocean floor as if falling from a great height. Like Icarus, Anna has the gift of perspective, but in her overexposure to the sublime works on display at the Uffizi, she has risked her vision by "flying too close to the sun." Just as Icarus melted the wax of his artificial wings and squandered his father's gift, Anna, utilizing her mother's gift of opening herself to works of art, also exposes herself to peril. Beneath Breughel's painted sea, Anna swims through the deep water, the cacophony of the sounds "above" the surface of the water now out of earshot and muted. An enormous, apparently benign, fish swims toward her, and Anna kisses its pronounced lips. Perhaps because the fish has "breathed new life" into her, but more likely because by kissing the site of her wound, the fish draws attention to the pain of her split lip, Anna regains her senses. The lips and the mouth, as the location of one of the body's portals allowing access and exit, return in a later scene illustrating the Ur-hallucination that marks the pathogenesis of Anna's case of the Stendhal syndrome.

Anna undergoes two forced and concurrent transformations in the film: the first concerning gender identification, the second related to her change from police office to killer. The visual coding of Anna's gender identification is achieved largely through costume and makeup.[68] Before the attacks, when still "herself," Anna wears the demure clothes becoming to a female police officer on or off duty. The light-colored blouse and the skirt that reaches below the knee that Anna wears at the start of the film are the civilian equivalent of the uniform of the female police officer we see at the Florentine hospital where Anna is treated after her attack. As she exits the Uffizi in a sort of fugue state following her hallucination, we see the dark stain of her blood on the cream-colored blouse. The blood from her split lip is stark against the light color field of her blouse, announcing a rupture. This is the first mark of Anna's difference and a sign of the transformation to come. In the hospital following her rape in Florence, Anna cuts her long hair to just above the ears. The shorn hair coupled with the dark, loose trousers and plaid shirts code Anna visually as "butch." At home in Viterbo, her brothers tease her about "looking like a boy" and sparring in her old gym. After her second rape and deadly revenge against Alfredo, Anna examines in a mirror the slash her attacker has made in her cheek and observes, "He has left his mark on me." Even though Anna has dispatched Alfredo to the rapids, he is still the Perseus (whose name means "to cut") to her Medusa. Like the blood from her split lip, the split flesh on her cheek flags a transformation, the last she will make.[69] In Rome, after the bloodbath in Viterbo, Anna adopts the visual codes of ultrafemininity, wearing flowing, feminine dresses, dark glasses, and a long blond wig that makes her look like film noir doyenne Veronica Lake, the femme fatale of such classics in the genre as *This Gun for Hire* (Frank Tuttle, 1942) and *The Blue Dahlia* (George Marshall, 1946).[70]

Changes in how the film represents visually coded gender norms correspond to Anna's progression from police officer to quasi-rapist to fugitive killer. Back in Rome after she is attacked in Florence, Anna resists her boyfriend Marco's (Marco Leonardi) sexual overtures, then aggressively asserts herself with notable physical force.[71] As she tells her therapist during court-ordered sessions, her force was an expression of wanting to "fuck (Marco) like a man." Given her aggression in the scene with Marco, it is clear that, for Anna at this juncture, "fucking like a man" means forcing her partner to do something he does not grant full consent to. When she throws Marco against the wall in her apartment, Anna's stance behind him easily recalls that of a police officer making an arrest. Anna reaches around his waist to forcibly rip open Marco's jeans and shove her hand down the front of his pants. The scene makes obvious how ill at ease Marco is: this is not rough foreplay, or if it is, Marco does not enjoy it. After this display of force in the face of her partner's lack of consent (to call her a rapist is to overstate), Anna becomes a killer.[72] Even though she regains possession of her gun from Alfredo and thus has the upper hand, and even though Alfredo reminds her that as a police officer, it is her duty to arrest him, Anna kills him. Although Anna kills serially—first Alfredo, then her boyfriend Marco, and finally her therapist, since the murders are unplanned, she cannot really be called a serial murderer.[73]

Argento's films, as Vito Zagarrio has recently observed, do not sit squarely within a single genre, something critics have noted in the unfolding of his career from a director of "thrilling" films to *giallo* to horror.[74] Given its "contamination" and partial adherence to different genres, the way *La Sindrome di Stendhal* disturbs the law and order of gendered subject formation is similarly partial. I am, perhaps, less sanguine than a critic such as Adam Knee, who believes that in Argento's films "as point of view is destabilized and undermined . . . so are 'norms' of gender and sexuality."[75] At the same time, the representation of destabilized gender in *La Sindrome di Stendhal* strikes me as grounds for being more optimistic than Jacqueline Reich's reading of *Suspiria* and *Inferno*; in those two films, she sees ossified notions of patriarchal law and order calling for the punishment and extermination of witch figures rather than the female subversion Argento may have intended.[76] Along the lines of Paul Smith's notions of the representation of masculinity in Clint Eastwood films, Argento does not subvert patriarchal conceptions of masculinity so much as "suspend" them. [77] One should expect no grand or even coherent subversion of patriarchal law and order in Argento's films, but one can identify the pulsation of micro-moments of resistance. Consideration along these lines might, therefore, address Deborah Toschi's concerns about the formulaic expectations and assessment of Argento's films with regard to issues of gender. She has noted in a recent essay on *La Sindrome di Stendhal* that "the game of identification Argento proposes will not be reduced to a dichotomy but, the director seems to suggest, a more complex and pliant mode."[78] Using strategies to destabilize geographical interior and exterior space, *La Sindrome di Stendhal* does not present the binaries of heteronormativity—woman and man, "butch" and "femme"—nor does he seem to assume that any of these positions on the spectrum of gender identity are fixed or unchanging.

FROM "HURTABLE" VISION TO VISION THAT HURTS: ARGENTO AND CENSORSHIP

Judging from Argento's experience with the censorship of his films within Italy, the fear of early cinema spectators that images would leap off the screen and assault them has not been completely conquered. As Argento has said, "All my films have had problems with censors."[79]

Distributors and producers seeking to secure the widest market possible try to ensure a rating that permits eventual television broadcast. This means avoiding Italy's designation of *"Vietato ai minori sotto 14 anni,"* children under the age of 14 will not be admitted. Although the age limit for a restricted audience in Italy is 14 and not 17 (as in the United States), this rating offers an equivalent to the Motion Picture Association of America's (MPAA) NC-17 rating.[80] Article 9 of the April 21, 1962, law governing censorship specifies that the following content will be subject to scrutiny: "vulgar gestures, amoral behavior, violent or erotic scenes, surgical operations, hypnotic or supernatural phenomena, hatred or revenge, crimes or forms of suicide that could cause emulation."[81]

Clearly, many, if not most, of these elements are present in Argento's cinema. Because article 528 of the Italian Penal Code stipulates that "obscene performances and publications" are punishable by law, Argento's films have undergone considerable review by the Ministero dei Beni culturali e le Attività Culturali.[82] The *nullosta* (no objection) is required for the disbursement of a subsidy from the state; since Argento had secured financing, his films sought to pass muster with the Ministero upon completion rather than before filming began.

The juridical definition of what is "obscene" changes over time. Article 529 of Italy's Penal Code defines it as "actions and objects considered

obscene are those which offend a common sense of modesty."[83] *Opera,*
from 1987, for example, appears to have elicited an extreme response
from the censors. Meant for a pre-Christmas release (17 December), it
did not gain the approval of the Commissione di Revisione di Secondo
Grado until January 15. The commissioners refused to grant even then
a rating of *Vietato ai minori,* forbidding entrance to minors without
specific cuts: the footage in which the theater manager's throat is cut in
the first killing, the footage in which scissors are stuck in the *costumière's*
mouth, and the footage in which the raven eats the eye of the villain after
gouging it out—a total of 50 meters and 20 centimeters of required cuts.[84]

For Argento, the notion that his films should provide the basis for
imitative violence is risible. If censorship aims to prevent mimetic examples of violent behavior from being sources of fantasy, then, he believes,
its efforts are misguided. As he has said, the hunt for the origin of violent
behavior has led to searching "in films, in television programs, without
understanding that the origin is social, certainly not in 'thrillers,' which
draw a certain sort of spectator and certainly not serial killers."[85] Argento's thoughts as a practitioner approximate the problem in critical
theory of the role of the scopic, or, visual identification in the dynamic
of the social subject's constitution. As Mark Seltzer has observed in his
work on serial killers in American culture, the problem lies in positing a
social subject who "filled . . . from the outside in. This assumes the sheer
transparency of interior states to external conditions and hence obviates
the necessity of theorizing those states, those panics, those desires."[86]

There is no consensus among theorists about whether violent acts
imitate external stimuli. In fact, the debate is polarized along disciplinary lines that are highly politicized. On one side are those interested in
establishing a relationship between the viewer and what he or she sees.
This group argues that it is possible that external stimuli shape behavior,
but they do not go so far as to abandon the notion of the autonomy of the
subject. In other words, for this group, the subject is affected by what she
or he sees, but the subject still has the capacity to filter this information.
Many proponents of this hypothesis work in the fields of film theory,
feminist theory, and theories of sexuality and gender. This field derives
from and tends to subscribe to psychoanalytic notions of the structure
of fantasy and the role it plays in identification and subject formation.[87]

This view does not tend to account for data from the fields of social psychology, cognitive psychology, or neuroscience. This perspective has filtered into mainstream society in the form of the idea that the effects of viewing violence on actual behavior are limited. This belief has been welcomed in the field of commerce, and it informs some social policies that would limit censorship.[88] Yet recent developments in social and cognitive psychology, neuroscience, and the philosophy of mind suggest a tighter relation between the viewing subject and the object that he or she views. New research has produced data that supports the idea that the human brain is hard-wired in terms of the relationship between exposure to violence and behavior. This perspective suggests that imitation may be what builds human behavior, culture, and language.[89] Those on the other side of the debate, who argue that the subject has cognitive autonomy, assert that violent images do not produce violent behavior; rather, they say, an individual who is inclined toward violence and aggressive behavior seeks out such visual stimuli.[90]

Given this debate, how can Argento be so confident that the violence made visual in his films does not incite imitation or catalyze latent tendencies into action? Giuseppe Alessandri, a chronicler of the "Monster" affair, believes that on-screen violence played an important role not only in the diffusion of the "Monster's" deviance, but also in its formation. Alessandri, who argues that Pietro Pacciani was in fact the only serial killer involved in the Florence killings, speculates that television offered Pacciani a direct link to the world of pornography. In the spring and summer of 1981, he says, Pacciani "(spent) hours glued to the set: he (watched) everything but especially porn and horror films."[91] During these marathons, Pacciani repeatedly saw a trailer for a film due to arrive in Florence's cinemas that fall: William Lustig's *Maniac,* which had been released in the United States in 1980.[92] Young couples do not fare well in the slasher genre in general and certainly no better in *Maniac.* The scene broadcast as the trailer for Lustig's film *"risulta a Pietro più che familiare"* (is more than familiar to Pietro).[93] This trailer, which lasted ninety seconds and "bombarded" Pacciani during May 1981, showed a young couple leaving a club in New York who stop to look at the view from the Verrazano Bridge and are gunned down by an unknown assailant. Alessandri tells his readers that Pacciani "(waited) for some time for the arrival of the film that (had) so struck him, but he (waited) in vain."[94] In August 1981, Ranieri Polese Remaggi, the film critic for *La Nazione,* reviewed Lustig's film under the headline "Così brutto e cattivo," and drew analogies between the filmed violence and the "Monster's" murders.[95] *Maniac* arrived in Florence's Cinema Nazionale in Via dei Cimatori on October 15, 1981. The bodies of Stefano Baldi and Susanna Cambi were found on October 23, victims in the same series that had already claimed two other couples.

These are the simple dots Alessandri wishes to connect: Pacciani is a murderer, Pacciani is drawn to pornography and to the spectacle of catastrophe, Pacciani likes to watch slasher-horror films about homicidal maniacs, and these films drove Pacciani to be a murderer again. Such circular logic reveals a limited understanding of the process of psychic identification, filling the subject from "the outside in."

But for Argento, the dots connect in another way, placing his cinema in the way of a cultural anxiety of being filled "from the outside." Despite the organic relation of Argento's films to those of such Italian directors as Riccardo Freda, Mario Bava, and Lucio Fulci—the so-called stepbrothers of Italian neorealism of the 1960s—reading Argento's cinematic practice as "Italian" betrays a rigid conception of national cinema that is particularly problematic given the kind of films he makes.[96] Cinema of the sort Argento purveys is hybrid in terms of audience demographics as well as genre.

⌣

The seven double homicides committed in Florence between 1974 and 1985 that were ascribed to the "Monster" of Florence generated disbelief, denial, and disavowal. Disbelief that serial murder could take place in the Florentine hinterland became a blanket rejection of the "Italianness" of the crimes. The Florentine police force imported forensic technology from the FBI, a New World prophylaxis to counter "New World" problems. When the anxiety over the "foreign" nature of the crimes was not displaced onto an extramural source, it was relegated to the world of folkways and anthropology. Frustration with the apparent inability of Italian law enforcement to apprehend the "Monster" was expressed in Italian literature and cinema. Amateur detectives and rogue agents spoke to a desire to work outside an unresponsive justice system. Finally, rather than solely testify to a cinema of violence that is autochthonous to Italy, the slasher films of Dario Argento also trouble the concept of "national cinema," allowing us to ask how this example of a "body genre" speaks to a phenomenon of violence that is more transnational in aim and, to be sure, in distribution. The ways *La Sindrome di Stendhal* illuminates the symbolic decoding and recoding of Italy's *città d'arte* act as corollary to the problem of the provenance of serial murder and its cultural representations in contemporary Italy.

Lombardy

Piedmont

Novi Ligure

Emilia-Romagna

Liguria

Susy Cassini and Gianluca De Nardo were
murdered on February 21st, 2001.

MAP 2. Novi Ligure, Piedmont, February 21, 2001.

PART TWO

Matricide and Fratricide

Erika, Omar, and Violent Youth in Italy

... ogni mattina lo specchio le rimandasse un piccolo
disagio, come di una faccia smarginata, scarsa di lineamenti
del tutto definiti: il dubbio di un lato in ombra.

—CLARA SERENI, "BORDERLINE"

(... each morning the mirror showed some slight unease, like
the face of some marginal person, without a distinct outline:
the doubt created by one side of the face in shadow.)

THE CENTER WILL NOT HOLD

TO BEGIN: AN IMAGE created discursively. The frame of the newspaper's
photograph shows several human figures from the waist up. (See Figure
II.1, "The Center Will Not Hold") At the borders of the image the figures
are clear and focused: men in winter clothing, one half-turned to the
camera, another with his back to it. These two visible figures flank two
others, obscured, at the center. The bodies are plainly discernible, but the
faces are blurred. The encrypted image, presumably censored to ensure
the individuals' privacy, does not offer complete anonymity, for gender
and age are easily deciphered. As Julian Stallabrass notes, "When video
rather than text is exchanged the conventional boundaries of identity
may be re-established."[1] One of the two figures with blurred faces is a
fairly tall young woman, slender in her dark blue ski jacket, with straight,

blonde hair. The body belonging to the second hazy face is in the foreground of the image, positioned in front of the young woman's. This is a
male body, like those hovering at the image's edges, although the slighter
stature suggests that this male is younger than the others. Dark short
hair disappears into the blur of what would be his identifying features.

Despite the encryption, or perhaps because of it, the identities of the
figures in this photographic image, initially captured by a camera opera-
tor for one of the RAI news services, are hardly secret.[2] Erika De Nardo
and Mauro "Omar" Fàvaro were minors when the image was captured
in February 2001 (16 and 17, respectively), the day following the brutal
murders of Susy Cassini, Erika's mother, and Gianluca De Nardo, her
younger brother, in their home in Novi Ligure. When the image was first
televised, and before Erika and Omar became the prime suspects in the
double homicide, beamed into millions of homes throughout Italy were
the faces of the bereaved daughter and her boyfriend being escorted past
the police cordon to the crime scene so that they might assist the police,
the carabinieri, and the State's Attorney's Office in understanding the
viciousness of the crimes committed by the Albanian intruders Erika
had identified as the killers. Shortly afterward, the young couple implicated themselves, and they were detained and charged. To protect their
identities as minors accused of a crime, organs of the press, one and all,
engaged in the common practice of encryption, erasing what had, only
shortly before, been plainly visible to any spectator.

Its constant use in various fora helped this particular image of Erika
and Omar attain iconic standing in the year 2001. The void at the center
of the still image (not a photograph, exactly) signifies the void of public
understanding of the ferocious stabbing murders of mother and son. But
the encryption also visibly marks a significant generation gap and the
failure of a cohort of parents, educators, spiritual leaders, and politicians
to comprehend the genesis of the crime and the way it spoke to young
Italians throughout the peninsula. Absent the facial features that serve
to assign precise identity, it appears that Erika and Omar symbolically
morph into the "Ragazza" and "Ragazzo Qualunque," or "Every Girl"
and "Every Boy," members of the misunderstood Italian "Everyteen"
generation.[3] While it is possible to argue that Erika's and Omar's rage
and homicidal violence are representative of Italian youth, my interest,

instead, is in the way the murders functioned as a cultural flashpoint, announcing generational méconnaissance, or a misrecognition of self, of the sort Clara Sereni comments on in the epigraph to this chapter.[4] In fact, the semiosis of the Erika and Omar "event," which includes literary expression as well as other cultural representations, argues for the reading of the homicides as a moment of the cultural articulation of the contemporary generation gap as seen from both sides. Omar, whose confession shortly after his arrest launched him anew onto the bosom of social piety, where he wept, declared remorse, and, consequently, received a welcome return, is ultimately less of a cipher than his former girlfriend, Erika. Her erasure, emptiness, and silence in the long narrative of her detainment and trial are nothing short of stunning. The inculpation of Erika for leading Omar into delinquency recalls the vilification of another promiscuous teenager, Miranda Bugli, erstwhile fiancée of Pietro Pacciani, whose trial for the crimes attributed to the "Monster" of Florence center part 1.

The 2001 Erika and Omar spectacle, which serves as the foundation for part 2, performs the drama of the contemporary, youthful subject's

FIGURE II.1. "The Center Will Not Hold."

unstable identity. Aided by instruments for the management and diffusion of information, the false binaries of self and other, fixed and fluid, and private and public loop endlessly on a closed circuit from which there appears no exit. Although the Erika and Omar media event illustrates the enactment of identity on several imbricating levels, including regional identity and national identity, my chief focus will be on generational identity. Youth culture was, in the first blush of cultural studies, considered self-same as popular culture. Consequently, youth culture was considered a site where issues devolving from class and consumer culture were sorted and studied. In the intervening years, however, this salutary attention has waned and, as Angela McRobbie has observed, there is need for renewed attention to youth culture as a critical field, in a contemporary context.[5] The Erika and Omar "event," the focus of chapter 4, works in tandem with contemporary narrative portraying the evanescent generation of Italian teenagers, the focus of chapter 5. Together, they help unravel these issues within a current Italian context. In chapter 4, my focus is the ways in which Italian adolescence is brought into being by contrasting and intersecting types of narrative, specifically, broadcast and print journalism and prose narrative, with some reference to cinematic narrative. The literary narratives of the so-called cannibal writers of the 1990s, and especially the violence that they portray, center chapter 5.

The brutal violence distinguishing Erika and Omar's crimes, which the Italian public found equally horrifying and riveting, is not accidental. Inexorably and pitilessly, the more than one hundred stab wounds inflicted on Susy Cassini and Gianluca stand as reminder that the struggle toward identity—psychosexual, social, geographic, or political—mirrors the struggle of birth. The birth of a subject, like that of most mammals, is, oftener than it is not, painful and bloody. The violence constitutive of the Erika and Omar story corresponds to violence common to contemporary Italian adolescents, articulated by scholarly and literary narrative alike.[6]

FOUR

Sono stati loro

Erika, Omar, and the Double Homicide of Susy
Cassini and Gianluca De Nardo in Novi Ligure

FEAR AND LOATHING IN NOVI LIGURE

ON THE AFTERNOON OF February 21, 2001, 42-year-old accountant
Susy Cassini picked up her 16-year-old daughter Erika De Nardo after
school at approximately 2:00 PM. They had lunch together at the family's
townhouse, then Erika studied at home until approximately 4:00 P.M.,
when she went to her boyfriend Mauro (nicknamed Omar) Fàvaro's
house. They spent a typical afternoon together: sex, drugs, music. Erika
returned to the De Nardo home on Via Beniamino Dacatra in Novi
Ligure at approximately 7:00 P.M. Susy had left the house to pick up
Erika's 12-year-old brother Gianluca from his afternoon sports practice.
Francesco De Nardo, Erika's father, was still at his weekly pick-up soccer match. Erika laid the dinner table for four, and Omar joined Erika
to wait for the family's arrival. Susy and Gianluca arrived home first.
Omar and Erika heard them in the garage before they entered through
the kitchen. Omar hid in the bathroom off the kitchen. Gianluca passed
through the kitchen on his way to bathe in the upstairs bathroom. Once
her brother was out of immediate earshot and the tub's faucets masked
the sounds downstairs, Erika took a kitchen knife and began stabbing
her mother, screaming "*Adesso muori!*" (Die now!) Omar left the downstairs bathroom and helped in the attack. Erika ran up the stairs and be-

gan attacking Gianluca, trying first to persuade him to eat a blue powder, rat poison that she and Omar had purchased some time earlier, planning to poison the entire family. Omar joined Erika upstairs, where they both stabbed Gianluca while he was in the filled tub. Autopsy results revealed that the boy eventually drowned. Omar left Via Dacatra, disposed of his clothes, and hid the second knife. Erika ran from the house. As she approached the roadway, her charade began.

The intruders had been Albanian and she had barely escaped attack, Erika claimed. The next day, February 22, the carabinieri questioned Erika and Omar and then took them to the De Nardo townhouse. The carabinieri did not believe either teen's version and began surveillance of the couple, which included recording their conversation at the carabinieri barracks with hidden cameras and electronically intercepting their telephone conversations. In this documented evidence, Erika assured Omar that "*non ci prenderanno mai*" (they'll never catch us) and "*ce l'abbiamo fatta*" (we did it).[1] The hidden cameras capture an exchange that exhibited a sort of ghoulish playfulness. "*Vieni qui, assassina*" (Come over here, you assassin), Omar invited Erika from across the interrogation room. Her retort, "*Assassino sei tu*" (You're the assassin), laid the ground for their later *battibecco,* or "he said, she said" opposition.[2]

Once the two were separated for further interviewing, Omar soon confessed. Erika confessed in turn, but not to participation in the attacks. That confession would not come until October. Erika changed her initial story that homicidal Albanian intruders were the murderers, claiming that Omar had attacked and killed both Gianluca and Susy. Both teenagers were detained in the Ferrante Aporti juvenile facility in Turin. To remove Erika from further contact with Omar and from public scrutiny in Piedmont, she was relocated to Carcere Minorile Beccaria, a facility for juvenile offenders, in Milan. Extensive psychiatric evaluations began in the spring and continued until late summer, when they were finished. The psychiatrists concluded that Erika was narcissistic and possibly had borderline personality disorder and that Omar was masochistically submissive to her. These diagnoses were disclosed to the press. A joint trial began November 28, at which date the teens' attorneys opted for a fast-track trial, which carries with it an automatic reduction of sentence by one-third. Since both teens were minors at the time of the crimes, life in prison was not a sentencing option. On December 3, the court issued its formal accusation: premeditated murder with several aggravating factors, including the couple's obstruction of justice and, in Erika's case, the killing of a sibling and a parent. On December 14, Erika was sentenced to sixteen years in prison and Omar to fourteen. Their sentences were confirmed on May 30, 2002.

The psychiatric experts' discussion of Erika's "borderline" personality disorder leads to the consideration of another borderland, that of Novi Ligure, and to the examination of the ways the Erika and Omar case spoke to identity as regionally formed. Significantly, regional affiliation, for the area surrounding Novi, is, like Erika's and Omar's faces in the images I referred to in the introduction to this part, blurred and indistinct. Roughly midway between Turin and Alessandria, Novi is positioned near the conjoining of Lombardy, Piedmont, Emilia-Romagna, and Liguria.[3] Even the town's name, Novi Ligure, suggests a Ligurian rather than Lombard seat. As in many small cities with an industrial base (the Pernigotti chocolate factory, where Francesco De Nardo works as a manager, is the chief employer in town) in northern Italy, Novi's population has grown since 1980 and counts among its inhabitants immigrants from North Africa and former Eastern bloc countries.

MORAL PANIC IN THE DEEP NORTH

The news of a double homicide in the affluent, suburban *profondo nord* (deep north) stunned the Italian public. In the previous fourteen months, the crimes against demi-celebrities (largely armed robbery) had been widely publicized in the press and attributed to illegal alien immigrants of Slavic descent.[4] Despite the fact that these crimes rarely ended in homicide, Erika's claim that the intruders were Albanian rooted immediately like a bad seed in loamy soil.[5] District Attorney Carlo Carlesi, filmed by news services outside the De Nardo *villetta* the night of the crime, asserted that "the murder had almost certainly taken place during an attempted robbery." Those that knew them refused to believe that either Erika ("*una ragazza a posto*" [a good girl]) or Omar ("*un ragazzo buono*" [a nice guy]) could be involved.[6] The intruders, they stated, were "North Africans . . . who have no scruples."[7] The title of Guido Chiesa's

2003 fictional documentary *Sono stati loro: 48 ore a Novi Ligure* (They did it: 48 hours in Novi Ligure) derives from the repeated avowals of numerous Novi residents that the perpetrators were interlopers, non-Novesi, non-Italians, menacing and indistinct "Slavs." This short feature–documentary blends actual reportage with staged interviews and commentary, complicating its generic designation.

The Novi Ligure homicides produced a classic configuration of elements that led to a moral panic.[8] The "Moroccans" or the "Albanians"—in other words, dark-skinned immigrants—were believed to have imported delinquent tendencies into the removed and protected Italian Northwest. With lightening speed, aided by extensive coverage by regional organs of the press as well as national news services, citizens clamored for political action to contain the perceived threat of invasion. Residents widely declaimed their dissatisfaction with the efforts of Mauro Lovelli, the mayor of Novi, to protect the area from *gli slavi,* the Slavs. Given the xenophobia of the teens' deception, the fact that Mauro had chosen the orientalized (Arabic, exotic) "Omar" as a nickname is as ironic as the fact that Erika was surrounded by young Albanian women in detention for a variety of crimes at the Beccaria facility in Milan.

True to the moral panic "script," parties on the right of the political spectrum capitalized on the extreme xenophobia that erupted, using it as fodder for the discussion about immigration in Italy. Chiesa's *Sono stati loro* highlights the fact that the national debate on immigration coincided precisely with the crimes in Novi Ligure.[9] Just as talk show host Bruno Vespa was staging a debate on immigration between Gianfranco Fini, founder of Alleanza nazionale (AN), or National Alliance, the party of the right, and Pietro Fassino of the Democratici di Sinistra (PDS), or Democratic Party of the Left, which replaced Italy's disbanded Communist Party, on RAI's *Porta a porta* broadcast of February 21, another channel was breaking the news of the double murder in Novi Ligure. While Umberto Bossi and other Lega Lombarda (Lombard League) leaders decried the crimes wrought "*in casa nostra*" (in our very homes), Francesco Rutelli (of the center-left Margherita Party) accused the media, and in particular Silvio Berlusconi's Mediaset conglomerate, of submitting the Italian public to "a mediatic bombardment on the topic of security." Although Rutelli "admitted that interest in the topic of security responds to a real need," he insisted that "certain newscasts focused maddeningly on crimes committed by foreigners."[10] The press fanned the flames of xenophobia, so that interest in expediting the Novi Ligure investigation reached the highest levels of the government.[11] For example, xenophobic panic delayed by several days an eyewitness account that placed Omar in blood-stained clothing in Via Dacatra at the time of the murders, even though he had claimed to be at home during the attacks. The witness regretted not coming forward until March 1. Even though he was "an immigrant with all his papers in order . . . he was afraid."[12]

The ways in which the political right painted with a broad brush the issues of immigration corresponds to the lack of distinct regional boundaries surrounding Novi, subsuming the problem under the wider umbrella of the less distinct "North" and, ultimately, "national," a designation that tends to undercut regional identity.[13] The rhetorical operations of AN and the Lega (the political party of the right, the Lega Nord, Northern League) also show how affiliation, and therefrom identity, can form across boundaries, over great distances, against cultural context, local histories, and practices in service to the creation of the "imagined" community that Benedict Anderson observes is constitutive of nation making.[14]

The blurred identity I have been referring to similarly describes the ways in which the case appealed to national identity. Chiesa's fictional documentary of the event is aptly named *Sono stati loro,* a title derived from the repeated avowals of numerous Novi residents, "Sono stati loro"; that is, "they" did it and, precisely, not "us." When at last it became clear that Erika and Omar were the murderers, the venerable journalist Enzo Biagi sadly accepted the teens and their ill-fated and poorly contained violence. "*Erika e Omar,*" he told the millions of viewers of *Il Fatto,* his nightly news commentary on RAI 1, "*sono nostri*" (are our own).[15]

The possessive predicate adjective *nostri* (ours) that Biagi so reluctantly used stands distinct from the *loro* (they) in Chiesa's film title— *Sono stati loro*—and returns to haunt the case and the many questions surrounding the etiology of violence. Concern about the way film and television, so available to young Italian audiences, might inculcate violence prompted then president of the Republic Carlo Azeglio Ciampi to assert that "our cinema does not nurture violence."[16] Filmmaker Bernardo Bertolucci agreed, stating that "Italian cinema only rarely nurtures a culture of death, that exaltation of extreme violence that can deeply affect viewers, especially youthful ones."[17] The linguistic binarism of "ours" and "theirs" recalls the importance of speech act theory to the dynamic production of identity, wherein "identity and boundaries of the individual ego are marked out by the use of what linguists call deictics or shifters (I/you, here/there, this/that, etc.), demonstratives (him, them, etc.), and performatives (I promise, I do, etc.)."[18] This split was captured in pop child psychologist Paolo Crepet's title for his 2003 book on Italian adolescence: *Voi, noi. Sull'indifferenza di giovani e adulti* (You. Us. On the indifference of young people and adults.)[19]

A shift in thinking from us/them to I/you precipitated the split between Erika and Omar. The psychiatric evaluations of the two teens revealed that as individuals, Erika and Omar were not predisposed to rage or poor impulse control. The catalyst lay in the third agent, the couple they had created that combined their forces.[20] After the murders, the previously inseparable couple began furious disavowals and betrayals in the interest of escaping punishment.[21]

At the beginning of the case, the media underscored Erika's youth in description worthy of fairy tale. She was reported as being fourteen (not sixteen), a young girl who was found barefoot in her pajamas in the middle of the street in the deep cold of a northern Italian winter night. One headline quoted Erika as saying: "Ho visto mia madre morire per salvarmi" ("I Saw My Mother Die Trying to Save Me").[22]

Once the facts were uncovered, though, the way Erika was represented changed significantly. Prosecutor Carlo Carlesi, who initially believed that the murders took place during a robbery, had changed his tune two days later. Erika "reconstructed the events with the precision of a thirty-year-old," he said.[23] Major (later Colonel) Luciano Garofano of the RIS (Reparto Investigazioni Scientifiche, the elite forensic analysis team of the carabinieri) similarly described Erika's behavior as mature and adult. As a guest on *TG 2 Dossier*, Garofano discussed some of the forensic facts and described Erika as having acted "*con grande freddezza . . . e lucidità*" (with great coldness . . . and clear-mindedness) after the murders.[24]

The investigation into Erika's behavior before the crimes revealed other details that contradicted the initial image the media created for her. She bought and took drugs and engaged in frequent and apparently aggressive sexual activity.[25] In addition, it became clear that she and Omar had plotted her family's annihilation for several weeks and had bought rat poison and the gloves they would wear during the attacks. In the couple's relationship, Erika was clearly the dominant one whom Omar sought to please. Several weeks before the murders, he had assaulted a classmate Erika did not like. Since the attack took place in the week of February 14, Erika considered it an act of Omar's devotion, her "Valentine's Day present."[26] Erika's calm and steely coldness after her arrest contrasted strikingly with Omar's behavior. He fell apart almost immediately, and was characterized in the press as "that big baby . . . his face crumpled by weeping, holding a handkerchief to his nose."[27]

POLICING PARENTING

In his 2001 study *Non siamo capaci di ascoltarli: riflessioni sull'infanzia e adolescenza,* (We are unable to hear them: reflections on childhood and adolescence), child psychologist and sociologist Paolo Crepet, a regular guest on televised talk shows that discussed the Novi Ligure murders, seeks to reveal the abyss between the experiences of contemporary Italian adolescents and their parents.[28] To a large extent, Crepet argues, this variance owes to the perceived permissiveness of the post-1968 generation. The gap between parents of that generation and their children has given rise to a mini-boom in parenting guides and in sociological investigations of the psychological character of juveniles. In addition to Crepet's *Non siamo capaci di ascoltarli,* the juvenile delinquency genre includes his *I figli non crescono più* (Children no longer grow up) (2005) as well the text he coauthored with magistrate and novelist Giancarlo De Cataldo, *I giorni dell'ira. Storie di matricidi* (Days of rage. Stories of matricides, 2002). Also included in this list are De Cataldo's monographs *Teneri assassini* (Young assassins, 2000) and *Il padre e lo straniero* (The father and the stranger, 2004). It takes a wry (and queer) ironist like Aldo Busi to lampoon books like these in his *Il manuale del perfetto papà (beati gli orfani)* (The perfect father's handbook (blessed be the orphans), 2001). It is significant that Niccolò Ammaniti, one of the so-called cannibal writers who, with tales of rape, murder, and apocalypse have contributed to the "exaltation" of violence that Bertolucci so disparaged, coauthored a book on adolescence with his father, an expert in child psychology, entitled *Nel nome del figlio: L'adolescenza raccontata da un padre e da un figlio* (In the name of the father: adolescence as told by a father and son, 1995).[29]

The investigations of Erika and Omar by journalists, agents of the police, educators, and psychiatric experts revealed the disconnect between adolescents' appearance and their behaviors. Repeatedly and from numerous sources, the pre-homicide Erika was remembered as "a fine girl," "athletic," and "*brava*" from supporters across the generational spectrum, including her Italian teacher, friends, classmates who knew her to varying degrees, and other adults, often her friends' parents. But after Erika's role in the murders was revealed, a range of behaviors that contradicted the appearance of "a fine girl" emerged from her text-messaging behavior. While journalists used "SMS" in its widely accepted meaning of "short message service" in their reportage, the term also came to stand for "*se mamma sapesse*" (should Mom suspect).[30] Renowned critic and television studies scholar Aldo Grasso wrote in *Il Corriere della Sera* that Erika frequently exchanged SMS messages with her boyfriend and that like all teenagers, the two were deeply immersed in cell phones, computers, and "every other type of electronic umbilical cord."[31] SMS is the mode of preferred communication among 14- to 18-year-olds in Italy; Centro Studi Investimenti Sociale (CENSIS) reported in 2004 that 79.7 percent of respondents in that age group described SMS as the primary function of the cellular telephone, as compared to 65.8 percent for those 19–24 years old and 46 percent for those in the 25–30 age group.[32] Young Italians are rarely far from their cell phones. As one interview subject for the CENSIS report noted, "they never unlatch themselves from it," adding that there are those who "sleep with it under their pillows."[33] This "wired existence," as Crepet puts it, makes contact between Italian teens constant and present.[34] The cell phone, CENSIS says, has become an extension of young Italians' bodies.[35] It has also contributed to the gulf between some teens and their parents; in their constant electronic contact with each other, teens freely discuss a world of desires and behaviors that most parents are not privy to.

The "wired" existence speaks not only to the omnipresence and importance of cellular technology, but also to the ways the Internet facilitates and fosters affiliation and identity formation.[36] New media technologies have transformed both social space and habitus, changing "the situational geography of human life."[37] The proximity to each other of young Italian-language-speakers via the Internet suggests the formation of a disembodied, virtual group.[38] The Erika and Omar case illustrates this. When the Internet site erikatiamo.com (the English translation of the URL is "Erika I love you") was launched on March 6, less than two months after the murders, it generated a virtual community that responded with strong opinions to the site's content. Authors of the site were not disclosed, but users appeared to be largely teenagers. Responses to the content of the site showed as much identification with Erika as criticism of her. On the day the site was launched, one reader commented "*Io mi identifico con Erika*" (I identify with Erika), while another rejected the site, judging it to be a "*sito da vomito, tetro e pericoloso*" (vomit Web site, dark and dangerous).[39] The clamor spilling into the next day's coverage continued this split reception. One user, perhaps with sarcasm (but surely in bad taste), wrote "Erika, you did good, I wish I had your courage," signing the posting "Hitler."[40] Other users (the disembodied apparatus of the Internet makes it impossible to determine gender, age, or other demographic traits) pondered the young couple's actions at greater length asking, "*Chi è il diavolo?*" (Who's the devil?) "Miao" offered a response: "Marilyn Manson, Puff Daddy, Erika and Omar? It's not a criticism, but events like these suggest just how incredibly different from normal that which is universally designated as 'normal' is. My God, are human beings difficult."[41] The reportage captured the last response in that particular discussion thread from "Uno," who said, "You all are philosophizing and (yet) two innocent people were massacred."[42]

Clearly Erika and Omar are not the first violent youth offenders to gain notoriety, nor are they unique in recent Italian history. Nearly all television programs covering the events, from the briefest to nearly epic in length, featured stock footage of four celebrated cases of young family annihilators. The Italian viewing public could not have forgotten these cases even if it wanted to.[43] In the first case, from Vercelli, in Piedmont, Doretta Graneris and her boyfriend, Sergio Baldini, killed her father, mother, brother, and grandparents on November 13, 1975, to secure her inheritance. In the second case, from Parma, Ferdinando Carretta killed his parents and brother on August 4, 1989. He claimed that they had all left the country to live in South America and he fled to London, where he lived until he returned to Italy nine years later to confess.[44] In the third case, Pietro Maso of Montecchia di Crosara (near Verona) enlisted the help of three friends to kill his parents in October 1991. The group then spent the night clubbing.[45] Of all the delinquents, his cool lack of affect proves the most remarkable to Italian collective memory. The last case history perpetually used to round out the group is that of Nadia Frigerio, who on November 4, 1994, in San Michele near Verona, killed her mother to secure her rent-stabilized apartment. One other case may be more pertinent to a discussion of Erika De Nardo, however. On June 4, 2000, four young women in Chiavenna killed Sister Maria Laura Mainetti in a ritual sacrifice. They were supposedly impelled by the "satanic" music of Marilyn Manson. Erika was not the first Italian young woman who escalated her antisocial behavior to murder.

In his 2000 study *I nuovi adolescenti: Padri e madri di fronte ad una sfida* (The new adolescents: mothers and fathers facing a challenge), Milan-based psychologist Gustavo Pietropolli Charmet identifies an increasingly violent society as one of the leading challenges to parents of adolescents. For Charmet, the etiology of violent behavior in young adults is usually attributable to violence endured during childhood.[46] Yet, unlike most documented violent youth offenders, Erika and Omar did not experience violence at the hands of family members or other adults. In fact, surprise or disbelief that two such seemingly "normal" teens could plan and commit such a violent crime is a recurring motif in media coverage of their actions. What was the source of such violence? Significantly, what passed between Erika and Omar during the brief moments they were left unattended in the police station was described by the press as *"un film d'orrore"* (a horror film). In fact, throughout the investigation and later trial, narrative (literary, cinematic, and musical) was thought to have influenced the young couple, particularly Erika.[47]

MIMETIC VIOLENCE: SEEING AND DOING, READING
AND REENACTING, HEARING AND HATING

In the week following the murders, while the RIS scoured the house for physical evidence, they made a discovery of apparent importance. On Erika's bedside table was a copy of late-nineteenth-century writer Giovanni Verga's short-story collection *Novelle rusticane* (*Little Novels of Sicily*). This fact is easily explained by reviewing the reading list in the parochial high school where Erika was a student: Verga the realist is required reading of all high-school-aged students in Italy. Yet Erika was no academic eagle and appeared not to take much pleasure in reading and study. In light of the accumulating evidence that pointed to Erika's participation and culpability, though, the fact that the story "Libertà" (Freedom) was heavily underlined took on great significance to investigators. Investigators also recovered Erika's diary in roughly the same place as the victims' bodies, and its contents seemed to underscore the importance of the Verga text.

Verga's 1883 short story is set in the small village on the slopes of Etna in 1860, as Garibaldi's Spedizione dei Mille (Expedition of the Thousand) makes its way through Sicily, "liberating" the island from both foreigners and its age-old feudalism, thus weaving it into the tapestry of events known as the Risorgimento. "Libertà" is a story of graphic violence and tremendous irony. Verga's prose describing the peasant uprising is as quick and choppy as the rise and fall of the hatchets, sickles, and scythes that the townsfolk employ to "cut themselves free" from the yoke of serfdom. These farm implements cut a swath through the crowd instead of through a field of wheat, quickly and inexorably mowing down landowners, lawyers, priests, and aristocrats, irrespective of gender or age. The short, staccato *"Viva la libertà!"* (Long live freedom!) punctuates nearly every dispassionate and realist description of violence.

The catharsis this unchoreographed bloodletting affords is quashed by a military restoration, whose mechanisms of law and order can neither explain nor tolerate the violent lawlessness the uprising displayed. The elliptical sentence that ends the story speaks volumes. En route to prison following a cursory trial, a condemned *carbonaio* exclaims: *"Se mi avevano detto che c'era la libertà . . . !"* (If they had told me that freedom . . . !)[48] If they had told him that freedom taken by violent means would end in the loss of every liberty, perhaps he would have reconsidered his actions.

Despite the apparent lack of motive, the RIS had suspected Erika nearly from the discovery of the bodies; thus, reports that they had recovered Verga's short story and that it was heavily annotated led the press to suppose Erika had drawn inspiration from it, seeking her own liberty from her parents' interference in her relationship with Omar. However, as the investigation showed, although Susy De Nardo had informed her daughter that she did not care for Omar, there was no evidence she had forbidden Erika to see him. What, then, did Erika need liberty from or for?

At the trial in closed court, a member of Erika's defense team proposed a link between the germ of the idea to slay Erika's family and her interest in the musical group fronted by Jim Morrison, the Doors, which Omar had described as "her passion." Omar testified that he had given her a copy of the 1991 Oliver Stone film about the band, starring Val Kilmer, as a gift. Fàvaro claimed they had watched it together countless times. One of the judges read aloud Jim Morrison's lyrics from the song "The End" in the courtroom.[49] Apocalyptic in tone, Morrison's ballad is located across a yawning chasm from the ballad Giubba the *cantastorie*—Tuscany's version of the story-telling griot present in some African cultures—sang in 1951, in which he immortalized Pietro Pacciani's murder in Tassinaia and which was examined in association with Florence's "Monster" event in chapter 1. The song Erika allegedly found inspiration from begins somberly, with Morrison intoning over a simple guitar line, "This is the end / Beautiful friend / This is the end." The verses that most interested prosecutors came somewhere in the middle:

> The killer awoke before dawn, he put his boots on
> He took a face from the ancient gallery
> And he walked on down the hall
> He went into the room where his sister lived, and . . . then he
> Paid a visit to his brother, and then
> He walked on down the hall, and
> And he came to a door . . . and he looked inside
> Father, yes son, I want to kill you
> Mother . . . I want to . . . fuck you

The salient verses concluded with the refrain *"Kill, kill, kill, kill, kill, kill."*[50]

Morrison's narrator succumbs to the deep structure of Oedipal jealousy and rage and lays waste to his family.[51] "Did those words inspire you?" one of the judges asked Erika. "Did you (and Omar) share that view?" Erika replied that "(she) liked the Doors but nothing more, they were Omar's passion."[52] Instead of providing a link between music and her behavior, Erika's response to the prosecutor's question distanced herself from the song.[53] The effort to establish a cultural expression that could serve as the source of Erika's alienation was about as successful as Giuseppe Alessandri's attempts to establish a direct correspondence between the violent horror and pornographic films that Pietro Pacciani allegedly watched and his reenactment of that violence in some of the Florentine serial murders.[54] Like Verga's short story, the ending to inquiry into the Doors' influence was inconclusive.

If narrative of various brands and vintages—that is, cinematic, literary, musical—was not blamed as having nourished Erika's morbid and violent tendencies in 2001, the issue of violence involving young people appeared relentlessly before the Italian public that year, on screens both large and small. Andrea Porporati's film *Luce negli occhi* (*Empty Eyes*) played to some critical acclaim and was nominated for several prizes.[55] This film tells the story of Marco (Fabrizio Gifuni), a troubled, violent teen. Like Erika and Omar, Marco's weapon of choice is the carving knife, which produces an intimacy when used as an instrument of violence that a firearm does not.[56] Like Erika and Omar, Marco's victim is a parent, his father.

Also in 2001, the shooting death of 23-year-old anti-globalism activist Carlo Giuliani during the 27th G8 Summit, held that July in Genoa, horrified television viewers across Italy, Europe, and the world. Competing narratives emerged about whether Giuliani's actions could have been construed as aggressively violent, as the squad of carabinieri that was dispatched to contain the protests during the summit claimed. Camera angles from which the still photos of various news services were taken tended to collapse distance between the protesters and the carabinieris' Jeep. This is particularly the case for the widely circulated photo taken from the rear with a telephoto lens, showing Giuliani positioned in the foreground with the Jeep behind him. (See Figure 4.1.) In this photo, Giuliani hoists a fire extinguisher, and appears to be closer to the Jeep than he does in the video footage or in any photograph taken from a different position. The police used still photos, and particularly this one, to support the contention that Giuliani appeared menacing and aggressive because he was so close to the vehicle and that the shot the young carabiniere, Mario Placanica, fired was made in defense of his life.

Moving pictures, on the other hand, told a different story. The footage of Genoa's chaotic Piazza Alimonda in the late afternoon of July 20, 2001, that was shot by a Reuters cameraman is more detailed than any of the still photographs of the protest. Francesca Comencini included this footage in her 2002 short film *Carlo Giuliani, Ragazzo* (Carlo Giuliani, boy). Comencini made her position about the injustice of Giuliani's death and his portrayal in the popular press clear, and she intercut footage of an interview with Giuliani's mother, Heidi Giuliani, throughout the documentary to support her argument. In a year in which adolescent violence was very much in the public eye and in public discourse, Gi-

FIGURE 4.1. Protests at the Piazza Alimonda, Genoa, July 20, 2001.

uliani's death caused another moral panic concerning Italian youth in the thrall of violence. In this light, and following the "script" of moral panic, the verdict that Placanica acted appropriately in shooting Giuliani seemed like a foregone conclusion.

<drawings>PRIVACY, CONTEMPORARY ITALIAN
YOUTH, AND A GENERATION GAP

The shocked response to Erika's and Omar's brutal, unexpected violence derived partially from the teens' secrecy but also from their parents' wish to respect the young couple's privacy. Although De Nardo family intimates stated that Susy had expressed concern over what she felt was her daughter's too-consuming relationship with Omar, no outright prohibitions appear to have been made. Establishing a love relationship is a "normal" phase, an adolescent's psychological separation from the parent, as Charmet and myriad other experts observe.[57] Coincidentally, several weeks after the Novi Ligure murders, a film about the adolescent's need for privacy premiered, Nanni Moretti's *La stanza del figlio* (*The Son's Room*).[58]

This successful and acclaimed film from 2001 about the accidental drowning death of a young man and its aftermath for his family revolves around secrecy and revelation. The habitus of privacy is inscribed by both the title and the camera. Andrea (Giuseppe Sanfelice), the teenaged son of the title, occupies his distinct architectural space, the room of the title, which is the repository of his secrets. The father, Giovanni (Nanni Moretti), who is a psychoanalyst, is often shown in his office, where he listens to his clients' secrets, private wishes, desires, and fears. Numerous tracking shots make clear how separation and union alternate seamlessly in this happy family. After Andrea drowns in a diving accident, his secrets begin to emerge. One of them involves the disappearance of a fossil from the laboratory of Andrea's school. Although Giovanni had publicly supported his son, insisting on his innocence, we learn that Andrea had confessed to his mother, Paola (Laura Morante), that in fact he and a friend had stolen the artifact. Andrea's confidence that Paola will keep this secret proves all the more devastating to her sense that she intimately understands her son when she learns of the beginnings of a romance he kept privately to himself, in the form of his correspondence with a girl named Arianna (Sofia Vigliar). The question of whether the family can survive the trauma of Andrea's death suggests that *La stanza del figlio* could be Moretti's most political film, as Guido Bonsaver has argued, and not solely the domestic drama most critics saw that, however well-acted, marked a retreat from the director's more engagé films.[59]

The family is a common thematic in Moretti's oeuvre. In fact, one of the fault lines of the director's corpus reaches from his role as a contrarian young adult in the 1970s (*Io sono un autarchico* (*I Am Self-sufficient*) and *Ecce Bombo,* 1976 and 1978, respectively) to his role as a father (*Aprile,* 1998).[60] More than one critic has observed that after celebrating his son's birth in *Aprile,* Moretti was forced to (symbolically) kill him off in his next film. The self-doubt lurking at the edges of *Aprile* (Will he be able to direct the musical? Be a success as a parent?), becomes the focus of *La stanza del figlio.* Over the course of his directorial career, Moretti has transformed from rebellious young man to an adult who reflects on the effects of his generation on Italian culture.

Author Lidia Ravera shares this reflectiveness with Moretti. Like the filmmaker, Ravera's debut dates from 1976. Her celebrated coauthored novel, *Porci con le ali: diario sessuo-politico di due adolescent* (Pigs with wings: a sexual-political diary of two youths) explores life from the point of view of two 16-year-olds buffeted by the winds of change of the 1970s. In addition to its trenchant social commentary on life and mores, the novel's salient characteristic is its dual, alternating narrative: the teens Rocco and Antonia share the narrative voice, which, significantly, corresponds to the novel's actual composition: *Porci con le ali* was written together by Ravera and Marco Lombardo Radice. For these authors, gender equality was not simply a theme for artistic exploration in their novel; it was their aesthetic and their ethical practice.

In her 2003 publication, *Il freddo dentro,* Ravera once more uses two adolescents as her subject. In this book, her "open letter" to Erika in the Beccaria prison in Milan, Ravera seeks to fill in the many gaps in the case about motivation, particularly Erika's. Ravera uses a fiction writer's tools to get at what lies beneath Erika's cool exterior as well as the truth beneath the surface of the case after it had suffered so much media handling. She contemplates Erika's psychology as a novelist, entertaining options from nonfiction assessments (Erika's narcissism, her inner conflict felt over separating from her parents and especially from her mother, the problem the "couple" created) as well as fictional ones (André Gide in his poems collected in *Fruits of the Earth* (1899), Lady Macbeth) in an attempt to understand what motivated Erika's actions. What emerges is a complicated, multifaceted portrait but, as in the case with any fictional character, one that changes according to perspective. In a July 2004 television appearance, Ravera was asked by audience members to compare Italian adolescents from the 1970s with those in contemporary Italy. Using Erika's case as an example, Ravera described her considerable concern over the state of the Italian family, which she described as the "microcosm of a rotten society."[61] She argued that the differing viewpoints between the two generations are common to both time periods but that the battles of the 1970s have given way to silence and secrecy for both generations. Toni, an audience member, commented that the Sessantottini, or the 1968ers, as the generation who engaged in student protests in 1968 is referred to, inveighed against a repressive, fossilized family structure but offered nothing in its place to their own children. (Recall the naked wish to annihilate the family that Jim Morrison vocalized in "The End.") That generation, Toni observed, "forced us to build our own parental figures."[62]

In his 2001 novel *Archeologia del presente* (Archaeology of the present), Sebastiano Vassalli arrives at a similar conclusion. The novel unambiguously refers the reader to the vicissitudes of the Erika and Omar case. Like Ravera's, Vassalli's perspective incorporates a generational reckoning. However, Vassalli's indictment of the utopian (yet anarchic) tendencies of the post-1968 generation in Italy is much more clear. This distinction may owe to the shift in genre from Ravera's hybrid, epistolary memoir to Vassalli's novel. Ravera's "open letter" to Erika, especially the familiar *tu* form of address used, suggests that the text is as much about Ravera as it is about her subject. The way Ravera alternates between the "you's" of the *tu* address—Erika and herself—recalls Luisa Passerini's collage of the 1968ers in her 1988 *Autoritratto di gruppo* (*Autobiography of a Generation*). In this text Passerini, an oral historian, alternates between interviews of her subjects in even-numbered chapters and passages from her own diaries in the odd-numbered chapters.

Vassalli's text, on the other hand, is fiction: the author made use of Turin's daily, *La Stampa,* to offer comments from his own subject position, and *Archeologia del passato* is deliberately dislocated in space, if not in time. Partially censoring place names throughout the novel (e.g., "Comune di ***"), Vassalli obviously wishes the location to be both imprecise and representative. *Archeologia del passato* is a bitter and ironic novel that explores developments in Italian society from 1970 onward. The main characters are an anonymous first-person narrator and his two friends, Leo and Michela Ferrari.[63] All the principal fictional characters are Sessantottini. Their naïve embrace of every social cause and movement from 1968 forward drives Vassalli's narrative. The Ferraris' engagement with movements that seek to open traditional locations of power in Italian society is exhaustive. They participate in movements for women's liberation, sexual liberation, gay rights, the rights of the psychiatrically challenged, the rights of animals, and peace. They also embrace transcendental meditation, work against nuclear armaments, and are members of Greenpeace. In an attempt to change traditional notions of family, Leo and Michela also adopt two children, Marlon (for Marlon Brando) and Aria.

Despite the largesse these fundamentally bourgeois do-gooders lavish on their children, Marlon and Aria suffer from a kind of reaction formation. Marlon becomes a member of the Guardie padane (read: neo-Nazi, skinhead) and strays from his parents' social conventions and political inclinations. After various run-ins with the law, Marlon and Gigliola, his unwholesome girlfriend, lay waste to the entire household, killing both parents and his adoptive sister. Because of the narrator's longstanding friendship with the Ferraris, the magistrate asks whether he could visit Marlon in detention in an effort to learn the underlying pathology that caused his actions.

> "Maybe Marlon will say something new," the judge added. "Maybe he'll explain to you why he and Gigliola decided to exterminate the Ferrari family. Whose idea it was and who the shooter was. To us the kid just keeps repeating the same story. . . . He says he acted in a daze and that Gigliola had nothing to do with the massacre. He keeps trying to get his girlfriend off the hook. She, on the other hand, does the exact opposite and doesn't hold back from accusing him of anything so long as it means she'll get off."[64]

The narrator's meeting with Marlon reveals no weighty epistemology of evil, which turns out to be as banal as Hannah Arendt supposed.[65] The structural similarities of the crimes Vassalli narrates to the Erika and Omar case are too obvious to disregard. The violence takes place in the home, a sibling is killed, and the initial blame is placed on immigrants. Further, the massacre takes place, as it did in the De Nardo case, in the barricaded hinterland of Italy's regional North, where, despite their parents' aim to shelter them, children are deeply familiar with sex, drugs, and rock and roll. The protectionist attitude of the embourgeoised enclaves of townhouses in the novel, like those in Novi Ligure, is the very thing Vassalli attacks in an article entitled "Odio e noia di provincia" (Hatred and boredom in the provinces), published four days after the Cassini–De Nardo murders. It is worth noting that Vassalli's book appeared in June 2001, before the reports of the psychiatric experts were completed or filed, during a time when speculation as to the motives Erika and Omar thrived.

Steeped in self-pity, Marlon tells the narrator during their prison interview: "My adoptive parents paid attention to me only so that I could become exactly like them. They wanted a kid that was a photocopy of themselves."[66] Ultimately, Vassalli's narrator agrees with Marlon's assessment that his parents were "*egoisti*" (selfish). As if his narrative were a film and the narrator a director, Vassalli concludes *Archeologia del presente* with a radical zoom out, so that Leo and Michela's deaths are seen as the necessary consequence of the social upheaval of 1968 and its aftermath. No Bertoluccian hagiography here as in the director's 2003 film *I Dreamers* (*The Dreamers*).[67] At novel's close, the narrator raises a glass in bitter toast: "To all those in every era who have spent their lives trying to make the world perfect and, at great cost and suffering and enormous efforts they managed to bring it to where it is now, that is, on the brink of its own demise. I shook my head. I repeated: What idiots."[68]

The one image of Erika and Omar that was taken before privacy laws protected their identity has been endlessly reproduced. It is blurry and out of focus. The obscured center of the infinitely reproduced image of Erika and Omar ideates the struggle that often characterizes the formation of identity. What once was clear and identifying is transformed, meaningfully, into a half-presence, a smudged image only partially knowable. The issues devolving from the murders of Susy Cassini and Gianluca De Nardo illustrate how various identities—gendered, generational, regional, and national—vie with one another for prominence and how moments of utter clarity, like the certifiable xenophobic panic that seized the area surrounding Novi Ligure in 2001, can be transformed into haze.

FIVE

The Raw and the Cooked

Transnational Media and Violence in Italy's
Cannibal Pulp Fiction of the 1990s

Il primo gennaio

So che si può vivere
non esistendo,
emersi da una quinta, da un fondale,
da un fuori che non c'è se mai nessuno
l'ha veduto.

—EUGENIO MONTALE

(I know that one can live
without existing,
emerging from offstage, or from behind a curtain,
from an outside that isn't there if no one
has ever seen it.)

THE PRECEDING CHAPTER, WHICH detailed the 2001 murders of Susy
Cassini and Gianluca De Nardo in Novi Ligure, began and ended with
a motif of indistinctness. I argued that the blur of the photographically
reproduced faces of the two adolescents, Erika De Nardo and Omar
Fàvaro, accused and convicted of premeditated double murder, came to
signify the blurry outlines of the rising generation of adolescents in Italy
at the waning of the twentieth century and the start of the twenty-first.

The motif of an indistinct and inscrutable younger generation in Italy continues in this chapter, which explores the violence in (and of) the work of a cohort of young writers who emerged in the second half of the 1990s, called the *"Giovani Cannibali,"* or Young Cannibals.

The Novi Ligure double homicide spawned twin moral panics: a xenophobic response to increases in criminal activity and concern about Italian youth at risk as victims and perpetrators of violence. Both were relieved by way of mechanisms of displacement and disavowal. The context of a more generalized violence was perceived as increasingly prevalent in Italian society in the 1990s, and its origins were displaced onto nonindigenous populations: Albanians, immigrants from the Balkans, and others from behind the recently raised Iron Curtain, believed to be criminally inclined. Though the assertion that "Albanians" had committed the murders was quick to take root, acceptance that De Nardo and Fàvaro were responsible was slower in coming. The provenance of the violence the two teens loosed in the murders was a source of speculation and puzzlement inside and outside the courtroom and reveals several successive acts of displacement. The locus of blame traveled from De Nardo, to the dangerous entity she and Fàvaro had created as a couple, to the nineteenth-century canonical writer Giovanni Verga, to Jim Morrison of the Doors, to filmmaker Oliver Stone. The attempt to identify the origins of De Nardo's and Fàvaro's violence is one matter, to locate it outside of Italy another. One would think that the slow but steady flow of young Italians annihilating their families since the Doretta Graneris case in 1975 would have offered preparation enough for the events that took place in Novi Ligure in January 2001.[1]

Sentencing in the trial phase of the case against De Nardo and Fàvaro concluded on December 11, 2001. This date fell several weeks shy of *il primo gennaio*, the first of January that Nobel laureate Eugenio Montale contemplates in his poem and that is presented as epigraph to this chapter. But the date of the poem's title was not as important to the district attorney, Livia Locci, as its content. Locci intoned Montale's poem as she called for the full sentencing of the teenagers allowable under Italian law. Locci herself, whom journalists described as *"durissima,"* stony, became emotional as she read the lines of Montale's poem, as if speaking for Erika's mother, both absent and present. Susy Cassini has not disappeared, Locci appears to say, if she can conjure her in that Turin courtroom. When the sentences were announced, endorsing the prosecutor's suggestion, with sixteen years for Erika and fourteen for Omar, Erika collapsed in "long sobs she could not control."[2] For his part, Omar "froze."[3]

Far from Montale's honored solemnity, yet reflecting the kind of violence that claimed Cassini's life, lies the work of the Young Cannibals. The shocking opening lines of "Bagnoschiuma," the lead story in the collection *Superwoobinda* (1998), by Aldo Nove, one of the authors associated with this group, offer an entry point to an exploration of literary texts associated with the Cannibals. "I killed my parents because of the absurd shower soap they used, Pure & Vegetal."[4] This one sentence neatly represents the hallmarks of the Young Cannibals' style: brand name consumerism, hyper- or surreal violence, and black humor. District Attorney Locci's declamation, on the other hand, offers a different view on the mutually informing and socially signifying practices of literature and the law. "Il primo gennaio" literally brings literary signification into the Turin court of law. The interstices, gaps, sutures, and bridges between the symbolic practices of the law, literature, and cinema will be examined as we go along.

The Young Cannibals is a group whose identity blurs at its edges. "Cannibal" narrative gives expression to the violence in contemporary Italian life, sometimes even wreaking violence upon the country's literary language. As generations of Italians had expressed dismay and disbelief at the kind of homicidal aggression De Nardo and Fàvaro gave vent to, the Italian literary establishment articulated comparable dismay at the "*contaminatio* of trashy, regional, media-derived scenes and dialogues" characteristic of the Young Cannibals' literary production.[5] To suggest, as some critics do, that the writers of the 1990s "killed" their literary predecessors is simplistic and reductive. However, as a generation, they challenge the "arcane literary 'mannerism'" that they felt had become "entrenched . . . in accepted 'serious' Italian literature subsequent to Italo Calvino's death in the mid-1980s."[6]

The foundational text of the Young Cannibals was a commercially successful anthology of short fiction entitled *Gioventù cannibale* (Cannibal Youth), edited by Daniele Brolli and published in 1996 in Einaudi's

Stile Libero series.[7] One would have thought the Cannibals strangers to the sort of nonbeing that Montale described in "Il primo gennaio." But the chilly reception by academics and critics—especially in Italy—gave the motley group some inkling of what it might be like to be willed into nonexistence.[8] While attempts were made to define them as a group or school, the narratives the Cannibals wrote resisted simple definition. The difficulty in demarcating the group's precise boundaries can be seen in the array of names used to characterize it: "pulp," "splatterpulp," "cyberpunk," "trash," "narrativa grunge," "spaghetti splatter." For those critics more open to the Cannibals, these subgenres feature as many commonalities as they do distinct attributes. Yet the common interest in violence and *orrore estremo,* extreme horror, the subtitle Brolli gave to *Gioventù cannibale,* diminishes divisions, drawing disparate texts into a common rubric. Brolli grouped the Cannibals' stories in three sections with titles flagging not only horror, but also the violence that begets it, at every step: *atrocità quotidiane, adolescenza feroce, malinconie di sangue* (daily atrocities, ferocious adolescence, bloody melancholy).

These young Italian writers investigate late-twentieth-century, largely urban settings. Their stories are about drugs, self-mutilation, the commodification of culture, and global media, among other things. Like the closer global contact facilitated by telecommunication, the characters who populate this literature are on the move: they leave the peninsula, either literally or virtually, for other outposts in the European Union, the United States, and beyond. The willingness of these writers to accept outside influences included a more avant-garde attitude toward transnational movements and trends.[9]

PAPER/GANG: GROUP IDENTITY AND VIOLENCE

In terms of crafting an identifiable voice for a "new" and "young" generation of writers that can succeed also as a commercial enterprise in the literary marketplace, there is safety in numbers. Anthologies provided this sort of safe haven.[10] Before *Gioventù cannibale* or *Cuore di pulp* (Heart of pulp), the 1997 collection edited by Giovannini and Tentori, some of the writers later associated with the Cannibal phenomenon got their start in Pier Vittorio Tondelli's series Progetto Under 25 (Under 25 Project), a series of anthologies that showcased young writers.[11] Three Under 25 Project collections were published: *Giovani Blues* (Young blues) in 1986, *Belli e perversi* (Beautiful and perverse) in 1987, and *Papergang* in 1990, one year before Tondelli's death, at the age of 36, from AIDS. Tondelli's editorial efforts helped identify an emerging generation of writers.

One member of the new generation of pulp writers whose work did not appear in these anthologies was Niccolò Ammaniti.[12] His short story "Rispetto" (Respect), published in his 1996 collection *Fango*, underscores the power of the group over the individual. Thinking back to the psychiatric evaluation of Erika De Nardo and Omar Fàvaro, we remember that the young pair were emboldened by their status as couple. Perhaps the individuals constituting the collective narrative voice of Ammaniti's short story might have resisted violent action, but the dangerous "we" takes another course. The aggregate of the verbal forms in Ammaniti's story is remarkable for its ability to portray a consensual, tribal voice and to capture the surge of collective power. "We" is the first word of the story; "Rispetto" begins with "We go out at dusk."[13] The young men in the story are not thirsty for blood, like the vampires with which they are subtly compared. Rather, they are "famished. Famished for cunt. Famished for tight cunt."[14] This is savage masculinity in numbers, whose aim is to satisfy its hunger.

"Rispetto" is a disturbing story of anonymous, tribal "fun" at a rave near the coast. The evening turns nightmarish for the three female victims. While the young women are named—Maria, Paola, and Amanda—the young men are part of an indistinct group that makes up the famished, narrating "us." The young men and women leave the dance club with the pack. They drive to the beach, and, in an alcoholic blur, two of the women are viciously raped. One is beaten and killed outright. Another is left for dead.

From the start, Ammaniti's story creates a pack mentality with repeated use of the "we" as distinct and separate from the "you all." The first page is littered with such verbal forms: *andiamo, sappiamo, saliamo, ridiamo, decidiamo, avvertiamo, aspiriamo* (we go, we know, we get into, we laugh, we decide, we notice, we breathe). This compact, united *noi*, or we, smashes into the *voi* (you all), daring "them" to respond. They taunt the others: "Come say something. Come on. Show us you've got balls."[15]

The stark division between "us" and "you all" invokes the *noi/voi* split discussed in the preceding chapter that rode high atop the wave of xenophobia in Italy's northern regions. When news of her mother's and brother's murder came out, Erika De Nardo had initially stabbed a finger in the general direction of Albanian immigrants, saying, "*Sono stati loro,*" They did it. The absence of a speaking "I" in "Rispetto" contributes to the blurriness of these Italian youth (in the eyes of others), who appeared remote and whose behavior was both secretive and inscrutable. In Ammaniti's story there is no *tu,* the intimate, individuated "you" so noticeable in Lidia Ravera's "open letter" to Erika De Nardo, *Il freddo dentro,* examined in the preceding chapter. In "Rispetto," there is no consciousness apart from that of the group. The story's narrator, that indistinct, indiscriminate *noi,* is a clannish pack of feral young men that eclipses a female voice nearly as successfully as the trial for matricide and fratricide silenced Erika De Nardo, producing her erasure.[16] This is the perilous side of collective identity.

As a story of senseless and unmotivated violence a defense against which is impossible, "Rispetto" is significant for its content as well as its collective voice, and the probable genealogy of Ammaniti's story is of at least as much interest as the cautionary tale it tells. It is very likely "Rispetto" was inspired by actual events that took place in the Roman hinterland in 1983 and that were later adapted in a variety of forms that brought them into public scrutiny and consideration. These forms include print and television reportage, cinema, fiction made for television, and true-crime literature.

The source for Ammaniti's story has never been firmly established, but it seems likely that he drew inspiration from the same events that journalist-novelist Andrea Carraro used for his 1993 novel *Il Branco* (The pack), which Marco Risi adapted for the screen the following year.[17] *Il Branco* tells the horrible, true story of two German women picked up while hitchhiking outside of Castellina, approximately 100 kilometers northeast of Rome, in 1983.[18] They are taken to a shack, where they are serially raped by a group of young men from the nearby town before being raped by virtually all the town's male residents over the age of fourteen. The novel and film single out one of these characters, 19-year-old Raniero, as a sort of filtering consciousness of the pack psychology.

Just two days before he will wed his fiancé, Esterina, and learn whether or not he will be accepted into the carabinieri corps and leave Castellina behind, Raniero is drawn into the dynamic of a group of six of his friends, some less morally evolved than others. Raniero and another young man choose not to participate in the rapes. Although they break free from the pack of rapists, they stand by and watch. Marion, the young German woman who is killed during the gang rapes, is tossed, like a bag of garbage, into the nearby waterfalls. Sylvia escapes, reaches safety, and reports the crimes. The film closes on the carabinieri arresting Raniero as Esterina, and we with her, passes by in the *corriere*, the commuter bus, on her way to work.

Ammaniti's story and Risi's film share a substantial number of characteristics. Both take place far on the outskirts of metropolises; both involve a "pack" of largely young men who rape women for sport; at least one of the women involved is killed; and there is enough moral opprobrium to spare.[19] The actual events on which *Il Branco* was based—shocking gang rapes and a homicide deep in the Tiburtina area in 1983—were widely acknowledged, unlike the context of Ammaniti's story as it has been critically received. Valerio Ferme comes closest when he identifies the "*fatti di cronaca*" (crime stories) that lie behind "Rispetto" and "Ti sogno, con terrore," another story in the collection.[20] The differences between *Il Branco* and "Rispetto" are scarce. The stage for the violence in Ammaniti's story is the beach as opposed to the landlocked location in Carraro's novel and Risi's film. But Ammaniti is Roman, like the settings for his early, short fiction.[21] It seems inconceivable that "Rispetto" does not at least allude to the 1983 events.

The transformation of the story of the rapes and homicide from a *cronaca* report to Risi's film adaptation is achieved by way of traversing varied forms, beginning with the press and telescoping out, like the generic itinerary of true crime, as outlined in the introduction. Risi's film is based on Carraro's novel, which, effectively censored by an industry that would not publish it in book form, was first published under the title "La Baracca" ("The shed") in the journal *Nuovi argomenti*. As the cover of that issue of the journal announced, the only other novel to be subjected to this recourse in the preceding thirty years had been Leonardo Sciascia's *Le parrocchie di Regalpietra* (*The Parishes of Regalpietra*).[22]

Carraro's novel, published in 1994 by Theoria simultaneously with the release of Risi's film, also used as a source Augusta (Tina) Lagostena Bassi's *L'avvocato delle donne* (The lawyer for women, 1991), a nonfiction book recounting twelve rape cases. After Risi's cinematic adaptation, the story of the rapes and homicide became the basis for a television miniseries, also titled *L'avvocato delle donne*, starring Mariangela Melato.[23]

The development of the *Il Branco* project linking *cronaca* to nonfiction narrative to novel and finally to screenplay enacts the kind of mediatic interweaving I have been describing throughout and also enacts the "contamination" the Cannibals were accused of. The project of *Il Branco,* in its many incarnations, lends support to the observation that "in the pages written by the *Cannibali* authors, reality dissolves as it is literally swallowed by the language and the facts connected to the media."[24]

VIETATO AI MAGGIORI: ADULTS OVER THE AGE OF 17 NOT ADMITTED

Referring to the Giovani Cannibali as pulp writers recalls both the influence of Quentin Tarantino's *Pulp Fiction* (1994) and the cheap, low-grade paper on which sensationalizing fiction was first published.[25] Of common (read: low) origin, the coarse pulp paper stock seemed to be a judgment on the kind of literature printed on it.[26] Pulp was popular, not necessarily "good," and its success depended on sales, not the opinions of publishers, editors, critics, or academics. The taste of the reading public that consumed this phenomenon ran toward the lurid. Pulp fiction told the stories of hard-boiled private detectives, gamblers, con artists, prostitutes—a group that lived and operated just outside the law. The characters of this literature—like the paper it was printed on—were abject: that which is expelled, wrung out; the detritus and surplus.

The field of Italian pulp fiction raises questions about pages of another "stock." The "parchments" Michel Foucault observes when describing the operation of genealogy, which I discuss in the introduction, invite examination of just the sort of phenomenon Italian pulp fiction presents, namely, varied cultural practices that constitute the power—institutional, social, cultural—that lies behind the crafting of aesthetics, canons, and public memory.[27] In the interest of reshuffling the parchments spelling out literary schools and movements, thereby interrogating the ways they have been shaped, I have deliberately distributed "cannibal" writers throughout *Murder Made in Italy*. The work of Andrea Pinketts, for example, whose story "Diamonds Are for Never" appeared in the anthology that gave its name to the movement—*Gioventù cannibale*—appears in chapter 2, which concerns the literary representation of serial killers. Simona Vinci, on the other hand, whose short novel *Dei bambini non si sa niente* (*A Game We Play*) might share some characteristics of the Cannibal movement, will be explored in part 3. Ammaniti functions as a bridge; his short fiction appeared in *Gioventù cannibale,* while his novels sit uncomfortably within the rubric of "cannibalism."

Not everyone agrees that Italy's Cannibal fiction shares traits with American exemplars of pulp such as Dashiell Hammet, Raymond Chandler, and Philip K. Dick.[28] For Gian Paolo Renello, "Italian *Cannibale* literature has nothing that can be assimilated to the actual pulp stylistic traits."[29] Like those cinema studies scholars who eschew the need to firmly distinguish between the various examples of the slasher-*giallo*-horror *filone*, Renello simply dispenses with false binaries of "schools" and "movements," *buonisti* and *cattivisti, vegetariani* and *cannibali,* or the "raw" and the "cooked" of this chapter's title, which glosses cultural anthropologist Claude Lévi-Strauss's description of the balance between competing cultural forces.[30] Yet, this blanket denial recalls some of the chauvinist inclinations of Giovannini and Tentori, who, in their introduction to *Cuore di pulp,* train on the national origins of the pulp movement. For these critics, pulp is located at the end of a trajectory whose origin is Italian, rather than a varietal of global splatter-pulp-horror writing.[31] Embracing the history of Italian pulp and "extreme" horror, however, contradicts the assertion that it does not exist. This tendency displaces onto non-Italian sources the "problem" of the expression of violence, making the displacement mechanism I have been discussing problematic. As a transnational phenomenon, the extreme horror of Italian pulp partakes of an array of histories and influences. While the provenance of pulp is contested, acknowledging the youth of its practitioners meets with almost universal agreement. Writing in *Europeo* in 1995, one journalist quipped that the novels of this emerging contingent of youthful writers were *"vietat(i) ai maggiori"* (adults not admitted unless in the company of a child).[32]

In homage to Tarantino, Italian pulp embraces and exudes violence.[33] The violence in the work of pulp writers is extreme, unrestrainable, and takes the form of patricide, matricide, homicide, femicide, the killing of pets, the killing of strangers, and the killing of *extracomunitari* (illegal aliens). Critics of such representation of violence perceived it as the product of an increasingly anonymous society in which the law's capacity to curb violence and aggression is impaired and derided, not what Montale's poem addresses, and not what District Attorney Locci hoped to remind the court of at the close of the De Nardo–Fàvaro trial by quoting it.

Those who look for influences from the well-established literary generation that preceded the Cannibals are likely to be frustrated. They drew upon the culture around them, not upon the culture of the past—even if we define "the past" as only a decade earlier—and certainly not high culture. With the increased speed and reach of global communications and the attendant development of global markets for the representation of violence, "influences" on the cadre of young writers are uncovered by the mere click of the computer's mouse. Like *bricoleurs,* young Italian authors responded to influences where they came upon them. Enrico Brizzi, the young Bolognese author of the best-selling 1993 *Jack Frusciante è uscito dal gruppo (Jack Frusciante Has Left the Group),* described his influences this way: "My readings are really disorganized . . . my cultural referents are a lot closer to (periodicals like) *Supertifo* (and) *Mountain Biking* than to good ol' Carlo Emilio Gadda."[34]

A lineage of influences on the Young Cannibals—like the one Brizzi describes—embraces the popular culture of the 1970s and later, and presents another side of the legacy of the 1968ers described in the preceding chapter, where both Lidia Ravera and Sebastiano Vassalli pointed to the erosion of a family structure that, once the Sessantottini had successfully torn it down, did nothing to configure something that could take its place. Out of the popular culture that emerged from the 1960s the Cannibals drew upon youth consumerism and commodity culture, interest in *cronaca* (journalism and also true crime), and a global outlook bolstered by such transnational multimedia influences as popular music, cinema, television, and the Internet. Of these, music and the visual media of television and cinema occupy me here.

TRANSNATIONAL MULTIMEDIA: MUSICAL VARIATIONS ON A THEME

Popular music serves a function that is at once thematic and formal in contemporary pulp fiction, what Renato Barilli has called its *"flusso sonoro"* (resonant flux).[35] Reference to rock music has the power to ground narrative in youth culture and a history of social change.[36] Giuseppe Caliceti's 1996 novel about clubbing in Emilia Romagna, *Fonderia Italghisa* (Italghisa foundry), thematizes rock music throughout; Caliceti mentions rock artists Vasco Rossi and Luciano Ligabue, the Neapolitan Rap group Articolo 31, and Frankie Hi Nrg. However, the music that pervades this literature is not as peninsular as this list of rock groups might lead us to believe. Giorgio van Straten's references to Bob Dylan in his novel 1987 *Generazione* (Generation) testify to the presence and cachet of a distinctly international musical menu.

However, most of the soundtrack to the fiction of the Young Cannibals is from a more recent period. The songs of social protest that were so popular with the student movement of the Sessantottini, or 1968ers, have given way to the high-decibel jeremiads of such groups from the 1990s as Nirvana, Pearl Jam, Fiona Apple, or Hole. As Brizzi observes,

> Anybody under twenty knows videos from MTV and Videomusic better than the music from the classic groups (of his generation). Maybe teenagers today don't have clear musical coordinates (commodification reduces their perspective), but even if we're talking about kids who actually listen to music and not Take That fans, I think the definition of rock is too limited; even two minutes of the Sex Pistols, on their own, isn't enough anymore. I think the imagination of my generation, and of the writers of my generation, has been colonized by the crossover phenomenon, of mixing different sounds with the fundamentals of punk. I find it really indicative that among today's most significant and influential groups are the Red Hot Chili Peppers, Green Day, or a band like Primus, which is never praised highly enough.[37]

The passage from Dylan to the Red Hot Chili Peppers, Green Day, and Primus tells another story, yet one of equal import. The solo singer-songwriter has been superseded by the grunge group. At the same time, a nostalgia for the stadium rock of classic bands such as Led Zeppelin, fronted by singer Robert Plant, hovers on the edges of *cannibale* fiction, as evidenced in Andrea Demarchi's *Sandrino e il canto celestiale di Robert Plant* (1996). The title—Sandrino and the heavenly song of Robert Plant—really says it all.

But more than flagging common cultural referents—anomie, AIDS, suicide, and Ecstasy—the presence of popular music also signifies formally for the pulp writers.[38] Cultural critic Enzo Siciliano observed, "Music is a mercurial element that brings together different levels of meaning. . . . Music moves wordlessly into the orbit of thought without the tiring deliberations of philosophy."[39] Music's ability to form connections between otherwise discrete disciplines is but one of the manifestations of its formal influence on pulp narrative. Giuseppe Culicchia recalls that the idea for organizing his 1994 novel *Tutti giù per terra* (*We All Fall Down,* adapted by Culicchia and Davide Ferrario for cinema in 1997) came to him while listening to the Ramones: "It occurred to me to take from the structure of those records, developing short chapters as if they were on an album."[40] Gabriele Romagnoli's 1994 collection, *Videocronache* (Videochronicles), is compiled in like fashion, complete with a proposed "soundtrack" that suggests specific songs and recording artists—Tears for Fears, Sting, Stadio, Bruce Springsteen, Jovanotti, Vasco Rossi, the Rolling Stones, Fiorella Mannoia—to accompany the reading of particular chapters.

Cannibal authors borrow from the world of music in another way, through the practice of "sampling"—*remixaggio* in Italian—that characterizes rap and hip-hop.[41] Sampling lifts a recognizable portion of a popular song (percussion, the musical line of a particular instrument, a specific melody, the trademark sound of a particular artist) and interpolates it into a new and different song. It is intrusive and deliberate. It exacts recognition.

In Italian pulp fiction, material for the sampling derives from a rich array of pop cultural expressions, including popular music, cinema, comic books (special praise is reserved for Tiziano Sclavi's serial comic *Dylan Dog* and for Andrea Pazienza), graphic novels, commercials and advertisements, and television.[42] Television writer Tommaso Labranca convinced Aldo Nove, Rossana Campo, Isabella Santacroce, and Tiziano Scarpa to revise some of their texts along the lines of "sampling" and even "scratching," another practice common in the clubs of the 1980s. Scratching consists of manually backspinning a record under the stylus, resulting in a considerable amount of static, hence its name. "To tell the truth," Gervasutti confesses, "the experiment was pretty disappointing, however, it shows once more the desire (in these writers) to fuse music and literature."[43]

I LIKE TO WATCH: TRANSNATIONAL VIOLENCE AND VISUAL MEDIA

Like popular music, visual media informs Italian pulp narrative from both a thematic and a formal perspective. The representation of myriad kinds of violence has particularly saturated visual media and has, in turn, played a significant role in the work of Italy's Cannibal writers. Whereas cinematic violence once required an act of will—buying a ticket, entering the theater—expanded television reportage has brought global violence into every home, accessible with a click of the remote control. Writer Fulvio Abbate remembers the chilling effect of watching the 1989 Rumanian tribunal that sentenced Nicolae and Elena Ceausescu on television, an event that produced an even greater impression once he realized that the viewers around the world were watching the proceedings with him *dal vivo*, live.[44]

Abbate was probably watching one of many broadcasts, similar in content, aired at staggered times, with commercial interruptions, rather than a simultaneous broadcast live from the scene. Yet, his remarks do recall another moment in Italian television history: the June 1981 attempt to rescue a young boy, Alfredino Rampi, who had become trapped in a well in Vermicino, near Frascati, in the central area of the Lazio region. Coverage of the Vermicino episode constitutes a unique moment in Italian television history. The well was only about a foot in diameter, but it was almost 263 feet deep. Rescuers, who estimated that the child had fallen about 118 feet, tried a number of strategies to rescue the child, including digging a tunnel. When they realized that the vibrations from the digging had caused the boy to fall still deeper, several rescuers lowered themselves down the well to attach a harness to young Alfredino. This effort also caused him to fall deeper into the well. Finally, after nearly two days, Alfredino died. RAI broadcast the child's dilemma for nearly twenty-one hours, with an estimated 28 million viewers.[45] It was, as journalist and cultural critic Furio Colombo described it, a "*gioco dell'orrore,*" a game of horror.[46]

The Vermicino broadcast set in motion a chain of events leading eventually to the sort of all-television all-the-time scenario that many Cannibals described as a constitutive element of their youth, distinguishing the youth culture of this generation of Italians from that of its predecessors. The uninterrupted broadcast illustrated the potential for spectatorship in unprecedented moments throughout the day, what were known as *fasce orarie*, or scheduling blocks. Not coincidentally, the privatization of Italian television, marked by the arrival of Silvio Berlusconi's Canale 5—launched in September 1980 and legally recognized as a broadcast company in March 1981—sought to capitalize on this newly recognized market. The launch of Canale 5's *Buongiorno, Italia* (Good morning, italy, modeled explicitly on ABC's *Good Morning, America*), in September 1981 exemplifies this trait.[47]

The *Secondo Lotto* (Second batch) of unfinished short stories in Aldo Nove's *Superwoobinda* is entitled "Vermicino," and concerns the televised coverage of the 1981 rescue attempt of Alfredino and television event. It is worth observing that Nove divides the collection's stories into *lotti* (batches), explicitly recalling the *lottizzazione* (parceling out) of the three RAI channels to different ruling political parties, created by Law 103 of April 14, 1975.[48] Nove's nameless narrator begins the brief story by noting that "it's important. It might be the most important thing to have something to remember like Vermicino."[49] The events are emblazoned in the narrator's memory. For the narrator, "Something solid remains. To tell to your grandchildren. History."[50] The narrator watches the episode unfold over the hours of coverage, noting that "we were in the millions and he was down there, alone."[51] Remarking on the passage of time since then, the narrator says that advertising would have posed challenges to any broadcast subsequent to 1981, particularly for private television. Directors would have waited for a "a neutral moment to air the ad for dog bones, like when the ball is kicked off field in the soccer match."[52]

In addition to marking the advent of a new era in Italian television as outlined above, Nove's story also introduces a hallmark of Cannibal style.[53] "Vermicino" ends in midsentence, more precisely in midword, as if the narrator has abruptly hung up the telephone line, changed the frequency on the radio dial, or changed channels ("zapped") with the remote control.[54] The narrative pause created by this truncation—the blank space—followed by the beginning of the next story tells the tale, *in nuce*, of Italian television's privatization. After the gap, "Pensieri" begins, "*Quando inizia* Non è la Rai, *abbasso tutte le tapparelle*" (When *It's Not the RAI* begins, I shut all the blinds).[55] The cover art to the softcover first edition features a television Cyclops, its somnolent eye beneath a heavy lid staring blankly back at the absent spectator. This attests to the sort of benign omnipresence the television had acquired by the mid-1980s and the shift in makeup of the audience. As Francesca Anania observes, while television audiences in the 1960s were largely middle-class and male, "as women and young people became more interested after 1975, there was practically no Italian who did not watch it, at least occasionally."[56]

The moral panic arising from the 2001 Novi Ligure murders, as I outlined in the preceding chapter, constellated first around issues of regional xenophobia and immigration and then concerns of a troubled generation of Italian youth perceived as threatened by a host of troublesome social pressures, including television. This generation, evidently failed by the parenting tactics of the Sessantottini, appeared particularly vulnerable to the kinds of influences that the Cannibals exercised in their work and that were thought to be pernicious precisely because of they were non-autochthonous. In other words, xenophobia in the cultural sphere. This is the sort of displacement at work in the social reception of the "Monster Event," as explored in part 1, with mechanisms including the initial refusal to contemplate an Italian killer and the vilification of cinematic representation of violence. As discussed in part 1, the etiology of the homicidal violence attributed to Pietro Pacciani fixed on his "monstrous" attachment to the transnational "body genres," as Linda Williams calls them, of pornography and slasher films. A similar search for the origin of the impulse of violence guides the De Nardo–Fàvaro trial, and the results were similarly elusive.[57]

Permeated by violent acts, Italian pulp fiction attests to the spread of the representation of violence throughout the global marketplace and marks the passage from the visual to literary representation. Cinema may provide the Young Cannibals with thematic content, but they also borrow from it certain narrative techniques. Editing techniques proper to visual media clearly inform recent fiction. We can see the relation of the jump cut, quick cutting, and the standard length of a cinematic shot in a mainstream film. We can also relate the more dilettantish notion of "zapping," or channel surfing, to the quick pace and brevity of this fiction. Poet-novelist Edoardo Albinati confesses that "even though I curse myself, I watch a lot of TV, and pull out things to transform it, raw material to work on. . . . I let myself become transfixed by the TV and hope something will come of it."[58] Aldo Nove dedicated his 1996 collection of ultra-short fiction to the 1970s fictional veterinarian Woobinda, the title character of an Australian television show that was part of RAI's programming for children and teenagers.[59] Whether or not television informs their writing in the same way or to the same degree, both Silvia Ballestra and Andrea Pinketts reveal it as a staple in their daily media diet.

～

The murders in Italy's "deep north" revealed anxieties concerning Italian youth's vulnerability to and proclivity for violence, as well as the dangers in collective behavior. As the preceding chapter noted, the psychiatric experts believed that, alone, neither De Nardo nor Fàvaro would have expressed such violent aggression. This chapter began with a meditation on the dangers of the "pack mentality" of a collective male narrator in Ammaniti and ends with a consideration of collective female aggression. Both Raffaella Krismer and Elena Stancanelli, each located on the blurred and permeable margins of the Cannibals, explore female union along a generational axis, whether tinged by erotic attraction or not. Like the Novi Ligure homicides, Stancanelli's novel *Benzina* (Gasoline, 1998) also "kills" the mother. Krismer's novel, on the other hand, explores intragenerational solidarity and friendship.

Raffaella Krismer's first novel, *Il signore della carne* (Lord of meat, 1997), uses some of the hallmarks of Cannibal writing, yet also charts different waters.[60] The novel celebrates and frequently refers to such transnational phenomena as science fiction and horror cinema, and the *scatola parlante,* the talking box, or television, is a faithful companion. An accomplished stylist, Krismer's short novel offers some singing sentences in a gripping story. In the sea of testosterone that characterizes the field of young writers of horror in Italy, this novel seems all the more refreshing for its embrace of wider themes and frames.[61] Exemplary of certain trends of the pulp genre as outlined, *Il signore della carne* also strikes out in new directions.

RAFFAELLA KRISMER'S *IL SIGNORE DELLA CARNE*: PULP, VIOLENCE

I settled myself more comfortably on the couch, I let the magic of the screen take me prisoner and the vision of the telepathic nightmares dispel my slight sleepiness.

2:20.

I had another hour and a half of amazing cellular transformation before going to my room. Okay, I said to myself. Let's get even more comfortable and let's try to keep our eyes really open. My chief problem was attending to the clues in the story, mining the narrative solutions that yielded a crescendo for suspense. You could learn a lot from a maestro like this.[62]

As the novel begins, Rita is ensconced on her sofa, watching a late-night rerun of David Cronenberg's science-fiction horror film *Scanners* on television. Rita shares an apartment in Bologna with Angela, and the first-person point of view alternates between them in the twenty-one chapters comprising the novel's four sections. Rita is a young writer who has apprenticed herself to masters like Cronenberg, from whom she hopes to learn ways to sculpt and perfect the crafting of her stories, borrowing especially "special effects . . . of a frightening brand of realism."[63] Rita is heavily influenced by Hollywood and American independent cinema, especially Robert Zemeckis, Steven Spielberg, and—her favorite—Quentin Tarantino. Influences of David Cronenberg, Francis Ford Coppola, Martin Scorsese, and Brian De Palma, all frequently cited by Italian pulp authors, are also noticeable.

Angela, who is the more devoted, though less gifted, student of the pair, tries desperately to achieve two goals: to pass her course on international law and to lose weight. As for many young women in Italy and elsewhere in the industrialized world, Angela's body falls far away from her desired body image. Her failed efforts to reduce dismay her. So convinced is she of this failure that she believes Dr. Milan, her nutritionist, has scheduled her appointments later and later in the evening so that she will not run into other equally neurotic patients in the waiting room. Although Rita does not share her roommate's compulsiveness toward food, she watches, perhaps obsessively, horror reruns for inspiration for her "extreme" short stories.

One evening after Rita leaves for a party, Angela invokes il Signore della Carne, the Lord of Meat. She is willing to make a pact with this devil, believing he will strip from her the unwanted *carne*, or flesh. Rita, en route to the party in town, gets caught in a diluvial rainstorm, a flood we take as a cue for what is to occur. Soaked to the skin when she arrives, Rita immediately goes to the bathroom to repair her "look." In the shower she is struck by a powerful, completely extraordinary, extraordinarily painful menses. At the same time, Angela, back in the apartment, also experiences a sudden onset of menses. In the bathroom at the party, Rita hears voices (easily recognized as Italian either spoken backwards or supplemented with extra, irregular syllables) and, through space and time, detects Angela's pleas and warnings. Angela implores Rita not to return home lest she encounter Osgood il Ripugnante, or, Repugnant, emissary of il Signore della Carne. Rita returns to find Angela in the thrall of a monstrous demon, whom she (Rita) subdues sexually and whom they eventually exorcise. This is, at least, what they believe. But a riot has gathered force, a legion of "great regional, reactionary demons" who attack Bologna, subdue the progressives, and rule the day.[64]

Blood is the sine qua non of splatter. Although blood has made a variety of appearances in horror literature and fiction, its appearance in the form of menstruation is rather uncommon. One significant appearance of menstruation in the genre occurs in *Carrie* (1976), directed by Brian De Palma. Close to the beginning of the film, Carrie White (Sissy Spacek) finishes gym class at her high school. The shower scene that follows is pleasant, warm, rosy, and—it is possible—an occasion for the private pleasure of masturbation. Shot in slow motion, this scene rhythmically corresponds to the climactic prom scene, where blood also figures prominently. Significantly, it is with the onset of menses that Carrie develops powers of telekinesis that form the basis of De Palma's film.

The problem with the film *Carrie,* at least for feminists, and at least according to Barbara Creed, is the way it signals misogynistic and conflict-ridden views of women's bodies without really extricating itself from the sign system that vilifies women's bodies and women's blood.[65] However much Carrie may tell her mother, a religious fanatic played by Piper Laurie, that it is "natural" that women have breasts and that they menstruate, the film also makes it seem natural that menstruating women, when physically and emotionally abused, will cause immolation, general mayhem, and the crucifixion of their mothers. Rather than live as a powerful witch, Carrie kills her classmates, her mother, and herself.

In her influential work on horror, Julia Kristeva discusses the tight weave of revulsion and the abject, of revulsion at the abject.[66] Those things expelled, or abjected, from the body—excreta, feces, urine, pus, blood—are the things that sicken us the most. Kristeva believes that the cadaver is the example par excellence of the abject, since it is the corporeal shell that the soul has expelled or left behind. Menses, like other bodily fluids, are expelled, the body rids itself of them, but they tend not to cause revulsion in the women whose bodies bleed monthly. There is no need to rehearse the ways in which menstruation has been reviled in Western culture. It suffices to remember the practice of the mikvah in Judaism, the ritual monthly purification of women from their "unclean state," as well as the work of the late-nineteenth- and early-twentieth-century forensic psychiatrist Cesare Lombroso, who capitalized the notion that women's criminality predicated on menstruation. Significantly, in De Palma's nonfeminist film, Carrie, whose mother has never told her about menstruation and who has always been an outsider among her own cohort, is initially terrified and made hysterical at the appearance of her own blood.

Krismer's sense of humor is a great anodyne to the potential violence against women that always seems near to hand in this genre. Menstrual blood, so reviled in *Carrie,* signals in Krismer's novel a solidarity between women that should make most feminists thrill. Not only have

Angela and Rita demonstrated the very real biochemical consequence of a saturation of human pheromones, which help synchronize hormonal cycles in a bounded community where more than one woman lives, the sudden onset of menstruation is brought on sympathetically, that is, a commiserative act. Other young women at the party try to help Rita. Importantly, no one maligns her. Different from Carrie's freakish isolation, for she is both out of place and out of time, Krismer uses menstruation to draw into temporal proximity Rita's and Angela's conditions (which is only the beginning of her revision).

Comically, when Rita returns home, she is greeted by the aroma of smoked trout and celery (remember, this was Angela the Plump's incantation) and finds her roommate barricaded, naturally, in the bathroom. Naturally, for where else should one encounter the abject save for the bathroom, the appropriate place for soil and that which the body expels? Tormented by Osgood, Angela requires her roommate's intercession. Rita sexually subdues Osgood, who, depleted, begins to resume his non-bestial and mortal identity. Osgood's shedding of scales and regaining of human form exactly recalls one image from the film *Hellbound*, the second of the *Hellraiser* film series inspired by Clive Barker's terrifying short story, "The Hellbound Heart", and strengthens the connection between Krismer's pulp and visual culture.[67] In fact, had Krismer not flagged Barker as an influence in the novel's first epigraph, a citation from Barker's *The Yattering and Jack,* one might be tempted to call this re-elaboration something more than allusion.[68]

Briefly, in *Hellraiser* (1987), Kirsty (Ashley Laurence) does battle with her fiendish uncle, Frank (Sean Chapman), who, by way of a device he bought in the Orient, a "chinese" box unlocked only if its puzzle is solved, opens the portal to Hell. But Hell turns out to be even worse than Frank imagined, a place where his body is ceaselessly tormented, flayed, ripped asunder, stitched back together, only to be flayed and ripped apart once more. With the help of Kirsty's evil stepmother, Julia (Claire Higgins), Uncle Frank seeks to become corporeal once again. Julie lures anonymous men to her house, kills them, drains their blood, and gives it to Frank, who, with the blood of each new victim, acquires one more dermal layer. He kills his brother, Kirsty's father, whom she tries to redeem from the underworld in *Hellbound* (Tony Randel, 1988).

Her conspirator in the second film in the series is Tiffany (Imogen Boorman), a traumatized, autistic young woman with a knack for puzzles. The fiendish physician of the insane asylum where the hysterical Kirsty has been placed at the end of the first film is, like Uncle Frank, slightly too interested in the parallel universe. He believes that Tiffany can help solve the riddle of Frank's rune and open the portal to hell. It is not what he expects, either, and a diabolical battle with the trademark *Hellraiser* character, the cenobite "Pinhead" (Doug Bradley)—familiar to Barker fans everywhere from the film's promotional campaign—ensues between the doctor and Julia and the two young women.

During this battle, at the film's climax, Tiffany falls over the edge of a cliff while in Hell. Peering over the edge and reaching out her hand to help is Julia, whom Tiffany knows to be diabolical. But she grabs Julia's hand, and, as she hoists herself up, her weight causes the skin on Julia's arm to peel away. But this is not the same stripping and flaying as elsewhere in the film, and the type I explored in part in chapter 2. Beneath Julia's skin lies Kirsty, who has donned her stepmother's skin and "passed" as Julia in order to win favor with the doctor. As Rita does for Angela in Krismer's novel, Kirsty saves her friend.

Barker and Krismer both resist what Carol Clover identifies as the "last girl" strategy. Tracing a genealogy of slasher pictures mostly from Hollywood, Clover identifies the "last girl" who defies the demonic forces of evil, and whom Argento queers in *La Sindrome di Stendhal,* examined in chapter 3.[69] Krismer, like Barker, doubles the "last girl," and they both locate her salvation in solidarity, for Barker between Kirsty and Tiffany, for Krismer between Angela and Rita. Kirsty in *Hellbound* will no more leave her friend Tiffany in Hell than Rita will leave Angela to the domination of Osgood the Repugnant.

Rita's allegiance to Angela and their friendship is the sort of thing that sets apart *Il signore della carne* from the random acts of violence so characteristic of the pulp genre. Not all pulp is violent in the way of visual media, especially, perhaps, pornography, where the representation of violence against women is the norm. By way of humor, *pulpiste*—female Italian pulp practitioners—such as Krismer and Santacroce, subvert current notions of pulp and Cannibal fiction in Italy.[70] The components that make this novel an exemplum of the pulp genre include the menace of violence, copious amounts of blood, and repeated references to an international market for horror. However, this particular novel distinguishes itself from so much of the contemporary testosterone-driven fiction by refusing to vilify women, their blood, and their relationships to other women.

(THE) MISSING MOM: STANCANELLI
AND THE SPECTRAL MOTHER

Female friendship does not fare as well in Ammaniti's collection *Fango* in general, to judge from "Rispetto," which was explored earlier, and the lengthy story "L'ultimo capodanno dell'umanità" ("Last New Year's Eve of Humanity").[71] Destruction threads Ammaniti's novella, which is set on an end-millennium New Year's Eve. "Le Isole, " or the Islands, a condominium community on Rome's Via Cassia, is at the antipodes of Lenni and Stella's deserted service station—nevertheless, an oasis for them—on the Via Flaminia in Stancanelli's *Benzina*. The Islands is secluded, a selective refuge from the looming metropolis. Ammaniti's story is operatic, weaving between narrative lines of wealthy executives who send their dutiful wives to the country so that they can engage in s/m practices for hire, aging aristocrats who throw lavish parties, stoned teenagers, and busloads of rambunctious soccer hooligans. Among this collection is Giulia, who is preparing for a party at the home she shares with her husband, Enzo. Through an accident of fate (a conversation between Enzo and Debby that was recorded on the answering machine) Giulia learns the two are having an affair.

For the residents of the Islands and their guests, the year will end in immolation and apocalypse.[72] The condominium complex will burst into flames and explode as the new year is ushered in. But before this final devastation, Giulia will take her revenge on those who have betrayed her. Channeling her own absent "Mamminacara," or Mommy dearest, Giulia arms herself with her husband's underwater rifle and metes out her own unrelenting justice.

The pair Angela and Rita in Krismer's short, irreverent novel leads to consideration of Lenni and Stella, the lesbian lovers at the center of *Benzina,* touched on at the start of this chapter. In *Benzina,* Lenni and Stella live a happy and isolated life together at a service station on the Via

Flaminia, outside the pale of the capital.[73] Lenni's mother, Giovanna, appears one day with cash and the intention to dragoon Lenni and forcibly return her to their comfortable middle-class life in Florence. Provoked by Giovanna's threats and Lenni's inability to resist them, Stella unpredictably seizes a wrench from her workbench and neatly fells Giovanna.[74] *Benzina* relates the couple's attempts to unload the body at the dump. Their efforts are thwarted as they encounter obstacle and peril at almost every turn. Unable to shed Giovanna's body, they travel in a circle, on the road to nowhere, returning to the service station where they began. With the eponymous gasoline spilled and spreading, one match ignites a general immolation, dispatching all three women to the beyond.

Giovanna's spectral presence in the text at once corresponds to, and differs from, Susy Cassini's absence in that Turin courtroom resurrected by Livia Locci and her declamation of "*Il primo gennaio.*" Giovanna's death, while not an accident, is not a matricide either.[75] Lenni's mother is a matricide only if Lenni and Stella are collapsed, if Giovanna becomes Stella's mother. It strikes me that this would silence the female voice— and sovereignty of the subject—as much as murdering the mother.

Alternatively, it is possible to read Giovanna's death as a symbolic matricide, within the diegesis of the novel, as well as within the signifying practice of the "mother-daughter" plot as a literary topos, discussed by Marianne Hirsch and others.[76] Stella's mother left her as a child. If she wants a maternal imago, she must conjure one. Patrizia Sambuco points out that Stella has never fantasized a mother like Giovanna. Staging her own interpretation of Freud's family romance, Stella imagines a mother much closer to the image she has of herself. Her fantasy mother is a rock star who had conceived her with a lifeguard from the nearby beaches at Ostia.[77] Significantly, this is a generationally continuous image of a mother, a useful fantasy to bear in mind when considering the matricide that has rooted this chapter and the preceding one.

Though dead, Giovanna has the power of narration. Her disembodied voice in Monica Stambrini's 2001 film adaptation of *Benzina* [*Gasoline*] effectively recalls Kaja Silverman's thoughts about the "sound regime" of cinema, starkly represented by the reproduction of her voice, all the while insisting on the invisibility of her body.[78] Significantly, Stancanelli's novel deprives Giovanna of life, but not of her narrating subjectivity, especially from beyond the grave. If Stella's wrench lays waste to the bourgeois family idyll in the shape of Giovanna's restorative fantasy—her daughter "cured" of same-sex desire, married, and returned to Florence—Stella destroys Giovanna's shackles at the same time.

Destruction of the ideal of family in contemporary Italy played a key role in the 2001 Cassini–De Nardo double homicide for which Erika De Nardo and Omar Fàvaro were convicted. The "Erika and Omar" sensation provided the subplot of the annihilation of the killer's adoptive Sessantottini parents in Sebastiano Vassalli's *Archeologia del presente,* as we saw in chapter 4. The murder case exacerbated concerns over the increasing accessibility of violent representations facilitated by developments in telecommunications. Yet, Erika De Nardo was hardly the only Italian teen at the start of the new millennium who engaged in "SMS behavior." "SMS Erika" provoked her boyfriend's aggression, took drugs, listened to doom rock music. Had there been any irony, black humor, or self-ridicule in the Erika De Nardo narrative, she could have been a character in a Cannibal short story. An appetite for violence that was becoming more acute threads the texts of the Cannibals and helps re-dimension the context in which the murders of Susy Cassini and Gianluca De Nardo took place.

Unprecedented violence and the destruction of the family forge ideal connections to the case making up the foundation of part 3, which follows. The murder of 3½-year-old Samuele Lorenzi took place in remote Cogne barely a year after the Novi Ligure homicides. If the murders of Susy Cassini and her son in Novi Ligure revealed that small town as prey to the kinds of violence thought constitutive of urban life, the murder of a toddler in Italy's remote Valle D'Aosta region made such unpredictable violence seem inescapable. The destruction of the family in our next murder case, in Cogne, however, was not engineered by representatives of an inscrutable teenaged generation. Rather, as part 3 will illustrate, the homicidal aggression belonged to a mother.

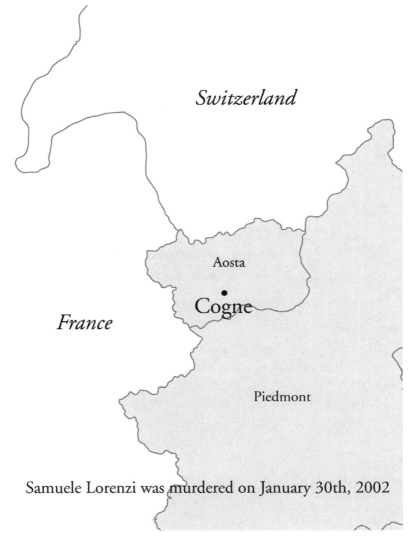

Switzerland

Aosta

Cogne

France

Piedmont

Samuele Lorenzi was murdered on January 30th, 2002

MAP 3. Cogne, Valle D'Aosta, January 30, 2002.

PART THREE

Filicide

The Bad/Mad Mother of Cogne
and Violence against Children

Any crime, because it draws attention to the frailty of the law, is abject, but premeditated crime, cunning murder, hypocritical revenge are even more so because they heighten the display of such frailty.

—JULIA KRISTEVA, *THE POWERS OF HORROR*

IN MAY 2008 the Corte di Cassazione (Court of Cassation), Italy's highest court, confirmed Annamaria Franzoni's conviction for the bludgeoning death of her 3-year-old son, Samuele. The murder occurred on January 30, 2002, in the Montroz section of the town of Cogne, in the Valle D'Aosta. Just as in other noteworthy cases of infanticide that received relentless press coverage (e.g., the 1980 case against Lindy Chamberlain in Australia, the 1993 case against Susan Smith and the 2001 case against Andrea Yates in the United States), the events in Cogne and Franzoni's trials, culminating with her 2004 conviction, became almost immediately a national media sensation. As RAI 1 correspondent Roberto Pozzan later described it, the murder of Samuele Lorenzi was quickly christened "the crime of the century," despite the fact that the century was but two years in the making.[1] On a similar note, Pino Corrias captured the public fascination for the sense of the violated and wounded Alpine hinterland, a theme similar to the politics of geography surrounding the double homicide in Novi Ligure. Like each of the two murders probed in the preceding parts of this volume, Samuele's murder in Cogne created a furor in terms of the popular perception of the geography of Italian crime. Sharply recalling the notion that emerged in the Novi Ligure double murder, Cogne, too, was rooted in the "deep North," a location believed sufficient defense against the sorts of violence and delinquency more characteristic of urban settings.[2]

The obsessive mediatic attention paid to the Cogne events produced significant juridical consequences. Television coverage in particular became a curious protagonist in the case. As Enzo Tardino, a former assistant district attorney in Bologna and member of the Cassation, remarks, the Cogne Affair produced the conditions in which "for the first time in the judicial history of the nation . . . the preliminary investigations were followed live in their entirety by the media."[3] Mediatic vigil of the case continued past the investigation to cover, in equally obsessive nature, the trials of Franzoni in the six years that followed, turning the case into the ballyhooed "judicial media circus."[4] While it is true that the Cogne case commanded a good deal of space in the front pages of Italian dailies, it is the televised coverage that transformed it into a "postmodern spectacle."[5] Consequently, TV coverage has a privileged place in these pages.

Out of a critical narrative of Annamaria Franzoni's trials for filicide emerges a matrix of interrelated issues that I pursue in part 3 of *Murder Made in Italy*. These issues are explored in fictional and nonfictional narrative forms that challenge the myths of family and childhood in contemporary Italy and are drawn alongside the Cogne case for evaluation and contrast. The matrix of issues I examine builds on the concept of "moral panic" as developed in the social sciences in the 1970s and 1980s and reconceived in the 1990s to acknowledge the impact of new media on the construction of "panic."[6] The themes I will explore include an examination of the technology of gender at work in this case, a topic that occasions exploration of the public discourse on maternity in contemporary Italy. A sociological issue of some moment in Italy concerns the current demographic situation and negative birthrate, a situation so acute in some regions that it has been described as one in which there are "more coffins than cradles."[7] In this context, Franzoni's conviction

FILICIDE 157

for filicide, the technical term for the killing of a child over the age of 18 months, stands as a cautionary tale for the welfare state, very much like Aesop's fable in which the couple kills the goose that laid the golden eggs.

A critical narrative of Franzoni's trials also draws attention to how her psychological affect and maternal demeanor conditioned legal procedure, something exemplified by the psychiatric evaluations called for in both the trial and appellate phases. That demeanor includes her "coldness" and apparent lack of hysterical mourning. Television personality Iva Zanicchi epitomizes the general perception of Franzoni's coldness when she asserted on the evening talk show *Porta a porta* that "I want to believe that she is innocent because if she's not, we're facing a monster of coldness."[8] Thus, chapter 7 trains on the spectacle of mourning in contemporary cultural articulations, most extensively in Sandro Veronesi's award-winning 2005 novel *Caos calmo*. The final issue stemming from the Cogne affair that I will examine concerns the ambiguity surrounding what Davide Lorenzi, Samuele's older brother, knew of the events. To this end, chapter 8 addresses the representation of the childhood experience of violence, as witness, victim, and perpetrator in the prose fiction of Susanna Tamaro, Simona Vinci, and Niccolò Ammaniti.

For the ways it illuminates and informs both the mother-child relation and the fascination with horror, the concept of the abject recurs in several of the examinations that follow. Infanticide in Italy, both in popular discourse and in the criminological literature, is often called "*La Sindrome Medea*," or Medea Syndrome, recalling the figure from Greek tragedy who killed her children as revenge against her husband.[9] Adriana Cavarero's recent exploration of the "ontological crime" of murder uses Euripedes's protagonist to represent the "slaughter of the innocents."[10] The slain innocents are the ones who, like children, are the least able to defend themselves. Cavarero's exploration of "horrorism" trains on the way that chance makes potential victims of us. Her interest in the common vulnerability drawing human beings together onto the stage of contemporary violence, where randomness discharges a key function, leads Cavarero to ponder the relation of the maternal as it signs the utter dependence of the infant who must rely on the caregiving of another.

If, however, the Cogne case became a media sensation that permits the examination of a set of interrelated issues, this is not only because of its novelty—the relative rarity of a *giallo* constituted by a case of a mother's filicide in a remote corner of Italy—but also because it resonates with a set of concerns antedating the crime and subsequent trials. The cultural expressions probed are not, consequently, seen as the reproduction of concerns deriving only from the case but, in some cases, as the registration of those concerns in the run-up to 2002. This operates similarly to the way the "prologue" of Pietro Pacciani's 1952 crime primed the pump of public perception of his involvement in the "Monster Event" in Florence thirty-five years later, or the way the violent narratives of the Young Cannibals from the 1990s prepared the way for the public reception of the homicidal violence unleashed by Erika De Nardo and Mauro "Omar" Fàvaro in 2001. In brief, the Cogne affair was able to achieve its status and notoriety because it fell on fertile ground, tilled and readied for planting by various narrative expressions.

SIX

The Yellow and the Black

Cogne; or, Crime of the Century

THE MORNING OF JANUARY 30, 2002, was reportedly both the same as and different from all other mornings at the small chalet in Cogne, in Italy's Valle D'Aosta, where Annamaria Franzoni lived with her husband, Stefano Lorenzi, and their two sons. Franzoni, thirty-one at the time, was alone in the house with her two children: Davide, aged seven-and-a-half, and Samuele, three. After Lorenzi left for work, Franzoni either prepared her older son for school in exactly the same way as she always had or took a wide detour from her typical routine.

The degree of sameness or distinction of this morning routine became crucial for the psychiatric experts engaged in the evaluation of the case as well as the narrative of the murder itself. Trying to determine whether Franzoni was subject to an underlying psychopathology—which would serve as a conditioning factor in sentencing—the psychiatric team probed the possibility of an extraordinary and temporary break in an otherwise established routine, particularly in Franzoni's actions following Samuele's death. The forensic team of the RIS confirmed the location of blood in the Lorenzi-Franzoni chalet, which served to establish the time of death, a possible narrative of the actions that followed the crime, and the viability of the theory that an intruder committed the murder.[1]

The psychiatrists involved in the evaluation during the trial part found Franzoni lucid at the time of the crime. Their colleagues involved in the evaluation in the appellate phase disagreed partially, but significantly. The jury in the appeals phase established that no mental defect had contributed to the defendant's actions and that, following some sort of brief cognitive break in which she killed her son, she had set out lucidly to cover her actions. This was the theory of the crime sanctioned by the Court of Cassation in May 2008.

JANUARY 30, 2002: "LITTLE" SAMUELE'S MURDER

On the day of Samuele Lorenzi's murder, at approximately 8:16 AM, Franzoni walked down the sloping driveway toward the school bus stop with her elder son, Davide. The driver said that he observed no unusual haste in either Franzoni's arrival or her return trip. Upon reentering the chalet at 8:24, she found her younger son, Samuele, in a pool of his own blood in her bed.

Franzoni's call to 118, the emergency number used in Italy to alert authorities and summon emergency medical care, was logged at 8:28 AM. She went to the window and called to her family doctor and neighbor, Ada Satragni, who arrived at 8:32. Satragni took the receiver from Franzoni and completed the call. Another neighbor, Daniela Ferrod, also came to the chalet. In the twenty minutes it took for the emergency medical team to arrive by helicopter, Satragni, with Franzoni's help, attempted to clean Samuele's massive head wounds and staunch the bleeding.

Dr. Satragni later stated that when she first saw him, Samuele Lorenzi was still alive. She testified, "When I entered (the room), the child was moaning. I had before me a child who was still alive."[2] She was worried that the medevac helicopter would have difficulty landing in the hilly Montroz area of Cogne, so Satragni and Franzoni wrapped Samuele in blankets against the late January cold and took him outdoors. Ivano Bianchi, one of the emergency medical technicians, believed that Samuele was dead, but the attending physician, Dr. Leonardo Iannizzi, declared him alive and gave orders to evacuate the child.[3]

Franzoni did not accompany Samuele in the medevac helicopter, a point later used to indicate her alleged "coldness" and indifference toward her son's predicament. Samuele died during the airlift to the hospital, Iannizzi said.[4] Death was declared at 9:47 AM.

PRIME SUSPECT

Annamaria Franzoni has never admitted that she took a blunt object and attacked her son, mortally wounding him, sometime between 7:40, when her husband left the house, and 8:16, when she and Davide left the house to meet the school bus. Her theory, which she stated coherently and consistently, is that an intruder entered the house through the unlocked door, found Samuele, who was located in his parents' bed (a departure from the normal routine), and killed him sometime during her eight-minute absence. Franzoni's version proposes that within those eight minutes, the killer donned Franzoni's pajamas and slippers, attacked Samuele, and then left the pajamas on the bed and the slippers on the floor. Franzoni asserts that the killer then washed her- or himself clean of any blood and left the chalet, leaving behind no traceable forensic evidence.

Franzoni's husband and his family have fully endorsed her story. Neither Stefano Lorenzi nor Franzoni's enormous family from Monteacuto, a small community outside Bologna, has ever publicly cast doubt on Franzoni's account of the facts. Indeed, it could be argued that their regular and frequent courtroom presence during the trials attested to their continued belief in her version of the events. The intruder Franzoni suspected and, with Lorenzi, accused in the summer of 2004 was Ulisse Guichardaz, the brother-in-law of her neighbor, Daniela Ferrod, whom Franzoni and Lorenzi also suspected. Unlike Erika De Nardo's blanket accusation that Albanians had killed her mother and brother in Novi Ligure the previous year, Franzoni and her husband accused a specific individual. Fabrizio Gandini, the GIP (*Giudice per le indagini preliminari*, judge for preliminary investigations), did not find these theories credible.[5] Franzoni's lead defense attorney, former minister of the interior Carlo Taormina, used Gandini's decision not to pursue another suspect as a reason to appeal his client's conviction.

The scene of the crime was universally described as a bloodbath. In her emergency call Franzoni had said that her son was vomiting blood and not breathing. Dr. Satragni, the first of the medical personnel to arrive, believed that the 3-year-old may have suffered some sort of aneurysm that, as Franzoni had said in her emergency call, had caused "his head to explode." The theory of the aneurysm was soon dismissed, and Satragni was publicly rebuked in the press by neurologists, who believed she should have been able to distinguish between the somatic effects of an aneurysm and blunt trauma to the 3-year-old's skull.[6]

The Franzoni defense team never formally embraced the aneurysm theory as a possible narrative of the crime. In fact, Carlo Taormina never argued for his client's innocence. Rather, he consistently drew attention to the dearth of evidence—most particularly, the absence of a definitive murder weapon—and the way the investigation was bungled.

THE MAD/BAD MOTHER: GENDER AND CRIMINALITY

Dr. Ada Satragni is one of the many women associated with the Cogne case. Indeed, the presence of so many women at different phases of the investigation and trial is significant precisely for the ways their presence served as one of the factors conditioning the construction of Franzoni's monstrous maternity. Other women who played significant roles were emergency medical technician Stefania Neri; district attorney for the Valle D'Aosta Maria del Savio Bonaudo; assistant district attorney for the Valle D'Aosta Stefania Cugge; and the public defender who took over Franzoni's case after Taormina resigned in March 2007, Paola Savio.

Cultural representations of monstrous mothers in Italian society are not new.[7] The construction of female criminality as generally "monstrous" or in some other way attributable to the realm of anthropology, myth, and folklore is also a well-accepted premise in feminist criminology. Frances Heidensohn observes that female criminals found to be "wicked, evil and beyond all reason" evoke the "witch of myth and legend."[8] Similarly, when the sexual deviancy of some female perpetrators is uncovered, they recall the harlot of yore.

In this period, any criminal wending through the various procedures and courts in the Valle D'Aosta would also have come under the auspices of Cugge and del Savio Bonaudo. They were not mothers accused of filicide. The density of women in the Italian public sphere occupying legitimating positions within various disciplinary institutions, both medical and juridical, produces specific effects and consequences.[9] The firm belief in Franzoni's guilt that del Savio Bonaudo repeatedly asserted is not evidence of extraordinary conditioning by the judicial system in which she participates. Yet as the district attorney herself stated that her womanhood—she called it her "instinct"—played a decisive role at a key moment in the investigations.

The prosecutor's decision to "keep the gloves on" during the interrogation of Franzoni in Turin's Le Vallette prison in March 2002 helped direct the investigation down the path of the *giallo,* as murder mysteries in Italy are called, rather than the *nero.* (*Cronaca nera* is the term historically used to describe journalistic reportage of violent crime.) The narrative that del Savio Bonaudo constructed featured a woman accused of the crime of killing her child, an accusation that was supported by evidence and in which no anthropological quest for "monsters" played a role. Heidensohn remarks that when "women are not conforming to stereotypes, the chances are that their behaviour will be so defined by the media, by the agents of social control, and perhaps even by women themselves."[10] The performance of outraged and victimized maternity for the press as well as other audiences (judicial, penal, psychiatric, television) before which Franzoni appeared in the six years required to bring the case to formal conclusion constitutes what Teresa de Lauretis has identified as a "technology of gender."[11]

It is clear that maternal subjects respond to and enact ideological formations of social subjectivity.[12] Contemporary Italian mothers respond as much to the maternal ideology of Italy's past as to formulations of that ideology in the present. This is what Rosi Braidotti means when she says, "'I, woman' am affected directly and in my everyday life by what has been made of the subject of woman; I have paid with my very body for all the metaphors and images that our culture has deemed fit to produce of woman."[13] Escape from such figurations of the maternal might be impossible. As Braidotti suggests, cultural expressions of the maternal abound and cut across historical periods.[14] Literary and other cultural elaborations are not the only source of data, as the following section reveals.

PRÉNATAL, MOMMY, AND ME: PREGNANCY AND PUERICULTURA IN CONTEMPORARY ITALY

The context of maternity in which the Cogne case unfolded is characterized by opposing forces. One side honors traditional figurations of the maternal, the feminine, and the family in Italy. Franzoni and her large family, with their observations of certain daily rhythms of Italian life such as sharing the midday meal, might be located in these ranks. The other side has been shaped by Italy's negative birthrate and a more modern version of family life. For example, women now learn about pregnancy and childrearing from sources other than the older women in their families.

Among the contemporary Italian cultural articulations of maternity (authored by either men or women), there are, to be sure, figurations that resist time-honored, stereotypical, or archetypal maternal representations. These representations should be considered alongside the contemporary phenomenon of Italy's birthrate, which is currently one of the lowest in the world. In 2008, the Population Reference Bureau, which compares demographic data from around the world, reported that Italian women give birth only 1.3 times in a lifetime. This datum is compared to the United States (2.1) and the Democratic Republic of Congo, which, with 6.5 births per lifetime of a female citizen, stands at the opposite end of the spectrum.[15] The data report that the annual number of births in Italy in 2008 (568,120) was exceeded by the annual number of deaths (575,300), evoking Mussolini's Fascist-era complaint that he saw "more coffins than cradles."[16] In addition to the negative birthrate, fully 20 percent of the Italian population is over the age of sixty-five, while the group under the age of fifteen represents only 14 percent. This is almost the exact inverse of the United States, where those aged sixty-five and older total 13 percent of the population, while the under-fifteen cohort stands at 20 percent. In brief, though contraception patterns vary in Italy according to region, class, and degree of secularization, on the whole not enough live births occur each year to replace Italians who have died. Demographers, sociologists, and human geographers consider this situation dire.[17]

These data indicate that Italian women are having fewer children. It is also the case that many women are delaying childbearing. This has resulted in a cultural shift in how information about childbirth and childrearing is transmitted to new mothers. Mothers and grandmothers are no longer the main source of information. Instead, many new mothers learn from childbirth manuals.[18] One aspect of the "maternity industry" in Italy that has not yet received much critical attention concerns the ways childbirth manuals and early-childhood pedagogy are shaping a discourse of maternity that is particular to Italy.

One of the richest sources of information concerning pregnancy, childbirth, and childrearing available to Italian women is *Guida Prénatal alla nascita: le cose da sapere, da fare e da decidere quando si fa un bambino* (The prenatal guide to birth: things to know, do, and decide when having a child), a manual that is manufactured and produced by Prénatal, the international conglomerate that specializes in maternity clothing and clothing for children from birth to the age of eleven.[19] The pedagogy Prénatal offers new mothers is a significant part of the social and cultural terrain of early-twenty-first-century Italy. Whether or not Annamaria Franzoni read the Prénatal manual, the new pedagogy of maternity Prénatal offers shaped the society in which she became a mother and raised her children. And it shaped the public world against which the moral panic of the Cogne Affair unfolded.

Since *Guida Prénatal alla nascita le cose da sapere, da fare e da decidere quando si fa un bambino* was first published in 1984, Prénatal has made considerable efforts to educate pregnant women and new mothers who may be removed from conventional familial networks in which transmission of information pertaining to maternity and childrearing might circulate. Prénatal's clothing and furnishings may not be free, but the information they circulate is.

Prénatal's shaping of information concerning childbirth and -rearing has expanded and transformed over the last three decades. *Guida* was reprinted ten times until, in 1998, revisions called for its replacement by two texts: *La mia gravidanza* (My pregnancy) and *Diventare genitori: Le leggi, l'assistenza sanitaria, gli aspetti medici, l'alimentazione* (Becoming parents: laws, health service, medical aspects, diet). The first contains a diary for expectant women to keep during pregnancy; in its fifth edition, published in 1992, approximately 1,400,000 copies have been distributed in Italy.[20] Since 2002, *Diventare genitori* has been made available solely online; it is easier for the company to revise the information it offers, which includes contact information and information about various state institutions and agencies associated with childbirth and childrearing in Italy. In addition, Prénatal publishes two reference manuals, *Libro aperto* (Open book) and *Vado alla scuola materna* (I'm going to nursery school). First published in 1996, *Libro aperto* is more specifically detailed than *Diventare genitori,* as demonstrated by the titles of its seven chapters: "L'attesa" (Waiting), "Il parto" (Delivery) "La nascita" (Birth) "Chi aiuta la mamma" (Who helps mom), "Il benessere" (Well-being), "Il tempo libero" (Free time), and "Numeri utili" (Useful numbers). *Vado alla scuola materna,* which provides information about different types of nursery schools, was published for the first time in 1999. A remarkable detail emerging from an examination of *Vado alla scuola materna* may be found in the information it yields concerning the increase of public interest in private nursery schools rather than those sponsored and supervised by the state. Such codification, or, rather, commodification, of the experience of pregnancy, childbirth, and childrearing illustrates the perceived need for such texts, if only within a certain class fraction.

Texts such as Prénatal's show the normalization of childbirth in contemporary Italy, where women delay pregnancy until achieving a certain level of either economic self-sufficiency or job security, two issues that do not always mutually entail each other. In addition to fewer Italian mothers overall, the average age of a first-time mother in Italy has risen over the last twenty years, a trend located in various narrative expressions. Observing his daughter-in-law Francesca, the narrator in Cristina Comencini's 2007 novel *L'illusione del bene* (The illusion of good) notes, "Children were not discussed. I tried out the topic. 'Sure, we'll have a kid. I'm 33 and I figured I still have a couple of more years: I mean to maximize my biological clock,' she'd replied."[21] Comencini's Francesca could end up like Giorgia (Stefania Rocca) in Stefano Incerti's 2003 film *La vita come viene* (Life as it comes) who, deep in her thirties, is childless. At an appointment with her gynecologist in one of the several interlocking narratives in the film, Giorgia expresses frustration that she and her husband have not yet been able to conceive. Overjoyed when her suspected pregnancy is finally confirmed, Giorgia rushes to find her husband, who is engaged in a mock military exercise for fun. Out of place and not knowing the rules of the game, she is mistakenly shot by her husband, whose rifle she herself loaded with live ammunition "as a joke" before he left the house that morning. Whether or not the film punishes Giorgia for her delayed maternity is left to the viewer to determine.

~

By all accounts, Franzoni's life in Monteacuto and her privileged place as the oldest daughter in a large family that observed such hallowed daily practices as eating together daily at midday would appear to obviate the need of such instruction as Prénatal was poised to offer. This notwithstanding, the Prénatal texts help describe the general context of preparation for maternity in Italy at this time. More interesting than Prénatal's texts are the *incontri* (gatherings) that the company has organized at its retail stores since 1988. *Incontri,* like the manuals, have transformed since their first appearance, when "an expert in children's clothing. . . explained in detail and with practical examples how to dress a newborn and use the necessary products in the first few weeks of life."[22] Of greater significance than the demonstration of Prénatal products is the information that from the outset, these meetings were not intended for mothers alone, but were also open to grandmothers and fathers. This reversed the generational transmission of information. Since, as Prénatal's director of marketing observes, the experience of childbirth has undergone "*cambiamenti dei costumi e dei linguaggi*" (changes in customs and language), the *incontro* seems less an opportunity for women of an older generation to impart their understanding of childbirth than a reversal of the transmission of information.

The *incontro* underwent substantial redesign in 2002 that significantly realigned its objectives. Prénatal divided the gatherings into two sessions, one that took place in the second trimester and a second during the final trimester. More than a retailing opportunity, the *incontri* aim at helping "future moms and . . . dads . . . live in peaceful awareness during pregnancy."[23] The first *incontro,* "La mia gravidanza," (My pregnancy) follows "a trip through the senses" and addresses "emotional and physiological changes in bonding, and relaxing to music."[24] The second gathering, "Neonato e Dintorni" (The newborn and surroundings), focuses on retail opportunities, but it also seeks to prepare new mothers for labor, childbirth, and the needs of a newborn. Prénatal estimates that the meetings are attended by approximately 60,000 women and 10,000 men annually.

Although Prénatal acknowledges "*i papà*" at the *incontri,* it is clear that the chief targets are pregnant women, in particular pregnant women of a certain social class and geographical location. Single fathers confound contemporary Italian society, whose gender norms change at a rate that can only be described as glacial.[25]

The downward turn in the birthrate in Italy began in the mid-1980s, coeval with the beginning of the Prénatal enterprise. The commodification of the child in Italian society, therefore, is but one consequence of this trend, which reifies the social importance of the child. This is similar to the instrumentalization Alfredo Carlo Moro notes, saying that the child has transformed into the "child-resource"; that is, the child as object or instrument of sheer gratification for the adult and the adult world.[26] Not only the source of individual gratification, the child clearly constitutes a resource for the social welfare state. Killing the goose that laid the golden egg, to refer again to Aesop's fable, sends a chill warning to an Italian polity seeking pensions and retirement forty years out.

As concerns Franzoni as the maternal subject, if, as I explored in the introduction, murder "undoes" the privileged position of the body in critical and theoretical considerations, then infanticide and filicide destabilize maternal identity.[27] The dead body of Samuele disrupts Franzoni's maternal identity. The fact that she was convicted of her son's murder impugns her claim on this maternal subject position. But Italy's justice system, finding it unlikely that Franzoni would reoffend and kill other children, released her from prison before her trial. She was free on her own recognizance from March 30, 2002, until May 2008, when the Court of Cassation confirmed her sentence. This was a longer period than anyone expected, long enough for Franzoni to conceive again and give birth to the Lorenzis' third child, Gioele, in January 2003. The final irony is that, as she is the mother of a child under the age of ten, Franzoni's prison sentence has been curtailed.[28]

INVESTIGATIONS AND MORAL PANIC: THE ALL-FRANZONI-ALL-THE-TIME CHANNEL

"There is no brute who is killing children, nor
is there a serial killer on the loose."

—Maria del Savio Bonaudo, district attorney, Aosta, February 4, 2002

When word of a mysterious murder in Italy's alpine hinterland spread to the peninsula's urban centers, home of daily newspapers and television studios, a veritable avalanche of journalists stormed the small town of Cogne, 25 kilometers south of the regional capital, Aosta. Against the backdrop of the mounting "mediatic delirium," the RIS's first forensic examinations and Samuele Lorenzi's funeral took place in Cogne. Much significance was attributed to Franzoni's behavior during the medics' attempts to revive Samuele and before and during the child's funeral on February 9. Mario Lorenzi, Franzoni's father-in-law, observed wisely that public opinion was remarkably unkind in its vilification of Franzoni during the time of the funeral, which focused on, for example, the alleged visit to the hairdresser before the funeral, the report that, in the presence of the carabinieri investigating the case, she said to her husband, "*Mi aiuti a fare un altro?*" (Will you help me have another (child)?), and the fact that she arranged for an orchestra to play at Samuele's funeral, something residents of Cogne were wholly unaccustomed to.[29] As Mario Lorenzi said,

> If this is the basis for measuring (her behavior), then I, too, could have killed my grandson. I also had sleepless nights, agitated nights when I dreamed of Samuele. Come morning, I didn't know where I was, if it had all been a nightmare or if it was real. I, too, could have been overcome by anxiety. My daughter-in-law's reactions after the crime cannot be judged precisely because they were influenced by the trauma she underwent.[30]

Although Franzoni was not formally named as the prime suspect until the beginning of March 2002, for the press she quickly emerged as a person of interest. She and the case became the source of endless reports on a variety of television programs. These ranged from relatively sober treatment of the case by various TG services, news broadcasts by the RAI and otherwise, and short news-based programs associated with TG3. Longer programs such as in-depth reports or entertainment programs did not treat the case with as much decorum. Programs such as *La vita in diretta* (Life, Live, shown in the late afternoons), *Domenica In* (Sunday in, shown on Sunday afternoons opposite soccer matches), and *Unomattina* (One morning, shown in the mornings on RAI 1) tend to be more lurid and are aimed principally at female viewers and, especially in the case of *La vita in diretta,* to a more senior audience. But the program with the widest audience demographic is the king of Italian evening talk shows, *Porta a porta,* shown usually after 10:00 PM, though the occasional prime-time special does occur. *Porta a porta* takes up issues of public interest and is a major shaper of public opinion. Its host, Bruno Vespa, embraces and encourages confrontation, orchestrating appearances of guests with opposing views on the same program. Though Vespa invites different experts for commentary via satellite, a cadre of stable guests return nightly. These include the journalist Barbara Palombelli, pop psychologist Paolo Crepet, and criminologists and various politicians, depending on the topic.

The Cogne events made for the perfect media storm. Kidd-Hewitt and Osborn have pointed out that popular culture is "undoubtedly obsessed with crime, and particularly violent crime, and television has developed this obsession with the forbidden into endless narrative strategies whose unconscious attraction to the viewer is a critical question in this area."[31] The popular interest in violent crime in general worked in tandem with the sensational aspects specific to Samuele's murder. Geographically remote Cogne is located in a cranny of the Valle D'Aosta, which gives its name to this region of several conjoining valleys. Crime statistics for this area are in the main low, and violent crime is an even less common occurrence. At first, the panicked community worried that the randomness of the crime meant the killer, still believed on the loose, would kill again, another sensationalizing factor. It is in this context that the district attorney, Maria del Savio Bonaudo, made the statement I have given at the start of this section: "There is no brute who is killing children, nor is there a serial killer on the loose."[32]

Rather than ebb over time, media coverage of the case intensified, and when Franzoni was named as suspect on March 14, media attention attached to another sensational aspect, the criminally dangerous woman. As media studies scholar Milly Bonanno observed in 1978, "*la donna fa notizia*" (women make the news), and a murderess captures interest even more efficiently.[33] Robert Reiner has pointed out that "both crime statistics and crime news portray offending as a predominantly male activity."[34] Moreover, "women murderers are interesting precisely because of their rarity," as Meda Chesney-Lind and Lisa Pasko have remarked.[35] Italy, much less the Cogne case, offers no exception to this general rule.

District Attorney del Savio Bonaudo found the case straightforward and believed it had been transformed into something more complicated than what it was, a simple domestic tragedy, not "*un'altra Via Poma*" (not another Via Poma), as she told the press on Feburary 8, referring to the unsolved 1990 murder case of Simonetta Cesaroni in Rome.[36] Yet the televised coverage of the Cogne case suggested a complicated crime, requiring repetition so viewers could easily digest the explanation of the case.

The stock footage used with greatest frequency shows Cogne from an aerial view in its alpine splendor. Similarly, when the RIS's investigations were reported on, long aerial shots showed the carabinieri forensic team like ants, clambering over the Franzoni-Lorenzi *baita,* as the mountain chalets are known, winding their way through the interior, and snaking Cogne's sewer system in the hopes of locating the murder weapon. The repetitive nature of the carabineri's movements, matched by its repetitive airing, begs comparison with the police detectives in Edgar Allen Poe's short story "The Purloined Letter," made famous by both Jacques Lacan and Jacques Derrida for the ways it illuminates Freud's notion of repetition compulsion, itself a concept related to the working through and mastery of trauma, in the original case of the child's anxiety over separation from his mother enacted in the play of the *fort-da.*[37] In the Cogne case, one might say that the reenactment functioned for the reverse reason, that is, not so much for the child's mastery of separation from the mother so much as the more generalized social anxiety over the child separated—by murder—from his family.

In Poe's acclaimed story, the minister has stolen a document compromising to the queen. Dupin, for his part, steals the document from the minister and stashes it in his apartment. He leaves home each evening so that the dimwitted police officers can, night after night, search the same places in the hopes of finding it. Like Poe's police agents, the carabinieri scoured the Franzoni-Lorenzi home as well as surrounding areas, looking for the blunt instrument used in the murder. Since blunt instruments abounded in the Franzoni-Lorenzi household, as they do in most households, I would suggest that, as the queen's stolen and probably treasonous letter hangs in the very center of Dupin's home in plain view in Poe's story, so the object used for bludgeoning Samuele was both everywhere and nowhere.

Television coverage included, in addition to news services, programs of entertainment. At times in the investigation of the murder, these programs took on added significance, becoming players in the drama of the case. An example of this is the *Porta a porta* episode that aired March 11, 2002. In marking the convergence of mediatic intervention with legal action, this episode, virtually coeval with the GIP's *avviso di garanzia* (arrest warrant), constitutes a flashpoint.[38] The episode featured the usual suspects with one exception: the addition of criminal defense attorney Carlo Taormina, whom the Franzoni-Lorenzis asked to lead Franzoni's defense after this television appearance.

The central focus of this airing of Vespa's program is the undeniably newsworthy interview with Franzoni, the first granted since Samuele's murder. This interview, exclusive to the dailies *Diciannovesimo secolo* (Genoa) and *Il Corriere della sera* (Milan), was brokered by a family friend, was conducted by veteran crime reporters Marco Imarisio and Alessandro Cassinis, and had appeared in the papers of the morning of March 11. Although the two journalists had tape-recorded Franzoni, the recording was not broadcast. Rather, the text from their interview was dramatically declaimed on *Porta a porta* by an uncredited actress. *Porta a porta* significantly eschewed a distinct embodiment, or embodied representation, of Franzoni; rather, the actress, like an informant whose identity must remain concealed, was barely visible in silhouette. Even a lookalike would have had difficulty competing with the saturated image of Franzoni's face in close-up, the preferred framing choice of the small screen.[39] The actress's voice, with her invisible face, recalls Kaja Silverman's thoughts about the way cinematic voice-over of a female character, following a Lacanian conception of the Symbolic, represents feminine lack, and was explored also in the form of the "missing" mother in the preceding chapter.[40]

The actress's voice cracked with emotion as she gave the narration all of Italy had been awaiting: the way Franzoni had safely stowed Samuele in her bed while she discharged morning tasks, the darkened master bedroom she returned to that, at first, seemed as safe a harbor as ever but quickly transformed into a charnel house, the horror uncovered in the parental bed, her son's small and battered body, and the tumult of activity and people that followed. The emotions laid claim to were on an equal footing with the sequence of the events. Significantly, it was Taormina who asked the journalists whether the actress credibly represented Franzoni's voice. Via satellite link, Imarisio observed that Franzoni's voice *"era ancora più drammatica"* (was even more dramatic) and Cassinis describes her as "a mother who sobs continually, who has tears in her eyes."[41] Other examples of the way television became a protagonist make their way into the appeals phase of Franzoni's case.

On February 1, 2002, following the conclusion of the autopsy, public prosecutor Stefania Cugge declared Samuele's death a homicide, formally opened the case, and began conducting interviews with individuals believed pertinent to an investigation. On March 5, Cugge added Franzoni's name to the list of suspects. She was arrested on March 14 while visiting her parents' home. From Monteacuto, Franzoni was taken to Turin's Le Vallette prison, where she was detained for two weeks before the *tribunale di riesame* (roughly equivalent to the arraignment in U.S. penal procedure) established that the evidence was insufficient to hold her in jail pending trial.

The interrogation that took place on March 18, 2002, was one del Savio Bonaudo considered signal and the key moment when she wishes she had probed more deeply and interrogated more aggressively. Once more describing her actions on the morning of January 30, Franzoni recounted, as she does in her memoir *La Verità,* her movements when she reentered the house. Hematological analyses confirmed that the blood found on Franzoni's slippers was Samuele's. The forensic explanation was that the slippers were worn during the murder. Both Ada Satragni and Daniela Ferrod had testified that Franzoni had worn her boots during the time they were in the chalet, following the alarm she raised.

Franzoni offered a different version and sequence of events. The morning of January 30 was filled with deviations from her daily routine. Due to the previous day's outing to Aosta, Samuele had skipped his afternoon nap and had consequently slept unusually late and heavily on the night between January 29 and 30.[42] When Davide woke, mother and son returned to her bed, where their games made them *"veramente in ritardo"* (really late) that particular morning.[43] With greater speed than usual, Franzoni said, she and Davide went upstairs to the kitchen, where he ate his cereal in silence, without the usual background noise of the television, which, Franzoni feared, would have made too much noise and wakened the still-sleeping Samuele. She hurried to her bedroom to change, leaving her pajamas on the bed. Given that Samuele was still sleeping, Franzoni took Davide's clothes upstairs so that he could dress in the kitchen. Just as she was about to leave with Davide, she testified, she found Samuele on the stairs, "half asleep" but also "desperate because he hadn't found Davide at his side."[44] She told Davide to head toward the bus stop. She took Samuele and placed him in her bed, where he could be comforted by "my smell on the pillow."[45] As she did this, she caught a glimpse of Davide, who had still not left the house, on the stairs. This exchange of glances, largely overlooked, suggests the possibility of a child witnessing violence, a theme I examine in the next chapter. Afraid that if Samuele heard his brother he would grow even more upset, she motioned to Davide to stay quiet and tucked Samuele into her bed. Franzoni decided not to lock the front door of the chalet because "Samuele surely would hear me."[46] She and Davide made their way to the bus.

This is not the State's reconstruction of the events, upheld on appeal and in Cassation and, therefore, its official, formal, and conclusive narrative. Although an underlying psychopathology was discounted, this is not to suggest that Franzoni was not experiencing difficulties in the period leading up to January 30. For example, at the sudden onset of Franzoni's malaise, Stefano Lorenzi phoned the Guardia medica, as the emergency medical technicians are called, at 5:30 the morning of January 30. Stefania Neri, a corps physician, came to the chalet. Unable to discern a specific complaint, she left. When Stefano Lorenzi left the house at 7:40, Franzoni, who had slept very little that night, was still in bed. Consistent in all narrative accounts is Franzoni's decision to move Samuele from his bed into his parents', but the precise time is not verifiable. Similarly, the precise time of the attack is not known nor, as the forensic pathologist on the case, Francesco Viglino, observed, is the exact time necessary in crafting a plausible theory of the crime.[47] Consequently, it is not known whether Samuele was attacked before or after Davide ate breakfast in the company of his mother in the second-floor kitchen.

All forensic experts, whether court-appointed or hired by the defense, confirmed that the assailant wore Franzoni's pajamas and attacked Samuele with some sort of blunt object made of copper. The Appellate Court determined that a lucid Franzoni hid the murder weapon, which they believed could have been any number of domestic objects. In closing arguments, Taormina bemoaned the absence of conclusive evidence demonstrating his client's guilt: the State had failed to locate a murder weapon or establish a motive, and the case in its trial phase had fallen victim to machinations of the media.[48] As evidence, the State had the cadaver of a 3-year-old who could have been killed with any one of many objects easily found in the home. Moreover, the State found impossibly brief the window of time to allow an intruder to have committed the crime. Finally, no blood was found outside the murder scene of the parental bedroom.

Blood, its patterns, and its absence centered the State's case against Franzoni. The RIS spent many months painstakingly collecting data. The fact that no blood was found outside the master bedroom indicated, for del Savio Bonaudo, that a household member had committed the crime. Dr. Satragni had testified that she saw Franzoni wearing boots (*stivaletti*) when she entered the chalet.

Franzoni's footwear the morning of Samuele's death became a central issue in the investigation and determination of a suspect in the murder. Blood-spray pattern analysis illustrated that the assailant wore Franzoni's clogs during the time of the attack. The centrality of the footwear in determining the suspect could be why Franzoni begins her memoir, *La Verità*, with a description of her actions upon reentering the chalet after taking Davide to the school bus. *La Verità* begins with

"I slip off my shoes leaving them on the floor and put on my slippers."[49]
Accounts of the events of that morning distinguish between two types of
footwear, those kinds worn inside the house (which included clogs (*zoc-
coli*) and slippers (*ciabatte*), two terms sometimes used interchangeably)
and those worn outside the house (shoes (*scarpe*) and boots (*stivaletti*)).
Although, when pressed during questioning, Satragni could not certify
what Franzoni wore on her feet during the time the two women waited
for the medevac helicopter, the doctor stated that at no time did she tell
Franzoni to get ready to leave. This contradicted Franzoni's statement
at the time (and reproduced in *La Verità*) that in order to help Satragni
ready Samuele for evacuation, Franzoni raced upstairs to put her shoes
on again.[50] Investigators reasoned that the blood found on the soles of
the clogs would have left traces on the stairs if Franzoni had worn them
upon reentering the house. Moreover, the blood had already dried by the
time Franzoni returned from the bus stop, helping fix the time frame
of the murder but also explaining why the boots Franzoni wore did not
track traces throughout the house. Finally, when questioned again on
January 31, Satragni stated that she had seen the clogs under the sink
in the bathroom in the main part of the house, not in the bedrooms.[51]

The Appellate Court surmised that the slippers had been moved
from the scene of the crime—by hand, not foot—but could not determine
when. Franzoni recalls that del Savio Bonaudo did not believe her version
of the events during interrogation. The Appeals Court believed instead
that, like hiding the murder weapon, this gesture displayed clearly a
woman intent on hiding actions that she knew were criminal. For the
court, Franzoni was not someone who, like an "automaton," was in a
trance, unable to discern the consequences. As Romano Pettinati, the
chief justice of the appellate court observed, "The important thing was
that she acted in such a way as to leave no sign. . . . This act could not have
been automatic. We assessed it as necessarily deliberate, conscious."[52]

Returning to the interrogation in Le Vallette on March 14, Franzoni
stated that when she had reentered the bedroom and before she could
really take in what had happened, she touched Samuele's scalp and when
she came away with brain matter on her fingers, tried to restore it. She
stated that "it seemed to me I had taken something that was his."[53] This
account struck del Savio Bonaudo as distinct and peculiar and accords

with the second team of psychiatric evaluators, who found the recall of that moment "anomalous." More importantly, forensic evidence belied the claim.

Franzoni's recalled gesture is remarkable for the way it illuminates pulsations of the abject, as proposed by Julia Kristeva and elaborated upon significantly by Elizabeth Grosz and Barbara Creed, among others.[54] As elaborated in the introduction, for Kristeva, the abject is an experience of limits and boundaries that signs identity. Kristeva links the abject to the prelinguistic realm of the maternal.[55] Attempts to determine fixed boundaries mirror the powerful fantasy of stable identity; as a consequence, signs of the abject, which are themselves often signs of flux and flow that is "out of place," underscore the dynamics of the search. Another notable aspect of the abject, that is, its verbal form that, when used, signifies expulsion, is addressed presently.

So much of the scene the morning of January 30, 2002, in the Franzoni-Lorenzi Cogne chalet recalls the abject. The description of the attempt to restore gray matter to Samuele's shattered skull is a clear example of the sort of abject scene Creed explores in her work on horror films. The scene clearly manifests "boundary" concerns. Samuele's gray matter is outside of its proper place, but, significantly, all witnesses described the scene as characterized by a quantity of blood and torn flesh worthy of a horror film à la Dario Argento, not to mention a source of terrified disgust. Moreover, Samuele's battered body in his parents' bed, while not an example of something necessarily improperly located, does recall fantasies of the primal scene, which, as Freud observed of his patients' fantasies, could be said to "adopt . . . a sadistic view of coition."[56] Geography should not overdetermine boundary issues attached to the abject, but the media drew attention to Cogne's extreme northwesterly position in the valley, abutting the French border. The nature of the crime, the youth of its victim, and its geographical setting—all produced the sense of a wound occurring in the most vulnerable instances of time and place: childhood and one of Italy's most remote corners. Along these lines, the Cogne case has appeared as the subject of an episode in RAI's series *Ferite d'Italia* (Italy's wounds).

The media's gravitation toward the Cogne case offers more than the sensational drive to ensure a share of the television audience. Coverage also spectacularly reproduced a blending of the kind of fascination deriving from the consumption of pornography, melodrama, or horror films.[57] Whether as phallic or archaic mother—to adopt Creed's rubric—the Annamaria Franzoni that emerged as the prime suspect in the murder of Samuele remarkably displayed the signs and symbols of monstrous femininity. Additional aspects of the abject as a sign in the Cogne case and the issues it gave rise to emerge in several of the analyses of the narratives that follow.

District attorney del Savio Bonaudo regrets that during the interrogation in Le Vallette in March 2002, she did not show Franzoni the autopsy photographs. The prosecutor describes the photos as "terrifying images, almost impossible to look at."[58] She described her hesitation as "an instinct," saying "my *conscience* won out . . . *my own compassion* for a mother whom I could not attack."[59] The district attorney kept the photos in front of her as she faced Franzoni across the table. Consequently, Franzoni could not see clearly—the photos were upside down for her—the result of the attack. Del Savio Bonaudo later said that "had I done that, perhaps the trial would have gone differently and we wouldn't have talked about a *giallo* all these years. Perhaps, had she seen the photos, she could have had a significant and clear reaction."[60]

Defense attorney Carlo Federico Grosso secured Franzoni's release on March 30. Requisite confirmation that the State's evidence against Franzoni was sufficient was not confirmed until October 4, 2002. In the interim, Franzoni had made television appearances, most noticeably on the *Maurizio Costanzo Show* that aired July 16, 2002. Although the question had not been covered in interview preparations, Costanzo asked Franzoni if what his sources had discovered was true, that she was expecting another child. A surprised and unsure Franzoni thus announced her pregnancy on the air in a moment that Francesco Barale, a psychiatrist participating on the first team of experts, described as "inauthentic." The fact that Franzoni was expecting a child so soon after Samuele's death fueled the public's belief that she had indeed said to Stefano on January 30, "*Mi aiuti a fare un altro?*" When the Cassation confirmed the October finding of the Tribunale di Riesame on January 31, 2003, Franzoni was a mother for the third time, having given birth to Gioele earlier that month.

About the first psychiatric evaluation, Franzoni writes in *La Verità* that she agreed to participate following her family's counsel. "To talk, to tell the story, to answer questions helps me," she writes.[61] However much relief the sessions with the psychiatric team may have provided, Franzoni, nevertheless, felt humiliated at "needing to demonstrate each time that I am not crazy, that I haven't forgotten anything."[62] The evaluation took several months, and after "interviews, tests, and exams the court appointed experts found me sane."[63]

One expert appointed by the State, however, Ugo Fornari, disagreed. In an interview in Feburary 2005 with the weekly magazine *Oggi*, he described Franzoni's behavior as consistent with a diagnosis of a "borderline personality disorder." This diagnosis recalls that of another "bad/mad" woman in *Murder Made in Italy*: Erika De Nardo. Barale and most of the others on the first team of experts found Franzoni lucid and, significantly, with her memory intact: in his estimation, no lacunae lurked in Franzoni's recall of the events that could signal a "twilight" state in which she may have killed her son and not realized, remembered, or believed it. Unable to determine an underlying psychopathology, Barale was not surprised that a second team of experts was convened to discredit the findings of the first. It is as Catanesi and Troccoli describe, in their important study 1994 study *La madre omicida* (The homicidal mother), an attitude that pervades Italy's magistrature: women are "mad," not "bad."[64]

Scholarship on the gendered reception to crime, and Italian crime in particular, would also register no surprise at the efforts to determine Franzoni's "madness." Michela Bani, who works at the intersection of crime and the media, makes quick work of the presumption, now obsolete, that once women participated to a higher degree in Italian public culture and society, the statistics for female criminal deviance in Italy would increase.[65] On the contrary, as she points out, "if we consider the official statistics of women who have been convicted, especially since the 1970s, the decade in which the education and participation in the workplace increased for women, it becomes clear that not only is there no increase in crimes authored by women, but an actual decrease has been documented."[66] Bronwyn Naylor demonstrates similar findings in the British context, showing that "the dominant explanations of women's

violence were about emotion, madness, and irrationality. The characterisation of women as 'bad' was rarely made. . . . The reluctance to ascribe
real wickedness (and, arguably, real violence) to women in many cases
. . . is likely to be connected to the implication of such characterisation
for this society's understandings of gender, especially the feminine."[67]
The Cogne case, its investigations, its trials, and the reportage it gave
rise to clearly manifest these tendencies.

THE TRIALS OF ANNAMARIA FRANZONI

If murder is a simple matter for reporting, trials offer different circumstances. The discovery of a body, especially that of a child, is considered
a simple matter for news reporting. Del Savio Bonaudo believed the
investigation and the trial of the murderer of Samuele Lorenzi should
have been a straightforward affair. It was not. This owed in part to the
mediatic circus, which many believed Franzoni's defense team and family manipulated themselves, but also to the legal manipulations of Carlo
Taormina, Franzoni's defense attorney after the respected Carlo Federico Grosso resigned in June 2002.

As spectacles, trials have a cast of characters. Franzoni's attorneys,
therefore, merit some attention. Carlo Federico Grosso acted as Franzoni's lawyer from shortly after the crime until June 2002, when he
demitted, indicating a difference in opinion as to legal strategy. Grosso's
stature in the Valle D'Aosta should not be underestimated; his legal and
political activities had garnered him attention and esteem. Before representing Franzoni, he had served as the vice mayor of Turin and vice
president of the Regional Council of Piedmont. Nominated by Minister
of Justice Giovanni Maria Flick, he had served on a national commis-
sion charged with revising the Italian penal code. Moreover, he was a
contributor on legal issues to Turin's daily, *La Stampa*. He had served
as legal representative of the civil interests of the families of the victims
of the slaughter in the Bologna train station in August 1980, as well as
in the case of the Strage del Rapido 904—also known as the Strage di
Natale—the 1984 attack on a Milan-bound train that left nearly twenty
dead in a valley outside Bologna. He had subsequently served also as the
legal representative of bondholders victimized by the "Parmalat crash,"

the 2003 scandal of fraud and price-fixing. Franzoni, however, claims she knew none of this about him, and had barely a nodding acquaintance with the man, whose second home was located down the road from her own in Cogne. Grosso's eminence as a jurist and public interlocutor instilled confidence and gravitas in Franzoni, her case, and her supporters. His substitution by Carlo Taormina, who joined the team in June 2002, significantly altered this.

Franzoni said that Grosso's decision to resign "makes me very sorry because the political aspect (Grosso on the left, Taormina on the right) holds no interest for me."[68] Taormina's political leanings are not the sole characteristic distinguishing him from Grosso. His legal tactics and strategies gravitate toward the sensational. Taormina defended officials accused of hiding evidence that could have clarified the mysterious events of the disabled Douglas DC-9 that plummeted from the skies above Ustica in June 1980, killing eighty-seven passengers. Taormina also participated in the much-publicized murder case of Marta Russo, a University of Rome law student who had been killed in mysterious circumstances in May 1997 while in the *città universitaria,* on campus.[69] Taormina accused the prosecuting attorneys of tampering with a recorded interview and abridging a witness's rights during interrogation. In addition to representing several individuals indicted in the Tangentopoli political corruption scandal of the mid-1990s, he also served as the defense attorney in former Nazi Erich Priebke's trial for war crimes. This media circus gained in legal importance when the defense strategy of Priebke, who stood accused of assisting in the massacre of the 335 partisans at the Fosse Ardeatine outside Rome in March 1944, introduced the claim that Priebke was "just following orders."

What Taormina's cases share is their ability to command public attention in the operation of moral panic, which I explored in the introduction. Variously, the cases' circumstances are particularly noteworthy historically, as in the examples of Priebke and the defense of some accused of involvement in the Tangentopoli scandals. Alternatively, the cases feature particularly mysterious circumstances, such as Ustica, or events of historical import that not only are mysterious but also feature a high degree of prurience, as in the Marta Russo murder case, high-profile pedophilia and sexual abuse cases, and, finally, the Cogne case. To his much-publicized cases we may also add Taormina's political cachet: he served as a member of Parliament of the Forza Italia party, as well as undersecretary of the interior in the second Berlusconi government. It is worth noting that Taormina later expressed regret over his involvement in the Franzoni trial. As he said in an interview, "I lost a lot in accepting this case, both in terms of my public image as well as in terms of the time I could have devoted to my own practice."[70] In Taormina's view, defending Priebke against the accusation of war crimes for involvement in the Fosse Ardeatine massacre did not tarnish his reputation so much as taking up Annamaria Franzoni's defense. Had he been convinced of Franzoni's innocence, one might have imagined this as reason enough to justify his participation in her defense. Notwithstanding his claims, the Franzoni trial served as the basis of at least two of Taormina's publications. The first, *La mia verità sul delitto di Cogne* (My truth about the Cogne crime), a slim volume published by and sold with the politically right daily *Il Giornale* in April 2007, lamented the absence of anything more than circumstantial evidence in the State's case against Franzoni. The second, *Il regime delle prove nel processo penale* (The regime of proof in criminal trials) (2007), pays less specific attention to the Franzoni case but works the same terrain and joins Taormina's other publications exploring Italian criminal procedure.[71]

The trial of Annamaria Franzoni began in the Aosta court in September 2003 and concluded in June of the following year. A bench trial, it was presided over by Eugenio Gramola. On June 28, 2004, Carlo Taormina requested a fast-track trial, which carries the advantage of an automatic reduction in sentence of one-third. Accused of a crime that would carry a 30-year sentence, Franzoni stood to gain, if convicted, ten years' liberty. Taormina always insisted that Franzoni's trials were a miscarriage of justice and credited his legal foresight with the reduced sentence Franzoni is now serving.

On July 19, 2004, Gramola announced the conviction of Franzoni to a 30-year prison sentence. Two months later, on September 1, 2004, the rationale behind the sentence was made public. Gramola adjudged that Franzoni "had all the time necessary to commit the murder, to remove the clothing used in the criminal act, to wash herself and resume anew coldness and rationality so as to demonstrate that, having committed the act, her priority was to ensure that her criminal responsibility would not be ascertained."[72]

The trial court's judicial rationale consisted of ten key points. First, the location of the chalet made unlikely the presence of assailants the Franzoni-Lorenzis did not know. Second, the accused lacked an alibi save for the eight minutes she was seen outside the house taking Davide to the bus stop. The third point consisted of the unique aspects of the circumstances of the morning of January 30, 2002: Samuele had been only rarely left alone in the house and Franzoni's explanation of the unlocked door was rejected. Points 4, 5, and 6 concern the clothing that the killer wore while committing the crime: point 4 maintained that the killer wore Franzoni's pajama bottoms, point five the pajama top, and point 6, Franzoni's footwear. The slippers (also referred to as clogs) return in point 7, where it was maintained that Franzoni had lied about when and where she had worn them. Point 8 drew attention to the fact that Franzoni did not immediately identify Samuele's condition when she phoned 118. The tenth and last point underscored the lack of rancor toward the Franzoni-Lorenzis in Cogne, making it unlikely that a killer was acting out of revenge. Point 9, however, was the most inflammatory, for Gramola underscored Franzoni's *"notevole e anomala freddezza,"* or her notable and anomalous coldness, in the period immediately following the murder.

Carlo Taormina began to search for an alternative theory of the crime, a mission that resulted also in a lawsuit for slander brought against Franzoni and Lorenzi. But this is not the only supplemental lawsuit, for Franzoni, Lorenzi, and Taormina himself were accused of obstruction of justice. This part of the trial narrative is entitled "Cogne bis," or "Cogne, Part II." In the first lawsuit, Franzoni and Lorenzi accused their neighbor, Daniela Ferrod's brother-in-law, Ulisse Guichardaz, of killing their son. Guichardaz, evidently the village eccentric, was interviewed on numerous occasions and was never called to testify because it was not believed his testimony held any probative value.

The obstruction charge of "Cogne bis" concerned the efforts of the Franzoni-Lorenzis and Taormina to produce additional exculpatory forensic evidence. One of the chief problems with Franzoni's narrative of the crime, del Savio Bonaudo had maintained, was the absence of blood linking the inside of the chalet to the outside, which could have demonstrated an intruder's presence. Taormina and company were believed to have manufactured evidence they claimed was forensically valuable. What had been taken for evidence of blood in a location that would have supported the theory of an intruder was instead found to be fossilized animal droppings. The great forensic pathology wars began.

The State based the forensic aspects of their case on the findings of the RIS, while Franzoni's defense team, on the other hand, had the right to call their own expert witnesses. Employing pathologists, hematologists, and various others expert in the reading of bloodstain projections and patterns, Taormina sought, to no avail, to dismantle the State's set of evidence. The ensuing *battibecco* (back and forth) protracted the appeals phase.

The appeal began in Turin on November 16, 2005. Several ordinary, structural changes accompany the case's entry into the appeals phase. First, a jury and not a lone member of the magistracy considers the case. Moreover, this jury is composed of *giudici togati*, jury members who are actual magistrates, and *giudici popolari,* "popular" jurors, analogous to those in the U.S. judicial system. Although the Corte di Assise d'Appello, like the appeals phase in other judicial systems, should restrict its consideration of the case to the elements present in the trial phase, in Franzoni's case, the court considered new developments. Taormina had formally requested that additional evidence be considered, and it is within the purview of the appeals court to make a determination. In fact, in keeping with the "mad/bad mother" exchange feminist criminologists had predicted, the appeals court sitting in judgment on Franzoni's case and presided over by Romano Pettinati called for additional psychiatric evaluation of the defendant.[73]

The convening of a second psychiatric evaluation, perhaps more than any other aspect of the case, reveals the gendering of the Italian justice system in Annamaria Franzoni's case. The split between the trial and appellate phases concerning Franzoni's possible mental defect reproduces a classic split in criminological studies of infanticide and filicide, as Catanesi and Troccoli have detailed.

Courts, and particularly in the Italian judicial system, seem unable to accept that a woman could kill her child unless plagued by mental defect. As they write, judges "are not satisfied by a technical opinion concerning the condition of illness that could bear on the indictability of the accused; they feel it necessary to 'understand,' to 'comprehend' how such a thing could have happened."[74] When they were called upon to conduct expert examination of women accused of murder, they found that "expectations of mental illness were so strong as to make it difficult for anyone, including the prosecutor, to accept reports that found no mental defect."[75]

Catanesi and Troccoli anticipated with great accuracy the events as they unfolded in Franzoni's appeal. Significantly, the prosecution (directed by Vittorio Corsi, who substituted Maria del Savio Bonaudo in this phase of the trial), and not Franzoni's defense team, called for the psychiatric evaluations. Typically, psychiatric evidence is used to establish an *attenuante*, an extenuating circumstance that could be used to reduce sentencing. Understandably, the prosecution does not often seek such factors. Franzoni refused to participate in the second evaluation. Consequently, the experts relied on videotaped interviews.

The small screen of the TV eerily morphed into a curious participant in the proceedings, either as witness to Franzoni's putative psychiatric unhinging during the exploratory phase of the investigation or, by way of the bizarre turn of events in December 2005, as a source of material for the psychiatric evaluation that the defendant refused to submit to.

The experts participating in the disputed psychiatric evaluation intended to focus on a series of television programs. These included Franzoni's 2002 appearance on the *Maurizio Costanzo Show*; a 2003 special investigation by Irene Pivetti, the president of Italy's lower chamber of Parliament; two airings of Bruno Vespa's *Porta a porta*; and the November 21, 2005, edition of *Matrix*. *La Repubblica* reported that "the cassettes will soon be secured, including the famed instance in which Franzoni asks off-air, 'Surely I didn't I cry too much?'"[76] As anyone who watched Franzoni's defense attorney react over the course of the trial and its appeal could have predicted, Taormina lashed out at authorities one and all: "The judges are mistaken: it is not possible to use material of this kind for a psychiatric evaluation."[77]

The report, filed on June 14, 2006, indicates a personality disorder, and in November of that year the team hypothesized that Franzoni could have been acting in *"uno stato crepuscolare,"* a "twilight" or fugue state in which swathes of memory can be repressed. In no uncertain terms, Franzoni denounced both the findings as well as the hypothesis a week later, on November 20. Perhaps any shadow cast on Franzoni's lucidity would have adversely affected sales of *La Verità,* which was just about to arrive in bookstores.

The disciplinary apparatuses of psychiatry and the judicial system clearly tried to make the defendant conform not only to societal stereotypes of femininity and maternity but also to judicial ones. The chapter that follows details the tension established between the construction of the maternal subject advanced in these discursive formations and the maternal subject discussed and detailed in Italian feminist epistemology.

SEVEN

Spectacular Grief and Public Mourning

THE PUTATIVE "COLDNESS" ATTRIBUTED to Annamaria Franzoni's behavior on January 30, 2002, and in the weeks that followed, indelibly
conditioned her reception by the public. Not native to the Valle D'Aosta,
Franzoni did not conform to the expectations of the Cogneins, the residents of Cogne. As detailed in the preceding chapter, the preparations
for Samuele's funeral were considered too grand and Franzoni's reported
attempts to make an appointment to have her hair done for the funeral an illustration of her callousness and superficiality. Since much
of Franzoni's behavior was documented by the media, and especially
television, the Cogne case illustrates what Peppino Ortoleva identifies
as the "lessons of grief" that the media, and especially broadcast media,
are poised to offer.[1] For Ortoleva, cinema especially enjoys hieratic, or,
priestly, power. Television's domestic omnipresence guarantees its power
to instruct and imprint. Franzoni's behavior was variously described,
as she enumerates herself in *La Verità*, as "cold, without affect, cynical,
mendacious, false."[2] Judge Eugenio Gramola, who presided over the
case in its trial phase, declared her to have murdered her son "with presence of mind, cynicism and relentless coldness" and to have displayed
"noteworthy and anomalous coldness."[3] As detailed in my investigation
of the Novi Ligure matricide and fratricide of 2001, for the Italian penal
code the murder of a family member is considered an *aggravante,* an aggravating factor, and carries an added penalty in sentencing. Franzoni's
alleged "coldness," everywhere captured and reproduced in the media,
served as an *aggravante* in her sentence in the court of public opinion.

LESSONS OF GRIEF

Franzoni's distress over the demise of her child—Samuele's death was not ruled a homicide until a week had passed—was not sufficiently acute, at least not when she was in the public eye. Moreover, when she did display distress, it was not considered adequate. Simply put, Franzoni was not suitably hysterical. She lacked, for example, the maternal melancholy Laura Morante had embodied as Paola in Nanni Moretti's *La stanza del figlio* (*The Son's Room*, 2001), released in Italy the spring before Samuele's murder. Morante's performance was singled out for significant critical acclaim, and Morante won the David di Donatello from the Accademia di cinema italiano (American Academy of Cinema) for Best Actress for her portrayal of a mother grieving the accidental death of her teenaged son.[4]

Moretti's *La Stanza del figlio* was briefly mentioned in relation to the Novi Ligure double murder, where it offered perspective on adolescent privacy, a central theme raised by the killings. As concerns the Cogne case, Moretti's film is of interest for the way it elucidates parental grief over the loss of a child. Briefly, a family of four—the "nuclear" ideal of the heteronormative marriage with two children, one of each sex—lives a fairly happy, fairly peaceful life. Their relative tranquility is shattered by the accidental death of Andrea (Giuseppe Sanfelice) while scuba diving in the Adriatic. Finding his son's death and his own grief too great a distraction during sessions, Giovanni (Moretti) announces the closing of his practice as a psychoanalyst. Paola (Morante) is undone by grief at the loss of their son. (See Figure 7.1.) Rattled by her brother's accident, Irene (Jasmine Trinca) begins to show signs of an aggression never before displayed. When Arianna (Sofia Vigliar) walks into their lives, she brings a secret Andrea had not disclosed to his family. Like her mythical forebear Ariadne, who helped Theseus escape the Minotaur, Arianna provides the family with a way out of the labyrinth of mourning with its dead ends, impasses, and unprofitable repetitions.[5] In telling the family that she and Andrea had been involved in a romance, Arianna breaks the seal of privacy of "the son's room," but she also shocks the family out of the stasis of their grief.

FIGURE 7.1. *La Stanza del Figlio* (The Son's Room) (Nanni Moretti, 2001).

Moretti's film exploring spectacular norms of parental grieving appeared before the Cogne events and provides a benchmark for the state of conditions in which the "perfect media storm" of the Cogne event gathered force. In her sui generis account of the Cogne events, Maria Grazia Torri observes the currency of a work such as Sandro Veronesi's best-selling 2005 novel *Caos calmo* (*Quiet Chaos: A Novel*) in the murder case against Franzoni. If *La Stanza del figlio* may be considered as an indication of the spectacular norms of mourning before Samuele's murder, Veronesi's novel—winner of Italy's most coveted literary prize, Il Premio Strega, in 2006—may be used to the same ends in the period after the child's death. In fact, as explored below, Moretti's film and Veronesi's novel are closely linked.

Grief over the unexpected death of a family member marks the dramatic beginning of *Caos calmo*. Torri underscores the role that Franzoni's reserve played in the public's perception of her, noting the way it resonated with Veronesi's novel, whose publication and reception correspond to the appeals phase of the murder trial. *Caos calmo* thematizes absent mourning and offers "a case of atypical reaction to pain. . . . The protagonist is calm, becomes a more loving father, an exemplary parent. . . . At times he steels himself for what may occur. But no: the grief bomb never drops."[6]

Torri's exposé offers a fair, albeit abbreviated, assessment of *Caos calmo* and its protagonist's inability to conform to public expectations of his grief.[7] Like the media's depiction of Franzoni's character, the novel contrasts private grief with its public performance and reception. Although they both cover similar terrain, Veronesi's novel departs from Moretti's film in several ways. Grief in *La stanza del figlio* may be as much about the concept of "family" itself as it is about Andrea's death. The novel transforms the loss of a child into that of a presumptive spouse. Significantly, although they had been a couple for nearly a decade, Pietro and Lara were only just about to embark on marriage at the time the action begins. The family in *La stanza del figlio* may always have carried within it the germ of its own unraveling, as Fabio Vighi has observed, rendered materially concrete in the film by the fossil Andrea steals and, when it breaks, worries he cannot replace, or the cracked teapot that Giovanni inveighs against, comparing it to the shards of his family.[8] In *Caos calmo*, the "family" is ruptured irreparably even before its civil sanction through matrimony. The narrative of the Cogne case reveals similar cracks in the foundation of the family structure. As one of the events of public record that "shook public opinion the most in the last twenty years," the murder of Samuele Lorenzi became a bellwether.[9] One of the reasons for this, Torri conjectured, rested on the way Samuele's killing showed how a sensational yet isolated event linked to widespread concerns about child welfare, the anxiety that children have as much, if not more, to fear from the enemy within the home as from the enemy outside of it. The enemy is no intruder, but, rather, the *nemico intimo*, or the intimate enemy, as Consuelo Corradi called it, working from within the family unit itself.[10]

Nanni Moretti himself clearly acts as an extra-cinematic link between *La stanza del figlio* and Antonello Grimaldi's 2008 screen adaptation of *Caos calmo,* in which Moretti stars as Pietro. Moretti's less explicit connection to Veronesi's novel took place before it was even written. Without knowing the subject of Moretti's film, Veronesi had approached the filmmaker with a screen treatment for another film toward the end of production for *La stanza del figlio.* Moretti hesitated to become involved with the project at that time. As Veronesi recounts, Moretti urged him to develop the story as a novel, eventually published as *Caos calmo.* It was producer Alfonso Proccacci who brought Moretti into the project as lead actor and co-screenwriter.[11]

SPECTACULAR MOURNING: MERGING AND PURGING

Caos calmo tells the story of a successful media executive in a multinational conglomerate and explores the general difficulties of mourning as they correspond to "merging" in several contexts. A Roman in Milan, Pietro, the executive, has for some years lived with Lara, with whom he has a daughter, Claudia, now close to ten years old. Lara's death from an aortal aneurysm days before their wedding emblematizes the difficulties of "merging" taking place in parallel fashion in the agency where Pietro works as a respected director. A merging of the different agencies in this global media conglomerate has thrown a wrench into office politics, relations, and friendships. The merger of the media conglomerate, with its emphasis on networks and networking, is the backdrop against which the action of the novel plays out mourning and loss in a series of performances that escalates from private to public, collapsing the distance between them. The merger of the media conglomerate for which Pietro works exemplifies the "processes of trans-national expansion," that William Uricchio and Susan Kinnebrock have discussed by which "global media hardware and content producers increasingly concentrated ownership and market share (the Sony and Bertelsmann empires, for example) (with which) the stage was set for an effective restructuring of the media's role in the public sphere."[12]

That Lara's death should occur just as Pietro and his brother, Carlo, struggle to save two drowning swimmers in the waters off Roccamare on the Tuscan coast underscores the novel's parallel mergers. Further, the opener overdetermines Pietro's ability to save a woman who means nothing to him while his future wife collapses in a heap on their drive-way, far from any help he could offer. Using Claudia's return to school following Lara's death as an excuse, Pietro abandons his office and sta-tions himself outside her school. From his perch on the park bench, Pietro means to offer a reassuring presence. Although initially viewed as paternal solidarity with Claudia, as the Milanese autumn turns wet and chilly, Pietro's days in front of her school appear increasingly curi-ous to those bearing witness to his presence. His sojourn in the park becomes more about his own difficulties than his daughter's. The longer his absence from the office, the more frequently do his coworkers seek him in the park. When they confess to him their various peccadilloes and worries, these colleagues make him into some kind of guru, priest, or, eventually, messiah, imbuing Pietro's self-imposed "exile" with alle-gorical overtones. Although at first it seems to dramatize his grief over the loss of his partner, Pietro's separation from others during the merger becomes a statement about the merger. His self-isolation is interpreted as a display of wisdom befitting the next chief of the Milan chapter of the media multinational, the position Pietro will eventually be offered. At the same time, Pietro's embodied presence on the park bench goes against the grain of the type of industry he works in. His physical pres-ence on the bench in front of Claudia's school seems quaint when com-pared to the disembodied media networks the agency seeks to expand.[13]

There are noticeable distinctions between the narrative of the Cogne case and Veronesi's novel. Pietro does not suffer loss as the result of vio-lence, for example, and the urban setting of Milan contrasts significantly with the ruptured pastoral setting of Cogne. Further, moving from a reading of the Cogne narrative to Veronesi's novel, while *Caos calmo* maintains the general concern of atypical grief, it shifts from parental to spousal mourning. The chief distinction between the cultural and the literary text, however, is the gendered difference between Veronesi's fictional protagonist and Franzoni.

It appears that Veronesi finds the gendered distinction between par-ents significant. Early in this novel, taking the form of a lengthy first-person narrative, Pietro observes that the bourgeois Milan in which he moves marvels at the attention he pays to Claudia following her mother's death. The subject of Pietro's narration, Claudia's psychology, remains as removed and inscrutable as, for example, Davide Lorenzi's with regard to the sudden death of his brother and the clamorous consequences. The parents of Claudia's classmates—largely but not solely mothers—seem surprised, "as if everyone took as a given that I wouldn't be able to take care of my daughter."[14]

Public reaction to Pietro as a solicitous single father resonates with other cultural expressions of paternity at the beginning of this century.[15] To return to the example of Prénatal's configuration of the discourse on maternity in contemporary Italy, a subject explored in the preceding chapter, we note that fathers appear almost as an afterthought in the preparation of parenting, as demonstrated by the way the Prénatal multinational orchestrates the *incontro*. To turn to additional expressions of contemporary fatherhood in Italy, the situation Veronesi's protagonist finds himself in echoes some aspects of the situation of Frigerio, narrator of Giuseppe Pontiggia's 2000 novel *Nati due volte* (*Born Twice*), winner of the Premio Campiello. Even more, Veronesi's novel recalls Gianni Amelio's direction of *Le chiavi di casa* (*The Keys to the House*), the 2004 film adaptation of *Nati due volte*.[16] In Amelio's film Paolo's mother dies during childbirth, leaving Gianni (Kim Rossi Stuart) alone with their severely handicapped son.

Like this film, *Caos calmo* portrays a father's loving care of a child following a mother's death. Pietro is besotted by the newfound intimacy with his daughter, the circumstances for which are created by Lara's untimely death. Linking to the Cogne case, the novel portrays a paradise lost and gained. Tiny Cogne is located in the valley of Il Gran Paradiso, or the Great Paradise, as this Italian national park is known. The murder of Samuele Lorenzi erupted in the small village like some *"flagello divino,"* or divine retribution, a phrase Veronesi uses repeatedly in the novel. But if the murder in Cogne flags a paradise lost, the traumatic loss of Lara in *Caos calmo* creates a paradise of a new sort for Pietro. His newly found parental reliability is something out of an earthly paradise regained. As he remarks to himself, "Wake Claudia, have breakfast with her, take her to school and wait for her here outside like every other day seemed to me all of a sudden like part of a Paradise lost."[17]

The cost of Pietro's attachment to Claudia following Lara's death is that neither he nor his daughter is granted the relief made available by grief. Pietro treats his grief as he does the hard drive for Lara's computer—he hits the F6 button and purges it manually. Pietro's other purges include fainting and vomiting at the meeting for parents of children who have experienced loss, and smoking opium with his brother, which is followed by another bout of vomiting.[18] Coincidentally, the purging of a hard drive is a central metaphor employed by the second team of psychiatric experts that examined Franzoni for the courts. This group of experts, which unlike their predecessors found her non compos mentis, likened the defendant's repression of the memory of murdering of her son to "a computer that erases its own files, but not definitively: it puts them in the trash, where, with the proper commands, it is possible to retrieve them."[19] The novel's resemblance to the Cogne event ends there: the dispute concerning Franzoni's ability to recall the events of the morning of January 30, 2002, will never be settled. Pietro, on the other hand, by the novel's conclusion, has ripened to the point of broaching and, it is presumed, eventually accepting his loss and grief and challenging the notion of expunging or eradicating his grief. I return to this point below.

Claudia's fifth-grade teacher starts the school year by encouraging her students to see the relation between palindromes and the mathematical concept of reversibility. Pietro worries that the process will lead her to contemplate the irreversibility of her mother's death. However, it is Claudia who encourages her father to reverse the effects of his fugue state and abandon his vigil. The decision, as she tells him at the novel's conclusion, "is reversible: you can hardly stay out there forever, can you?"[20] The novel closes on a fantasy enactment of reversibility, sketching a broad imaginary network of recipients of phone calls from Pietro, who is interested in settling accounts. Veronesi's earlier novel *La forza del passato* (*The Force of the Past: A Novel*) focused on the past exerting constant pressure on the present. *Caos calmo* takes up an analogous theme. Pietro's long series of fantasized telephone calls turns the tables on history, reversing its flow. When he reaches Lara in the final phone call, it marks his farewell to her, the source of his grief, and the end of the novel. Taking its cue from the oxymoron offered in its title, *Caos calmo* ultimately reaches back to the future.

Pietro's reaction to Lara's death is, in fact, unusual, and Claudia becomes the screen onto which grief may be projected, measured, and evaluated. While driving her to the first day of school, he notes that "Claudia seems to follow my lead: distracted, stunned, but still far from the true pain of it. We've always been together in this maelstrom . . . and we've even done the most ordinary of things. . . . And each time I think will be the last. . . . But each time, to my great surprise, we emerge unscathed."[21]

Months pass. When Pietro and Claudia return to Roccamare for an unseasonably warm Halloween, the dreaded confrontation with grief's abyss does not occur. Even Carlo is surprised by the duo's equanimity. To the question of how Claudia has reacted to being back in the place where she witnessed her mother's unexpected death, Pietro responds that she is "really well. As if nothing happened."[22] As Pietro tells Carlo when he visits Milan, Claudia maintains the most fragile of balances. She will seem normal, he cautions, telling his brother that "her reaction is a mystery and I haven't dared to take it on."[23] Carlo, however, finds Claudia's behavior transparent, telling his brother that she "is only imitating you. She sees that you don't suffer and so she doesn't either."[24] Marta, Lara's sister, is less philosophical in her assessment of Pietro and Claudia's behavior. She says sarcastically, "Lara dies and you two aren't sad: that's great."[25]

Pietro oscillates between repressing and postponing grief. In the first instance, he believes that he can mechanically wipe the slate clean and, with it, either eradicate or substantially delay mourning, as he does when purging the computer's hard drive. Despite claiming the contrary to Marta, Pietro does fear the emergence of an unknown Lara in the belongings she has left behind. An epic e-mail message from Gianni Orzan to Lara reveals a friendship he was altogether unaware of. This is the sort of mediated "friendship" that Pietro's industry in some ways enables, but it also reveals an unknown aspect to his now dead partner: what else might he not have known about her? Forging a link to the Cogne case, it is worth noting that Stefano Lorenzi has never publicly doubted his wife's version of the events of that January morning in their chalet in Cogne. Lorenzi's understanding of the events is as remote as his son,

Davide's, possible witness of Samuele's murder. Unlike Franzoni's possible recuperation of memory that might answer questions about the circumstances in which her son died, in *Caos calmo,* Pietro makes the bold and irreversible decision to delete all e-mail files on Lara's computer. "I'll destroy that mail, I'll destroy it all, and I won't make the same mistake as before. . . . *It's simple: Edit. Select all. 4332 items selected. Delete.* Zap, deleted, without even going into the trash. Lara's e-mail is no more."[26]

Several aspects of Gianni's e-mail missive are worth noting. First, Veronesi indeed illustrates "the force of the past" exerted on his own prose, since Gianni Orzan is the protagonist of *La forza del passato.* Further, Orzan, the author of the children's book *Le Avventure di Pizzano Pizza,* is adult and long-winded in his e-mail, contrasting to both the style and tone of his publications in the children's book market. This logorrhea of the disembodied e-mail communications provides sharp contrasts to public economy of words in Pietro's first-person narrative. Cast routinely as the listener in *Caos calmo,* Pietro is himself taciturn. He may be a media executive with expert understanding of communications networks, but his own interpersonal communications skills are rarely put to the test. Pietro's contributions to dialogue are scarce, contrasting greatly with the crowded, almost suffocating, interior monologue that makes up the rest of the novel, foreshadowed by the near-drowning episode with which it opens.

Purging Lara's hard drive is the closest Pietro comes to deleting the experience of her death. Although Marta, along with everyone else, waits for Pietro to lose his mind to grief, this is a banalization Veronesi withholds. It is not clear that Pietro searches for release in drugs or sex, though it is clear he does not find it there. Even though it is he who is named "Peter" and not his brother; it is Carlo who embraces the Neverland ethos of refusal. This motif is made clear both by the poster of J. M. Barrie that Carlo hangs on the wall of his bedroom in Rome and by the name of his perennially lucrative clothing line, "Barrie." The opium interlude with Carlo (more Thomas de Quincey than J. M. Barrie) reveals who the "real" Peter Pan is. Pietro himself is aware that he is not repressing grief so much as delaying it, as Peter Pan denies and delays maturity. He sees that "We're not suffering yet, we just took it in this way for now or, rather, we haven't taken it in yet at all."[27]

NETWORKING GRIEF: FROM LOCAL TO GLOBAL

Pietro's vigil in the park is a performance in search of an audience, those witnesses that increase and widen in scope from individuals to classes to groups of people and eventually to nations. A wide range of individuals take note of his actual, physical and embodied presence on the park bench. These include Signor Taramanni, the older Roman widower who lives in the apartment house opposite the park and invites Pietro to lunch; Marta; Matteo, the boy with Down Syndrome who passes Pietro daily on his way to therapy; Jolanda, the dog owner who "does spinning"; and, chief among these, Claudia. Looking at the windows of the school, Pietro realizes he wishes that Claudia would issue some sign of acknowledgment. As he says, "I'd like it if she looked out the window and saw me. I'd like to be aware of it, I mean."[28] Such contact—here the visual recognition of his presence—is a far cry from the sort of distant *esistenza cablata*, or wired existence, that surfaced as a characteristic of the daily life of young adults in the Novi Ligure case. No text message from his daughter will suffice, providing Pietro with another one of those quaint, "old school" moments concerning communication, here between parent and child.[29]

As Pietro's elaboration of grief moves from private performances for individuals to classes observing the mourning spectacle, the grief grows less personal, less particular, and more anonymous. After the wave of Claudia's classmates and their parents, a constant stream of coworkers arrives at Pietro's bench. They have clearly come to share grief, but their own, not Pietro's. His coworkers, he says, "have come here to dump their pain on me, blindly, relentlessly, in front of this school."[30] But the self-pity of others helps Pietro understand that "I must protect myself. I must defend myself if I don't want to find myself, while I am still able to avoid my own pain, plunging into other people's at night. . . . It's important to remember that *I am not them*.[31] Of these visits, Piquet's and Enoch's figure most prominently.

Piquet underscores Pietro's qualities of confessor and explicitly addresses the performance of grief and loss when he broaches the topic of the "*teatralizzazione del rifiuto*," the theatricalization of denial, his son's diagnosis. Piquet responds to Pietro's priestly demeanor and tells him "You're the only one I trust" as he launches into a full confession.[32] Piquet has left his wife and child for the youthful Francesca, whom he adores. His devotion notwithstanding, he is troubled by Francesa's bizarre double-speak that she either cannot identify or refuses to acknowledge. On numerous occasions, Francesca has spontaneously loosed obscenities that, when Piquet asks her about them, she flatly denies having pronounced. The parallel structure of what Piquet believes she has said and what she states she has said relates to the way the expectation of a public display of grief runs parallel to the inability, or refusal, to satisfy the expectation, so central to the novel and to the Cogne filicide trial.

More significant than the notion of a parallel reality is the reaction of Saverio, Piquet's son, following his father's departure, which the boy perceives as abandonment. Piquet's presence appears to block others in their verbal expression: Francesca lapses into coprolalia, Saverio stutters severely, and Piquet leaves little to no room for Pietro's response. Saverio's theatricalization or performance of denial is the somatic response to the loss of his father and provides an obvious counterpoint to Claudia, whose own loss, by comparison, is certainly more profound and irremediable.[33] Yet, the girl nonetheless soldiers on as if nothing has happened.[34] Like her father, Claudia eschews any public outpouring of grief.

Enoch's several visits to Pietro move the discourse about loss and the anxiety of grief to the corporate level.[35] At work, Pietro's story has become inextricably linked to that of the merger. As Pietro himself remarks, "They talk more about me than about the merger over there and anyway the two topics are considered closely tied."[36] As with the arrival of grief and the accompanying pain, the novel also waits with anxiety for the *fusione* (merger) to take place. Pietro and his closest colleague, Jean-Claude, had always opposed the merger with the slogan, "No merger! This is what happened. This was our pact."[37] Enoch's grand treatise on the merger, a tremendous statement on management and labor, moves grief from corporate to global and, ultimately, theological levels.

But in its methodical development from personal to global, the novel's interconnected issues of loss, grief, and merging are played out by another class of people in another arena that I explore here briefly before returning to the allegory of the corporate merger. During his visit, Carlo tells Pietro that he has become "very popular since you plunked down here. Judging from the way they peppered me with questions I'd say that this town's haute bourgeoisie is passionately following your case."[38] In Carlo's opiatic estimation, the merger extends to include everything, and therefore also links Pietro's corporate fate with that of Eleonora Simoncini, the wealthy Swiss heiress he saved on a beach in Tuscany as Lara lay dying.

Even the (in)famous sodomy scene with Eleonora at Roccamare offers, in its own way, a meditation on merging.[39] As preface to the climactic scene that brings the novel's second section to a crashing, symphonic halt, Pietro tells the story of Lara and Marta's lawyer who, in order to settle the estate of their dead mother, "needed to sodomize them both, first one and then the other."[40] An equal opportunity offender, the attorney requests the same of Pietro when he makes efforts on the sisters' behalf. The memory of what ensued gives rise to Pietro's contemplations of sodomy as a pact of solidarity. As Pietro recalls, the lawyer explains that "for historical and indisputable reasons sodomy was the sole instrument to ensure a solid and enduring relationship, and went into the building of that *ineradicable unicum* that he called the 'symbiotic association.'"[41] In Eleonora's experience of near-death and salvation followed by the summary exile of the husband who would have let her drown, Pietro sees reflections of his own turmoil. He recognizes that "what happened two months ago awakened in you as in me something repressed and unconfessable."[42] But Pietro's merging with this unknown, and judging from her reception to his advances, unexplored, point of entry to Eleonora's body produces no symbiosis. Their greater familiarity, however, does serve to connect Pietro's private and individual tragedy to loss that is both corporate and global in nature.

Together with Enoch, Eleonora ushers the theme of merger and grief to a global, then theological, level. In the sodomy scene, the emphasis given to the coupling of "ineradicable" and "unicum" anticipates the other traumatic grief addressed in the novel. The Nazi genocide of Jews during the Holocaust parallels Pietro's loss on a global level and in a historical frame. Isaac Steiner, the Canadian Jew who is the North American CEO of Pietro's agency, seeks just reparations for European

Jews who had been stripped of their wealth and material goods during the Holocaust. As Steiner says to Pietro, for "rich Jews there was a double Holocaust, because it laid waste both people *and* material goods."[43]

Steiner seeks closure through the justice system, entering into legal negotiations with representatives of various Swiss banking institutions that have withheld funds for decades from the dormant accounts of Jews who perished in the Holocaust. He felt "invincible, because I was working for the dead."[44] Although Steiner had hoped his business association with Eleonora Simoncini's father would provide valuable leverage with the Swiss, he learns the bitter lesson of justice unfulfilled and grief unrelieved. He fails to secure reparations, and when his American colleague succeeds, the "Canadian with a conscience" experiences it as the bitterest defeat of his life, far worse than any failed business deal or merger gone awry. The world Jewish federation for which he worked, sensing his mortification, assured him that his efforts would never come to light. Like Pietro's absent mourning for Lara, in the way that Claudia goes forward into each day "as if nothing had happened," the federation maintained strict silence about his failure, making it appear as though Steiner's unsuccessful negotiation had "never taken place."[45] There will be no theatricalization of grief for Steiner, nor for those defrauded Jews on whose behalf he worked.

Steiner's efforts to secure reparations on a global scale tally with the "annihilation" Pietro's coworkers fear will accompany the Grande Fusione in Avvicinamento (the Great Merger Drawing Nigh). Significantly, during this time of merger, as at the time of the Shoah, Jewish material wealth will be appropriated, as Steiner predicted. Enoch's theory of the merger links explicitly to the religious backgrounds of Steiner and Boesson, the European bureau chief. Indeed, his solution hinges on the greatest fusion of all, that manifest in the Christian holy trinity, which furnishes Enoch with a metaphor for the possible solution of corporate management and the division of power.

Both titans of industry hew to national and religious provenance, Steiner the Canadian to Judaism, albeit in attenuated and secular form, and Boesson the Frenchman to firm, almost ascetic, Catholicism. Steiner's model for the merger mirrors Judaic law, which Enoch finds "hierarchical and immutable."[46] Boesson's model, on the other hand, corresponds to the "elastic and complex" model of Catholicism.[47] As Enoch explains it, Judaism's weakness is its radically patriarchal nature, displayed in the sort of vertical genealogy found in Genesis. In his view, Judaism is "rigid, heavy, completely absent of the kinds of contingencies brought to light by Christianity which is, not accidentally, a more recent, modern religion."[48] Once the elderly, womanizing Steiner expires and is succeeded by his son—"Il Figlio," or The Son, as Enoch stresses—Boesson will easily seize power once more and the flexible, adaptable Trinity will triumph, perhaps even with Pietro as the holy spirit. When he rehearses the hypothesis for Boesson, without attributing it to Enoch, Pietro is hailed as a genius. Assuming the mantle of director of the Milan office, he would constitute the third divinity described as "neutral, abstract, powerless, that stays at bay, without influence but nevertheless necessary, to stabilize the relationship between the other two."[49]

Grief, in *Caos calmo*, is like the new Peugeot parked on the street near Pietro's park bench: an accident waiting to happen. At first, Marta, while parking her own car, smashes in the Peugeot's side panel. Although the damage is not of his doing, Pietro, nevertheless, feels compelled to take responsibility and leaves his contact information on the windshield. In the days that follow, Pietro's business card begins slowly to disintegrate in the rain as, curiously, the battered Peugeot remains unclaimed. When moving day arrives for Signor Taramanni, who had invited Pietro to lunch, the van, left briefly driverless, crashes into the Peugeot, demolishing it. In the ensuing hubbub, Pietro retrieves his business card from the windshield: he has been liberated from any responsibility of damage.[50] With Radiohead, whose music returns as a refrain throughout the novel, Pietro remarks silently that "we are accidents waiting to happen."[51] As with the Peugeot, there may seem no need for a reckoning. But, like Isaac Steiner who carries his failure to "repair"—that is, secure reparations—alongside his grief, Pietro knows better.

The claim that the media can present the consumer with "lessons of grief" by offering a space for their theatricalization or performance is something it appears that Annamaria Franzoni neither mastered nor understood. Neither she nor her defense team, including the media-savvy criminal defense attorney, Carlo Taormina, were able to counter the mediatic representation of her inadequate hysterical grief over the wrongful death of her child. Franzoni's later attempts to harness the energies of the media were, by her own account, too little and too late.[52]

As I indicated in the introduction, probing the cultural expressions of the concerns raised by the homicide cases in *Murder Made in Italy* is not a matter of equivalency. Written and published principally during the Cogne Affair, *Caos calmo* makes the problem of inadequate public mourning thematic. For Veronesi, grief requires theatricalization, by which I mean the embodied and shared expression that constitutes theatrical representation. Such embodiment is distinct from its mediatic counterpart, which is disembodied, remote, and, not to put too fine a point on it, mediated. Pietro's bodily presence in the park registers with his daily "spectators," not least of whom his daughter. This somatic registration contrasts with the hierarchy of grief as it extends into the corporate and global arena. If the Weltschmerz (lit. "world hurt") of something like the unicum of the Holocaust cannot be adequately salved, as Steiner's parallel story illustrates, what difference does the personal loss make? In an age of transnational media, personal loss, Veronesi clarifies, is never simply personal. The fact that Pietro does not seek to enact or work through his grief in a public way is immaterial: his spectators will do that for him. From personal traumatic loss, a network of grief radiates outward, extending to encompass various classes. Reaching from family to friends to colleagues in Milan and then Paris and Canada, grief is never properly personal, nor, as Steiner's case shows, properly acknowledged. The setting of *Caos calmo,* the nervous merger of a media multinational, dramatizes the networked aspect of the spectacular display of grief and its elaboration.

EIGHT

Unspeakable Crimes

Children as Witnesses, Victims, and Perpetrators

SEVERAL YEARS AFTER THE events of the day her son died, Franzoni wrote her memoir for publication. *La Verità* (The truth) was released in November 2006 and went into a fourth printing by the end of the month. Given its brisk sales, one is tempted to quip that Franzoni "made a killing" with her version of the events of January 30, 2002, the day her son, Samuele, was found murdered in their house. In her book, Franzoni responded to public opinion about her, her family, and her role in the crime with choice words for the role the media played in shaping the public's reception of her.

Three days after the homicide, she writes of her elder son, Davide, who blamed himself—and her—for his younger brother's death. He says to her, "I told you I could get to the bus by myself . . . if you had stayed with Samuele nothing would have happened."[1] By all accounts from neighbors, friends, and relatives, Franzoni had good relationships with her sons. Thus, when she heard a news service several months later in which commentators pointed to Davide as the possible murderer, she grew understandably protective of him.[2] Refuting any participation on Davide's part, accidental or otherwise, opens a third possibility. Davide was not the perpetrator, but he may have witnessed the events or have some other knowledge of what occurred.

Franzoni maintains that on the day that Samuele was murdered, her morning routine had been atypical, including dressing Davide for school in the upstairs kitchen. She wrote that when she was just about to leave the house, she realized that Samuele was awake. Looking at Davide as he waited on the stairs, Franzoni wrote, "I make a sign for him to stay quiet."[3] An indication that her son should remain silent is chilling. What was Davide meant to stay quiet about? Franzoni—who has always maintained her innocence—clearly means to indicate that, since Samuele was still alive when she left the house, she wants Davide to stay quiet so as not to rouse and upset his younger brother. If, however, one does not believe in Franzoni's sequencing of the events on the morning of January 30, 2002—and three levels of the Italian justice system have found it untenable—then the wish for Davide to remain silent suggests something different.

Gianrico Carofiglio's 2002 novel, *Testimone inconsapevole* (*Involuntary Witness*), tells the story of a Senegalese immigrant in Bari accused of the murder of a child in one of the beachfront communities in the largest town in the region of Puglia. Even though Carofiglio's focus in the novel is the racial tension leading to the false accusation of Abdou Thiam, the novel yields a memorable image representing the intersection of children and crime.

The body of 9-year-old Francesco "Ciccio" Rubino is found in a well, where it has been stowed after his murder by strangulation. The scenario of a child languishing in a well recalls the tragic situation of Alfredino Rampi in June 1981, described in chapter 5, where it served to mark the end of the RAI's monopoly on television and passage into the age of "Neotelevision." Two decades later, Ciccio cannot garner the same attention. Despite the "umbilical cord" that cell-phone technology has created for parents and children, the texts examined in this chapter suggest that rather than technology creating potentially more secure circumstances, children are—perhaps more than ever—at risk.[4] Ciccio is, in effect, killed twice by Carofiglio's novel, first by a never-identified assailant, second by narrative neglect. This is explained by the author's greater interest in courtroom drama and the malicious prosecution of Thiam than in the child's death.[5]

The cultural representations I explore concern childhood witness of crime as both victim and perpetrator. In some ways, these narratives redress the silencing of children at the scene of the crime. At other times, they reinforce it. In the Cogne case, these articulations resonate with silence, not only of Samuele—though his silence endures—but also of his brother Davide, a potential witness.

At a methodological level, reading these texts closely helps ground the concerns regarding murder, children, and violence. Throughout, *Murder Made in Italy* offers close readings in order to punctuate and shore up the theoretical assertions. Offering close readings of literary texts in chapter 5 acknowledges and valorizes the methodological imperative of joining text and context, the specific to the general, the micro example to the macro concern.

Threading this chapter are references to concepts of the abject, a topic that has also appeared at several other junctures in *Murder Made in Italy*. The narrative of Samuele's murder in chapter 6 takes note of the many witnesses describing the abject state of the crime scene. Further, in the telling March 2002 interview at Turin's Le Vallette prison, as well as in subsequent re-narrations, Franzoni's description of what she found upon entering her bedroom is remarkable for how it conjoins different aspects of the abject. Before she could discern the extent of her son's wounds, she touched his scalp, her hand coming away with gray matter. Franzoni recounted how, when she realized what it was, she tried to "return" her son's brain tissue to him, a detail in Franzoni's account that struck psychiatric evaluators and law enforcement officials as unusual. This viscera, effluvia, blood, and revulsion that take part in the dynamic of the abject—all documented in chapter 3, particularly, in their representation in Italian horror/slasher cinema—is something we note in the narratives retelling childhood, adolescence, crime, and its witness.

The imperiled state of childhood, the myriad ways children are exposed to violence, and violent behavior among children did not begin—or end—with the Cogne event. For that reason, I explore narrative representations that precede the Cogne affair, are coeval with its various phases, and succeed it, in the interest of the thickest description possible, to use Clifford Geertz's designation, of the phenomenon of the childhood witness and practice of crime in contemporary Italy.

THE ABJECT STATE OF CHILDHOOD: SUSANNA TAMARO'S *PER VOCE SOLA* AND THE IMITATION OF VIOLENCE

The stories in Susanna Tamaro's 1991 collection *Per voce sola* (*For Solo Voice*) sketch the arc of a lifetime. My interest lies in two of the stories—the first and the third—which, together, illustrate childhood and adolescence. These stories are "Di nuovo lunedì" ("Monday Again") and "Un'infanzia" ("A Childhood").[6] Each story characterizes childhood as an imperiled state for which no claims of innocence can be made. As Giovanni, the narrator of the third story, "Un'infanzia," observes, "nowadays, six-year-olds know everything already."[7] Set deliberately in vague urban centers of industrialized countries, the stories portray the ritualization of pain in the portrayal of childhood throughout Tamaro's oeuvre.[8] Yet, these stories also reveal the danger of imitative violence and the incremental transition from victim to perpetrator that results from the witness and experience of violence and abuse, whether within the household or family or outside it.[9]

In addition to the issue of violence, another element linking Tamaro's collection to concerns raised by the Cogne event is the way the collection represents contemporary childlessness. Italy's birthrate, a cause of concern for demographers, has been declining at least since the late 1980s. Chapter 6 explored the ways in which the murder of a child rang the "moral panic" alarm of the welfare state. Italy's ability to pay for social welfare programs in forty years requires an increase in the natality rate so as to countermand the annual number of deaths.[10] Anticipating the now much publicized, and feared, zero birthrate in contemporary Italy, Tamaro's first story delineates the reproductive challenges many Italian couples face, which began to receive some attention from demographers in the 1990s. For example, Jeff and his wife felt great joy at the possibility of adopting Dorrie, for "from the moment it was determined we could not have children we wished for nothing else."[11]

The first story in Tamaro's collection, "Di nuovo lunedì," emphasizes the split between competing fictions and realities concerning childhood. From between these fissures emerges the story of the nameless narrator, her husband, Jeff, and their adoptive daughter, Dorrie, related in the form of the narrator's diary entries. The narrator does not identify the domestic violence she witnesses and experiences. Her diary entries composing the story are remarkable for the way violence is disclosed to the reader and, simultaneously, denied by the narrator. When the collection's first story shifts abruptly at the end to close on Dorrie's brief narrative—the story she has been trying to write for homework—it reveals a damaged and wary child.

As the editor of a newly launched series of children's books, the narrator insists that it reflect her vision, however distorted, of a happy, carefree childhood state. Although a colleague "says that now's the time to break out the horrifying tales . . . monsters, giants foaming at the mouth, terrible, flesh-eating stepfathers," the narrator hopes instead to make young readers "dream" and undertakes writing the first book herself.[12] The difference in opinion as to what might best serve young readers indicates other splitting and doubling techniques at work in this story, manifest, for example, in Dorrie's life split into two parallel versions. The story opens with belated recognition of Dorrie's "second birthday," not her actual date of birth, but the day she was placed with her adoptive parents. Discovered in a trash bin, Dorrie's story reminds Jeff of the fairy tales his wife publishes. He suggests that she stand in as protagonist of the narrator's story. She agrees, noting that Dorrie's "story really does have a happy ending. (It's) a real fable."[13]

If the narrator is the unreliable character whose diary is not to be believed, Dorrie is, following Joseph Conrad, her "secret sharer," the inconvenient witness to the violence at home. Jeff's hostility victimizes first mother and then daughter, a reenactment of the "cycle of violence" characteristic of child abuse. But the cycle continues. Dorrie plays the role of the narrator in miniature, and has a miniature of herself, her doll, whose arms she has pointedly ripped off. Throughout the story, the narrator distracts herself by knitting a sweater for the little girl, a literal attempt to stitch together her rips and tears. When the narrator asks Dorrie to try it on, she "repeatedly presented th(e arms) she had ripped off her doll. So I said that, if she liked, after I had finished her sweater, I could make an identical one for her doll. She held out her little hands and let me drape the sweater on her."[14]

The doll is a miniature Dorrie and undergoes the same violence as the little girl. At the same time, Dorrie is a younger version of the narrator and, underscoring the reenactment of violence, what Dorrie has witnessed she has now begun to repeat. It is likelier that Dorrie is seeking a way to represent her own wounds, but the mimetic aspect of the violence cannot be ignored.

Like the narrator's colleagues, Dorrie prefers bleak fairy tales and "will, as always, want to hear Bluebeard or Tom Thumb."[15] The story of

Bluebeard hinges on the difference between perception and appearance. Is Bluebeard a proper aristocrat whose wives have mysteriously disappeared? Or is he an assassin responsible for the grotesque array of the wives' cadavers that his new bride sees when she penetrates the locked room? The veiled diary entries reveal the narrator as the obedient wife who, if Tamaro's story follows the trajectory of the Bluebeard fable, will soon suffer more than the beatings Jeff gives her. But Dorrie seeks to be on the other side of the locked door and beyond "penetration." When she asks the narrator to lock the bedroom door on her way out, her mother refuses, saying that the only locked door is the front door to the house.

But the Tom Thumb reference is no less important than Bluebeard, particularly for the way it resonates with childlessness and adoption. Whatever the story's provenance, Tom Thumb recounts the escapades of a minute child conjured to console the loneliness of an old and childless couple, like Isaac for Abraham and Sarah and not unlike Pinocchio for Geppetto, although the latter's single status produces different consequences. Like Tom Thumb, Dorrie is a foundling for the childless narrator.

Kristeva's notion of the abject finds acute expression in Tamaro's story. Abandoned at birth on the rubbish heap, Dorrie is like the rhetorical figure of a synecdoche, pointing to an abject state of which she is part.[16] Dorrie recalls the other disposable girls, victims of random violence, that Eraldo Baldini's *Bambine* identified, described in chapter 5. Other disposable little girls appear in the texts examined in this chapter.

When asked for a conference with Dorrie's teacher, the narrator knows what topics of discussion will be broached: "the little girl is thin, inattentive, and seems worn out. It's not the first time. I told this teacher what I had told the others: about how we don't know who her parents are, about her first hours in the world among the refuse, in the worst conditions possible."[17] The abject returns forcefully at the story's end in the most appropriate of settings—the bathroom—and with the most appropriate of characters, her mother, for it is "mother's" task to instruct children on the proper and hygienic protocol for the disposal of that which must be expelled, abjected, and cleared away.

Although Dorrie works up the courage to ask Jeff for permission to take dance class, it appears as though Jeff prefers to give the girl lessons himself. As she passes the bathroom, the narrator sees the pair "dancing." She sees that Jeff "had raised her up in his strong arms, making her pirouette in the air (and) when she fell, he gathered her up again and threw her high once more."[18] After Jeff leaves for work, the narrator discovers Dorrie in the tub, a place of peril that recurs in *Per voce sola's* subsequent stories.

What was found in the trash has returned to the place where civilized society abjects its waste, separates the impure from the pure, and enjoys architectural guarantee of the opportunity to wash away the trace. Deciding to let Dorrie stay home from school, her mother tries once more to see if the sweater fits. Significantly, the narrator is sizing the sleeves, as though this could erase Dorrie's armless doll. Even though the girl "couldn't get up . . . she wanted me to dress her in her dance outfit."[19] At this point, "she wet herself, like when she was little. Then she vomited up her breakfast on the lace collar."[20] The multiple markers of the abject—the bathroom as the repository for waste, the urine, the vomit—all return in the stories that follow in Tamaro's collection.

"Un'infanzia," the third story in *Per voce sola*, forms clear links to the two previous stories, carrying forward themes such as the avian motif (particularly of eggs and chicks), the power of incantation, abject markers of blood and vomit, the bathroom as a lethal or dangerous place, a cycle of violence that is ineluctable, and unwanted pregnancy. Told in the form of fifteen transcribed interviews between Giovanni and a mental health care worker, "Un'infanzia" tells of Giovanni's descent into serial sexual violence. From the setting—a psychiatric institute—the reader waits only for the unraveling of the plot to explain what criminal act he has committed that resulted in his incarceration.

The intertext between "Un'infanzia" and the preceding stories is clear. Dorrie's difficulty in writing a school composition about "my Dad" easily compares to Giovanni's humiliation when he takes up the same topic. Recalling his first sexual assault of a classmate subsequent to that episode at school and the beating from his mother that followed, Giovanni comments on his own illegitimacy and the thought that his mother may have wanted to abort the pregnancy. But, as the transcript of this conversation reads, "by then it was too late. I was already big inside her, she couldn't get rid of me anymore," suggesting that possibly this is the pregnancy that Vesna, the Rom protagonist of the second story that I do not examine here, brought to term.[21] "Un'infanzia" traces chronologically episodes from Giovanni's life, beginning with his early childhood spent alone with his single mother, the arrival of his stepfather, his time in boarding school, and events of escalating violence that end with serial killing, cannibalism, and his detention in, it is likely, an institute for the criminally insane where the conversations take place.

The transcribed interviews of this story are the generic counterpart to the narrator's diary entries in "Di nuovo lunedì." Both narrators tell their first-person narratives in segments noting temporal progression. In both stories, a cycle of violence and misery is invoked, either with reference to the Monday "syndrome" or, in "Un'infanzia," the change of the seasons. Giovanni sees himself as the rotten, putrid thing "sotto," or underneath, from which new birth will arise. When his younger brother arrives, it is hardly surprising that he is given the name "Benvenuto," or welcome, for welcomed he is into the legitimacy of marriage, heteronormativity, and society.

The putrescence lurking beneath recalls some of the cinematic representations of the abject explored in chapter 3. In "Un'infanzia," what pulsates beneath is not water, blood, or other human effluvia but, rather, rage in a stratum of dangerous, seething magma seeking release. This geological image derives from young Giovanni's fascination with stones. In the fifth interview, he tells of being six and taken by his mother's companion for a Sunday drive to the beach. As the "uncle" skips stones across the surface of the water, he invites Giovanni to do the same, and tells him that he will soon marry Giovanni's mother. Once home, Giovanni takes to his bed and begins to cry for what he says is the first time in his life. No skimming the surfaces for him; the young geologist is already aware that "underneath the earth's hard surface is a molten heart of fire. Everything is shut up down there, compressed, but if something bursts ... the molten heart rises and rises until it even gets into the faucets and one day comes out instead of water and kills everyone."[22]

Giovanni believes that life is a result of chance, good and bad, and not of inherent qualities, one of the reasons he distinguishes himself

from his absent father. More than innate evil, Giovanni's violent behavior is engrained by lessons learned, ironically, in the very place intended to reform him. When they are not busy molesting the captive
boys themselves, the priests and other wardens at the reform school
where Giovanni is sent try to prevent the boys from congregating, because they feared "*simpatia*" would lead straight to "*quella cosa*" (that
thing: sodomy).[23] Such interdiction notwithstanding, same-sex encounters are, as Giovanni notes, always available either at night or in the
toilets. Although he understands the transgression for which he has been
sent away, Giovanni had no knowledge of "*quella cosa*" before arriving
at the reformatory.[24] But it does not take long for him to see what role it
plays. As he remarks, "they did it to me in those first months and then I
started doing it to others."[25]

In addition to lessons learned within the setting of a disciplinary
institution, the violence Giovanni mimics also has display in the animal
kingdom and, of course, within those volcanic geological paradigms that
have so beguiled him. Before being sent to the reformatory, Giovanni
asks for, and is given, a pair of budgies. He is certain that their love will
produce offspring, which he awaits with excitement. The chicks arrive,
but they do not last long. Returning one day from school, he finds the
bottom of the birdcage littered with their tiny corpses, each with its
breast ripped open. Giovanni is stunned and does not understand how
the birds could have been killed: they did not know how to fly and they
are far from the nest. Despite the tender ministrations that Giovanni
had witnessed and recorded, the adult budgies appear unaffected by
the death of their chicks, disproving the boy's theorems about loving
reproduction. Parents do, in fact, kill their young.

The tiny organs espied through the chicks' breast feathers link to the
image of the "molten heart" seething beneath, which returns in great
goriness at the story's close. When he runs away from the reformatory
and returns to his mother's house, Giovanni, now a teenager, finds his
infant brother, but not the love he had imagined "spreading," like an oil
stain, to engulf him. His mother and stepfather behave as though he does
not exist, and the domestic arrangement quickly deteriorates.

After attempting to murder his stepfather, Giovanni wanders
through the city for several days on a murder spree during which he

rapes and murders children whom he lures from school playgrounds. The last of his victims affords him the chance to reenact the death of the budgie chicks. With a knife, he slashes open his victim's tender torso. From within he takes his young victim's heart, and then he eats it, a gesture that, finally, gives him peace.[26]

SIMONA VINCI'S *DEI BAMBINI NON SI SA NIENTE*: "RISE UP SWEET WOMAN CHILD"

Dei bambini non si sa niente (*A Game We Play*), Simona Vinci's first novel (1997), negotiates a series of inside-outside binaries, transactions that convey the alternations between a recognition of the law and its transgression, of the allowable and the impossible, of the knowable and the inscrutable.[27] Interestingly, these exchanges do not materialize along gender lines, with some attributes associated with either males or females for the purposes of contrast. Vinci instead establishes a composite, heterogeneous—and heteronormative, a point I return to—group entity within which these issues are negotiated. The notion of group identity among young adults was discussed in part 2 in relation to the Novi Ligure murders, and in Vinci's novel, that notion shifts downward in age. *Dei bambini* is particularly useful for the way it inches up to the various boundaries mentioned, until, when the limit is finally breached, it is an act that seems horribly inevitable.[28]

While Tamaro's stories, published earlier in the decade, gave expression to one facet of the abject, concentrating on what is expelled and consigned to the place of disposal, Vinci's novel illustrates other aspects of Kristeva's concept. Employing Mary Douglas's important 1966 anthropological explorations of the opposition of the clean to the impure, Kristeva examines the collapse of the distinction between self and other, finding that the "abject has only one quality of the object— that of being opposed to *I*."[29] Signs of the nonexistence abound, and we are constantly reminded of the frailty of being when confronted with the manifestation of nonbeing. As Kristeva observes, "loathing an item of food, a piece or filth, waste, or dung. . . . Food loathing is perhaps the most archaic form of abjection."[30] Other examples of the abject include sewage, vomit, a wound with pus or blood, menstruation, excrement, and the soulless corpse. Human reaction to these signs tends toward the physical and includes retching, nausea, gagging, spasms, and general repugnance.

Chief in Kristeva's elaborations of the abject is the dual and contradictory function of the skin, which both contains that which it protects and keeps at bay that which it defends against. This contiguity marks constant peril. Chapters 2 and 3 examined the motif of the slashing or shredding of protective skin in various contemporary Italian cultural expressions of serial murder. What Vinci's novel demonstrates is not only how fragile is any protective casing (skin, hymen, colon), but also, given the contiguity just described, how threats to its integrity are imminent. The contradictory relation of the skin is hinted at in the incoherence of the lyric "Rise up sweet *woman child*" (my italics). This lyric, from a Skunk Anansie song played on Mirko's boom box one afternoon in the *capannone,* or shack, in *Dei bambini*—which I use as the heading for this section—blurs the distinction between adult and child, who in the song become rhythmically fused.

The collapse of the distinction between child and adult lies at the heart of Vinci's novel, complicating issues of responsibility, criminal or otherwise. Like the skin, which only partially protects what lies beneath it from external threats, the fluid and unstable figure of the woman-child reveals the partial and very incomplete protection that contemporary childhood affords. It is no accident that *Dei bambini non si sa niente* culminates with a rupture that, in its violence and location, clearly recalls the process of abjection and its relation to horror. Nor is the choice of the ultimate victim, the "woman-child" Greta, a casual one.

Dei bambini non si sa niente tells a horrific coming-of-age story in suburban Emilia-Romagna, where a group of five adolescents ranging in age from ten to fifteen begins on a path toward sexual exploration that culminates in the violent death of one member.[31] Told as a lengthy flashback, this brief novel illustrates the problem of children's witness of violence, its consequences, and the way it is absorbed and comprehended. Vinci's interest lies in the group as a whole rather than any single member, something the narrative achieves with shifting perspectives, as well as the absence of direct discourse. Some of the indirect discourse is easily attributable to specific characters, just as the point of view is sometimes clearly identifiable, but Vinci focuses firmly on the group of three males and two females who come together in the *capannone,* located in the abandoned farmland not far from their suburban apartment complex near Granarolo, some 10 kilometers outside of Bologna. Although Vinci's children are not yet old enough to travel the Via Emilia—which, as Lucarelli remarks in his fiction as detailed in chapter 2, merges locales in the greater Bologna area—they, nevertheless, encounter some of the same urban threats.

Greta and Martina are the group's two preadolescent female members and, like the third, Matteo, are ten years old. Luca is fourteen, Mirko fifteen. Mirko is the novel's protagonist in the classic sense of principally advancing the plot. He selects potential members and invites them to join the group, decides that the group will meet in the *capannone,* or the shed, instructs the others to stock the hangout with their favorite possessions, and supplies the print pornography that inspires the members to explore their bodies and sexuality by reenacting the scenarios suggested by the magazines' pictorials. Mirko is the character solicited by two older men to take photographs of group members engaged in sexually explicit activity. It is Mirko who surpasses all limits of previous activities when, at the novel's horrible climax, he anally rapes Greta with the handle of a tennis racket, rupturing her bowel and, consequently, killing her. As if Greta's cadaver did not suffice as marker of the abject, then the disposal of her body, covered in the excrement and blood that has seeped out of it, makes the reference clear: with "the *ass* of the car" facing the door of the *capannone,* Mirko tosses Greta's body and all incriminating evidence of her murder in the trunk, "as if they were the same thing: *garbage,* broken things, (stuff) to be thrown out."[32]

Dei bambini non si sa niente tracks the group members' gradual absorption of print pornography and, in so doing, illustrates a gradual awakening of both sexuality and violence. When Barilli criticizes Vinci, saying that psychoanalytic theory "has provided us with adequate instructions, informing us that it (childhood) is most certainly not the realm of innocence" he appears unable to reach beyond a Freudian conception of infantile sexuality, as Vinci does, to study *both* the effect of sexuality explored in a group setting *and* an understanding of it that acknowledges gendered difference.[33]

The children's witness of violence and its consequences does not suggest that the process is purely imitative, though imitation is a key component in the novel. Rather, Vinci complicates this process by demonstrating how the children's curiosity is piqued by the photographs they study.[34] The passage of print pornography to Mirko from other, older men recalls the circulation of pornographic materials and photographs among the guardoni, the voyeurs in the Florentine hinterland who played a minor role in the investigation of the "Monster's" crimes, as detailed in chapter 1.

Vinci's group are all quite willing to study the pornography. The issue is not one of consent; given that the age required to provide legal consent in Italy is 14 and all the main characters save one are therefore ineligible by definition, the issue is moot.[35] Rather, Vinci's interest is accountability: however gruesome the outcome, Vinci does not demonize the children for their sexual curiosity, nor does she strip them of their limited responsibility for the consequences.

Photography, from which realist print pornography is composed, is a purely visual and still medium. Focus on the ways violence affects children is, therefore, necessarily limited to the violence these children witness as mediated by still photography. In other words, the discussion is not about the effects of violence transmitted via film, television, or other electronic forms wherein movement of the image is paramount, which has been a chief focus in parts 1 and 2. Distinguishing between a "real" death and a fictional one, the narrator observes that children are frightened of all cadavers save the simulated ones of television and film, who are "actors who pretend to be dead, or maybe they're really dead, but they are only *images that pass quickly on a flat screen*."[36] Focus is not on any type of physical violence children may suffer or witness directly, as either victims of domestic abuse or its witnesses, nor does it extend to encompass violent conditions produced by war to which children are subject.

Matteo may have brought the group "the world," figuratively, in the form of his prized possession, an illuminated globe, but it is Mirko who brings the underworld of the traffic in children, pederasty, pedophilia, and violence into the *capannone*. The group's acceptance of, and interest in, the magazines Mirko supplies is gradual. Some, like Greta, will be victimized by the exposure, others—perhaps, like Greta, victims, too—will be galvanized into violent behavior. Just as Greta dies only after many summer afternoons spent in exploration, so, too, does the interest in the pornographic pictorials increase by degree.

Like the development of the group's sexual curiosity, interest in the magazines is also gradual. What at first appears as the glamour of fantasy only afterward reveals itself frighteningly real. In the first maga- zine Mirko shows them, the men's and women's bodies are displayed in a glossy photo spread. The magazine appears to be of some quality: the paper is substantial stock, it is printed in costly large format, and the photographs were shot and reproduced in color—all factors that indi- cate a certain financial backing. In terms of the content, the reception of the magazine is filtered through Martina's consciousness. She finds the photographed subjects simultaneously beautiful and repulsive. The sexual encounter that follows, the first in the group atmosphere, features Mirko masturbating behind Martina, with both gazing at the magazine's titillating centerfold.[37] When print pornography next appears several chapters later, its standards and contents have changed. To convince Martina to allow him to penetrate her for the first time, Mirko shows her a magazine ragged from use whose cover shows an Asian woman sur- rounded by three men with the caption "'Gang bang,' in big red letters."[38] Nothing about the model's Asianness is remarkable to the children: as with other "body genres," the pornographic image—whether visualized in print, cinematic, or electronic form—observes no linguistic, national, ethnic, or cultural distinctions.[39] The body trumps all other categories of identity.

With an uptick in narrative pace, the magazines appear again one chapter later (chapter 12), by which time they have already been banal- ized by repetitive consumption, indicated by use of the imperfect nar- rative tense. The group members "acted out by turns the games in the magazine" and "they always looked at different magazines and tried out the positions."[40]

These glossy, costly magazines give way to amateurish rags for which the disappearance of certain standards (e.g., paper stock or color photog- raphy) indicates an absence of professional engagement—art directors, photographers, publishers. Eventually, Mirko brings to the *capannone* clandestine magazines treating subjects of increasingly transgressive violence. One afternoon, he appears with a bundle of magazines, that when tossed on the bed "made a sharp and violent sound, like the crack of a whip," hinting at the violence to come.[41] These new arrivals are different from those they have become inured to. One magazine in particular draws their attention. The diminished quality of the photography, the unsubstantial stock, and the poor lighting sign the gateway to a realm of increasingly taboo subjects. From where she sits at the foot of the bed, Greta cannot see the photos. This is significant, given the fact that for her more than the others the consumption of pornographic photography will have the greatest effect.

These grainy and poor photos show adult subjects in s/m poses. Another magazine from the bundle appears at first to contrast these disquieting images. Its lovely photos depict young children playing on a beach, like so many wood nymphs in a pastoral setting. But following the attraction to the formal beauty of the portraits and the seaside idyll, the group's attention is drawn to several photographs toward the back of the magazine showing young children engaged in practices as brutalizing as those documented in the other magazines. As in the other clandestine rags, the photography is poor and the lighting casts shadows that seem to threaten the human subjects. Significantly, even though no adults are visible, "you felt their presence, they were there, like animals lying in wait, with their claws already planted in the flesh of their victims."[42]

Merging Greta with the photographed subject of underground pornography corresponds to another significant episode wherein photography foreshadows her death. Before the summer afternoons in the *capannone*, the children in the elementary school pose for their annual end-of-year portrait. The fifth-grade class photo shows Greta's uneasy presence in the group. Just as the photographer releases the camera's shutter, Greta bends over and the final product shows a girl who "*sembra sul punto di schizzare via dalla foto, in una torsione violenta e repressa, fermata dalla pellicola*" (appears on the verge of shooting out of the frame, in a violent, sharp twist, cut short by the film).[43] The camera cuts short Greta's violent and contained (or sharp) twist, the verb *fermare* denoting a host of possibilities, including to arrest, to fix (as in a color), to halt, to stop, to hold. Notwithstanding the subtle differences in the definitions, the verb underscores a fierce (*violenta*) desire for movement that is truncated. Greta's death at Mirko's hands can be interpreted as the truncation of her short life, but it may also be seen as ambivalence or a symbol of hesitancy that corresponds to the novel's pulsations between the opposing issues of acceptability and transgression.

In the environment of the *capannone,* immobility and silence have been taken as the continued consensus previously assumed though never explicitly stated. Greta has never openly agreed to any of the corporeal explorations—none of the children has. It is understandable that her earlier tacit acquiescence continues, particularly in the absence of any indication to the contrary. Like her choice "(to) leap out of the photo" only after the decisive click of the shutter has sounded, Greta's kinetic response to her attack arrives too late to serve as deterrent. The episode culminating in Greta's rape operates on a continuum, beginning some afternoons earlier with the insertion of a small object into her anus, to which she submits. The handle of a pink Hello Kitty toothbrush is, quite simply, child's play, and Greta laughs, saying it reminds her of the doctor taking her temperature when she was little. Such levity makes the assumption of Greta's consent, and the group's understanding of it, plausible.

The atmosphere of compliance and silence continues over the course of many afternoons in which "that miniscule and strange area had become the center of some experiments."[44] In this way, Mirko brings the s/m magazine *Japanese Fist* to the *capannone* and begins to reenact one of the pictorials only after the group's consent, which is always implied, has been attained. Greta's pain is obvious even from the start of what eventually turns into a rape (that is, the absence of consent, already problematized by the juridical impossibility of that consent). This notwithstanding, she "continued to cry but in a submissive way, hardly audible . . . and she didn't say anything."[45] The choice of the conjunction "and" rather than the disjunction "but" that might have been expected is significant for the way it underscores the continuity of the group perception of Greta's consent. Her own colon by now ruptured, she breaks the silence of the group only after Mirko has exercised an uncharacteristic violence that surprises everyone. "It only took a motion from Greta who tried to raise herself and rip the tape from her mouth with her hand" for the group's paralysis to disintegrate.[46]

The collective has far greater importance than the individual in *Dei bambini non si sa niente* and contributes to that part of Kristeva's conception of the abject in its erosion of the sovereign social subject. In the way of the Novi Ligure case, explored in part 2, in which the court-appointed psychiatric experts determined that the two teens committed the murders only when emboldened through their identity as a couple, Vinci's novel demonstrates the strength—and peril—of group identification. Some members, like Martina, find solace in a group environment where "you can hide, you can be quiet, like you were alone, and no one could ever tell."[47] To maintain the order and privilege of the group identity, Mirko, their undisputed leader, forbids the formation of couples. When together as a group,

> the relationships were definite and at the same time fluid . . . what made things less clear was that precise moment when they were naked in front of each other, they became the same. Their bodies looked alike, girls and boys were different, sure, but only because of that one detail. They all had the same flat chest and smooth, small hips. They had the same smooth, taut skin, without wrinkles or hairs.[48]

Yet, the sameness of their naked bodies does not always obtain, which is illustrated by the game, a sort of Blind Man's Bluff. The children touch and lick each other, trying to guess the identity of the unknown other. The only one to sit out the game is the older, more hirsute Mirko, whose secondary sex characteristics have made him too recognizable in the game of blind groping.

The children do, however, discover their one irreducibly similar anatomical characteristic. The anal cavity common to them all irrespective of sex serves to homogenize the group, and the children explore their common space long before the tragic escalation that leads to Greta's death. "The boys had allowed the girls to put their fingers inside of those places and they had learned that they were more or less all the same there. All differences were erased in that tiny place."[49]

Anal eroticism never appears in the form of sodomy between the boys and is not a predictor of homosexual attraction: regardless of the supposed equality of, and fluidity between, their bodies, it is, nevertheless, a heteronormative context in which women are shared in a group context in which male-on-male sex is absent.

Group identity remains a fluid process throughout the novel, outside the confines of the *capannone*. Martina observes that, for her teacher, the idea "of coupling or twinning was fixed, all she did was repeat it, a kind of obsession."[50] The twinning or compilation of the three youngest members of the group—Martina, Greta, and Matteo—is the most successful of fusions, leaving Mirko and Luca relatively autonomous actors. This could be why Mirko is the agent of violence, with Luca's tennis racquet—the prized possession he has bought to the *capannone*—his weapon of choice. While Martina and Greta are both students in the same fifth-grade class, Matteo is in the "twin" fifth-grade classroom across the hallway. For the ways in which their coming together and growing apart illustrates the fluidity of the group plural identity, the different groupings—Greta and Martina, Matteo and Martina—warrant differentiated examination.

Vinci frequently brings Martina and Greta together so that she can alternate between them in the narrative, much in the way that the boys substitute Greta for and with Martina in a classic reenactment of what Gayle Rubin has called "the traffic in women."[51] When they frequently hold hands, for example, the girls are literally linked. More figuratively, they both lose their virginity within days of each other, events significantly staged within the same brief chapter. Martina loans Greta a book about identical twins, and Greta's inability to finish it (unlike Martina, she is not an advanced reader for her age) illustrates Vinci's aim not to equate the two girls so much as rotate between them.

On the day Mirko takes Martina's virginity, the girl looks beyond the circle of boys reconstituting the "Gang Bang" pictorial and exchanges a look with Greta. But the identification and empathy Martina feels for Greta does not translate into any action of solidarity that could save the other girl. Gazing at the abject scene of Greta's death, Martina tries to comfort the other girl in a long soliloquy in which she describes a bucolic, nocturnal locale where "maybe we could go by ourselves some time."[52] It is only after the long monologue that the reader and Martina mark simultaneously her silence, for she has in fact said nothing of the calm she intended to transmit to Greta in extremis, if not already dead.

As Martina observes of herself, "she seemed to be speaking and instead she wasn't saying anything."[53]

The incongruity of knowing sexual desire expressed in not yet sexually mature bodies is something the three younger members share, and the text links Matteo to both girls in various scenes. Vinci repeatedly reminds the reader of Matteo's sexual immaturity, perhaps most pointedly in the scene where Martina fellates him and then asks why he does not ejaculate like Mirko. Significantly, Matteo understands the fluid and interchangeable identities of individual group members and that any of the others, except Mirko, could have met Greta's end. During the attack he wonders "why Greta was the center of attention. She was a cavity and she seemed to accept it. No one really knew why it was her and not Martina, Luca or Matteo. It just happened that way."[54] Matteo's salvation from a fate similar to Greta's owes, then, to serendipity. Shifting back to the Cogne case momentarily, if Samuele's death was the result of an accident of any kind, whether instigated by Annamaria Franzoni or not, then Davide's delivery from his brother's fate is similarly serendipitous.

Reading, as I noted above, links Martina to Greta and appears at a bedtime scene that links Martina and Matteo. As Erika De Nardo's bedside reading of Verga illustrates, young readers do not always distinguish themselves by their abilities to digest what they read. Yet, in *Dei bambini,* Martina falls asleep reading *Pippi Longstocking,* an ironic contrast to her own non-childhood. Matteo is folded into a version of this bedtime fairy tale when he climbs into bed with his pajamas decorated with little boats. The interchangeability of Matteo and Martina is further underscored by the fact that at first he alone was allowed to ride behind Mirko. Martina will literally substitute Matteo before too much time passes.

The most significant link between Matteo and Martina, however, is their uncanny recognition of the sensation of sexual pleasure that preexists any of the summer afternoon explorations. The innocuous games of all the children living in the apartment complex display the children's recognition of the conventional limits of acceptable sexual curiosity. But the awareness of infantile sexuality has already long since come alive. Martina immediately accepts Mirko's invitation to join the group, while Greta displays some reluctance. Martina's silent acceptance as compared to Greta's more reluctant complaining foreshadows the tremendous, mute monologue toward the novel's conclusion detailed above.

Martina's sense of readiness, or openness, to what may come is something that has in fact already taken place in a dream. When shown print pornography for the first time in the *capannone,* Martina sees that while the women's expressions in the photographs were something "she had never seen"; nevertheless, she feels "a familiar twinge between her thighs, a shiver she had already been feeling for some time."[55]

On the back of Mirko's scooter as she approaches the *capannone* for the first time, Martina remembers a dream in which she and Mirko race through her school's hallways at night pursued by some unknown presence. She sees "a window up high with a strange light coming through it."[56] When Mirko hoists her up, she "looked outside and outside was an inside."[57] On her way home from that first afternoon, Martina's thoughts about the afternoon's activities in the *capannone* link directly to this strange window in her dream. The *capannone* marks the beginning of "this different thing that was them together (that) came to exist with *no one looking in.*"[58]

In addition to sketching the ambiguous limits of inside and out-side—which recalls the binary oppositions I discussed at the beginning of this section, as well as the abject with relation to the Cogne case—the dream also expresses the desire for common activity with Mirko, as seen in the way they run together pursued by an unidentified "someone." The recounting of the dream flows seamlessly into other thoughts Martina has as she rides the scooter, like Greta and memories of her own pleasure. These thoughts are not juxtaposed so much as linked sequentially so that Martina may alternate between them with little effort, like the alternating modus operandi of the narrative. An organic connection of the elements nevertheless results for the reader, who reconciles the differences.

Mirko serves as the firm reminder of Martina's earliest feelings of sexual pleasure. For example, appearing once more in the same paragraph, Martina recalls Mirko's hand resting on her shoulder as he masturbates in the scene already detailed. The first time Martina takes Mirko's penis in her hand, she notices that "it was something unknown and familiar at the same time. As if it were a thing she knew, had known, but who knows why had forgotten about."[59] Almost immediately, Martina recalls her nursery school. Like the *capannone,* this is another space wherein a jumble of bodies comes together. She remarks on the "*tanti corpi stesi e respiri calmi*" (many reclining bodies and calm breathing) of the children as they lie in their cots napping.[60] Martina lies in this comforting albeit distinct group with her hand on her "*posto segreto*" (secret spot).[61] One of the teachers becomes aware that Martina is masturbating and orders her to stop. This screen memory connects directly to the dream Martina later recalls en route to the *capannone* for the first time.[62] The shadow that the teacher throws is associated with social control blocking her path toward orgasm. The shadow is also the unidentifiable presence chasing Martina and Mirko in her dream.

The uncanny sensation Martina feels is repeatedly captured by the use of the pluperfect tense (that which has already occurred by the time of its later narration, in grammatical terms), and links her sexual awareness to Matteo's. When Matteo first regards and then touches the genitalia of one of the two girls, unnamed and, therefore, identical, "he too had thought that it was strange and that it resembled something he knew."[63]

The narrative's fuller fusion of Martina and Matteo manifests also in their response to Greta's death. Each child vomits, a classic response to the abject also seen earlier in this chapter in Tamaro's stories, and, significantly, at either end of the flashback that constitutes the narrative. Before the reader can know the reason for Matteo's disquiet at the start of the novel, the boy experiences an almost existential alienation from his everyday life. So as not to invite his mother's inquisitiveness, Matteo goes to the bathroom and vomits into the toilet, the proper place for the improper, which is to say, out of place, abject thing. His vomit is a literalization of Matteo's guilt and fear of reprisal: he is afraid of what might spill out of him should his mother inquire.

Martina's response to the abject circumstances of Greta's death comes almost immediately. Having dumped Greta's corpse into the trunk of the car like so much garbage, and with Matteo and Luca riding the scooter back to the apartment house, Martina leans over and vomits on herself. Absent a proper receptacle for waste, Martina is unable to rid herself of the vomit; it stays visibly on her knee, a double indicator of her own abject state. From the experience of witnessing the chief indicator of the abject, a soulless cadaver, the subject herself engages in abjection (explusion). When no one was "looking in" to the *capannone,* as in Martina's dream, the distinction between what was inside and what was outside (e.g., the in/outside of Greta's body, of a game, of consent, of the law, of their neighborhood) was blurred to the point of dilemma.

Adjacent to refuse and located outside of protected boundaries, the *capannone* is the logical place for the reenactment of the abject. The two electronic sensors at the gate of the children's Granarolo apartment complex demonstrate an effort to protect and control entrance and exit into the community. They are useless against threats outside their boundaries and illustrate how centrally located the source of a threat can be: within its very confines. A place like the *capannone,* notwithstanding its position beyond the pale, enacts its own laws. Certain hierarchies inhere at the *capannone,* "a place apart, with its own laws."[64] Like the cesspool in Dario Argento's 1985 *Phenomena* or the culvert in his *Sindrome di Stendhal,* the *capannone* is not only the location for this abjection, the ejection of the inanimate, of excreta, of the soul, it sits adjacent to a dumping spot of the region's unwanted refuse. Given the progression of violence that ends in Greta's death from a ruptured colon, the proximity to such refuse is significant, for it reveals the *capannone,* with its appointments from the trash heap, as the place of the abject. But the situation of the *capannone* is also paramount to the group's actions for two chief reasons: it is beyond the pale of the law and it is simultaneously the place where the group identity is constituted and enabled.

Like Martina's self-reflexive indication of her own abject state, Greta's inert body is too abject even for the *capannone.* Much as she had hoped, Martina does indeed escort Greta to a private and bucolic locale, only not during the girl's lifetime. The group buries Greta in a shallow grave far from either the *capannone* or the palazzo. To reach the grave, one must go "straight for five minutes in the fields, then still straight, following the ditch, among the herbs, the yellow and purple flowers, the insects. Inside the ditch with the frogs, keep going straight, until the end. With the corn tall above that barely moves in the breeze. A few more weeks, maybe a few more days, and they'll cut it all down."[65] These words recur in Vinci's novel like a mantra, very close to its beginning and again at its conclusion. Measured and regular, the refrain nevertheless accelerates toward the novel's end, as the reader realizes that this is the place the group inters Greta and, with her, their childhood. As the Skunk Anansie lyric had forecast, childhood has been truncated, collapsed abruptly into adulthood.

IN THE NAME OF THE FATHER: FATHERS, SONS, AND VIOLENCE IN NICCOLÒ AMMANITI

The cadence of the mantra closing Simona Vinci's novel suggests liturgical intonation. Mourning and similar biblical overtones of a paradise lost will surface in Ammaniti's novel *Io non ho paura* and receive guaranteed visual recognition in Salvatores's film adaptation. To visually ensure that the notion of an exile from Eden obtains, Salvatores, with Italo Petriccione, who won the David di Donatello for best cinematography, repeatedly shoot idyllic fields of grain, the peaceful home to any number of small animals and insects (grasshoppers, rabbits) that serve as stand-ins for the children. As in *Dei bambini non si sa niente,* where these fields might survive, Salvatores, too, visualizes a certain loss of innocence when the threshers and combines appear on the hills of grain, like horsemen of the apocalypse ready to begin the harvest and destroy the homeland of the small and as yet defenseless animals. This sense of postdiluvian loss, I argue, finds tremendous resonance in the reportage covering the murder of Samuele Lorenzi in the valley known as Il Gran paradiso, the great paradise.

The transmission of violence from parent to child—specifically from father to son—underpins much of the prose narrative of Niccolò Ammaniti, whose short fiction I explored in part 2. My chief focus in this section is on Ammaniti's best-selling novels, whose popularity (and cultural diffusion) have been further enhanced by their film adaptations, and for which Ammaniti has also received a considerable amount of acclaim.[66] *Io non ho paura* (*I'm Not Scared*), for example, won the 2001 Premio Viareggio; and in 2006, Ammaniti won the Premio Strega for *Come Dio comanda* (*As God Commands*).

Yet, despite such accolades—or perhaps because of them—his work has invited relatively little critical exploration. A project such as *Murder Made in Italy* finds valuable "parchments," as Michel Foucault would call them, in varied places and genres, including best-selling novels such as Sandro Veronesi's *Caos calmo,* detailed in the preceding chapter, and Ammaniti's.[67] Much of Ammaniti's work explores violence as it intertwines with and affects the lives of young protagonists, nearly all of them adolescent or preteen males. This section traces how these young men are indoctrinated into violence, a theme that becomes increasingly explicit with each successive Ammaniti novel. The violent acts of adult men (often but not only fathers) inure the young male narrators to the violence they witness. Indoctrination into violent behavior relates to the concern about imitative violence, explored in part 2 in relation to the Novi Ligure case, but also to the Cogne case in terms of Davide Lorenzi's putative witness—visual or auditory—of the violent attack of his brother in January 2002.

In Ammaniti's novels, violence begins with its passive, almost incidental, acceptance in *Ti prendo e ti porto via* (*Steal You Away*, 1999), and transforms, in *Io non ho paura* (2001), to open resistance to the witness of adult violence.[68] Although the adults in these two novels do not aim to habituate a younger generation to violent behavior, this cannot be said of *Come Dio comanda*, which tells the story of the explicit transmission of violent values from father to son. The progression I have been describing is clarified by a capsule review of the novels' titles. The juvenile first person of *Ti prendo e ti porto via* and *Io non ho paura*, for example, is replaced by an omnipotent third person in Ammaniti's most recent novel, and not just any instantiation of God, but the God of the Old Testament, Moses's law-giver, dictator of the commandments.

Ti prendo e ti porto via presents the parallel stories of two pairs of characters: middle-schoolers Pietro Moroni and Gloria Celani and their adult counterparts, Graziano Biglia and Flora Palmieri, a teacher in the children's school. Their fates converge in the provincial Tuscan town of Ischiano Scalo. Pietro is the younger son of a brutish, uneducated shepherd and a clinically depressed, overmedicated mother. He usually manages to evade the local bullies, often by seeking out his best friend, Gloria, the only child of the well-to-do director of the local bank. One autumn night, he is drawn by the town hooligans, largely against his will, into vandalizing the middle school. Although all the boys are suspended, only Pietro is made to repeat the school year, nominally because neither of his parents attends the mandatory conference, but chiefly because the school staff interprets Pietro's passivity as immaturity.

Pietro's passive acceptance seems to invite taunting. As Pierini, one of the bullies observes, it almost does not matter what form the ridicule takes. Reprising the way Greta's silence is construed as consent for the violence against her in Simona Vinci's *Dei bambini non si sa niente,* precisely because of Pietro's mute acceptance of what the bullies dole out, Pierini feels that Pietro "made him want to do weird things. Violent things."[69] In fact, it is the sight of Pierini and his mates giving Pietro a beating that allows the story to draw Graziano and Pietro into proximity.

Pietro and Graziano occupy opposite ends of an inclination toward flight. In his early middle age, Graziano wants to stop globe-trotting and bed-hopping and return to Ischiano Scalo to start a family with Erica, the stunning go-go dancer he meets while working as a deejay in a Ravenna nightclub. When their stormy relationship ends abruptly and Graziano returns to his native Ischiano Scalo, he takes up with Flora, whom he quickly abandons once Erica unpredictably reenters his life. The couple leaves for Jamaica. He and Erica part ways, she for Hollywood, he for his provincial hometown, where he hopes to reunite with Flora. His first stop upon return is Flora's house, and, at first, Graziano thinks the ambulance he sees must be for the invalid mother she has cared for all her adult life, but it is Flora's body that is being removed by the orderlies. Pietro will confess to killing her.

Agitated by the news that he has failed school and holding Flora responsible, Pietro allows Gloria to convince him to break into the teacher's house and stage a practical joke. He finds her in the bathtub, unhinged by pregnancy and Graziano's sudden departure several months earlier. With her mother lying dead in another room, Flora informs him of the real reason he has been held back. The administration had no other choice but to pass Pierini, who was too great a troublemaker to be held back. Pietro, on the other hand, has been deemed immature and childish. She underscores his passivity, saying, "You don't react. You're shy. . . . You've got no backbone. They failed you because you let others make you do things you don't want to do."[70] It only takes a moment, Pietro thinks, "one damn moment that can change your life," and, at last the architect of his own actions, he steps on the electrical cord that pulls the tape deck down into the bathtub.[71]

The current that kills Flora also electrifies Pietro in some way, galvanizing him into action. Remorseful for what he has done, he nevertheless finds the independence previously unavailable to him. He attacks Ronca, one of the local bullies, when taunted about his failure at school. Pinning him to the ground, Pietro "let loose a torrent of punches to his face, his neck, his shoulders, muttering strange, hoarse words. If Pierini hadn't been there . . . who knows what he would have done to him."[72] In the aftermath of the fight, Pierini tells Pietro that their teacher has died. As if pummeling Ronca insufficiently demonstrated his newfound autonomy, Pietro "looked him in the eye. And he said it. 'I know. I was the one who killed her.'"[73]

Although Flora's death appears unintentional, Pietro, nevertheless, considers himself a murderer. As the novel's conclusion shows, Pietro recognizes his underlying desire to commit an act of delinquency so grave that authorities will be forced to remove the threat he poses to society, something that would also liberate him from his family. If Flora had not been the victim of a chain of events he set in motion (he knowingly steps on the electrical cord that consequently tips the tape recorder into her bath), then, Pietro reasons, someone else would have fallen victim to an act he would have committed to ensure his removal from society. As the novel's conclusion—a letter to Gloria dated six years later—reveals, Pietro was aware that punishable violence provided the only way out of his violent home and bleak future.

Reform school, where Pietro spends the six years following Flora's death, provides the time and setting for accepting and understanding the consequences of his actions. The narrative flags Pietro's development. The letter to Gloria that concludes the novel is the first appearance (apart from the title) of first-person narration.[74] At first, Pietro writes, he believed he had told Pierini because he wanted to refute Flora's description of his passivity. But with the passage of time, Pietro comes to see that he blurted out the truth as a way to separate radically from his family. With his eighteenth birthday, he notes, "*sarò un uomo*" (I'll be a man).[75] Man enough perhaps to enable Gloria's fantasy of passivity and flight from the path set out for her by her parents. This motivates the inclusion of the postscript that ends the novel and furnishes its title. As an afterthought, Pietro writes: "P.S. Better get ready, because when I come to Bologna I'm going to grab you and carry you off."[76]

Michele Amitrano, the 9-year-old protagonist of *Io non ho paura*, published in 2001, is in some ways Pietro's opposite, although the two novels share some common attributes. What the pair has in common is the juvenile male protagonists' desire to flee their provincial outbacks, in Michele's case Acque traverse in an undisclosed "South" of Italy. The settings of both novels lie far outside an industrialized Italian landscape: Pietro's father is a shepherd and Michele's a truck driver whose long hauls take him far from the remote location of their home.

Yet the texts also differ significantly. Whereas Pietro is relatively passive until Flora's accidental electrocution, Michele displays greater initiative in response to the knowledge that his father and mother, and, with them, the entire adult community of Acque traverse, have orchestrated the kidnapping of Filippo Carducci, the 9-year-old scion of a wealthy family from Pavia. In *Ti prendo e ti porto via*, Pietro silently resents his father and never challenges his poor decisions. Pietro is helpless in the face of his father's dominance and lacks the initiative to find an alternative solution. *Io non ho paura*, on the other hand, tracks the episodes of Michele's repeated resistance to his father, Pino, as he returns time and again to visit Filippo, his secret sharer, the twin he reckons being separated from at birth.[77] As concerns ethical reckoning of the individual's rights and responsibilities, Michele occupies an absolutist position that may owe to his tender age, whereas Pietro has already slipped into moral relativism. Michele's empathy for, and identification with, Filippo finds some correspondence in the empathy Pietro discovers once he has been confined to the reform school, empathy that was conspicuously unavailable to him in the episode in Flora's bathroom.

Gabriele Salvatores's acclaimed 2003 film adaptation of Ammaniti's novel maintains a unity of time not featured in the prose narrative. The film unfolds within a short period in the late summer of 1978, while the novel stages the story from the point of view of an adult Michele looking back on the events from a distance of more than ten years.[78] In addition to changing the text's representation of, and relation to, history, the film's unity locks down Michele's moral certitude.[79]

The presence of the adult Michele in Ammaniti's novel is fleeting. The prose narrative offers no information about him, nor does this adult narrator comment substantively on the past. Ammaniti withholds information concerning the adult narrator's evaluation of the assertion of his autonomy at the age of nine. In his rare and irregular incursions into the recounting of the 1978 events, the adult narrator reveals no retrospective assessment of events that he set in motion. These events are of some moment and include the denunciation of his father, the dissolution of his family, and the imprisonment of half the adults of his small town for being accessories to the crime or accomplices after the fact, none of which would make for simple psychological absorption.

The novel's omission of an evaluation of the events permits Salvatores to exclude the mechanism of an adult narrator from the film's narrative frame. My aim here is not a sustained examination of the film adaptation, nor an extended comparison of the novel and film. Of interest, instead, is the contemplation of what such an omission may mean. In both novel and film, I argue, rather than allegiance to family or social hierarchy, Michele's loyalty goes out to a contemporary, a child of his generation.

Io non ho paura closes on the split between the different generations of father and son, who, despite the affective attachment joining them, are, nevertheless, clearly distinct. Having disobeyed Pino's explicit instructions never to return to Filippo's underground cell, Michele makes a last, mad dash through the southern landscape. Throughout the novel, Ammaniti has privileged landscape as a place of comfort and refuge. The hill the children must climb on their bicycles, for example, is described as a "*panettone*," the sweet bread often associated with Christmas. The surrounding countryside offers refuge to the many small animals that make it their home: porcupines, crickets, bats.[80] Salvatores makes good use of this motif, and when the four threshers appear on the hillside to cut the wheat, they signal the end of the summer. Like the four horseman of the apocalypse, they augur the unrest to come.

Certain that Filippo will die as a result of his actions, Michele flies to his "twin's" aid. The adults of Acque traverse follow. In the confusion that ensues, Pino accidentally shoots Michele. As Pino stands over him, Michele exhorts his father to escape and save himself from the authorities who have descended on Acque traverse in a helicopter whose metallic whir recalls the threshers, their mechanized form, and their power to overcome the naturalized landscape. More concerned with his son's welfare than with his own possible escape, Pino stays by his side. Michele feels his presence and notes that *"ora c'era di nuovo buio. E c'era papà. E c'ero io"* (there was darkness now. And there was my Dad. And there was me).[81] Ammaniti's conspicuous punctuation already divides these three short sentences. Graphically speaking, however, they are actually typeset as three distinct and brief paragraphs, a hallmark of the author's often terse prose style. Thus, instead of joining father and son, for example in a single paragraph, the novel seeks to isolate them, underscoring their difference at the structurally prominent place of the conclusion.

Such an ending allows no narrative intervention from the adult Michele. The novel ends as it begins, in the consciousness of a 9-year-old narrator. Absent a reckoning of the events, this loyalty and the child-like, innocent attachment to it maintain their integrity. Consequently, what emerges from *Io non ho paura* is a nostalgia for the empathic child guided by a sense of moral justice, one who makes the "right" decisions despite the poor modeling of moral choices displayed by the older generation. Often aligned with the small animals seeking refuge, the children in *Io non ho paura* are as naturalized as the landscape. Like Rousseau's noble savages, they make decisions guided by an innate sense of justice. As we have seen, nothing could be further from the sort of childhood aggression and imitative violence present in, for example, Tamaro's and Vinci's work.

First Michele's curiosity about, and then his empathy for, the sequestered boy drives him to visit Filippo's underground cell, which in turn powers the plot. Shortly after his first visit, when he happens on Filippo while exploring with the other children, Michele dreams of Jesus and Lazarus, a theme that will recur in *Come Dio comanda*. In this frightening dream of frustration, Jesus hails Lazarus, but instead of rising and exiting the cave, Lazarus is "all used up, lying on the ground."[82] Jesus consequently approaches the figure and "start(s) to shake him like a doll and Lazzaro finally (gets) up and rip(s) his throat out."[83] The message is clear: offer assistance, but be prepared to pay the price.

Come Dio comanda, published in 2006, tells a story of biblical proportions. The novel recounts six days in the lives of several chief characters, as well as a host of minor players who come into their path. The
characters in this "apocalyptic fable," include Cristiano Zena, who, like
Pietro in *Ti prendo e ti porto via,* is in his last year of middle school.
Cristiano lives in an unfinished house next to an industrial park on an
imprecisely located plain somewhere in Italy's central North with his
father, Rino, a skinhead with inclinations toward Nazism that are milder
than might be anticipated. *Come Dio comanda* widens the narrative
geography of Ammaniti's repertory, reaching outward from his native
Rome, which dominated the early fiction, namely *Fango* and the 1997
novel *Branchie* (Gills). Following the unique instance of a sustained setting outside of Italy that *Branchie* offers in Marco Donati's trip to India,
Ammaniti has reached out, to Tuscany in *Ti prendo e ti porto via,* to a
deep southern pocket of Italy in *Io non ho paura,* and to the northern
plain in *Come Dio comanda.* Such decentered geography that spans
the peninsula corresponds to the observation that Rino "zonked on a
cocktail of beer and grappa, is a Hitler-adoring inadequate who rails
against Jews and African immigrants while watching endless cable TV.
Berlusconi's brave new Italy is populated by just such goons, Ammaniti
seems to be suggesting."[84] But by decentering his narratives, setting them
throughout Italy, Ammaniti also aims at the sort of lack of regionality
that my examination of contemporary crime literature revealed.

Father and son scrape by, with Rino eking out a living as a day
laborer for a construction company. If he loses work to the underpaid
alien immigrants, illegal and otherwise, his response is less virulent
than one might expect from an avowed racist living too far off the grid
for something as politically organized as the Northern League. Rather
than on racial hatred, Rino's attention is more truly directed throughout
the novel toward his friends, Danilo and Quattro Formaggi, and a heist
they hope to pull off at the local bank. Of these three, Rino emerges as
the most able, and, in fact, is the only one of the trio to survive. Danilo,
divorced and alcoholic, is crippled with guilt over the death of his daughter Laura, which happened on his watch, and will die in a drunk-driving
accident before the novel concludes. Quattro Formaggi, who has suffered
serious neurological impairment from accidental electrocution some

time before the action of the novel, is the agent of destruction, his own and others'.

Come Dio comanda takes place under the sign of catastrophe that, once set in motion, cannot be curtailed or contained. Force majeure—or the hand of God—must be allowed to run its course and is symbolized in the novel by the two tremendous storms, at the beginning and climax, as well as the neurological storm gathering in Rino's brain in the form of an aneurysm that will implode, coinciding with the deluge of biblical proportions. Irrespective of the characters' attempts to control fate, a force greater than their own intervenes, curbing their autonomy. External forces also serve to diminish the characters' responsibility for their actions, and the novel charts the ways they navigate these interventions. In an alcoholic haze, Danilo loses control of his car and his life in the torrential rains of the novel's climax. The same night, Quattro Formaggi, misguided by his sizzled synapses, loses his wits and kills Fabiana, the flesh-and-blood recreation of "Ramona," his favorite porn character. Despite his muscled body, Rino the Übermensch, who is compared in the novel to Bruce Willis and Mel Gibson or *"uno che andava in Vietnam"* (a guy who went to Viet Nam) is felled by an aneurysm the night of the climactic downpour.[85] Giuseppe Trecca, the social worker assigned to the Zenas' case, is the only character to move in the direction of actualizing his desires and exerting control over his destiny, illustrated by his rejection of religious superstition and his bold announcement of his intentions toward Ida, the wife of a coworker.

A major snowstorm signs the novel's beginning, which Ammaniti sets apart as a prologue. The nearly 500 pages making up *Come Dio comanda* are arranged in four parts of unequal length: the relatively brief "Prologo" (Prologue); and the more evenly appointed "Prima" (Before), "La notte" (The night), and "Dopo" (After). The prologue sets the bleak mood. Unable to sleep because of a bad headache (the symptom not of drunkenness but of his slumbering aneurysm), Rino sends Cristiano out in a storm to kill the watchdog at the furniture warehouse next door. Not only is Cristiano not unwilling to use the pistol his father gives him, but he is actually already inured to violence of this sort, and his reluctance owes not to some moral repugnance over killing the dog but to his preference for a warm bed. Ammaniti cordons off Cristiano's unwillingness to act on his father's instructions by placing it in the prologue, significantly excluding it from the body of the novel so that it can be seen as a pre-existing condition. Violence, in other words, is a lesson Cristiano has already learned. Executing the guard dog, which he does with one shot to its head, stands as prologue to a series of violent acts and their acceptance: vandalizing Tekken's motorcycle, attacking the young man with a bat and nearly killing him, preparing Fabiana for her shroud, and accepting the thought that his father may have raped and murdered his classmate, the unraveling of which draws the novel to its end.

The three Ammaniti novels I have been discussing show a clear trajectory concerning a child or adolescent's response to moral conundrum. In *Io non ho paura*, Michele's actions steer clearly toward the absolute moral good of restoring Filippo to the family from which he has been unlawfully ripped. Michele's path laid out in the novel is less unerring than that of the film, as already noted, and guarantees the portrayal of Michele's response to Filippo's dilemma as one of automatic solidarity in which he never questions what is morally legitimate. By the end of *Ti prendo e ti porto via*, Pietro arrives at his capacity for wrongdoing.

Come Dio comanda begins where *Ti prendo e ti porto via* leaves off. The prologue—not flashback but rather precursor to the events that will happen in the six days that immediately follow—establishes Cristiano as already lost to the violence that constitutes his world. Despite the anguish he feels when recalling how Peppina, his dog, was killed by a speeding truck, he is largely without empathy. As Trecca tells Cristiano, who is reluctant to attend Fabiana's funeral, "You should know what it means to suffer and to be compassionate. Do you know what compassion is?"[86] The close of *Come Dio comanda* may feature a Cristiano remorseful for his lack of empathy, but it will not cost him his resolute and unconditional defense of his father.

As he sits during the Mass for Fabiana, Cristiano bemoans his own lack of empathy. Cristiano admits that he dragged Fabiana's body "*imbrattato di sangue senza provare nessuna pena . . . senza sentire vergogna . . . senza nessun rimorso*" (drenched in her own blood without feeling any pain . . . without feeling ashamed . . . with no remorse) and is certain that he is a monster that does not deserve to be forgiven.[87] However, Cristiano does have significant empathy for his father, whom he forgives almost fiercely. In a way, one could say that Cristiano's acceptance of his father at the novel's conclusion is in fact very *Christian,* and it is his forgiveness that raises Rino from the dead. The reader assumes that Rino, resurrected in the penultimate paragraph, will untangle the story of Fabiana's murder and tell Cristiano when he next sees him that Quattro Formaggi was responsible for the girl's death. The novel ends not with a father-son reunion and proof that Cristiano was right to have maintained his father's innocence, but with Fabiana's funeral. Applause drowns out Cristiano's defiant shout *"Non è stato mio padre!* " (My father didn't do it!)[88] The last sentence of the novel is *"Ma nessuno lo sentì,"* (But no one heard him), which could just as easily mean "And no one cared."[89]

It would be simple to lay the blame for Cristiano's lack of empathy at the doorstep of his violent, neo-Nazi, skinhead father, but Ammaniti complicates the matter. The neurosurgeon assures Cristiano that Rino's aneurysm was not brought on by any action (viz., bashing in the skull of a 14-year-old girl he had sexually assaulted) but was congenital in nature. Similarly, Cristiano's violence can be seen as an admixture of nature and nurture, something that corresponds to Cristiano's understanding of Rino, which alternates between seeing him as "good" and as "bad." Meditating during the funeral, he recognizes:

> My father was a bad man. He raped and murdered an innocent young girl. He deserves to end up in Hell. And me too because I helped. I don't know why I helped. I swear I don't know. My father was a drunk, violent, good-for-nothing. He beat up everyone. My father taught me how to shoot a gun, my father taught me how to give a beating to a guy whose motorcycle I had vandalized. My father was beside me since the day I was born. My mom abandoned us and he brought me up. My father took me fishing. My father was a Nazi but he was good. He believed in God and didn't take His name in vain. He loved me and he loved Quattro Formaggi and Danilo. My father knew right from wrong. My father did not kill Fabiana. I know he didn't.[90]

Two significant episodes illustrate Rino's sense of having failed Cristiano as a father. The first concerns Cristiano's school essay on the rise of neo-Nazism in 1930s Germany, the second with Rino's failure to teach his son how to fight. Ammaniti principally accomplishes two things with Cristiano's essay. Cristiano is not an accomplished, mature racist;

his essay—Ammaniti offers a draft only, not the final version—could be easily dismissed as lacking in logic, evidence, and, therefore, suasion. However, rather than minimize racialized discourse, the critique is aimed at Cristiano's environment, for the essay is testimony to the education he has received at Rino's hand. Yet when Cristiano shows his father the essay, Rino becomes enraged. The problem is not the content; for Rino, revealing racist beliefs is the problem, not adopting them. Rino is certain that if Cristiano's essay and the racist beliefs it espoused were revealed to school authorities and subsequently to social services, they would establish grounds for the loss of the custody of his son. And "without Cristiano he was nothing."[91]

Revealing anything to the world outside their lair is problematic for Rino. He repeatedly tells Cristiano that he "always keep his guard up" and try not to betray and weakness or vulnerability.[92] Returning home after the beating Tekken gives him, Rino chastises himself. Having a weakness—like being a racist—is not the problem that revealing it is. Rino tells his son in no uncertain terms:

> No one should beat you up. Never again. . . . You're not some faggot who lets himself get beaten up by the first guy who plants himself in front of you. I wish, and you don't know how much, I could help you but I can't. You've got to deal with your own stuff yourself. And that's why there's only one way to be: you've got to get mean. . . . You're too good. You're soft. You're mushy. Where are your balls?[93]

Rino's lessons, and his transmission of a Neanderthal-like masculinity, are clear.

Rino is not the only parent who has abdicated responsibility. Teenagers Fabiana and her sidekick Esmeralda do only as they wish (typically, smoking a lot of marijuana and shoplifting at the mall) with no parental interference, not even from Esmeralda's candid and, evidently, caring mother. Quattro Formaggi's mother deposits her illegitimate son on the threshold of the orphanage. Danilo's daughter, Laura, dies while in his care. Cristiano's mother flees and is nowhere mentioned. Even Trecca, assigned by social services to the Zenas' case, has risible notions of parenting that seem to consist largely in role-playing, and, stating that Rino drinks too much, he suggests that Rino try attending Alcoholics Anonymous, which would send social services a clear message.

Trecca the social worker is situated as Rino's counterpart and a paternal surrogate for Cristiano. Trecca literally takes Rino's place as Cristiano's guardian after "La notte." He wonders, shortly after news of Rino's stroke reaches him, whether he could adopt Cristiano and they could live together in the Zenas' bunker. Trecca clearly reaches toward instruction of the paternal kind when he tries to sway Cristiano to a more compassionate outlook concerning Fabiana.[94] Finally, Ammaniti links Rino to Trecca by way of the Lazarus motif. Rino rising from his coma, as I mentioned earlier, is reminiscent of Filippo's surge from his cave into light and life in *Io non ho paura*. Trecca also turns to the story of Lazarus, albeit haphazardly, searching for biblical corroboration for the too-hasty pledge he has made to renounce Ida.

Returning home from his tryst with Ida, Trecca nearly kills an African immigrant waiting for the bus in the torrential downpour and swears to surrender something important in exchange for the life of a man who, like Lazarus, rises from the dead. This is the symbolic gesture that he had advised for Rino, and while at first the gesture suffices, as the privileged character who undergoes change during the course of the novel, Trecca eventually adopts positions that increase in depth, commitment, and maturity. The novel ends with his homily on compassion, his rejection of a pledge he had made out of superstition, and a reckoning of his actions that will, we are left to assume, result in the breakup of Ida's marriage and the constitution of a new family consisting of him, Ida, and her three children.

Of the children the novel presents, the girls fare worse than their male counterparts. The girls in *Come Dio comanda,* even if relatively scarce in this narrative thick with male presence and preoccupations, seem subject to dangers that do not plague the boys. The death of Laura the toddler offers an example. Ironically, although the car seat was intended for her safety, Laura died because of a defective buckle that prevented Danilo from extricating her in an emergency. All children, whether male or female, run a similar danger. In light of the senseless murder of Fabiana, upon which the novel predicates, Laura's death makes it seem that even the daughters of dutiful parents are endangered. Like Danilo, Fabiana's father at first blames himself for allowing his daughter to have a scooter: had he not succumbed to her insistence, perhaps she would not have been exposed to the dangers, natural and otherwise, of the downpour. Consequently, Fabiana *Ponticelli* might not have ended up under a *bridge,* floating, like the other garbage the storm has brought in its wake.[95]

Characterized by proximity to garbage, Fabiana becomes, like the other children but especially the girls in Tamaro's and Vinci's works explored earlier in this chapter, the colophon indicating the abject. This is made nowhere clearer than in Quattro Formaggi's decision, as God commands, to include Fabiana in his crèche, which is made of ragtag objects reminiscent of the symbolically broken dolls in the work of both Susanna Tamaro (explored earlier in this chapter) and Eraldo Baldini (explored in chapter 2).

Quattro Formaggi lavishes energy on a crèche in his apartment that he allows no one to see and that in many ways constitutes his life's work. The crèche features

> thousands of figurines recovered from dumpsters, found at the dump, or forgotten in parks by children.

> Atop the tallest mountain was the manger with baby Jesus, Mary, Joseph, the ox and the donkey. Sister Margherita had given those to him for Christmas when he was ten. Quattro Formaggi, moving with unantici-pated grace, crossed the crèche without knocking anything down and adjusted the bridge across which advanced a column of blue Trolls with a Pokemon as their captain.[96]

This universe assembled out of detritus is the antithesis to the natural-ized landscape in *Io non ho paura.* No noble savage, Quattro Formaggi makes decisions that appear to be unaided by an innate sense of right and wrong. For Quattro Formaggi, who navigates this trash universe with unusual grace, Fabiana has always been linked with the flotsam of the crèche as well as with the protagonist of his favorite porno film. One night while rooting around in the public park he sees Fabiana. After finding "a King Kong figure without an arm . . . he saw the blonde arrive with a guy on a motorcycle."[97]

In the period of decompensation following Fabiana's murder, believ-ing he has also killed Rino, Quattro Formaggi tries to soothe himself by regarding the crèche, his privileged object and the universe he, not God, has created. The stress of his situation, however, interrupts whatever consolation may be found in the familiar landscape, and "he realize(s) how wrong everything (is)."[98] He believes he must recuperate Fabiana's body "and put her in the crèche. This was why he had killed her. And God would help him."[99] He will surround Fabiana's body with "toy soldiers, shepherds, toy cars. On her small breasts spiders and iguanas and sheep. On her dark nipples little green crocodiles. Among her pussy hairs, dinosaurs and toy soldiers."[100] But Quattro Formaggi cannot add Fabiana to the crèche because Cristiano, believing her death may have been Rino's doing, has removed her, enshrouded her, and set her down in the river where she may be washed out to sea, far from Varano.

His daughter violated and left for garbage, Fabiana's father lashes out at those gathered for her funeral in a spectacle of grief that conforms with public expectation, to capture one of the themes explored in conjunction with the murder of Samuele Lorenzi. Since young girls are seldom raped and murdered in the protected *"profondo nord,"* a theme examined in conjunction with the double homicide in Novi Ligure in part 2, Fabiana's funeral is covered by all the news services. As the family members enter the church, "some people raised their cell phones up high to be able to take pictures or videos," and "they had them sit in the first row next to the mayor, a bunch of important people and policemen in uniform."[101] Fabiana's grieving mother "took her son in her arms as the TV cameras zoomed in for a close-up."[102] Like the unyielding Old Testament God, the very one from which the novel draws its title, Signor Ponticelli calls for vengeance and reprises the Franzoni-Lorenzi defense that "there is a monster hidden among us" who has killed his daughter and who must pay for the crime committed.

Redemption is not available to Cristiano, a name laden with meaning in a book entitled *Come Dio comanda*. The story told by the prologue creates some ambiguity. Readers of Ammaniti's more mid-career fiction might think that the resistance Cristiano shows to his father's plans heralds the return of the morally upstanding Michele of *Io non ho paura* or of Pietro before he sets in motion the chain of events leading to Flora's death in *Ti prendo e ti porto via*. Such resistance, however, as the novel reveals, evaporates in the face of moral relativism and feral loyalty.

The spectacle of Fabiana's funeral that draws *Come Dio comanda* to a thundering close returns us to a key theme that arose from the Cogne affair that followed the killing of Samuele Lorenzi on January 30, 2002—namely, the spectacle of grief and mourning. Children are disposable, these narratives tell us. Childhood is bleak, perilous, and often too short. The image from Carofiglio's novel of the child's corpse languishing in the well recalled the predicament of another child, Alfredino Rampi, whose dilemma is outlined in the beginning to this chapter, as well as in chapter 5. Significant about this was the Italian state television's nonstop coverage of the death of this boy. In terms of constancy, the broadcast coverage of Samuele Lorenzi's tragedy was similar to the RAI blitz of 1981. The proliferation of private channels in Italy since 1981, however, creates a stark distinction in reportage of the events. Alfredino's dilemma was broadcast in real time throughout Italy, establishing homogenous conditions for its reception. The multiplication of privately owned television channels fragmented the coverage of developments in the investigation of Samuele's case. The increase of images—televised, print, via Internet news services—created conditions that were ripe for moral panic. Stories spread of possible "Brutes," to use District Attorney Maria del Savio Bonaudo's sarcastic language, prowling through the bucolic Gran Paradiso. This is the backdrop against which the trial of Annamaria Franzoni—whether in the courtroom, in the court of public opinion, or in the virtual public sphere made possible by advances in telecommunications—took place. As Enzo Tardino observed, the Cogne affair was the first in Italian judicial history in which "the preliminary investigations were followed live in their entirety by the media."[103]

Rumor, the classical poet Vergil wrote in the *Aeneid*, is a monstrous, fabricated bird that has an eye for every feather. Rumors of the Cogne case multiplied, circulated, and affected the investigations. Although Rumor's flight cast a shadow on the Italian polity's perception of the case, it seems not to have clouded the vision of the Italian justice system, which concurred at all three levels, confirming the guilty verdict for Annamaria Franzoni.

Perugia

Umbria

Meredith Kercher was murdered on the
night of November 1st, 2007

MAP 4. Perugia, Umbria, November 2, 2007.

EPILOGUE

Kiss Me Deadly

TRANSNATIONAL MURDER IN PERUGIA: MEDITATIONS
ON THE AMANDA KNOX MURDER TRIAL

There are all sorts of seeming anomalies, in connection with murder
and *** (*sic*), in the human race. People are oftentimes as sick as the
secrets they hold. Amanda Knox may not be the "little girl" that her
mother believes she still is. The face she presented to her mother,
and the face she presented to others, were perhaps quite different.

—MISSINGPLEC1[1]

The parents of Amanda Knox are very certain she was charged
and convicted unfairly. How can they be so sure? I doubt it was
a crime planned out but an event that went the wrong way. I feel
for both Amanda's parents because they are determined to get her
released and yet the evidence was strong enough to convict her.
Every parent with a child going overseas to study or travel should
require their child to read the Knox story. She, by her actions, joking,
comments . . . etc.—some likely taken wrong has really destroyed
so many lives. A sad lesson to learn with huge consequences.

—LIN, SEATTLE[2]

THE MURDER OF MEREDITH KERCHER

On November 2, 2007, the slain body of Meredith Kercher, a 20-year-old Briton studying in Italy, was found in her rented *villetta*, or cottage, in Via della Pergola in Perugia, Italy. The news of the murder of a young foreign woman found in her home with her throat slashed and evidence of sexual assault shocked the Umbrian town, where foreigners abound. With approximately 40,000 foreign students attending annually Perugia's well-known and respected Università per Stranieri, the center of town has become largely populated by non-Italian students renting apartments from Perugians.[3] Perugia's center offers temporary housing to the annual flux of students arriving and departing and contrasts to the more permanent residences at the city's edges and beyond. The difference between the center of Perugia and its edges recalls the blur at the center of the photographic image of Erika De Nardo and Mauro "Omar" Fàvaro, whose encryption was explored in relation to regional identity in part 2. Perugia, with its center leased to non-Italians, generates similar issues concerning identity in contemporary Italy, where tourism, immigration, the study-abroad industry, and other transnational forces produce a flow of people who will leave behind, it is hoped, a trace of capital, not cadavers.[4] The transnational aspect of Kercher's murder was immediately established by the suspects detained several days after the murder: Amanda Knox, 20, a U.S. citizen; Diya "Patrick" Lumumba, 44, originally from the Republic of Congo but a legal resident in Italy; Raffaele Sollecito, 24, who, from Giovinazzo, in Puglia, was the only Italian national implicated. Rudy Hermann Guede, 22, born in the Republic of Côte d'Ivoire but reared in Italy, joined the three suspects several weeks later.

The interrogations of Knox, Lumumba, and Sollecito produced substantially different narratives. At first, Knox stated that she was not in Via della Pergola on the night of November 1. She said she had spent the night with Sollecito, whom she had been dating since they met on October 25, at his apartment. During her interrogation by Perugia police on the night between November 6 and 7, 2007—evidence from which was later thrown out, since Knox had not been given her opportunity for guaranteed legal representation—her story changed. She admitted to being in the *villetta* the night Kercher was killed. From the kitchen, she stated, even with her hands over her ears, she could hear Kercher's screams provoked by her attacker, Lumumba. Although this statement could not be admitted in the criminal case against her, the memorandum Knox wrote while in lock-up on November 6 was another matter. This memorandum chiefly confirmed the earlier statement. And although inadmissible in the criminal case, Knox's November 5 statement was admissible in Lumumba's civil suit against her.[5] This version tallied more closely with testimony provided by a witness, who stated that he had seen both Knox and Sollecito outside the Via della Pergola house at 9:30 PM on the night of the murder.[6] Notwithstanding his vigorous protestations of innocence and denials of any involvement, Lumumba was arrested and jailed for two weeks. After evidence implicated Guede, Lumumba was released November 20, 2007. Sollecito denied any involvement, though trace DNA at the scene undermined the credibility of his claim—until, that is, the credibility of the DNA evidence was itself undermined in the great transatlantic forensic wars that arose during the murder case. Guede, who had left Italy, was picked up by German police on the train outside Mainz, Germany. Believing he was conversing via Skype with a friend while the latter was in the privacy of his home, Guede revealed his whereabouts; the friend, however, was in Perugia's police headquarters at the time of the Skype exchange.[7] German police detained Guede for questioning, ultimately extraditing him to Italy. Upon return to Perugia, Guede substituted Lumumba as the third person needed for the District Attorney's Office theory of the crime.

Perugia's district attorney, Giuliano Mignini—who was also the prosecutor in the trial of the "Monster" of Florence and who subscribed to the *pista perugina* theory in that case—believed that Meredith Kercher died as a result of a sex game run amok.[8] This theory of Kercher's murder proposed that Kercher was killed when she resisted, with Guede restraining her, Sollecito holding a knife to her throat, and Knox responsible for stabbing her in the throat with the murder weapon.[9]

Sollecito and Knox were held in prison, awaiting arraignment. Under Italian law, *custodia tutelare,* or preventive detention, can last up to twelve months, at which point an extension can be sought or charges can be filed. In October 2008, as the regular period for preventive detention elapsed, the GIP, Guidice per le investigazioni preliminari, or the magistrate overseeing the investigative phase of the case, determined that Knox and Sollecito would stand trial for Kercher's murder in the scenario that Mignini advanced as the State's theory of the crime. By the end of October 2008, Guede had already been tried for his role in the crime, having requested and received a fast-track trial. A guilty verdict was delivered, and Guede was sentenced to a 30-year prison term, automatically reduced to 20 in accordance with the sentencing protocols available for defendants choosing fast-track trials. Slightly more than a year later, on December 5, 2009, the court delivered two more guilty verdicts: Sollecito was sentenced to 25 years for his role in the murder, while Amanda Knox received a 26-year sentence. The difference of one year between the two sentences reflects the court's determination that Knox was also guilty of libel when she accused Lumumba of committing the murder. The prosecution had asked for life sentences, for each; consequently, defense attorneys for both Knox and Sollecito believe the sentences demonstrate doubts about the case and the evidence. These doubts constituted the bases for appeal of Knox's and Sollecito's sentences, which began in late 2010 and concluded October 3, 2011, when both Knox and Sollecito were acquitted of the murder of Meridith Kercher.[10]

PERUGIA: GLOBAL CROSSROADS

The murder trial of Amanda Knox picks up on several strands threading arguments in all three parts of this volume. A murder in this calm, small city shocked the Perugians in the way the Florentines, Novesi, and Cogneins responded to the murders that shook their faith in the public safety of their towns. In the weeks and months that followed Kercher's murder, Perugia itself felt under attack. As a headline from *La Repubblica,* dated November 7, 2007, reads: "Perugia is incredulous and in shock. Those killers were among us."[11] The geography of crime revealed by the murders probed in *Murder Made in Italy* reorders perceived notions of criminal violence in Italy. Violence, specifically murder, does not exclusively represent Italy from Rome southward, something contemporary Italian murder mysteries make especially clear.[12] The notion of a pristine landscape that has been despoiled (read: raped) is evident in the

"Monster" murder case in Florence, where the "lovers' lanes" of the bucolic Florentine hinterland became grisly crime scenes. This is the sort of invasion that Dario Argento refigures in *La Sindrome di Stendhal* (1996), where the landscape of central Italy has been raped and plundered by the speculative public works projects associated with the Tangentopoli corruption crisis of the mid-90s. At the same time, as chapter 3 details, Italy's *città d'arte,* or cities of noteworthy artistic patrimony, have been invaded by the golden horde of tourists. Continuing with geographic affinities, it is only incidental that Sollecito is from the town of Giovinazzo in Puglia. In Italian, the suffix *-azzo,* like *-accio,* is pejorative. One could speculate on the ironies that Sollecito, convicted for the Kercher slaying, corresponds to his native Giovinazzo, understood as "nasty" (*-azzo*) young man (*giovin*).[13]

In addition to plotting coordinates in the revised geographical understanding of the location of murder in Italy, the Kercher slaying raised issues concerning the increased presence of immigrants, xenophobia, and the justice system's treatment of immigrants suspected or accused of crimes. The investigation's exchange of one African man, Guede, for another, Lumumba, suggests the heightened vulnerability of black male immigrants in contemporary Italy, where a moral panic has emerged at the intersection of crime and immigration.[14] In this regard, the Lumumba-Guede exchange sharply recalls Erika De Nardo's repeated assertion that "*sono stati loro,*" it was "those other" Albanian immigrants who were responsible for her mother and brother's death in Novi Ligure in 2001. Yet the investigation of Kercher's murder in Perugia, with its facile switch of one black male perpetrator for another, might derive as much—if not more—from the sort of "racial profiling" of "superpredators" in the United States, given that it was Knox who set these mechanisms in motion, whether deliberately or as a result of a memory made hazy by too many drugs and too much alcohol.[15] This is moral panic in Italy with a transnational edge, reenacting some of the classic anxieties about the predictability of criminal dangerousness of black men.[16] As in the double homicide in Novi Ligure and the investigation of the murder of Samuele Lorenzi in Cogne, the raising of the specter of moral panic in the Kercher murder case threw a wrench into the works of the investigation.

Perceived sexual prurience presented itself again in Italian court-rooms as it had during Pietro Pacciani's trial for the crimes ascribed to the "Monster" of Florence. However, the youth of defendants Knox, Sollecito, and Guede and the bewilderment over sexual practices of a younger generation are reminiscent, once again, of the trial of Erika De Nardo. Knox, described as "cool," with "icy eyes," brings to mind repre-sentations in the media, as well as in the justice system, of the other two female murder defendants whose stories are explored here, De Nardo and Annamaria Franzoni. As for Knox, the courtroom affect and demeanor of both De Nardo and Franzoni were repeatedly called into question.[17] Their "coldness" was underscored. When De Nardo stubbornly main-tained the story that her boyfriend, Fàvaro, was the chief architect and protagonist of the murders, the press described her as the stony succubus to a hapless Omar, much in the way that Sollecito's family laid the blame for Raffaele's circumstances on Knox. Franzoni's putative coldness on the day of her son's murder and in subsequent court appearances actually constituted evidence and conditioned her judicial sentence.

The "diabolical couple" in the Perugia murder, Knox and Sollecito, further evokes the situation of De Nardo and Fàvaro. The recording of De Nardo and Fàvaro's banter while inside the barracks of the cara-binieri, in which they teasingly called each other "*assassina*" and "*as-sassino*" (murderers), was matched by reports of Sollecito accompanying Knox on a shopping trip to buy lingerie shortly after Kercher's murder. Both couples came to stand for the perceived inscrutability of a younger generation that appeared increasingly susceptible to the transnational commodification of violence in the form of literature, cinema, and other cultural texts. Moreover, the rumors of the possible role group sex may have had in Kercher's murder bring to mind some of the explorations of group identity represented in texts of the emerging generation of writers in Italy in the 1990s, as chapter 5 illustrates in texts by Niccolò Ammaniti, Marco Risi, Andrea Carraro, and Aldo Nove, among other practitioners in the 1990s. The observations "Missingplec1" offers at the beginning of this epilogue call attention to the possibility of Knox's dif-ferent personae and resonate clearly with the notion of De Nardo's "SMS behavior." Instead of "short messaging system" technology, SMS came to stand for "*Se mamma sapesse*" (should Mom know) and underscored the different faces De Nardo showed to Susy Cassini, the mother she was convicted of murdering. It is hardly surprising that the investigation of Kercher's murder began with the discovery of lost cell phones—Kercher's—in the garden of an apartment not far from the *villetta* that she shared with Knox and other roommates.

At the same time that Perugia attracts students from all corners of the globe to its Università degli Stranieri, it is also a site of global export. Perugia marks the location of the headquarters for Baci Perugina, producers of the internationally exported "Baci," the chocolate drops with the amorous fortune cookie–like messages that resemble Hershey's chocolate kisses. Hershey's product was launched in 1907, and the 1921 development of machine wrapping antedated by one year Baci Perugina's launch of the *bacio*.[18] Visits to Hershey, Pennsylvania, or to Perugia can occasion similar quips: You went to Hershey, how were the kisses? or *Come sono i baci a Perugia?* The title of this epilogue, "Kiss Me Deadly," refers to the kisses, of course, and to Perugia, the location of Meredith Kercher's murder. It hints, too, at the prosecutor's theory of the murder as a possible sex game gone off its rails. Beyond this, the title "Kiss Me Deadly" also recalls Mickey Spillane's homonymous pulp novel from 1952 and its film adaptation three years later.

A vehicle for Spillane's gumshoe detective, Mike Hammer, *Kiss Me Deadly* harks back to the noir-pulp-slasher hybrid *filone* of Italy's Young Cannibal movement in the 1990s.[19] The film explicitly recalls screenwriter and director Quentin Tarantino's 1994 film, *Pulp Fiction*, which, in turn, influenced in myriad ways a number of the Young Cannibals, as chapter 5 detailed.[20] Alternately maligned and embraced by differing generations of critics, the young Italian prose writers of the 1990s embraced and participated in a global market of violence believed to more accurately depict contemporary life both within Italy and outside the country. The trial of Knox for Kercher's murder should be seen against the backdrop of these cultural tensions and contexts. Moreover, "Foxy Knoxy," or "*faccia d'angelo*"—angel face—embodies the part of the femme fatale, an essential component of noir fiction.[21]

I have never called for the equivalency of crimes to their representations in various texts, whether literary, cinematic, or televised. With the objective of offering a "thicker description," to use Clifford Geertz's significant and powerful portrayal of the aims of cultural anthropology, this study has explored three acclaimed murder cases in contemporary Italy in their specific contexts.[22] My interest in the Kercher murder and the Knox trial is as an epilogue to three notorious murder cases "made in Italy." I am interested in distinguishing between the media landscape of the Knox case as it compares to the investigations and trials of Pietro Pacciani, Erika De Nardo and Omar Fàvaro, and Annamaria Franzoni. It is clear that information about the Knox case—and its cultural signification—was facilitated by "viral" distribution mechanisms that are made possible by increased speed of access to the Internet posting and that do not accurately characterize any of the three cases that serve as my chief focus. All four cases share the common attributes of a "judicial media circus" in the way Daniel Larivière-Soulez describes, but they are worlds—and mediascapes—apart. Attending to the kind of media, the breadth of its reach, and the cultural and historical context in which that media system is embedded has been my principal aim.[23]

Exploring the genealogies of the crimes ascribed to the "Monster" of Florence, the Novi Ligure double homicide, and the Cogne filicide has necessitated an examination of cultural texts—with Michel Foucault, I have sometimes referred to them as "parchments"—of varied sorts.[24] Some texts have derived from the literary efforts of the so-called Young Cannibals, and others stem from contemporary writers who cannot be considered part of the movement. Still others have no literary provenance at all; rather, they come from the nonfiction sector of the marketplace for books or from journalistic reportage, in either print or other media.

Throughout, I have argued for an evaluation of murder that is local, embedded in particular cultural, historical, and juridical contexts. Apart from cases of war crimes or genocide, murder is a local offense, adjudicated within the jurisdiction where the murder has occurred. The body, a recurring and key concept in these pages, is paramount in a murder case. Discussion of the representation of violence underscores the repeated and omnipresent motif of flayed tissue, which, I have contended, signifies the fragile tissue of the *social* body. Kercher's corpse is such a body. The media coverage transformed Kercher's murder, the investigation of the crime, and the trial of those who stood accused of it into the sort of "body genre" that Linda Williams has identified in cinematic forms such as pornography or martial arts, where the indelible visibility of the body trumps the *énoncée,* or linguistic utterance. In this way, the transnational consumption of the mediatic images and journalistic coverage of her murder at once reifies notions of the "national" body and effaces them.

The gendered, classed, and nationalized states of Kercher's corpse pressure notions such as "national" and "global." A citizen of Great Britain, Kercher was, according to the verdict, slain by two *extracomunitari* (Knox and Guede) and one Italian (Sollecito). The trial for Kercher's killing took place under the aegis of the Italian justice system, which was invested with the authority to adjudicate a crime that took place on sovereign Italian soil. Yet the long-held legal convention of local jurisdiction held no sway in the arena of international scrutiny, where many non-Italian observers lamented what they perceived as a miscarriage of justice. Criticism, emanating principally from consumers of a Knox-friendly media in the United States, rained down on the Italian justice system, taking the form of editorials in daily newspapers (in print and electronic versions), newscasts and news programs on radio and television, a host of Internet sources, and even formal censure from a U.S. senator—Washington's Maria Cantwell. An excellent representation of the perceived flaws in Italian justice as manifest in the Knox case can be found in the points enumerated on the Web site injusticeinperugia. org.[25] Although Knox's family and friends described her as having been "railroaded" by the Italian justice system, Knox's own opinion of the trial differs: on several occasions she has remarked that she thought the trial was run in a manner that was "correct."[26]

The CBS investigative news program *48 Hours* developed an episode out of the Amanda Knox trial, "A Long Way from Home," which aired in April 2008.[27] It challenged the competence of the police involved in the case. An organization called Friends of Amanda Knox engaged Seattle-based defense trial lawyer Anne Bremner, who systematically challenged all of the evidence gathered by the ERT, or the Esperti ricerca trace, the forensic arm of the Italian state police. A video released on the Internet, which was picked up by various U.S. television news programs and finally made its way to Corriere TV, showed breaches in protocol for the gathering of evidence that could have resulted in its contamination.[28]

At least one viewer of the *48 Hours* episode was skeptical and posted a comment to the program's blog, remarking, "This was completely one sided. (The private investigator hired by CBS) simply trashed the Italian police and this 20 year old black kid (Rudy Guede). He never once refuted the police's evidence with anything credible."[29] Diminishing police credibility and eroding faith in organs of the law appears to be the task of private investigators, whether Italian or not, as chapter 2 clarifies. In an interesting reversal of the "Monster" case, Italy—and not the United States—now purports to be the leading expert in forensic analysis. In response to criticisms of the gathering and analysis of forensic data at the Via della Pergola *villetta*, Francesco Maresca, who represented Kercher's family in the trial, stated that Italian analysts were "teaching the whole world and the United States how to collect, analyse and evaluate scientific technical aspects of the case."[30] Yet even the *colpevolisti,* or those who believed in Knox's guilt, acknowledged that collection of forensic evidence had at points been haphazard and, consequently, impeachable.[31]

Claims of anti-Americanism in the Knox trial correspond to other recent trials of note in Italy. The *Corriere della Sera* published an editorial stating: "The first rule when an American citizen is accused of a crime abroad is that it does not matter whether he or she is innocent or guilty, what matters is that he or she has a US passport, which carries even more weight than an alibi."[32] As evidence of a pattern in which American citizens committing crimes on sovereign Italian soil were subsequently found not criminally liable, the *Corriere della Sera* referred to the 1998 incident of U.S. Marines pilot Captain Richard Ashby, who had flown through the cable of a gondola carrying skiers in Cavalese, Italy, a community in the Dolomite mountains approximately 25 miles northeast of Trento. Its support cable sliced, the gondola crashed, killing twenty. Ashby, who was convicted of obstruction of justice in May 1998 for removing a recording device from his plane at the NATO base in Aviano, Italy, was sentenced to six months in prison and dismissal from the Marine Corps.[33] Further evidence supporting the perception that Americans skated on the surface of the law, albeit in an international arena, was found in the shooting death of Nicola Calipari in 2007 in

Baghdad. An Italian secret service agent, Calipari had been engaged in the rescue mission of a kidnapped Italian citizen when he was shot and killed at an American roadblock.[34]

The protocols concerned with the redress of Kercher's murder play out at intersecting local, regional, national, and international levels. The slaying signals Italy's geopolitical position in the transnational movement of people and capital in a postcolonial era. Despite its relatively scarce colonial experience, Italy has found itself as one of the most trafficked portals into the European Union for immigrants from North Africa, Albania, and the Middle East in the last two decades of the twentieth century.[35] Italy's position as entry point in the Mediterranean to greater Europe (and the European Union) has never been clearer than the present: in Spring 2011, refugees fleeing political unrest in northern Africa began making their way across the water, stopping first on the small island of Lampedusa, equidistant between the eastern coast of Sicily and the western coast of Tunisia. The mix of North African immigrants in Italy has not always been a happy one. The xenophobia against "the Albanians" that erupted so quickly and easily in the Novi Ligure case, for example, testifies to the readiness to blame *extracomunitari* for social ills associated with cities and the alchemy of foreign elements and immigrants.

As noted, the substitution of Guede for Lumumba in the investigation of Kercher's murder suggests circumstances in which black men are homogenized and easily exchangeable despite their differences, whether national, cultural, or physical. Knox later apologized to Lumumba, whom she knew from working at the Perugian pub Le Chic, for her false accusation. He initiated civil proceedings against her for the defamation of his character. Significantly, it was not Lumumba's residence in Perugia since 1988, when he arrived as a student of political science, nor his reputation that exonerated him. Rather, DNA incompatible with his own found at the scene of the crime eliminated him as a suspect.[36] After two weeks' incarceration and Guede's extradition to Italy, Lumumba was released, restored to work, family life, and guest spots on various televised talk shows.[37]

Yet, Perugia, with its legion of young foreign students, was not known for the sort of xenophobia displayed in the cases of serial murder in Florence or the double domestic homicides in Novi Ligure, shortly after which De Nardo announced "they," Albanian immigrants, had committed the murders. As magistrates assigned to the Kercher case wrote, "Perugia can boast of a long history of civility and tolerance. . . . In its streets, piazzas, and public spaces one hears the happy and multi-racial voices of a multitude of students of all ages and from all corners of the globe that attend both its celebrated universities."[38] When Lumumba was exonerated and suspicion deepened concerning the participation of Rafaelle Sollecito—the "native son," as it were, in the case—a graf-fito appeared on the door of Le Chic reading "*W Lumumba, Sollecito dentro*" (Long live Lumumba, jail for Sollecito).[39] As he left detention on November 20, Lumumba said, "I'm happy to be going home. . . . I thank God and all my friends from Perugia who defended me."[40]

Gestures of solidarity with Lumumba, a known presence in the community for twenty years, advance an image of a Perugia that tallies with Claudio Cupellini's 2007 comedy, *Lezioni di cioccolato* (Chocolate lessons), where the city is portrayed as an oasis of intercultural under-standing. This comedy, released November 23, 2007, just weeks after Kercher's November 2 murder and three days after Lumumba's release, is set in the context of Perugia's chief employer, Baci Perugina.

The timing of its release helps make the jolly *Lezioni di cioccolato* a sort of moment of articulation measuring racial dissonance. Cupellini's film tells the story of Mattia (Luca Argentero), an egotistical housing contractor, who hires non-Italian workers—some undocumented, oth-ers with their papers in order—so that he can underbid competitors. One worker, Kamal (Hassani Shapi), breaks both arms one day on the work site. He is devastated because, an expert pastry chef who has emi-grated from Egypt, he was about to embark on a rare open apprentice-ship in the art of chocolate crafting that Baci Perugina had organized to commemorate the institution's centennial. Although he could de-nounce Mattia for injuries sustained on an unsafe site, the two reach an accommodation. Mattia will masquerade as Kamal, earn a certificate, and avoid entanglements with labor authorities. First, however, Mattia must conform to the ways Kamal wishes to present "himself" in public. Mattia must cut his longish and effeminate hair, wear clothes befitting an *extracomunitario* construction worker, exchange his fancy car for

Kamal's battered one, and, to pass for a credible North African, darken his skin, which he achieves through yeoman effort on a tanning bed so that ultimately he approaches Kamal's hue. Together, Mattia and Kamal develop a chocolate that marries the finest and most delicate of tastes from the northern and southern edges of the Mediterranean, respectively, hazelnuts native to Umbria and dates, which represent Kamal's national Egyptian pride.

This chocolate creation, and the note of friendship and collaboration on which the film ends, may be understood in the context of a less cheery union of an Italian and a North African from one year prior to the film's release. In the July 2006 World Cup soccer championship final between France and Italy, Zinedine Zidane, the legendary French footballer born in Marseilles whose family hails from Algeria, headbutted Marco Materazzi following the Italian's taunting insults. With Zidane sidelined for the penalty kicks, France lost to Italy, with the final score of 5 to 3.

Since the exchange between the two players was neither broadcast nor recorded, there was great speculation as to the content of Materazzi's comments. Indeed, if *Lezioni di cioccolato* films one (fictional) story of an association between an Italian and a North African, its predecessor, the "silent film" of the 2006 World Cup Final, tells another. Save for the din of the Berlin stadium soundscape, the image of the exchange is mute. The Brazilian television channel *Globo* announced that their hired lip-readers had deciphered Materazzi's side of the exchange, but one need not have read much postmodern critical theory to see that the precise content of Materazzi's comments mattered less than what its context revealed.[41] Whatever the content of Materazzi's provocative comment, almost immediately after hearing it, a very seasoned and senior soccer professional offered an aggressive nonverbal response to his equally seasoned opponent.

Reports in the press suggested myriad possibilities, ranging from Materazzi having called Zidane "a terrorist" (as the UK's *Guardian* reported) to having called his sister "a prostitute" (*Globo*).[42] One British sportswriter even suggested Materazzi had simply made a snide comment about Zidane's lapsing contract, inviting him to come play for the Milan club, Inter.[43] The British tabloid, *Daily Mail,* printed headlines so sensational, including both racist and sexist speculations, that Materazzi eventually was awarded damages in a lawsuit that he brought against the newspaper.[44]

In the days that followed, Materazzi categorically denied having said anything about Zidane's mother or terrorism. He was reported as stating that *"per me la mamma è sacra, lo sapete"* (mothers are sacred for me, you know that).[45] Materazzi may not have paid the same respect to other female members of Zidane's family.[46] John Foot offers the footballer's revelation to staff writers of *Sorrisi e canzoni TV* as the exchange that took place with Zidane. According to Foot, Materazzi said, "Zidane: 'If you want my shirt, I'll give it to you at the end.' Materazzi: *'Preferisco la puttana di tua sorella'"* (I prefer your whore of a sister).[47]

Even if the substance of Materazzi's remarks had never been made explicit, one notes the relative slipperiness of the racialized terrain on which one "other" is exchangeable for another of the same group.[48] Conjecture in the United States that Materazzi's comments included anti-Arabic invective is not surprising. The *New York Times* of July 11, 2006, for example, reported that Zidane's family had confirmed that Materazzi had called him a terrorist, triggering his quick response. Suppositions that racism lay at the heart of the exchange make sense in post–September 11 circumstances in North America, and, specifically, the United States. The racist logic in this instance functions similarly to the logic—or, rather, its absence—rooted at the foundation of moral panic: all "others" (black males, people of Arabic origins, homosexuals) are alike, easily exchangeable, and equally threatening.

Framed in its Italian context, however, speculation concerning the racist content of Materazzi's comments was dismissed. Announcing his own "ignorance," the soccer player himself flatly denied having referenced terrorism at all.[49] In an article in the *Corriere della sera* on July 13, 2006, television studies scholar and critic Aldo Grasso surmised that Materazzi's comments had concerned female members of Zidane's family, and that *"il razzismo non c'entra"* (racism has nothing to do with it).[50] That thoughts of *"la più ridicola e grandiosa esegesi collettiva"* (the most ridiculous and grandiose collective exegesis) should have turned almost immediately to concerns of "terrorism" reveals, in a European perspective, slight understanding of the *Mediterranean* context of the

Materazzi-Zidane exchange. Insulting the honor of an opponent's female family member may not be racist so much as sexist, adhering to a classical sense of patriarchy displayed in customs and practices from "continental" Italy—as Sicilian writer Leonardo Sciascia would have said—to Sicily and from there to Algeria and beyond. Women's "honor" is between men.[51]

The film *Lezioni di cioccolato* goes to some effort to rehabilitate the game of soccer tainted by the racialized violence of a year prior to its release. This is made explicit in the scene in which Mattia and Kamal watch a televised soccer match together. Shadows of Euro-colonialism persist in Perugia, not so much the setting of the intercultural respect and collaboration that Cupellini's film portrays, as the site where Guede "substitutes" Lumumba. Fleshing out the postcolonial portrait, it is only coincidental irony that Lumumba's nickname—Patrick—derives from Patrice Lumumba, the celebrated anti-colonial activist who helped Zaire gain freedom from Belgium in 1960 and founded the Republic of Congo.[52]

Nor is Amanda Knox a citizen of the European Union. In some ways, her citizenship confirms the disavowals throughout *Murder Made in Italy* that seek to displace "foreign" or "unknown" violence and aggression onto non-Italian sources, typically cultural products (television, film, graphic novels, pornography) "Made in the USA." Despite the anti-Italian rhetoric that erupted, it does not appear as though college students from the United States, such as Knox, will stop choosing Italy as a study site any time in the near future.[53] Italy is the top destination for United States students studying abroad in a country where English is not the lingua franca.[54] Writing in response to Sophie Egan's widely read December 2007 guest essay in the *New York Times*, "Junior Fear Abroad," Elaine Fallon observed that "while it is true that American students often behave badly while studying abroad, we should remember that American colleges have created a revenue bonanza by sending their students abroad on programs that provide little in the way of structure or serious academic obligations."[55] "lin," whose comments I quote at the beginning of this epilogue, sees Kercher's murder and Knox's trial as a cautionary tale for any student contemplating study abroad. The inclusive advice extends to European exchange students constituting the ERASMUS cohort that Meredith Kercher was part of.

LA DONNA FA NOTIZIA: WOMEN MAKE THE NEWS

Media studies scholar Milly Bonanno has observed that "*la donna fa no-tizia*" (women make the news). The murders in Novi Ligure and Cogne attest to this, as does the coverage on Kercher and, especially, on Knox. Veteran crime reporter for the Florentine daily *La Nazione*, Mario Spezi, also the coauthor, with Douglas Preston, of *The Monster of Florence* (2008), described the lack of readiness for the advent of crimes like those of the serial murders ascribed to the "Monster" of Florence between 1974 and 1985. Journalists, law enforcement agencies, the public, in fine, the city of Florence and, with it, the rest of Italy, were unprepared for such grisly homicides.[56] The intervening twenty-five years, however, and the uptick in violence that was both indigenous and imported more than adequately prepared the Italian media machine for the arrival of "La luciferina," the "little Lucifer," as Knox was christened by the press. This was in fact what Carlo Pacelli, Lumumba's lawyer, called Knox in his closing statement for the civil suit against her, which ran concurrently with the criminal case.[57]

When testimony about his unsavory behavior was broadcast on television during hearings in the U.S. Senate in 1991 to confirm his nomination to the Supreme Court, the Hon. Clarence Thomas labeled it character defamation, calling it a "high tech lynching."[58] But the technological capabilities of spreading the kind of *Mala famum,* or Rumor, that Virgil describes in the *Aeneid,* only increased—one might argue exponentially—in the intervening sixteen years. Images of Perugia, Kercher, Knox, Sollecito, Lumumba, Guede, and even unofficial footage of Kercher's abject, dead body filmed by the forensic team flooded social networking websites, YouTube, and other Internet Web sites.[59] It would not be surprising if Knox expressed regret over her self-presentation on the social networking sites MySpace and Facebook. Although her alcoholic imprecations and behavior do not appear beyond the pale of late adolescence, she still gave the impression of a "girl gone wild."[60] Nor could the moniker "Foxyknoxy" be explained away. Knox's mother, Edda Mellas, tried to give the nickname some context—her fleet daughter wending her way through opponents on the soccer field had made her seem like a "fox" to teammates—but the explanations did not appear to make many inroads into the use of the nickname in the tabloids, which, along with Internet crime blogs, followed developments in the case almost relentlessly.[61]

Media scrutiny of Knox was constant in both Italian and English. It was at its most merciless in the British tabloids. Unintentionally recalling the characterizations of both De Nardo and Franzoni, Great Britain's middle-brow *Daily Mail* reported that "Italian press reports frequently describe what are termed her 'icy' blue eyes, and her attention to men and standoffishness with women."[62] Some of the headlines in the more sensationalizing British tabloids read: "The Twisted World of Foxy Knoxy," "The Dark Angel of Seattle," "Orgy of Death," and "Amanda Was a Drugged-Up Tart." But Italian newspapers—not tabloids but the venerable *Corriere della sera* and *La Repubblica*—also sensationalized coverage of the case.[63] In her guest essay for the *New York Times,* Egan wrote that "every day brings a new headline or television report about Amanda Knox. 'Man-hunter, insatiable in bed,' was the first line in an article in *Corriere della Sera,* Italy's leading daily newspaper. 'She lives only for pleasure,' *La Repubblica* reported."[64]

Knox has responded. During her detention in Perugia's Casa Circondariale Capanne, known locally also as the Carcere di Capanne, she kept a diary, entitled "My Prison." Echoes of Silvio Pellico's noted work of the same name, *Le mie prigioni*—written during his detention in the Brno prison, Spielberg, between 1822 and 1830—did not evade notice.[65] A patriot eager to further the unification of Italy, Pellico begins his text with the question, "Have I written these memoirs from a feeling of vanity, or a desire to talk about myself? I hope this is not the case; and as far as one is able to judge one's own cause, I think I was actuated by better motives."[66] Knox's tone and subject differ. She observes her notoriety, writing, "I received 23 fan letters (. . .) That makes the count up to 35 letters."[67] Further, she writes that she has been described by the press "as a man-eater, they've said the list of men I've had goes up to here, but I've only had two lovers while in Italy."[68] Yet the list of names of the seven men with whom she had had sex with while in Italy that she had given police when, in an effort to gather more data, they had falsely told her she had tested positive for HIV, gave the lie to the lower number later registered in her diary.[69]

In "My Prison," Knox registers disbelief at her circumstances, at the accusations charging her with murder, and offers alternative theories of the crime. Like De Nardo and Franzoni, Knox speculates about possibilities that an intruder played a role. Evidently as aphoristic as the notes Antonio Gramsci kept in prison, *I quaderni del carcere* (*Prison Notebooks*), which were thematically organized for the first time only when they appeared in English translation, Knox also examines a variety of texts. Like Gramsci—who was also a student of linguistics—Knox is often guided by her curiosity about the Italian language. Working to improve her Italian, the reason that made Perugia her destination, she has recorded the litany of profanity heard from fellow inmates. Despite initial descriptions of Knox as "well off," she worked to save the money for her study stay and, once there, worked in Le Chic.[70] "My Prison" substantiates the claim that prison in Italy has functioned as the "*università proletaria*" (the proletarian university).[71] Such attentiveness to linguistic nuance has delivered results. For example, during her appearance in court in June 2009, Knox's testimony was offered in "fluent Italian."[72] Since her sentencing in December of that year, Knox's interest in languages has extended to include Chinese and Russian. With the Japanese she had studied in high school as well as the German she knew before arriving in Italy, Knox's linguistic repertory is expanding.

Knox was not the only chronicler of a stay in prison pending trial for the murder of Meredith Kercher. Sollecito's writings from his cell have made their way to the press. Imagining that Guede also may have recorded some thoughts during detention, *La Repubblica* columnist Meo Ponte wrote that "three diaries . . . seem all ready for transposition into a television screenplay while Perugia's murder mystery, a month after the discovery of the dead body of an English student, has yet to be told."[73]

Murder Made in Italy began with a contested accusation and a division: the separation of the *colpevolisti* over and against the *innocentisti* in the case for serial murder against Pietro Pacciani in 1994 corresponds to the heated contestation (this time with a greater transatlantic edge) in Amanda Knox's trial for the murder of Meredith Kercher. Similarly, on the terrain of cultural expressions, Roberto Benigni's film *Il mostro* (*The Monster*), which parodies the fruitless search for the killer, came out slightly before the guilty verdict in the first Pacciani trial. Cupellini's gay

comedy of interracial cooperation in Perugia, on the other hand, was released in November 2007, just as Amanda Knox's defamation of Patrick
Lumumba was coming to the surface. As I write this epilogue, Amanda
Knox's appeal of her guilty verdict has just begun. In February 2011,
the Italian pop music star Al Bano premiered a song at the annual pop
music festival in Sanremo dedicated to Amanda and entitled "Amanda
è libera," Amanda is free. On February 21, 2011, the Lifetime channel premiered its dramatization of the case against Knox for Kercher's
murder in *Amanda Knox: Murder on Trial in Italy*. Between ads for the
Lifetime series *Army Wives* and upcoming coverage of the royal wedding
of Prince William and Kate Middleton, the made-for-television movie
features a largely bitchy Meredith and scheming Italians. But perhaps the
most startling moment comes when Knox's sentence is handed down.
The made-for-television film makes it appear as though Knox's mother,
Edda Mellas (Oscar winner Marcia Gay Harden) is the only mother to
"lose" her daughter, despite the fact that Arline Kercher (Meredith's
mother, played by Shooboo Kapoor) is also present in the courtroom.[74]
The investigation, the media coverage, the public responses in Italy and
abroad—all illustrate themes examined in case studies I have presented.
By bringing into proximity the signifying practices of the literature and
narrative—literary, cinematic, and televised—*Murder Made in Italy* has
shown the shifts in discursive power concerning three specific murder
cases in Italy in the last quarter-century. The power of legal narratives
and journalistic coverage, in tandem with the increased rapidity of the
exchange of information in the twenty years, have disclosed the assemblage of elements required for murder "made in Italy."

NOTES

Introduction

1. To call attention to the putative singular (as opposed to plural) identity of the murderer, I use quotation marks for the singular noun "Monster" throughout these pages. The reasons for this are given below.

2. See Paul Ginsborg, *Silvio Berlusconi: Television, Power and Patrimony* (London: Verso, 2004); Zygmunt Baranski and Robert Lumley, eds., *Culture and Conflict in Postwar Italy. Essays on Mass and Popular Culture* (New York: St. Martin's Press, 1990), esp. 245–336; Stephen Gundle and Noëlleanne O'Sullivan, "The Mass Media and the Political Crisis," in *The New Italian Republic: From the Fall of the Berlin Wall to Berlusconi*, ed. Stephen Gundle and Simon Parker (London: Routledge, 1996), 206–220; and Stephen Gundle, "RAI and Fininvest in the Year of Berlusconi," in *Italian Politics: The Year of the Tycoon*, ed. Richard Katz and Piero Ignazi (Bologna: Istituto Cattaneo, 1996), 195–218.

3. The designation of "thick description" is Clifford Geertz's. See his "Description: Toward and Interpretive Theory of Culture," in Geertz, *The Interpretation of Culture* (New York: Basic Books, 1973), 3–30. Most of the films discussed in these pages are available in wide distribution. Similarly, and thanks to the recent industry of a knot of translators, the novels are almost as equally accessible in English editions.

4. *Il Mostro* (*The Monster*), dir. Roberto Benigni (Columbia TriStar Home Video, 1994).

Please see the Preface for an explanation of the conventions of translation and titles. If a work appears in the notes only, its title remains untranslated.

5. All translations are my own unless otherwise noted.

6. Lino Micciché, *Cinema italiano: gli anni '60 e oltre* (Venice: Marsilio, 2002), 394.

7. *Berlinguer ti voglio bene* (*Berlinguer: I Love You*), dir. Giuseppe Bertolucci (Korch Lorber Films, 1977).

8. *Johnny Stecchino*, dir. Roberto Benigni (Dutch FilmWorks, 1991).

9. Gian Piero Brunetta, *Storia del cinema italiano*, vol. 4 (Rome: Riuniti Editore, 1998), 500.

10. The film had made 50 million lire by September of the following year. See *Segnocinema* 15, no. 75 (1995): 38–39.

11. *Chiedo asilo* (*Seeking Asylum*, Kinowelt Home Entertainment), written by Benigni, was released on October 24, 1979, but is distinct from the other films listed in that Marco Ferreri directed; *Johnny Stecchino* was released on October 24, 1991; *La vita è bella* (*Life Is Beautiful*, New Films International), which won the Oscar for best foreign language film and for which Benigni won the Oscar as best actor, on October 23, 1998; *Pinocchio* (Miramax Home Entertainment), on October 11, 2002; and *La tigre e la neve* (*The Tiger and the Snow*, 01 Distribuzione), on October 14, 2005. Il *Piccolo diavolo* (*The Little Devil*), which he also wrote and directed, was released in July 1988 and forms the exception to the general October rule.

12. John Francis Lane believes the setting is "a tower block in a vast suburb of Rome." Although he notes "digs" at Berlusconi that serve to fix the film's historical time frame, Lane does not mention any specific link to the "Monster" of Florence, despite the obvious allusion of the title. See John Francis Lane, review, "The Monster," *Screen International* 982 (November 4, 1994): 41.

13. Whether recounted as fiction in prose narrative or as fact in historical accounts, court documents, and media coverage, crime narratives reveal operations of power and knowledge. A reckoning of the shifts of power from one institutional site—or narrative form—to another accords with Michel Foucault's interest in discerning and understanding discursive formations. Whoever seeks to track competing narrative forms and shifts of power and knowledge is engaged in a practice Foucault deemed "genealogical." See Michel Foucault, "Nietzsche Genealogy History," in *Language, Counter-Memory, Practice: Selected Essays and Interviews,* ed. Donald Bouchard, trans. Donald Bouchard and Sherry Simon (Ithaca: Cornell University Press, 1977), 139.

14. See Gianni Losito, *Il potere dei media* (Rome: Carocci, 1994), 85. See also Felice Froio, *L'informazione spettacolo: giornali e giornalisti oggi* (Rome: Riuniti, 2000).

15. Inquiry into moral panics, as McRobbie and Thornton explain, helps expose the mechanism of hegemony and lay bare "the social conditions of consent . . . necessary for the construction of a society more focused toward law and order." Angela McRobbie and Sarah Thornton, "Rethinking Moral Panic for Multi-Mediated Social Worlds," *British Journal of Sociology* 46, no. 4 (1995): 562. See also Stuart Hall, "Encoding/Decoding," in *Culture, Media, and Language,* ed. Stuart Hall, Dorothy Hobson, Andrew Lowe, and Paul Willis (London: Hutchison, 1980), 128–138. Classic studies of moral panic can be found in Stanley Cohen's study of "folk devils," the clashes in the United Kingdom in the 1960s between the "mods" and the "rockers," and in the alleged crimes of Afro-Caribbean males and their "menace" to British city-dwellers. See Stanley Cohen, *Folk Devils and Moral Panics: The Creation of the Mods and the Rockers* (Oxford: Basil Blackwell, 1972); and *Policing the Crisis: Mugging, the State, and Law and Order,* ed. Stuart Hall (London: MacMillan, 1978). See also *The Manufacture of the News: Deviance, Social Problems and the Mass Media,* ed. Stanley Cohen and Jock Young (London: Constable Press, 1973); and Sheila Brown, *Crime and Law in Media Culture* (Buckingham: Open University Press, 2003).

16. Robert Gordon discusses recent event narratives in Italy in "Pasolini's Murder: Interpretation, Event Narratives, and Postmodern *Impegno*," in *Assassinations and Murder in Modern Italy: Transformations in Society and Culture*, ed. Stephen Gundle and Lucia Rinaldi (New York: Palgrave, 2007), 153–165. The notion of "intermediality" is useful in a discussion of studies of "event narratives," particularly for its ability to address the ways cultural expressions of events that take varied generic forms share among and between them a set of common aims in the representation of the event. See the essays collected in *Narrative across Media: The Languages of Storytelling*, ed. Marie-Laure Ryan (Lincoln: University of Nebraska Press, 2004), esp. 41–45. See also Nicoletta Marini-Maio's forthcoming study focusing on intermediality in cultural expressions of the Aldo Moro kidnapping, with the projected title "A Specter Is Haunting Italy: The Double Plot of the Aldo Moro Case in Film and Theater."

I use "case," "affair," and "event" interchangeably in reference to the three examples of murder I study. "Affair" is a deliberate reference to Leonardo Sciascia's interrogation of the events leading up to the 1978 assassination of former prime minister and president of the Christian Democrats, Aldo Moro. Sciascia's own use of the French *affaire* recalled the acclaimed Dreyfus Affair of 1894, in which a young French Jew, Alfred Dreyfus, a captain in the army, was accused of treason, convicted, and sentenced to life in prison, then later exonerated. Emile Zola's famed "J'accuse," his accusation that the military had trumped up charges and engaged in fanning the flame of anti-Semitism, aided Dreyfus's case and is the rhetorical strategy Sciascia adopted in his pamphlet, which was submitted as the minority report for the Italian Parliament's investigation of the events. See Leonardo Sciascia, *L'Affaire Moro* (Palermo: Sellerio Editore, 1978).

17. Sociologist Nicola Mai's work on the xenophobic responses in Italy to Albanian and Rumanian immigrants is especially useful. See his "Myths and Moral Panics: Italian Identity and the Media Representation of Albanian Immigration," in *The Politics of Recognising Difference: Multiculturalism Italian Style*, ed. R. D. Grillo and J. Pratt (Aldershot: Ashgate, 2002), 77–95. See also Piero Vereni, *Identità catodiche: Rappresentazioni mediatiche di appartenenze collettive* (Rome: Meltemi, 2008), 69–99; Nicola Mai and Russell King, *Out of Albania: From Crisis Migration to Social Inclusion in Italy* (New York: Berghahn, 2008); and Derek Duncan, "Italy's Postcolonial Cinema and Its Histories of Representation," *Italian Studies* 62, no. 2 (2008): 195–211.

18. As Consuelo Corradi assessed it, both the Novi Ligure and Cogne crimes revealed the *nemico intimo*, the enemy intimate; see Corradi, *Il nemico intimo: una lettura sociologica dei casi di Novi Ligure e Cogne* (Rome: Meltemi, 2005). Like the Lacanian concept of *extimité*, both murder cases reveal threats to the family from within its structure, not imposed from without. See also Fabio Vighi, "Unravelling Moretti's (Political) Unconscious: The Abyss of the Subject in *La Stanza del figlio*," *Journal of Romance Studies* 3, no. 2 (2003): 83.

19. Knox's trial for murder compares to the trials I take as my subject in the way that my foci compare to Karen Pinkus's treatment of the 1953 Wilma Montesi scandal. See Karen Pinkus, *The Montesi Scandal: The Death of Wilma Montesi and the Birth of the Paparazzi in Fellini's Rome* (Chicago: University of Chicago Press,

2003); and Daniel Soulez-Larivière, *Il circo mediatico-giudiziario,* trans. Maria Giustozzi (Macerata: Liberilibri, 1994). For an exploration of the Fadda murder trial, its mediatic circus, and the way it resonated in the newly unified Italian State at the end of the 19th century, see Thomas Simpson's *Murder and Media in the New Rome: The Fadda Affair* (New York: Palgrave MacMillan, 2010).

20. Gundle and Rinaldi's *Assassinations and Murder in Modern Italy* covers this terrain, as do several essays in *Imagining Terrorism: The Rhetoric and Representation of Political Violence,* ed. Pierpaolo Antonello and Alan O'Leary (Leeds: Legenda, 2009). But the three murders examined here do not produce "excellent cadavers" as the result of murder committed by the Mafia, a type of murder Alexander Stille explored in *Excellent Cadavers* (New York: Vintage, 1996). These are the sort of "little murders" whose effect on the social fabric of New York Jules Pfeiffer charted in his 1969 off-broadway play of the same name, later developed into the 1971 film directed by Alan Arkin: *Little Murders* (1971, Key Video).

21. The murders explored in *Murder Made in Italy* lie somewhere between the "misteri d'Italia" and the "ferite d'Italia," (Italy's wounds). "Misteri d'Italia" include, for example, the death of Wilma Montesi in mysterious circumstances in 1953, the mysterious death of energy maverick Enrico Mattei in 1962, and, especially, the death of Pier Paolo Pasolini in 1975, the Red Brigades' execution of former prime minister and secretary of the Christian Democrats Aldo Moro in 1978, the mysterious downing over Ustica of Itavia flight 870 in June 1980, killing 81 passengers. Some of the "misteri d'Italia" are murders in the terms and context of the state like those explored in the essays collected in Gundle and Rinaldi's *Assassinations and Murder in Modern Italy.* Carlo Lucarelli's RAI 3 series *Blu Notte* also covers this ground. For representations on television of the Misteri d'Italia, see Giancarlo Lombardi, "I misteri d'Italia nella fiction TV," in *Strane storie. Il cinema e i misteri d'Italia,* ed. Christian Uva (Rome: Rubbettino, 2011), 182–195. On the Moro affair, see Antonello and O'Leary, *Imagining Terrorism*; Robin Wagner-Pacifici, *The Aldo Moro Morality Play: Terrorism as Social Drama* (Chicago: University of Chicago Press, 1986); and *Remembering Moro: Historiographical and Cultural Representations of the Moro Affair,* eds Ruth S. Glynn and Giancarlo Lombardi (Oxford: Legenda, forthcoming 2012). "Ferite d'Italia," on the other hand, is a program on RAI 2 conducted by Monica Leofreddi and Milo Infante, and has featured as Italy's "wounds" both the Novi Ligure as well as the Cogne case.

22. The attempt to reconcile large-scale notions of interpellation, underscoring operations of hegemony happening on (at least) two fronts, corresponds to Jean-François Lyotard's description of a postmodern society that, while it acknowledges the historical moment of grand narratives, pays attention in an unprecedented way to little ones. Mark Currie, *Transitions: Postmodern Narrative Theory* (New York: St. Martin's Press, 1996), 13. See also Jean-François Lyotard, *The Postmodern Condition: A Report on Knowledge,* trans. Geoff Bennington and Brian Massumi (Minneapolis: University of Minnesota Press, 1984).

23. See Soulez-Larivière, *Il circo mediatico-giudiziario.* This tallies with Guy Debord's notions of the "society of the spectacle." Debord illuminates the processes of interpellation, understood in the sense Louis Althusser intended, and spectacle, a constitutive element of the three cases I examine here. Any individual, and in-

deed lone, social subject will be "hailed" by ideology in the operation of interpellation. However, as Debord observes, this process is greatly affected if spectacle forces interpellation into a forum made ever more accessible by way of new media. "The spectacle is the acme of ideology," Debord asserts, "for in its full flower it exposes and manifests the essence of all ideological systems: the impoverishment, enslavement, and negation of real life." Moreover, for Debord, spectacle is capable of "eras(ing) the dividing line between self and world in that self, under siege by the presence/absence of the world, is eventually overwhelmed." Guy Debord, *The Society of Spectacle,* trans. Donald Nicholson Smith (New York: Zone Books, 1995). Althusser's formulation is most clearly expressed in his *Lenin and Philosophy and Other Essays,* trans. Ben Brewster (New York and London: Monthly Review, 1971), esp. 164 and 175. See also Paul Virilio, *La bomba informatica* (Milan: Cortina, 2000).

24. See CENSIS-U.C.S.I., *Quarto rapporto sulla comunicazione in Italia. I Media che vorrei* (Milan: FrancoAngeli, 2005), 71 and 72. The *Rapporto* is conducted annually by the Centro Studi Investimenti Sociali (CENSIS) in conjunction with UCSI (Unione Cattolica della Stampa Italiana), and the 2005 report, based on research conducted in the previous year, marks data at the conclusion of the investigative phases of all the cases I explore here. The appeals phase of the Cogne case was still in process.

25. The more literal translation of *Se mamma sapesse* is "if Mom only knew," but "Should Mom Suspect" preserves the acronym SMS without losing the essential meaning of the expression.

26. Using technology to create community has been of social interest and importance at least since the end of the 18th century. Armand Mattelart discusses the use of the missionary press to "amplify the faith in all corners of the world" as part of the communicative and colonial strategies of the Catholic Church. See his *The Invention of Communication,* trans. Susan Emanuel (Minneapolis: University of Minnesota Press, 1996), 179–186. For the ways that these types of affiliative processes are transformed in the Internet age, see Armand Mattelart, *Networking the World: 1794–2000,* trans. Liz Carey-Librecht and James Cohen (Minneapolis: University of Minnesota Press, 2000), esp. 75–96; Joshua Meyrowitz's discussion of the public sense of loss and mourning over "media friends" in *No Sense of Place: The Impact of Electronic Media on Social Behavior* (Oxford: Oxford University Press, 1985), 118–122; William Mitchell, *e-topia* (Cambridge, Mass.: MIT Press, 1999), 84–97; "Introduction," in *Media Worlds: Anthropology on New Terrain,* ed. Faye Ginsburg, Lila Abu-Lughod, and Brian Larkin (Berkeley: University of California Press, 2002), 1–38; and Franco La Cecla, *Surrogati di presenza. Media e vita quotidiana* (Milan: Bruno Mondadori, 2006). See also Don Slater, "Social Relationships and Identity On-Line and Off-Line," in *Handbook of New Media: Social Shaping and Consequences of ICTs,* ed. Leah Lievrouw and Sonia Livingstone (Thousand Oaks, Calif.: Sage Publications: 2002), 533–543; and David Morley, "Belongings: Place, Space and Identity in a Mediated World," *European Journal of Cultural Studies* 4, no. 4 (2001): 425–448.

27. "*Per la prima volta nella storia giudiziaria del nostro paese*" there existed conditions in which "*le indagini preliminari . . . sono state integralmente seguite in*

diretta dai mezzi di comunicazione." Enzo Tardino, *"Chi ha uccisio Samuele?"* Il *racconto dell'assassinio di Cogne* (Ferrara: Gabriele Corbo, 2003), 7.

28. Moretti rejected the designation "episode" for "In Vespa," "Isole," and "Medici," the three parts that comprise *Caro diario* (New Line Cinema, 1994), preferring "chapter." See Flavio De Bernardinis, *Nanni Moretti* (Milan: Il Castoro, 2001), 128.

29. This cinematic maneuver anticipates Moretti's 1998 release *Aprile,* in which the protagonist (Moretti playing himself) is engulfed by a wallpaper-sized newspaper quilted together from an enormous selection of periodicals that, despite the broad spectrum from which they come, display a narrow ideological frame.

30. This sequence is visible on YouTube at http://www.youtube.com/watch?v=KVHbbT-rUMQ&feature=related (accessed June 11, 2011). My interest in this episode of Moretti's film, first explored in my "Monstrous Murder: Serial Killers and Detectives in Contemporary Italian Fiction," in *Monsters in the Italian Literary Imagination,* ed. Keala Jewell (Detroit: Wayne State University Press, 2001), is consonant with yet differs from Robert Gordon's more recent interpretation. Gordon is interested in the broader context of the representation of Pasolini's murder. My focus is on the specific and technical shifts in filmic discourses in the segment from mockumentary to fiction to documentary. See Gordon, "Pasolini's Murder: Interpretation, Event Narratives, and Postmodern *Impegno.*"

31. The Vespa acts clearly as a unifying element, no more conspicuously than in the sequence in which Moretti rides out to Ostia, the scene of the vicious murder of Pasolini on November 2, 1975. The part of the trip Moretti shows is located at some point on the continuum of cinematic time between documentary "real time" and "fictional" time, wherein the magic of editing collapses time and space. True to the hybrid nature of "In Vespa" as a whole, the chapter's final sequence is edited for sound and set to the oceanic first part of Keith Jarrett's legendary Köln concert of January 1975. In an uninterrupted tracking shot, the camera follows Moretti for about four minutes as he makes his way to the site of Pasolini's murder. Clearly, it takes longer than four minutes to ride out to the coastal site of Ostia from Rome, and this is one of the moments bridging "real" and "fictional" time. This lengthy shot is interrupted only when Moretti dismounts, signaling the return of deliberate editing and cutting to a point-of-view long shot as Moretti regards the commemorative statue. The improvisational aspect of the live recording punctuates the documentary-feature hybridity of the film.

32. See the essays collected in Nicoletta Di Ciolla MacGowan and Mirna Cicioni, eds., *Differences, Deceits, and Desires: Murder and Mayhem in Italian Crime Fiction* (Dover: University of Delaware Press, 2008); Maurizio Pistelli and Norberto Cacciaglia, eds., *Perugia in giallo: indagine sul poliziesco italiano* (Rome: Donzelli, 2009); and Dieter Vermandere, Monica Jansen, and Inge Lanslots, eds., *Noir de noir: un'indagine pluridisciplinare* (Bruxelles and New York: Peter Lang, 2010). See also Costantino Maeder, "Italian Crime Novels," in *Investigating Identities: Questions of Identity in Contemporary International Crime Fiction* (Amsterdam: Rodopi Press, 2009), 261–276; Maja Mikula, "Displacement and Shifting Geographies in the Noir Fiction of Cesare Battisti," in *Exile Cultures, Misplaced Identities,* ed. Paul Allatson and Jo McCormack (Amsterdam: Rodopi Press, 2008), 209–223. The television series *Time Shift* on BBC4 also aired a valuable episode entitled "Italian Noir: The Story of

Italian Crime Fiction," on December 27, 2010. Several valuable essays by Di Ciolla MacGowan focus particularly on the gendered aspects of contemporary crime literature; see "The Eternal City as Dystopia. Or Perfect Imperfection," *Romance Studies* 25, no. 4 (2007): 297–307; "Perfecting Females/Pursuing Truths: Texts, Subtexts and Postmodern Genre-Crossing in Salvatori's Noir, *Sublime anima di donna*," in *Trends in Contemporary Italian Narrative, 1980–2007*, ed. Gillian Ania and Ann Hallamore Caesar (Newcastle upon Tyne, England: Cambridge Scholars, 2007), 29–49; and "Relative Values: Resisting Desire and Individuation in Barbara Garlaschelli's *Alice nell'ombra* and *Sorelle*," *Rivista di Studi Italiani* 21, no. 1 (2003): 119–133.

33. *Mani pulite* probes uncovered an almost ecumenical spread of corruption throughout the Italian political landscape regardless of party affiliation. See Stephen Gundle and Simon Parker, "Introduction: The New Italian Republic," in *The New Italian Republic: From the Fall of the Berlin Wall to Berlusconi*, ed. Stephen Gundle and Simon Parker (London: Routledge, 1996), 3. See also Vittorio Bufacchi and Simon Burgess, *Italy Since 1989: Events and Interpretations* (London, MacMillan, 1998), esp. 62–107.

34. See also Tobias Jones, *Dark Heart of Italy* (New York: Farrar, Strauss, Giroux, 2003). Glossing the "dark" aspect of Jones' title, Alan O'Leary has commented on the "chiaroscuro" representation of Italy and Italian society, which vacillates between the "light" and "dark," between the base and the beautiful, the classic and the corrupt, etc., traveling between them as, for example, Moretti's Vespa travels between modes of representation. I am grateful to O'Leary for these observations.

35. John Dickie, "Analysis: Fantasy Maps," in *Italian Cultural Studies, An Introduction*, ed. David Forgacs and Robert Lumley (New York and Oxford: Oxford University Press, 1996), 103.

36. See the section entitled "Geography" in Forgacs and Lumley, *Italian Cultural Studies*; Carl Levy, ed., *Italian Regionalism: History, Identity, Politics* (Oxford: Berg Press, 1996), esp. 1–80; Anna Cento Bull, *Social Identities and Political Cultures in Italy: Catholic, Communist, and "Leghist" Communities between Civicness and Localism* (New York: Berghahn Books, 2000); John Agnew, *Place and Politics in Modern Italy* (Chicago: University of Chicago Press, 2002); and Albarosa Macrì Tronci, "Regionalismo, identità nazionale e vocazione europea: un prezioso sistema di forze," *Otto/Novecento* 26, no. 3 (2002): 129–144.

37. See Massimo Carloni, "La geografia metropolitana del *giallo* italiano contemporaneo: Roma e Milano," *Letteratura italiana contemporana* II (1984): 247–252; and Massimo Carloni, *L'Italia in giallo. Geografia e storia del giallo italiano contemporaneo* (Reggio Emilia: Diabasis, 1994). See also Marc Augé, *Non-Places: Introduction to an Anthropology of Supermodernity*, trans. John Howe (London: Verso, 1995).

38. Paul Ginsborg, *Italy and Its Discontents: Family, Civil Society, State, 1980–2001* (New York: Palgrave MacMillan, 2003), 201.

39. Letizia Paoli, "Crime, Italian Style," *Daedalus* 130, no. 3 (2001): 158.

40. Home Office, *Criminal Statistics, England and Wales 1997* (London: Stationery Office, 1998), 210–222, cited in Paoli, "Crime, Italian Style,"180.

41. Marzio Barbagli, "Lost Primacy: Crime in Italy at the End of the Twentieth Century," *Journal of Modern Italian Studies* 9, no. 2 (2004): 148. See also Marzio

Barbagli and Laura Sartori, "Law Enforcement Activities in Italy," *Journal of Modern Italian Studies* 9, no. 2 (2004): 161–185.

42. Consider *Il rapporto sulla sicurezza,* 2006. This 500-page document is available as a PDF for downloading at http://www.interno.it/mininterno/export/sites/default/it/sezioni/sala_stampa/notizie/sicurezza/0993_20_06_2007_Rapporto_Sicurezza_2006.html (accessed June 11, 2011).

43. See Mikel Koven, *La Dolce Morte: Vernacular Cinema and the Italian Giallo Film* (Lanham, Md.: Scarecrow Press, 2006).

44. The genre features both seasoned practitioners such as Giorgio Scerbanenco, Lorenzo Machiavelli, and Laura Grimaldi and those more newly arrived to the field, such as Andrea Pinketts, Carlo Lucarelli, Andrea Camilleri, Diego De Silva, Giancarlo De Cataldo, Gianrico Carofiglio, Sandrone Dazieri, Massimo Carlotto, among others.

45. Laura Browder, "Dystopian Romance: True Crime and the Female Reader," *Journal of Popular Culture* 39, no. 6 (2006): 933. See also Brown, *Crime and Law in Media Culture,* esp. 35–76.

46. Annalee Newitz, "Serial Killers, True Crime, and Economic Performance Anxiety," in *Mythologies of Violence in Postmodern Media,* ed. Christopher Sharrett (Detroit: Wayne State University Press, 1999), 66. See also Mark Seltzer, *True Crime: Observations on Violence and Modernity* (New York and London: Routlege, 2007), 16 and 35.

47. For an exploration of the genre of the nonfiction novel that uses *In Cold Blood* as a test case, see Eric Heyne, "Toward a Theory of Literary Nonfiction," *Modern Fiction Studies* 33, no. 3 (1987): 480 and esp. 481–483. Janet Malcolm also describes the slipperiness of generic boundaries and form concerning the presentation of murder to a reading public. See her *The Journalist and the Murderer* (New York: Vintage, 1990), esp. 14–20 along with her *Iphigenia in Forest Hills: Anatomy of a Murder Trial* (New Haven: Yale University Press, 2011). See also Calvin Trillin's *Killings* (New York: Ticknor and Fields, 1984).

48. I include works by Nino Filastò, Francesco Ferri, and Michele Giuttari and a study of the television appearances of Carlo Lucarelli, moonlighting as the host for *Blu Notte,* the popular television program dedicated to cold cases and other "Italian mysteries."

49. Mary Jean DeMarr, "True Crime Books: Socio-Psycho-Babble or Socially Redeeming Voyeurism," *Clues: A Journal of Detection* 17, no. 2 (1996): 1–18.

50. My review includes works by journalist Ilaria Cavo, Franzoni's memoir *La Verità* (co-written with *Gente* columnist De Gennaro), and the genre-disrupting study by Maria Grazia Torri. Torri is a journalist who wrote on culture for various periodicals, including *Donna* and *Kult,* but who undertook the "medical mystery" of Samuele Lorenzi's death, arguing that he died not of unnatural causes but of an aneurysm. I consider the rejection of her claim by the Italian medical establishment and forensic authorities in part 3.

51. Mark Seltzer, *Serial Killers: Death and Life in America's Wound Culture* (New York: Routledge, 1998), 2.

52. Since it became a topic for structuralists close to half a century ago, critical theory has explored the relation between culture and violence. From such theorists

as Jean-Pierre Vernant, Marcel Detienne, and (perhaps especially) René Girard, we came to understand that narratives of violence reveal the complex relay between power and knowledge. See René Girard, *Violence and the Sacred,* trans. Patrick Gregory (Baltimore: Johns Hopkins University Press, 1977); Walter Burkert, René Girard, and Jonathan Z. Smith, *Violent Origins* (Stanford, Calif.: Stanford University Press, 1989); and Jean-Pierre Vernant and Marcel Detienne, *Cuisine of Sacrifice among the Greeks,* trans. Paula Wissing (Chicago: University of Chicago Press, 1989).

53. In the generation that followed the structuralists, feminist inquiry in a wide variety of academic disciplines underscored just how vital the body was to the operations of hegemony, which are multiform, fluid, in a state of becoming. On the question of embodiment and normativity, see, among others, Rosi Braidotti, *Nomadic Subjects: Embodiment and Sexual Difference in Contemporary Feminist Theory* (New York: Columbia University Press, 1994); Alison Jaggar, "Introduction: Living with Contradictions," in *Living with Contradictions: Controversies in Feminist Social Ethics,* ed. Alison Jaggar (Boulder, Colo.: Westview Press, 1994), 1–12; Judith Butler, "Doing Justice to Someone," in Butler, *Undoing Gender* (New York: Routledge, 2004), 57–74; and Patricia Williams, "On Being the Object of Property," in *Theorizing Feminism: Parallel Trends in the Humanities and Social Sciences,* ed. Anne C. Herrmann and Abigail J. Stewart (Boulder, Colo.: Westview Press, 1994), 198–213.

54. Julia Kristeva, *The Powers of Horror: An Essay on Abjection,* trans. Leon Roudiez (New York: Columbia University Press, 1982); Barbara Creed, *The Monstrous-Feminine: Film, Psychoanalysis, and Feminism* (London: Routledge, 1993); and Elizabeth Grosz, *Sexual Subversions: Three French Feminists* (Sydney: Allen & Unwin, 1989).

55. This is more than the opposition of a Lacanian imaginary and its relation to the maternal and the symbolic, as constituted by paternal law, for the signs of defilement associated with the abject are often blurred and indistinct (viz., blood, viscera, excrement).

56. Barbara Creed offers a useful example in her discussion of a scene from *The Exorcist,* dir. William Friedkin (1973) when she addresses the confluence of menstrual blood and the blood flowing from Regan's mutilated genitalia. The inability to distinguish between the two illuminates the ambiguity in the sign of the abject I wish to draw attention to.

57. See Gilles Deleuze and Félix Guattari's notion of a "minor" literature in *Kafka: Toward Minor Literature,* trans. Dana Polan (Minneapolis: University of Minnesota Press, 1986).

Part 1: Serial Killing

1. Throughout these pages I will use quotation marks for the term "Monster" in order to underscore the constructed aspect of this identity.

2. Karen Pinkus's *The Montesi Scandal* (Chicago: University of Chicago Press, 2003) outlined the role of the press, particularly paparazzi photography, in the mysterious death of Wilma Montesi in 1953 outside Rome and the scandal that ensued. See also note 19 in the introduction, above.

3. Mark Seltzer, *Serial Killers: Death and Life in America's Wound Culture* (New York: Routledge, 1998), 3.

4. Concerning cultural representations of monsters in Italy, see *Monsters in the Italian Literary Imagination,* ed. Keala Jewell (Detroit: Wayne State University Press, 2001), esp. Keala Jewell, "Introduction: Monsters and Discourse on the Human."

5. *"Come la maggioranza degli italiani, conosco il caso del Mostro di Firenze per sentito dire."* Manlio Cancogni, "Presentazione," in Francesco Ferri, *Il caso Pacciani: Storia di una colonna infame?* (Florence: Edizioni Pananti, 1997), v. This and all other translations are my own unless otherwise indicated.

6. Michel Foucault, "Nietzsche Geneaology History," in *Language, Counter-Memory, Practice: Selected Essays and Interviews,* ed. Donald Bouchard, trans. Donald Bouchard and Sherry Simon (Ithaca, N.Y.: Cornell University Press, 1977), 139.

7. *Blu Notte,* RAI 3, February 16, 2003. *Blu Notte,* the popular true crime series that Lucarelli has written and hosted on Italian public television (RAI 3) since 1998, focuses on cold cases and *"misteri d'Italia,"* or unsolved crime cases in Italy. When first broadcast, the case of the "Monster" of Florence was split into two episodes airing February 16 and 23, 2003. The program, which was initially entitled *Mistero in blu,* is estimated to have attracted approximately 15 percent of the evening public broadcast market at peak moments of interest. See http://www.carlolucarelli.net/blunotte.htm (accessed August 26, 2009). These cases were written first for television and then published in three volumes by Carlo Lucarelli: *Mistero in blue* (Turin: Einaudi, 1999); *Misteri d'Italia: i casi di Blu Notte* (Turin: Einaudi, 2002); and *Nuovi misteri d'Italia: i casi di Blu notte* (Turin: Einaudi, 2004). *Blu Notte* has also been released on DVD.

8. The alignment of sight with knowledge and (consequently) control derives from Foucault's thoughts about panopticism. See his *Discipline and Punish: The Birth of the Prison,* trans. Alan Sheridan (New York: Vintage, 1979), 195–228. See also Sari Kawana, *Murder Most Modern: Detective Fiction and Japanese Culture* (Minneapolis: University of Minnesota Press, 2008), esp. 29–68.

9. The designation "hurtable vision" is Carol Clover's. See her *Men, Women, and Chainsaws: Gender in the Modern Horror Film* (Princeton, N.J.: Princeton University Press, 1992), 205. See also Susan Crutchfield, "Touching Scenes and Finishing Touches: Blindness in the Slasher Film," in *Mythologies of Violence in Postmodern Media,* ed. Christopher Sharrett (Detroit: Wayne State University Press, 1999), 275–299.

1. The "Monster" of Florence

1. Including in the "Monster's" crimes the 1968 double homicide of Barbara Locci and Antonio Lo Bianco in Signa is problematic for reasons that will be clarified below.

2. Douglas Preston with Mario Spezi, *The Monster of Florence* (New York: Grand Central Publishing, 2008), 5.

3. See the introduction to this volume, note 55.

4. As theories about the identity of the "Monster" alternate between possibilities, it is important to note another geographical pattern. Although the location of the victims appears to be random, a pattern that alternates between positions north and south becomes visible when the crimes are regarded both temporally and geographically. This alternation is evident with regard both to the city of Florence and to the previous murder in the series of homicides. The 1974 murder of Pettini and Gentilcore took place between Borgo San Lorenzo and Vicchio, approximately 30 kilometers northeast of Florence in the Mugello area. The June 1981 murder of De Nuccio and Foggi took place in Via dell'Arrigo, located on the far side of Florence's suburb of Scandicci. Via dell'Arrigo is close to 10 kilometers southwest of the city of Florence in a position nearly diametrically opposed, across the Florentine valley, to the location of the 1974 killings. The murders of Cambi and Baldi four months later—the third in the "Monster" series—were committed close to 20 kilometers northwest of Florence in a rural area just outside Calenzano. The fourth double homicide, of Migliorini and Mainardi in July 1982, took place again to the south of the previous murder, in Montespertoli, which lies 25 kilometers to Florence's southwest. The subsequent double murder of the two German tourists, Meyer and Rüsch, the fifth in the series, marked a return to the vicinity of the June 1981 murders and took place in Giogoli, near Scandicci. The July 1984 murders of Rontini and Stefanacci, the sixth in the series, were committed approximately 15 kilometers east of the first homicides, once again in the Mugello area located approximately 35 kilometers to the northeast of Florence. The final double homicide in September 1985 of the French tourists Mauriot and Kraveichili was committed near San Casciano, approximately 20 kilometers south of Florence. Thus, the murders alternate between the north and south and between the city of Florence and the nearby rural areas. This pattern defamiliarizes the Tuscan hinterland, recasting the former bucolic and pastoral areas outlying Florence's center as depraved and dangerous. Please see also map 1.

5. Bibliography concerning Italy as a tourist destination, especially in the era of the Grand Tour, is considerable and generally organized around nationality of the tourists, historical period, and destination (e.g., Rome, Venice, Naples, and so forth). Tuscany has enjoyed some attention, especially its literary construction in the works of E. M. Forster (*Where Angels Fear to Tread* (1905) and *Room with a View* (1908)). For a more contemporary view of Tuscany specifically in travel narratives and Italian and North American narrative fiction, see Silvia Ross, *Tuscan Spaces: Literary Construction of Space* (Toronto: University of Toronto Press, 2010), esp. ch. 5, "Going Native: Tuscan Houses and Italian Others in Contemporary American Travel Writing," 120–141.

6. The defamiliarization of geography attendant on each murder case is reminiscent of the notion of deterritorialization that French philosophers Gilles Deleuze and Félix Guattari probe, but I do not suggest that it is a perfect instantiation of the notion. I explore this concept in greater detail in chapters 2 and 3. See Gilles Deleuze and Félix Guattari, *Anti-Oedipus: Capitalism and Schizophrenia,* trans. Robert Hurley, Mark Seem, and Helen Lane (Minneapolis: University of Minnesota Press, 1983), 139–145 and 184–192.

7. See Mark Seltzer, *Serial Killers: Life and Death in America's Wound Culture* New York: Routlege, 1998), 17 and 31. Baseball statistician Bill James brings a dif-

ferent perspective to bear on the notion of "murder by numbers." See his *Popular Crime: Reflections on the Celebration of Violence* (New York: Scribner, 2011).

8. The removal of the breast recalls the taking of war trophies from the ranks of the enemy dead. See Joanna Bourke, *An Intimate History of Killing: Face-to-Face Killing in Twentieth-Century Warfare* (New York: Granta, 1999).

9. Preston with Spezi, *The Monster of Florence*, 17–18.

10. "*Viene privilegiata la pista del guardone maniaco.*" Michele Giuttari and Carlo Lucarelli, *Compagni di sangue* (Florence: Le Lettere, 1998), 11.

11. Preston with Spezi, *The Monster of Florence*, 114.

12. *Squadra mobile,* literally meaning the "flying squad," was named after the London Metropolitan Police Service unit bearing an identical name. The Squadra mobile is a division of the Italian national police, of which there are five organs: Polizia di Stato, Carabinieri, Polizia Pentienziaria, Guardia di Finanza, and Corpo Fortestale. Squadre mobili are attached to precinct houses of the municipal police in each city and collaborate with local law enforcement.

13. Preston with Spezi, *The Monster of Florence*, 159.

14. *Blu Notte*, RAI 3, February 16, 2003.

15. "*Ricostruire la personalità dell'aggressore individuandone le caratteristiche fisiche, la razza, l'età presumibile, il tipo di lavoro, il livello sociale, le tendenze sessuali, il quoziente intellettivo, l'istruzione, la religione, e via elencando.*" Emilio Radice, "Si fa presto a dire Serial Killer," *La Repubblica*, August 11, 1987. Perugini and the other *acchiappamostri* (monster snatchers) are slightly ahead of the curve in Italian popular culture when it comes to tracking serial killing. In 2004, Col. Luciano Garofano, former head of the RIS (Reparto investigazioni scientifiche), the elite section of the Carabinieri, published the first volume of *Delitti imperfetti,* his popular explorations of unsolved crimes. The television series *RIS, delitti imperfetti,* broadcast on Canale 5 beginning in 2005, is inspired by the success of the CBS series *CSI: Crime Scene Investigation,* which appears in popular syndication in Italy. However, the *RIS* episodes are based on Garofano's work.

16. Ferri, *Il Caso Pacciani*, 23.

17. See Ruggero Perugini, *Un uomo abbastanza normale: la caccia al mostro di Firenze* (Milan: Mondadori, 1995), 51–65.

18. For my description of the use of Foucault's description of "parchments" and a genealogical methodology and its significance to this study, see the introduction, note 13. See the introduction also for a review of Daniel Soulez-Larivière work on the mediatic judicial circus.

19. Preston identifies Giubba as Aldo Fezzi. Evidently, the *cantastorie* was called "*il giubba per l'inseparabile giacca che indossava anche d'estate*" ("the giubba" because of the jacket that he constantly wore, even in the summer). See the section on Aldo Fezzi on the *Insufficienze di prove* Web site, http://insufficienzadiprove. blogspot.com/2008/12/aldo-fezzi.html (accessed March 27, 2011). As David Forgacs has observed, criticism has "undervalue(d) the many non-print channels by which national culture could be mediated and disseminated even in the pre-film and pre-radio era, from local intellectuals (priests, mayors, party officials) and the itinerant singers and poets known as *poeti a braccio* or *cantastorie*." See Forgacs, "The Mass Media and the Question of National Identity in Italy," in *The Politics of Italian Na-*

tional Identity, ed. Gino Bedani and Bruce Haddock (Cardiff: University of Wales Press, 2000), 148.

20. Given in Italian in Giuseppe Alessandri, *La leggenda del Vampa: La storia del Mostro di Firenze?* (Florence: Loggia de Lanzi, 1995), 30–31.

21. Indeed, all major Italian dailies picked up the trail of the 1951 murder.

22. Umberto Eco, *Sette anni di desiderio* (Milan: Bompiani, 1983). See also Gian Paolo Caprettini, *La scatola parlante* (Rome: Editori Riuniti, 1996), 34–35; and "paleotelevisione," in *Enciclopedia della televisione,* ed. Aldo Grasso (Milan: Garzanti, 2002), 502.

23. A complete review of the network of media in the time frame spanned by the "Monster" narrative is beyond my scope here. My interest lies in the way the trials of Pietro Pacciani for murder correspond to the development of divers media in Italian culture and society and document how shifts between "information ages" may be unpredictable, halting, or incomplete. In *Mass Culture and Italian Society from Fascism to the Cold War* (Bloomington: Indiana University Press, 2007), David Forgacs and Stephen Gundle undertake a detailed review of these developments in a period spanning the 1930s to 1954, marking, as they go along, the ways in which fascist-era media mechanisms continued the same practices in the postwar period. For my purposes, part 2, "Cultural Industries and Markets," 95–194, of this study is particularly useful for the way it documents developments in a variety of media including radio, cinema, and publishing (principally books and periodicals).

24. Forgacs and Gundle observe that in the 1930s, Italy's consumption of periodicals was among the highest in Europe. The publishing industry, especially for periodicals, remained high after the war. See Forgacs and Gundle, *Mass Culture and Italian Society,* 97–112. At the same time, as Forgacs has observed, newspaper sales "remained more or less static at around 5 million copies a day from 1915 to 1980." See David Forgacs, *Italian Culture in the Industrial Era* (Manchester: Manchester University Press, 1990), 33.

25. See also Lorenzo Denicolai, "L'oralità tecnologica e la sua religione: il caso della televisione e le sue declinazioni," *Turin D@MS Review,* May 26, 2008, available as a download at http://www.turindamsreview.unito.it/sezione.php?idart=410 (accessed April 11, 2011).

26. See "Neotelevisione," in Grasso, *Enciclopedia della television,* 472. Speaking of the ramped-up media output surrounding the 1978 Aldo Moro kidnapping and assassination, Alan O'Leary draws attention to how this constituted "the first example of (twenty-four-hour news reporting) at work in the Italian context." See Alan O'Leary, "Dead Man Walking: The Aldo Moro Kidnap and Palimpsest History in Buongiorno Note," *New Cinemas: Journal of Contemporary Film* 6, no. 1 (2008): 38.

27. *Blu Notte,* February 16, 2003.

28. It seems hard to believe that crime reporters and law enforcement officials would not have felt "prepared" by such sensational news as, for example, the David ("Son of Sam") Berkowitz serial murders in New York City in 1976–1977. Spezi does not describe himself as "surprised," which is consonant with his subsequent appearances on *Blu Notte,* where he paints the picture of a Florence that is no stranger to violence. See previous note.

29. Preston with Spezi, *The Monster of Florence,* 19.

30. It is perhaps only coincidence that 1994 also marks the first, brief term of the media titan Silvio Berlusconi as Italy's prime minster. For Forgacs and Gundle, Berlusconi's "intertwining of political power, media ownership and control in election campaigns and governments" is but an "extreme phase of a process rooted way back in the past." See Forgacs and Gundle, *Mass Culture and Italian Society*, 2.

31. There is substantial footage available of Pacciani's 1994 trial as well as the trials, two years later, of Lotti and Vanni. The many programs devoted to coverage of the "Monster" (approximately 150 television transmissions on RAI alone) use the stock footage, often the same, for numerous broadcasts. Here I am referring to the episode of *Un giorno in pretura* that aired in February 2, 2004. There are also various clips of Pacciani and the proceedings available on YouTube, including this one from his deposition: http://www.youtube.com/watch?v=p7anj7RHgfU, accessed April 1, 2011.

32. Forgacs and Gundle, *Mass Culture and Italian Society*, 17. See also Tullio De Mauro, *Storia linguistica dell'Italia unita* (Bari: Laterza, 1963), 123–126.

33. For standardizing trends in the Italian Language see Anna Laura Lepschy and Arturo Tosi, eds., *Languages and Italy: Histories and Dictionaries* (Ravenna: Longo Editore, 2007), and Giulio Lepschy, *Mother Tongues and Other Reflections on the Italian Language* (Toronto: University of Toronto Press, 2002).

34. De Mauro himself remarked on the incomplete shift that the Italian populace, faced with an ever-evolving mediascape, made to standard Italian. As he noted, "even in 1991 less than half of the population used standard Italian regularly with friends and colleagues and a third used solely their dialect or language at home." Quoted in Paul Ginsborg, *Stato dell'Italia* (Milan: Il Saggiatore, 1994), 66.

35. "*Ce ne sono tanti e tutti lo sanno, ma sembra che se ne rendano conto solo in quel momento.*" *Blu Notte*, RAI 3, February 23, 2003.

36. Preston with Spezi, *The Monster of Florence*, 19.

37. "*Gente nota . . . stimati professionisti.*" *Blu Notte*, RAI 3, February 16, 2003.

38. Preston with Spezi, *The Monster of Florence*, 20.

39. See Judith Walkowitz, *The City of Dreadful Delight: Narratives of Sexual Danger in Late-Victorian London* (Chicago: University of Chicago Press, 1992). See also Gayle Rubin, "Thinking Sex: Notes for a Radical Theory of the Politics of Sexuality," in *Pleasure and Danger*, ed. Carole Vance (London: Routledge & Kegan, Paul, 1984); and Simon Watney, *Policing Desire: Pornography, AIDS, and the Media* (London: Methuen Press, 1987).

40. "*Momento di gioia, di affermazione della loro giovinezza.*" *Blu Notte*, RAI 3, February 16, 2003.

41. Preston with Spezi, *The Monster of Florence*, 22.

42. Ibid., 33.

43. Ibid.

44. Ibid., 85.

45. Ibid., 86. This is given in English, but it probably refers to "*albergo ad ore,*" popularized in a 1969 Gino Paoli song of the same name. A loose translation of this could be "rooms by the hour" or "no-tell motel." This sort of establishment differs in tenor and type from the *case chiuse*, the formerly state-sanctioned brothels.

46. See my *Prison Terms: Representing Confinement during and after Italian Fascism* (Toronto: University of Toronto Press, 2001), esp. 105–136. See also Lina Merlin

and Carla Barberis, eds., *Lettere dalla casa chiuse* (Milan-Rome: Edizioni Avanti!, 1955); and Aldo Casalinuovo, "Un nuovo capitolo nella storia del diritto italiano: Le norme penali della legge Merlin," *Rivista penale* 38 (1958), 553–572.

47. See Leopoldo Ortu, *La questione sarda tra Ottocento e Novecento: aspetti e problemi* (Cagliari: CUEC, 2005), esp. 214–234. See also Martin Clark, "Sardinia: Cheese and Modernization," in *Italian Regionalism: History, Identity, and Politics,* ed. Carl Levy (Oxford: Berg Press, 1996), 81–106.

48. Preston with Spezi, *The Monster of Florence,* 57. See Alessandri, *La leggenda del Vampa,* 101–107. The notion of the "traffic" in women derives from Gayle Rubin's influential essay, "The Traffic in Women: Notes on the 'Political Economy' of Sex," in *Toward an Anthropology of Women,* ed. Rayna Reiter (New York: Monthly Review Press, 1975), 157–210.

49. Preston with Spezi, *The Monster of Florence,* 99–102.

50. Ibid., 118.

51. Ibid., 57.

52. Ibid., 56.

53. See Alessandro Bucarelli, *Criminalità e giustizia penale nella Sardegna del periodo Sabaudo* (Cagliari: Scuola Sarda, 1998); Tonino Serra, *Violenza, criminalità e giustizia in Sardegna dal 1500 al 1871* (Sestu: Zonza, 2007); and Comitato di Solidarietà con il Proletariato Prigioniero Sardo Deportato, *Colonizzazione, autodeterminazione,"criminalità" in Sardegna: l'altra storia del banditismo,* preface by C. Cavalleri (Guasila: Editziones de su Arkiviu Bibrioteka, 1993).

54. Preston with Spezi, *The Monster of Florence,* 188.

55. Ibid., 84.

56. Preston writes, "In 1960, almost nobody in Sardinia spoke Italian." *The Monster of Florence,* 53.

57. *Blu Notte,* RAI 3, February 23, 2003.

58. Ibid.

59. *"Una potente setta internazionale."* *Giallo 1* began broadcasting on the Mediaset network in December 2004. Prior to this, Pivetti, a one-time member of the Lega Nord (Northern League), had served in the Italian Parliament from 1992 to 2001. She was president of the Camera dei Deputati for the XII Legislature of the Republic of Italy from 1994 to 1996.

60. Preston with Spezi, *The Monster of Florence,* 128–132. The English translation of the FBI profile is available online; see "'Monster of Florence' Profiled by FBI," *Dateline NBC* Web site, June 20, 2007, http://www.msnbc.msn.com/id/19313866/print/1/displaymode/1098/.

61. *Blu Notte,* RAI 3, February 23, 2003.

62. Angela McRobbie and Sarah Thornton, "Rethinking Moral Panic for Multi-Mediated Social Worlds," *British Journal of Sociology* 46, no. 4 (1995): 562.

63. See Barbie Latza Nardeau, *Angel Face: The True Story of Student Killer Amanda Knox* (New York: Beast Books, 2010), 95–96.

64. Preston with Spezi, *The Monster of Florence,* 304 (my italics).

65. See Donatella della Porta, *Lo scambio occulto: Casi di corruzione politica in Italia* (Bologna: Il Mulino, 1992); Carlo Guarnieri, *Magistratura e politica: pesi senza contrappesi* (Bologna: Il Mulino, 1993); and David Nelken, "A Legal Revolution?

The Judges and *Tangentopoli*," in *The New Italian Republic: From the Fall of the Berlin Wall to Berlusconi,* ed. Stephen Gundle and Simon Parker (London: Routledge, 1996), 191–205.

66. Preston with Spezi, *The Monster of Florence,* 267–268.

67. Ibid., 300. Both Giuliano Mignini and Michele Giuttari were found guilty of abuse of office for their investigation of the crimes attributed to the "Monster." On January 23, 2010, they were given sixteen and eighteen months' suspended sentences, respectively, by Florence's district court. See "Mostro di Firenze, indagini illecite Colpevoli Mignini e Giuttari," *La Repubblica,* January 23, 2010, http://ricerca.repubblica.it/repubblica/archivio/repubblica/2010/01/23/mostro-di-firenze-indagini-illecite-colpevoli-mignini.html (accessed April 21, 2010); and Richard Owen, "Amanda Knox Prosecutor Giuliano Mignini Convicted of 'Abuse of Office,'" *Sunday Times* (London), January 23, 2010, http://www.timesonline.co.uk/tol/news/world/europe/article6999196.ece (accessed April 21, 2010).

68. Mistrust of authority is not limited to residents of Sardinia. On the fairly standard mistrust of the police among Italians, see John Davis, *Conflict and Control: Law and Order in Nineteenth-Century Italy* (London: MacMillan, 1998).

69. "*Un luogo in cui non penseresti mai che accaddesero cose del genere. La campagna toscana.*" *Blu Notte,* RAI 3, February 16, 2003.

70. Massimo Carloni argues that after 1978 the reconfigured geography of Italy produced less of a regional inflection and greater geographical diffusion. See Carloni, *L'Italia in giallo: Geografia e storia del giallo italiano contemporaneo* (Reggio Emilia: Diabasis, 1994).

71. See, for example, Umberto Eco, *Opera aperta: forma e indeterminazione nelle poetiche contemporanee* (Milan: Bompiani, 1969).

72. See Giorgio Agamben, *State of Exception,* trans. Kevin Attell (Chicago: University of Chicago Press, 2005); and Santiago Zabala, "'Weak Thought' and the Reduction of Violence: A Dialogue with Gianni Vattimo," trans. Yaakov Mascetti, *Common Knowledge* 8, no. 3 (2002): 452–463.

73. See Jacques Derrida, "Force of Law," trans. Mary Quaintance, in *Deconstruction and the Possibility of Justice,* ed. Drucilla Cornell, Michael Rosenfeld, and David Gray Carlson (New York: Routledge, 1992), 3–67. See also Geoffrey Bennington, *Interrupting Derrida* (London: Routledge, 2000).

74. This excludes coverage on Italy's cable television network, including Sky and Mediaset channels, which have numerous subscription holders. As a publicly owned and operated network, the RAI is obliged by law to archive its programming; private networks are under no such obligation. Holdings of the RAI *teche,* as the various archives are known, are extensive and remarkable for their organization.

75. Richard Owen, "The Monster Hunter," *Sunday Times* (London), February 20, 2004, http://www.timesonline.co.uk/tol/life_and_style/article1024109.ece (accessed August 25, 2009).

76. Preston with Spezi, *The Monster of Florence,* 168.

77. "*A differenza dei gialli di carta, un'indagine vera non procede a colpi di scena ma si alimenta di piccoli passi che si conquistano in una routine quotidiana apparentemente piatta e noiosa.*" Michele Giuttari, *Il mostro: anatomia di un'indagine* (Milan: Rizzoli, 2006), 187.

78. Preston with Spezi, *The Monster of Florence*, 5.
79. Ibid., 268.
80. Preston with Spezi, *The Monster of Florence*, 186.
81. Ibid., 2.
82. Ibid., 264.
83. Ibid., 302.
84. Ibid., 228.

2. Monstrous Murder

1. Carlo Lucarelli, *Lupo mannaro* (Rome: Edizioni Theoria, 1994), 33 (emphasis in the original). All translations are my own unless otherwise indicated.

2. When speaking about the "Monster" of Florence in the April 15, 2004, episode of *Blu Notte*, Lucarelli makes a point of underscoring the "monstrousness" of the serial homicides in Florence. Although the word "monster" is no longer used to designate serial killers in Italy, Lucarelli says, "Ci sentiamo di usarla" (We feel the need to use it). *Blu Notte*, RAI 3, April 15, 2004.

3. Lucarelli, 33.

4. This follows the notion of a Foucauldian discursive tic. See Michel Foucault, "The Confession of the Flesh," in *Power/Knowledge,* ed. Colin Gordon (New York: Pantheon Books, 1980), 211.

5. See Marina Garbesi, *I serial killers* (Rome: Edizioni Theoria, 1996); Paolo De Pasquali, *Serial Killer in Italia: Un'analisi psicologica, criminologica, e psichiatrico-forense* (Milan: FrancoAngeli, 2001); and Carlo Lucarelli and Massimo Picozzi, *Serial Killers: Storie di ossessione omicida* (Milan: Mondadori, 2003).

6. See note 37 of the introduction.

7. See, for example, William J. Mitchell, *E-Topia: "Urban Life, Jim—But Not as We Know It"* (Cambridge, Mass.: MIT Press, 1999).

8. See Luciano Garofano, *Delitti Imperfetti, Atto I e Atto II* (Milan: Marco Tropea Editore, 2006), 257–322.

9. For the relation of the no-placeness and yet ubiquitous aspect of train travel, see Michel de Certeau, *The Practice of Everyday Life,* trans. Steven Rendall (Berkeley: University of California Press, 1988), esp. 117.

10. "*Assassinio seriale*" is also used, albeit infrequently. In the rapidly expanding bibliography concerning serial killers and popular culture (construed largely as American or Northern European), see Mark Seltzer, *Serial Killers: Death and Life in America's Wound Culture* (New York: Routledge, 1998), Jane Caputi, *The Age of Sex Crime* (Bowling Green, Ohio: Bowling Green State University Popular Press, 1987); Steve Egger, *The Killers among Us: An Examination of Serial Killers* (Upper Saddle River, N.J.: Prentice Hall, 1997); Carla Freccero, "Historical Violence, Censorship, and the Serial Killer: The Case of *American Psycho,*" *Diacritics* 27, no. 2 (1997): 44–58; Stephen Giannangelo, *The Psychopathology of Serial Murder: A Theory of Violence* (Westport, Conn.: Praeger Press, 1997); Philip Jenkins, *Using Murder: The Social Construction of Serial Homicide* (New York: Aldine de Gruyter, 1994); and Richard Tithecott, *Of Men and Monsters: Jeffrey Dahmer and the Construction of the Serial Killer* (Madison: University of Wisconsin Press, 1997).

11. "Serial killer" was first coined by FBI Special Agent Robert Ressler, whose accounts of tracking celebrated serial killers have enjoyed tremendous popularity in the U.S. market. See Seltzer, *Serial Killers*, 16.

12. Cited in Tithecott, *Of Men and Monsters*, ix.

13. See Edward Ingebretsen, "The Monster in the Home: True Crime and the Traffic in Body Parts," *Journal of American Culture* 21, no. 1 (1998): 27–34.

14. Giorgio Agamben, *Means without End: Notes on Politics*, trans. Vincenzo Binetti and Cesare Casarino (Minneapolis: University of Minnesota Press, 2000), 23.

15. Elaine Chang, "Spaghetti Eastern: Mutating Mass Culture, Transforming Ethnicity," in *Revisioning Italy: National Identity and Global Culture*, ed. Beverly Allen and Mary Russo (Minneapolis: University of Minnesota Press, 1998), 292–296.

16. These are the body genres, so called for the centering of the body that has trumped the linguistic *enoncée*; under this rubric we might fit genres such as pornography, martial arts, and films in the slasher/horror genre. In this regard, work like that of the *cannibali*, as a group of young writers in the 1990s became designated, is particularly suggestive. This indisputable extrapeninsular influence on the "pulp fiction" of the "cannibals" is a topic I explore in chapter 5. The designation "body genre" is from Linda Williams, "Body Genres," in *The Oxford Guide to Film Studies*, ed. John Hill, Pamela Gibson, Richard Dyer, E. Ann Kaplan, and Paul Willemen (New York: Oxford University Press, 1998), 339–341.

17. For the way contemporary crime fiction troubles the city-country binary, see David Schmid, "Imagining Safe Urban Space: the Contribution of Detective Fiction to Radical Geography," *Antipode* 27 (1995): 242–269. For the Italian literary *giallo*, see Giuliana Pieri, "Crime and the City in the Detective Fiction of Giorgio Scerbanenco," in *Italian Cityscapes: Culture and Urban Change in Contemporary Italy*, ed. Robert Lumley and John Foot (Exeter: University of Exeter Press, 2004), 144–155. See also John Agnew, *Place and Politics in Modern Italy* (Chicago: University of Chicago Press, 2002).

18. "*Un serial killer in Emilia Romagna, nel paese del Lambrusco!*" Lucarelli, *Lupo mannaro*, 51.

19. "*In effetti, se ci si pensa bene questa regione la può vedere come un'unica grande città che da Reggio arriva fino a Cattolica . . . una specie di Los Angeles con qualche milione di abitanti e una superficie estesissima e la via Emilia* on the road." Ibid., 51.

20. Cited in Judith Halberstam, "Skinflick: Posthuman Gender in Jonathan Demme's *The Silence of the Lambs*," *Camera Obscura* 27 (September 1991): 37–53. Velasco's figuration as a vampire in the age of Berlusconi, which I detail more fully below, also speaks to Bram Stoker's use of Dracula as a critique of capital. See Franco Moretti, *Signs Taken for Wonders: Essays in the Sociology of Literary Forms*, trans. Susan Fischer, David Forgacs, and David Miller (London: Verso, 1993).

21. In his sleepless state, Romeo resembles another of Lucarelli's disheveled detectives, Commissario De Luca, of the "historic" trilogy *Carta bianca L'estate torbida*; and *Via delle Oche* (Palermo: Sellerio Editore, 1990, 1991, and 1996).

22. Lucarelli, *Lupo mannaro*, 34.

23. Carla Freccero reminds us that Patrick Bateman, the narrator, protagonist, and serial killer of *American Psycho*, works for the aptly named Wall Street firm of

Pierce and Pierce. See Freccero, "Historical Violence, Censorship, and the Serial Killer," 51.

24. See Klaus Theweleit, *Male Fantasies*, vol. 1, *Women, Floods, Bodies, History*, trans. Steven Conway (Minneapolis: University of Minnesota Press, 1987).

25. Seltzer writes: "The social ego (is) formed from the outside in, *its social substitute skin* forming its insectlike exoskeleton. And this is exactly the ego of the kind one finds described, again and again, in accounts of the serial killer. If the serial killer . . . 'fades back,' chameleonlike, 'into society,' he seems to depend utterly on the support of this social exoskeleton." See Mark Seltzer, "Serial Killers (II): The Pathological Public Sphere," *Critical Inquiry* 22, no. 1 (1995): 147–148 (my italics). The quest for and conquest of the victim's skin could be seen as a literalization of this mechanism.

26. Kristeva puts it this way: "It is as if the skin, a fragile container, no longer guaranteed the integrity of 'one's own and clean self' but, scraped or transparent, invisible or taut, gave way before the dejection of its contents. Urine, blood, sperm, excrement then show up in order to reassure a subject that is lacking its 'own and clean self.'" Julia Kristeva, *The Powers of Horror: An Essay on Abjection*, trans. Leon Roudiez (New York: Columbia University Press, 1982), 53.

27. Ibid., 4. See Mary Douglas, who observes that "reflection on dirt involves reflection on the relation of order to disorder, being to non-being, form to formlessness, life to death." Douglas, *Purity and Danger: An Analysis of Conceptions of Pollution and Taboo* (London: Routledge and Kegan Paul, 1966), 5.

28. In an ultimately too optimistic reading of Jonathan Demme's 1991 film *The Silence of the Lambs*, Elizabeth Young believes that skin functions as the sign pointing to "a second model of gender . . . that offers a critique of sexual difference by transcending, rather than exaggerating, traditional oppositions between genders. . . . Thus, even as these two killers enact forms of violence against women, they also, in the objects and forms of their crimes, translate physical violence from a gender-specific act to a potentially unisexual set of bodily violations." Young, "*The Silence of the Lambs* and the Flaying of Feminist Theory," *Camera Obscura* 27 (1991): 12–13. I will query the notion that the rending of skin can sign a more neutral system in which violence strikes irrespective of gender in my consideration of the fashion industry as portrayed in Pinketts's noir novel *Il senso della frase*.

29. Of Italians' attitudes about organ donation, Allen and Russo write, "Belying their reputation as a consumately generous people, the Italians have the smallest donor bank of all developed countries. According to press reports, it is simply not the national custom to give up organs. Is there a shared revulsion to giving up or receiving parts of the body as 'natural symbols' of the nation?" Allen and Russo, *Revisioning Italy*, 2. For "natural symbols," see Mary Douglas, *Natural Symbols: Explorations in Cosmology* (London: Pantheon, Penguin, 1970).

30. Jenkins, *Using Murder*, 112.

31. "*I segni bluastri dei denti sulle gambe della ragazza, i buchi violacei che le scavano la pelle in una corona stretta e profonda, perfettamente circolare. E vedo anche quelli sul sedere, tanti e scuri, quando il dottore l'afferra per un braccio per voltarla sul tavolo di marmo con uno schiocco molle e sgonfio che mi sorprende.*" Lucarelli, *Lupo mannaro*, 19.

32. *"Mi fa star meglio. . . . È un modo di eliminare lo stress e in un lavoro da dirigente . . . se ne accumula parecchio."* Ibid., 64.

33. *"L'unica cosa che non so è perchè le mordo."* Ibid., 65–66.

34. *"Liscia e rosea, quasi senza rughe, distesa come un bambino."* Ibid., 38.

35. My focus is on Lucarelli's novel, but it should be noted that *Almost Blue*, a Cecchi Gori production, was adapted for the screen in 2000 by Sergio Donati and Alex Infascelli, directed by Infascelli, with Lorenza Indovina as Grazia and Claudio Santamaria as Simone.

36. *"Qua non siamo in America, qua siamo in Italia."* Carlo Lucarelli, *Almost Blue* (Turin: Einaudi, 1997), 22.

37. In the enormous bibliography informing these discussions that dates to the period when Lucarelli wrote *Almost Blue* and to a time before the "viral" aspects of the Internet, see Mitchell, *E-Topia*; Zygmunt Bauman, *Postmodernity and Its Discontents* (New York: New York University Press, 1999), esp. 186–208; Armand Mattelart, *Networking the World, 1794–2000*, trans. Liz Carey-Libbrecht and James Cohen (Minneapolis: Minnesota University Press, 2000), esp. 75–120; Cass Sunstein, *Republic.Com* (Princeton, N.J.: Princeton University Press, 2001); Andrew Feenberg and Maria Bakardjieva, "Consumers or Citizens? The Online Comunity Debate," in *Community in the Digital Age: Philosophy and Practice,* ed. Andrew Feenberg and Maria Bakardjieva (Lanham, Md.: Rowman and Littlefield, 2004), 1–28; and Anabel Quan-Haase and Barry Wellman, with James Witt and Keith Hampton, "Capitalizing on the Net: Social Contact, Civic Engagement, and Sense of Community," in *The Internet in Everyday Life,* ed. Barry Wellman and Caroline Haythornthwaite (London: Blackwell, 2002), esp. 292–297.

38. Glen Harper remarked of *Almost Blue* that "one thing about rereading a 10-year-old novel, though (especially one that wore its technology on its sleeve as *Almost Blue* does)—life is changing very fast, making large chunks of the narrative seem dated (almost historical): noisy modems, e-mail downloaded from Eudora, and that radio scanner's access to e-mail (though Grazia notes that the GSM phones already in circulation in Italy at that time were immune to the scanners)." Glen Harper, "The Other Carlo Lucarelli," *International Noir Fiction* (Weblog), July 8, 2008, http://internationalnoir.blogspot.com/2008/07/other-carlo-lucarelli.html (accessed August 25, 2009).

39. For a discussion of the potential impact of technology on the public sphere that is coeval with Lucarelli's book, see Anna Camaiti Hostert, *Passing: Dissolvere le identità, superare le differenze* (Rome: Castelvecchi, 1996).

40. See Kaja Silverman, *The Acoustic Mirror: The Female Voice in Psychoanalysis and Cinema* (Bloomington: Indiana University Press, 1988), esp. 42–50.

41. The fear of violation from without corresponds to Seltzer's assertion that the social subject is "in a state of shock" as a result of the trauma of repetitive violence that constitutes the machine age. "One might say that the subject of shock or trauma is thus inseparable from the notion of the cultural construction or historical determination of the subject as such, the subject determined from the outside in." Seltzer, *Serial Killers*, 71. Recent developments in neuroscience regarding the pathological imitation of violence have shed light on how the human brain is "hardwired" with regard to the consumption of violence. See, for example, Giacomo Riz-

zolatti, Leonardo Fogassi, and Vittorio Gallese, "Neuropsychological Mechanisms Underlying the Understanding and Imitation of Action," *Nature Reviews: Neuroscience* 2 (September 2001): 661–670; Wolfgang Prinz, "An Ideomotor Approach to Imitation," in *Perspectives on Imitation: From Neuroscience to Social Science,* ed. Susan Hurley and Nick Chater (Cambridge, Mass.: MIT Press, 2005), 1:141–156; Susan Hurley, "Imitation, Media Violence, and Freedom of Speech," *Philosophical Studies: An International Journal for Philosophy in the Analytic Tradition* 117 (2004): 165–218; and Susan Hurley and Nick Chater, "Introduction: Why Imitation Matters," in *Perspectives on Imitation: From Neuroscience to Social Science,* ed. Susan Hurley and N. Chater (Cambridge, Mass.: MIT Press, 2005), 2:1–52.

42. *"Ecco perchè ammazza la gente. Di più: la sbrana, la spappola, la distrugge. L'annienta. La spoglia nuda, si spoglia nudo e ne assume l'aspetto, come se si rivestisse di una seconda pella."* Lucarelli, *Almost Blue,* 97.

43. Adriana Cavarero, *Horrorism: Naming Contemporary Violence,* trans. Brian McGuaig (New York: Columbia University Press, 2009), 29.

44. For Jame Gumb, the missing "s" of his first name, initially just a typographical error on his birth certificate, plants the idea that he should be shed of that other curved presence, the one on his body: the penis he seeks to be rid of through gender reassignment surgery. Jonathan Demme's popular 1991 film adaptation of Harris's novel was released in Italy the same year under the title *Il Silenzio degli Innocenti.*

45. Harris's reference is both to Robert Louis Stevenson's 1886 novella *Dr. Jekyll and Mr. Hyde* and to the phoneme "hide," underscoring the killer's quest for a new skin and a new identity.

46. *"Un drago coperto da squame che . . . gli saltava sul petto e gli mangiava la faccia."* Lucarelli, *Almost Blue,* 85 (emphasis in the original).

47. Accepting a more "rhizomatic" understanding of the genealogy of influences, to follow Deleuze and Guattari, we might say that if reference to Thomas Harris led to Robert Louis Stevenson, so too Ortese loops back to the nineteenth-century British novelist. Like Stevenson in his 1883 adventure novel *Treasure Island,* Ortese christened the island locale Ocaña in her fable-like novel. For the rhizome, see Gilles Deleuze and Felix Guattari, *A Thousand Plateaus: Capitalism and Schizophrenia,* trans. Brian Massumi (Minneapolis: University of Minnesota Press, 1987) 25.

48. Concerning a potential Deleuzian reading of Ortese and the prospects of a fluid (and constant) state of gender transformation, see Concetta Chiappetta-Miller's dissertation, "Projections: Monster and Diva from Vision to Voice" (New York University, 2005). See also Adria Frizzi, "Performance, or Getting a Piece of the Other, or In the Name of the Father, or The Dark Continent of Femininity, or Just Like a Woman: Anna Maria Ortese's *L'iguana,*" *Italica* 79, no. 3 (2002): 379–390; and Flora Maria Ghezzo, "Paesaggi del desiderio, ovvero *devenir femme* tra terra e acqua," in ". . . *e c'e di mezzo il mare": lingua, letteratura e civiltà marina,* ed. Art van den Bossche, Michael Bastiansen, and Corinna Salvadori Lonergan (Florence: Franco Cesati Editore, 2002), 265–278.

49. For valuable explorations of gender and true crime in contemporary Italian fiction, see Nicoletta Di Ciolla MacGowan, "Perfecting Females/Pursuing Truths: Texts, Subtexts and Postmodern Genre-Crossing in Salvatori's Noir, *Sublime anima*

di donna," in *Trends in Contemporary Italian Narrative, 1980–2007,* ed. Gillian Ania and Ann Hallamore Caesar (Newcastle upon Tyne, England: Cambridge Scholars, 2007), 29–49; and Nicoletta Di Ciolla MacGowan, "Relative Values: Resisting Desire and Individuation in Barbara Garlaschelli's *Alice nell'ombra and Sorelle,"* *Rivista di Studi Italiani,* 21, no. 1 (2003): 119–133.

50. *"Io non mi chiamo Callaghan ma Negro. E sono di Nardò, in provincia di Lecce."* Lucarelli, *Almost Blue,* 55.

51. *"Io vi conosco voi donne nella polizia . . . sempre incazzatissime per far vedere che sono meglio degli uomini . . . e poi, Cristo, vestitovi un po' da donne!"* Ibid., 56.

52. *"Non ci divento commissario capo perché non sono laureata"; "Mi ci vestirei anche da donna, ma poi la pistola dove cazzo la metto?"* Ibid.

53. The emphasis laid on Grazia's youth, class, and rank differ widely from, for example, two popular representations of competent British policewomen in the mid-1990s. Jane Tennant (Helen Mirren) of the BBC series *Prime Suspect* (broadcast in the UK in 1991 and for the first time in Europe the following year) successfully solves her cases. In contrast, the female protagonist-narrator of Martin Amis's 1997 novel *Night Train* begins the story with her declaration, "I am a police." Contrasting with Tennant, Amis's Mike Hoolihan is a mid-rank inspector on the London police force who sees no gender in her job: police are police, irrespective of gender. Lucarelli and Argento, as we see in the chapter that follows, find otherwise.

54. *"Certe volte c'è qualcosa che mi striscia sotto la pelle, come un animale."* Lucarelli, *Almost Blue,* 51.

55. So attired, she seems in many ways the precursor to the character Giorgia, a private investigator whose principal beat is Bologna, in Grazia Verasani's 2004 novel *Quo vadis, baby?* adapted for the screen by Gabriele Salvatores the following year.

56. *"Non è un odore gradevole, il suo. È odore di fumo vecchio assorbito dalla stoffa fredda del giubbotto, acido di sudore e un po' dolce, come sangue, come quello di sua madre in certi giorni."* Lucarelli, *Almost Blue,* 91.

57. See Cavarero, *Horrorism,* esp. 10–13 and 106–115.

58. " . . . *quelle cose. Quei feticci mi venne da pensare. Bambole e bambolotti di plastica scolorita, raccolti forse in qualche discarica, o lungo la sponda di uno dei tanti canali della zona, dove la corrente lascia spesso cose buttate via. Vidi . . . le loro chiome svolazzare. Sembravano . . . piccoli, nudi, e macabri trofei."* Eraldo Baldini, *Bambine* (Rome: Ritmi Theoria, 1995), 15–16.

59. *Bambine* anticipates my discussion of disposable children in part 3, which uses the 2002 murder of Samuele Lorenzi in Italy's remote Valle D'Aosta as a point of departure.

60. Tithecott, *Of Men and Monsters,* 57.

61. In *Torture and Truth: the New Ancient World,* Page Du Bois writes: "The female body—among others—is still represented as the locus of truth . . . and the philosophical subject needs to find the truth, needs to locate truth elsewhere in the body of another, employs torture or sexual abuse against the other because he finds that he does not know the truth, because the truth has been defined as a secret . . . one that eludes the subject, must be discovered, unveiled and that truth will continue to beckon the torturer, the sexual abuser, who will find in the other—slave, woman, revolutionary—silent or not, secret or not, the receding phantasm of a

truth that must be hunted down, extracted, torn out in torture." Quoted in Freccero, "Historical Violence," 53.

62. Gremmi's recycling tendencies correspond significantly to the presumed killer in Mauro Covacich's *Colpo di Lama* (Vicenza: Neri Pozza, 1995), a man named Lama whose remarkable ability to reclaim Pordenone's discarded flotsam makes him an attractive candidate for a specialized welfare program

63. On the representation of Milan as a noir locus, see Giuliana Pieri, "Milano nera: Representing and Imagining Milan in Italian Noir and Crime Fiction," *Romance Studies* 25, no. 2 (2007): 123–135, which details imaging of the city in a range of *giallisti* by such vintage writers as Augusto De Angelis, Renato Olivieri, Antonio Perria, Giovanni Testori, and the eminent Giorgio Scerbanenco, as well as by newcomers such as Piero Colaprico, Giuseppe Genna, Sandrone Dazieri, and Gianni Biondillo. Pieri mentions Pinketts's work but focuses on the rich examples found in other authors. On De Angelis and Milan, see Luca Somigli, "The Realism of Detective Fiction: Augusto De Angelis. Theorist of the Italian *giallo*," *Symposium* 59 (2005): 70–83.

64. "*Non voglio denunciar(lo). Voglio punirlo.*" Andrea Pinketts, *Il senso della frase* (Milan: Feltrinelli, 1995), 213.

65. See Pieri, "Milano nera," 123; and John Foot, *Milan since the Miracle: City, Culture, and Identity* (Oxford: Berg, 2001).

66. " . . . *è la via in cui idealmente si congiungono la vita e la morte. La vita è rappresentata da bar in cui si stazionano le modelle americane affammate di copertine e di cappuccini. La morte è nella sobrietà di via Vincenzo Monti.*" Pinketts, *Il senso della frase*, 37. This moribund face of Milan is something Sandrone Dazieri remarked on in his 1999 novel *Attenti al gorilla*, whose narrator observes that Milan disappoints nearly everyone who goes or lives there. "*Sognano il verde . . . trovano solo qualche albero morente*" (They dream of green (but) find only some dying tree). See Dazieri, *Attenti al gorilla* (Milan: Mondadori, 1999), 12, quoted in Pieri, "Milano nera," 130.

67. " . . . *tappezzate dai 'composite' di modelli e modelle. Una tappezzeria umana. . . . i composite erano proprio questo:* la versione patinata delle foto sulle tombe. *Il certificato di morte.*" Pinketts, *Il senso della frase*, 38 (my emphasis).

68. In *Il senso della frase*, Pinketts makes Olegario's monstrousness clear on numerous occasions: "Olegario is the name of *that monster*. . . . I've seen him, he's horrible. Two meters high, like I said, and he looks like a giant vulture." Olegario's size tallies with the identikit profile of the "Monster" derived from evidence: footprints at the Florentine crime scenes indicated a very large, probably tall individual. Pinketts wrote that Ulli "seemed enthusiastic. But when I was obliged to tell her that in order to do me a favor she would have had to bait a probable serial killer two meters tall she hung up"; and, finally, like a fetching Frankenstein, Lazzaro sees (that) "Olegario was, sure, a jumble of incompatible features but taken altogether it was a patchwork of singular beauty." Ibid., 162, 169, and 183, respectively.

69. "*Gigantografie. Le foto rappresentavano soggetti diversi, soggetti ridotti a oggetti, nudi per lo più. C'erano bende, scudisci, catene, pinze all'opera. Sarebbe stato del banale materiale sadomaso, se non per i protagonisti delle scene. Ogni tipo di deformità era rappresentata, dalla più innocua alla più scioccante.*" Ibid., 232.

70. Seltzer notes that Dennis Cooper points to the primary role of seeing photographic evidence of pornographic violence in serial murder: "Maybe if I hadn't seen this . . . snuff. Photographs," the killer/narrator of Cooper's novel *Frisk* (first published in 1991) says. Later he says, "By the time I found out they were posed photographs, it was too late. I already wanted to live in a world where some boy I didn't know could be killed and his corpse could be made available to the public." Quoted in Seltzer, *Serial Murders,* 188.

71. See Carloni, "La geografia metropolitana."

72. British psychiatrist Robert Brittain observed in 1970 that part of the psychosexual composition of the serial killer includes "obsessive interest in forms of photography, representation, and 'mirroring' in general." Robert Brittain, "The Sadistic Murderer," *Medicine, Science, and the Law* 10 (1970), quoted in Seltzer, *Serial Murders,* 130 and 151n22.

73. Vincent Leitch linked the words "disciplinary apparatus" to fashion in "Costly Compensations: Postmodern Fashion, Politics, Identity," *Modern Fiction Studies* 42, no. 1 (1996): 111–128.

74. Pinketts, *Il senso della frase,* 232.

75. Chapter 5 explores in greater detail the subject of Italian "pulp fiction" of the 1990s.

76. Curzio Malaparte, *The Skin,* trans. David Moore (Marlboro, Vt.: Marlboro Press, 1952), 126. In the Italian, Malaparte, writing in the immediate postwar period, uses the word *schifosa,* which actually means "disgusting" or "repellent" more than it does "loathsome," which could be construed as more passive.

77. Please see note 34 in the introduction, where I discuss the contradictory pull between the real and the represented and, as Alan O'Leary has suggested, the "chiaro" and the "oscuro."

3. "Penile" Procedure

1. The role of visual scrutiny and the need for a blow-up is crucial to Michelangelo Antonioni's 1968 film of the same name—*Blow-up*—which also concerns the inability to solve a murder for which there exists ample evidence demonstrating culpability. It is worth noting the element of casting that will link Antonioni's film to Argento, the subject of this chapter: David Hemmings played both the mod photographer, Thomas, in *Blow-up* and Marc in *Profondo rosso,* which I discuss below. Both Antonioni's film and Pinketts's novel may also link to Elio Petri's 1970 film, *Indagine su un cittadino al di sopra di ogni sospetto,* in which the protagonist, il Dottore (Gian Maria Volonté), plants a series of very obvious and self-incriminating articles of evidence demonstrating that he is the murderer of Augusta Terzi (Florinda Balkan). When the Dottore walks through the crime lab and through enormous blow-ups of fingerprints the size of bedsheets, he faints. The message is clear: despite overwhelming evidence—and the Dottore is overwhelmed, fainting at the end of the scene—he is still "beyond suspicion" in the way of Olegario, an industrial titan from Milan.

2. "*C'erano stati nel mondo germanico ed anglosassone, mai in quello latino.*" Ferri, *Il Caso Pacciani,* 34. All translations are my own unless otherwise indicated.

3. Mary Wood, *Italian Cinema* (New York: Berg, 2005), 11; and Mikel Koven, *La Dolce Morte: Vernacular Cinema and the Italian Giallo Film* (Lanham, Md.: Scarecrow Press, 2006), v.

4. Wood, *Italian Cinema*, 57. See also Roberto Pugliese, *Dario Argento* (Milan: Il Castoro, 1996); and Teo Mora, *Storia del cinema dell'orrore*, vol. 1, *Dal 1957 al 1966* (Rome: Fanucci, 2002); and Mora, *Storia del cinema dell'orrore*, vol. 2, *Dal 1966 al 1978* (Rome: Fanucci, 2003).

5. Wood, *Italian Cinema*, 57.

6. The term "stepbrothers of neorealism" is from Stefano della Casa, *27th International Film Festival Rotterdam Catalogue* (1997), 288. On Margheriti and other participants in the *filone* of zombie apocalypse (read: horror, slasher, and other abject forms), see Dana Renga's essay "Pastapocalypse!: New York Revisited in the Italian Exploitation Film" in the summer 2011 special issue of *The Italianist* dedicated to contemporary Italian cinema.

7. I will refer to Argento's films by their Italian titles. The filmography that follows is in chronological order by date of initial release; names of U.S. DVD distributors are provided in parentheses . *L'uccello dalle piume di cristallo* (*The Bird with the Crystal Plumage*), 1970 (VC 1 Home Video); *Il gatto a nove code* (*Cat o' Nine Tails*), 1971 (Anchor Bay Entertainment); *Quattro mosche di velluto grigio* (*Four Flies on Grey Velvet*), 1971 (Ryko Distribution); *Profondo rosso* (*Deep Red*), 1975 (Anchor Bay Entertainment); *Suspiria*, 1977 (Anchor Bay Entertainment); *Inferno*, 1980 (Anchor Bay Entertainment); *Tenebre* (*Tenebrae/Unsane*), 1982 (Anchor Bay Entertainment); *Fenomena* (*Creepers*), 1985 (Anchor Bay Entertainment); *Opera* (*Opera*; *Terror at the Opera*), 1987 (Anchor Bay Entertainment); *Trauma* (*Trauma*), 1993 (Anchor Bay Entertainment); *La Sindrome di Stendhal* (*The Stendhal Syndrome*), 1996 (Troma Video); *Il fantasma dell'opera* (*The Phantom of the Opera*), 1998 (Ardustry Home Entertainment); *Non ho sonno* (*Sleepless*), 2001 (Artisan); *Il Cartaio* (*The Card Player*), 2004 (Anchor Bay Entertainment); *La Terza Madre* (*Mother of Tears*), 2007 (Dimension Extreme).

8. Maitland McDonagh, *Broken Mirrors/Broken Minds: The Dark Dreams of Dario Argento* (New York: Citadel, 1994), 244.

9. Mark Seltzer, *Serial Killers: Death and Life in America's Wound Culture* (New York: Routledge, 1998), esp. 53n10. See also Annalee Newitz, "Serial Killers, True Crime, and Economic Performance Anxiety," in *Mythologies of Violence in Postmodern Media*, ed. Christopher Sharrett (Detroit: Wayne State University Press, 1999), 65–83.

10. *Blu Notte*, RAI 3, February 16, 2003.

11. Carol Clover, *Men, Women, and Chainsaws* (Princeton, N.J.: Princeton University Press, 1992), 205.

12. Vivian Sobchak, *The Address of the Eye: A Phenomenology of Film Experience* (Princeton, N.J.: Princeton University Press, 1992), 93.

13. Quoted in Susan Crutchfield, "Touching Scenes and Finishing Touches,": Blindness in the Slasher Film, in *Mythologies of Violence in Postmodern Media*, ed. Christopher Sharrett (Detroit: Wayne State University Press, 1999), 279.

14. It was believed that images in early cinema could leap off the screen and therefore posed a danger to the audience. See Mary Ann Doane, "Technology's

Body: Cinematic Vision in Modernity," *differences: A Journal of Feminist Cultural Studies* 5, no. 2 (1993): 1–21.

15. See Linda Williams's considerations of this film in "An Eye for an Eye," *Sight and Sound* 4, no. 4 (1994): 4–16. See also Chris Gallant, "Threatening Glances, Voyeurism, Eye Violation: From *Peeping Tom* to *Opera*," in *Art of Darkness: The Cinema of Dario Argento*, ed. Chris Gallant (Godalming, UK: FAB Press, 2001), 11. For an exploration of the vulnerability of the eyes in *Due occhi diabolici (Two Evil Eyes)*, see also James Gracey, *Dario Argento* (Harpenden: Herts, 2010), 114.

16. Argento believes in the bad luck that *Macbeth* brings, calling the filming "overall . . . a terrible experience" and citing a string of misfortunes that included the loss of Vanessa Redgrave's participation, the deaths of one of the actors as well as his father during shooting, and the breaking off of his own engagement. See McDonagh, *Broken Mirrors/Broken Minds*, 248.

17. See Vito Zagarrio, "Perdere la testa (per Argento)," in *Argento vivo: Il cinema di Dario Argento tra genere e autorialità*, ed. Vito Zagarrio (Venice: Marsilio, 2008), 25.

18. Argento had been asked to direct a theatrical staging of an opera, but this did not materialize. See McDonagh, *Broken Mirrors/Broken Minds*, 247.

19. See Linda Williams, "When the Woman Looks," in *The Dread of Difference*, ed. Barry Grant (Austin: University of Texas Press, 1996), 15–34.

20. This sequence from *La Sindrome di Stendhal* is visible on YouTube. In the nine-minute sequence, the relevant segment begins at approximately minute 4:00. See http://www.youtube.com/watch?v=E7_89xO2dgw (accessed April 11, 2011).

21. Gracey notes that it took "five artists two days to create the grimy and depraved grafitti that stains the walls of this location." See Gracey, *Dario Argento*, 129.

22. See "Stendhal Syndrome" at Paul McFedries's *Wordspy.com*, http://www.wordspy.com/words/Syendhalssyndrome.asp (accessed March 12, 2011).

23. Ibid.

24. "*Sensazioni di piacere e di dolore si confondono, strane curiosità lo divorano, di sapere 'quello che [sta]dietro, dentro, non davanti.' La parola 'dentro' gli torna nelle rievocazioni con unusitata frequenza: dentro, al quadro, dentro di sé.*" Graziella Magherini, *La Sindrome di Stendhal* (Florence: Ponte alle Grazie, 1989), 51.

25. This excludes films based directly on the events, like the two released in 1986, *Il mostro di Firenze,* directed by Cesare Ferrario, and *Firenze: L'assassino è ancora tra di noi,* directed by Camillo Teti.

26. For dates of filming, see Gracey, *Dario Argento*, 125.

27. "*Ha impiegato quasi tre anni a condurre in porto l'ambizioso progetto.*" Michele Anselmi, *L'Unità*, January, 24, 1996, quoted in "La Sindrome di Stendhal," *Dario Argento*, ed. Gabrielle Lucantonio (Rome: Dino Audino Editore, 2001), 78.

28. See Antonio Tentori, *Dario Argento: sensualità dell'omicidio* (Alessandria: Edizioni Falsopiano, 1997), 28.

29. John Francis Lane believes the setting is "a tower block in a vast suburb of Rome." As concerns the social and political context of the film, although Lane notes "digs" at Berlusconi, there is no mention of any specific link to the "Monster" of Florence, despite the obvious allusion of the title. See *Screen International* 982 (November 4, 1994), 41.

30. Gracey explores what he describes as Argento's use of "art as weapon," describing also *Tenebre* (*Tenebrae/Unsane*), to make his point. See Gracey, *Dario Argento*, 30.

31. See Marcia Landy, *Italian Film* (Cambridge: Cambridge University Press, 2000), 357.

32. See McDonagh, *Broken Mirrors/Broken Minds*, 53–54.

33. Fabio Maiello, *L'occhio che uccide* (Naples: Edizioni Scientifiche, 1996), 72.

34. Ibid.

35. See note 1 for this chapter, above: the extra-diegetic intertext with Antonioni's *Blow-Up* (1966) is clear: in Antonioni's film, Hemmings plays a photographer who cannot "see" what has happened until he makes his series of blow-ups. See Zagarrio, "Aprire le finestre alle emozioni. Argento on Argento," in *Argento vivo*, 31.

36. Vito Zagarrio discusses other examples of who "lose their heads" in Argento's corpus. See Zagarrio, "Perdere la testa (per Argento)," 13–28.

37. Susannah Radstone, quoted in Ann Kaplan, *Trauma Culture: The Politics of Terror and Loss in Media and Literature* (New Brunswick, N.J.: Rutgers University Press, 2005), 35. See also Giacomo Manzoli, "Il trauma e la trama," in *L'eccesso della visione: Il cinema di Dario Argento*, ed. Giulia Carluccio, Giacomo Manzoli, and Roy Menarini (Turin: Lindau, 2003), 39–53.

38. Cavarero, *Horrorism*, 14–19.

39. The Bosnian War, I suggest, makes up part of the context that frames rape in *La Sindrome di Stendhal*. Reports of Serb soldiers systematically raping Muslim women were frequent and extensive in the European media, no less so in Italy, where greater proximity to the Balkan theater of war produced some different perceptions of the genocidal rape taking place there. See, for example, Beverly Allen, *Rape Warfare: The Hidden Genocide in Bosnia-Herzegovina and Croatia* (Minneapolis: University of Minnesota Press, 1996).

40. See Antonio Tentori's interview with the director in Tentori, *Dario Argento*, 30–31.

41. My use of place follows Michel de Certeau's. He conceived of place as "the order . . . in accord with which the elements are distributed in relationships of co-existence. . . . It implies an indication of stability." Space, on the other hand, considers "vectors of direction, velocities, and time variables. . . . In short, *space is practiced place*." See Michel de Certeau, *The Practice of Everyday Life*, trans. Steven Rendall (Berkeley: University of California Press, 1988), 117. Elizabeth Grosz draws a similar distinction, and, thus, "place" is constituted by being occupied or dwelled in and "space" is thought of as "territory which is mappable." See Grosz, *Space, Time and Perversion* (London: Routledge, 1995), 123.

42. Roy Menarini observes that "*è un vero peccato che Deleuze non abbia scritto di Argento perchè ne avrebbe avuto e recato soddisfazione,*" (it's a shame that Deleuze did not write about Argento because he would have found satisfaction in doing so and provided satisfaction as well). Roy Menarini, "Tutto l'orrore che c'è," in *Argento vivo: Il cinema di Dario Argento tra genere e autorialità*, ed. Vito Zagarrio (Venice: Marsilio, 2008), 78. Critics who have hazarded a Deleuzian reading of Argento—and not simply wished for one, as Menarini does—such as Giulia Carluccio, focus on a more evident point in Deleuze's thoughts about cinema, the "action

image." See Carluccio, "Poetica dell'erranza: Flâneries, architetture, percorsi della visione," in *L'eccesso della visione. Il cinema di Dario Argento,* ed. Giulia Carluccio, Giacomo Manzoli, and Roy Menarini (Turin: Lindau, 2003), 55–62. See also Anna Powell's expressly Deleuzian reading of *Suspiria* in her *Deleuze and the Horror Film* (Edinburgh: Edinburgh University Press, 2005), 142–145. Colette Balmain has also attempted a Deleuzian reading of *La Sindrome di Stendhal* in "Female Subjectivity and the Politics of 'Becoming Other,'" *Kinoeye: New Perspectives on European Film* 2, no. 12 (2002), available at http://www.kinoeye.org/02/12/balmain12.php (accessed 12 March 2011). My reading differs from Balmain's in two significant ways. First, Balmain focuses on the effect of masculinity on female identity. Second, her interest is mapped by way of reference to a rhizomatic understanding of cinematic space.

43. See Deleuze and Guattari, *Anti-Oedipus,* 139–145 and 184–192.

44. Silvia Ross also offers a reading of Argento's film in a context considering tourism's effect on Florence. See her *Tuscan Spaces, Literary Construction of Place* (Toronto: University of Toronto Press, 2010), 110–119. Ross's interest is principally in the French tourist Stendhal and his travel writings about Florence and, following from this, Argento's film.

45. What a difference twenty years will make: following the 2002 murder of Samuele Lorenzi, Cogne, located in the Valle D'Aosta, actually experienced an up-tick in "horror" tourism based on travelers visiting the site of the murder. For the analogous scenario concerning tourism and the Holocaust, see Nancy Harrowitz, "Primo Levi and Holocaust Tourism," in *Primo Levi: The Austere Humanist,* ed. Joseph Farrell (Oxford: Peter Lang, 2004), 203–214. See also Mark Lewandoski, "Tourist Season at Auschwitz," *Gettysburg Review* 12, no. 2 (1999): 293–302.

46. See Sarah Dunant, "A Florentine Death by Michele Giuttari," *Sunday Times* (London), http://entertainment.timesonline.co.uk/tol/arts_and_entertainment/books/fiction/article1971789.ece (accessed March 10, 2011). This remark recalls the notion of "chiaroscuro" with regard to the representation of Italy and Italian culture. See note 34 of the introduction. Chiaroscuro takes on greater significance, given the primacy of painting in Argento's work, and *La Sindrome di Stendhal* in particular.

47. *"Firenze è una città cattiva e lo è sempre stata." Blu Notte,* February 16, 2003.

48. The phrase "dream of Italy" is the name of a travel agency specializing in organized tours of Italy; see their Web site at http://www.dreamofitaly.com/. Please see http://www.dreamofitaly.com/public/112.cfm, accessed 17 August 2009, for a 2005 edition of the agency's brochure, which features an interview with the American author Frances Mayes, whose *Under the Tuscan Sun* was first published by Chronicle Books in 1996, the same year Argento's film was released. Like other travel writing about Italy written by foreigners, Mayes's encounter with Cortona, where she buys an abandoned house, offers the chance to refashion self and identity. As Silvia Ross observes, those interested in a second home in Italy are interested in a place that "embodies lifestyle" in a place that is foreign but not alienating. See Ross, *Tuscan Spaces: Literary Construction of Place* (Toronto: University of Toronto Press, 2010), 135.

49. Concerning the practice of *errance* and the way it recalls the freedom of navigation of the *flâneur,* by which new and unusual itineraries are charted, see Carluccio, "Poetica dell'erranza," 55–64. See also Koven, *La Dolce Morte,* 92–95.

50. *"Fin dall'inizio ho pensato che non ero costretto nella prigione della città. . . . Per me saltare da una città ad un'altra, tenendo una certa omogeneità di racconto, era normalissimo."* Zagarrio, "Aprire le finestre alle emozioni," 38.

51. This sequence is visible on YouTube. See http://www.youtube.com/watch?v=E B3rbOkFpoQ&feature=related (accessed September 15, 2009).

52. *"C'è una persona che cammina lungo una strada che è a Milano, prosegue e scende da una scala che è a Torino. Nessuno però ha notato."* Zagarrio, "Aprire le finestre alle emozioni," Zagarrio, "Aprire le finestre alle emozioni," 38.

53. *"C'è Perugia, c'è Roma, c'è Torino, c'è un pezzetto di Milano. Non si nota."* Ibid.

54. This is the typical jumping-off point for critics (and fans), who appear to appreciate the "late" Argento less than his earlier *giallo* films. See Claudio Bisoni, "Dal rifiuto alla celebrazione. Dario Argento e la critica," in *Argento vivo: Il cinema di Dario Argento tra genere e autorialità*, ed. Vito Zagarrio (Venice: Marsilio, 2008), 53–62; and Stefano della Casa, "Il nuovo cinema di Dario Argento," in *Argento vivo*, 68–72.

55. *"Che non poteva (sic) fare un film sull'arte a Phoenix. Era veramente impossibile . . . Non si può rimanere turbati, addirittura svenire, davanti a un grattacielo oppure di fronte a un ponte, per quanto magnifico sia. Un ponte e un grattacielo non possono sostituire Raffaello. Vedere Raffaello è come ricevere una pugnalata al cuore."* Daniele Costantini and Francesco Dal Bosco, "L'assassino potrei essere io," in *Nuovo cinema Inferno: L'opera di Dario Argento* (Milan: Pratiche, 1997), 169–170. Gracey also observes that Argento "had had enough of America and wanted to return to his roots." See Gracey, *Dario Argento*, 125.

56. Paul Ginsborg, *Italy and Its Discontents: Family, Civil Society, State, 1980–2001* (London: Penguin, 2001), 314. See also Aurelio Lepre, *Storia della prima repubblica. L'Italia dal 1943 al 2003* (Bologna: Il Mulino, 2004), 231–241.

57. The maze of waterways recalls the other mazes, usually subterranean, that Argento visualizes in his films, but also the bleed of categories of representation that I described in the introduction. The culvert where Anna is held prisoner and the waterways Alfredo's body travels through function as connectors, not unlike the London sewer system, which Paul Dobraszczk sees as a system that shuffles, like the monstrous, between the real and the imagined. See Dobraszczk, "'Monstrous Sewers': Experiencing London's Main Drainage System," in *Monsters and the Monstrous: Myths and Metaphors of Enduring Evil*, ed. Niall Scott (Amsterdam: Rodopi, 2007), 9–32.

58. See Carol Clover, *Men, Women, and Chainsaws: Gender in the Modern Horror Film* (Princeton: Princeton University Press, 1992); Clover, "Her Body, Himself: Gender in the Slasher Film," *Representations* 20 (1987):187–228; and Linda Williams, "Film Bodies: Gender, Genre, and Excess," *Film Quarterly* 44, no. 4 (1991): 2–13. Criticism that addresses the possibilities for reading possible realignments of gender normativity in Argento's films is split. Adam Knee, for example, rules favorably, and Jacqueline Reich offers a more skeptical view. My position lies between these, similar to the way Rhona Berenstein responds to Williams and Clover in *Attack of the Leading Ladies: Gender, Sexuality, and Spectatorship in Classic Horror Cinema* (New York: Columbia University Press, 1996). See Adam Knee, "Gender, Genre, Argento,"

in *The Dread of Difference,* ed. Barry Grant (Austin: University of Texas Press, 1996), 213–230; and Jacqueline Reich, "The Mother of All Horror: Witches, Gender, and the Films of Dario Argento," in *Monsters in the Italian Literary Imagination,* ed. Keala Jewell (Detroit: Wayne State University Press, 2001), 89–105.

59. For recent demographic trends in Argento's fan base, see Raiford Guins, "Blood and Black Gloves on Shiny Discs: New Media, Old Taste, and the Remediation of Italian Horror Films in the United States," in *Horror International,* ed. Stephen Schneider and Tony Williams (Detroit: Wayne State University Press, 2005), 15–32.

60. This sequence is visible on YouTube at http://www.youtube.com/watch?v=cGHULdKWF7I (accessed June 13, 2011).

61. In preparation for filming, Argento visited museums *"per vedere le immagini più perturbanti, per vedere le reazioni di tutti coloro che si fermavano davanti. . . . Li catalogavo a secondo dell'età, del tipo sociale, della nazionalità"* (to see the most disturbing images, to see the reactions of those who stopped in front of them . . . I catalogued them by their age, social type and nationality). Zagarrio, "Aprire le finestre alle emozioni," 33.

62. Visible on YouTube at. http://www.youtube.com/watch?v=cGHULdKWF7I (accessed June 13, 2011).

63. Sigmund Freud's essay "Medusa's Head," written in 1922 but published posthumously, lays out the motif of castration for a classic psychoanalytic critique. In Sigmund Freud, *Sexuality and the Psychology of Love* (New York: Collier, 1963), 212–213.

64. This sequence is visible on YouTube at http://www.youtube.com/watch?v=cGHULdKWF7I (accessed June 13, 2011).

65. In a later scene, a flashback shows the onset of the syndrome when Anna is a child. Similar to the Uffizi sequence, the flashback is meant to take place in the National Museum in Viterbo, where Anna grew up. The work of art that afflicts Anna with the onset of the syndrome, however, is the well-known Etruscan *Sarcophagus of the Spouses* from Cerveteri, ca. 500 BCE. This piece is rather famously on display at Rome's Villa Giulia, not in Viterbo's museum of Etruscan art.

66. In addition to influence of Hopper on Argento, cinematographer Vittorio Storaro, director of photography for *L'uccello dalle piume di cristallo,* also observed the influence of the violent paintings by German artists Otto Dix, Georg Grosz, and Konrad Fitzmueller. See in *Dario Argento,* ed. Gabrielle Lucantonio (Rome: Dino Audino Editore, 2001), 18. For the relation between these painters and serial killing, see Helen Tatar, *Lustmord: Sexual Murder in Weimar Germany* (Princeton, N.J.: Princeton University Press, 1995).

67. *"Ho battuto tutta l'Europa, visitando i più grandi musei, proprio per avere una sensazione più vera, più profonda, di questa famosa sindrome."* Zagarrio, "Aprire le finestre alle emozioni," 33.

68. For a retrospective of female figures in Argento's cinema, see Olivier Nelli, "L'image de la femme chez Dario Argento," http://www.lefantastique.net/cinema/dossiers/argento/femme_argento.htm (accessed 25 August 2009).

69. Cf. Adriana Cavarero, *Horrorism: Naming Contemporary Violence,* tran. Brian McGuaig (New York: Columbia University Press, 2009), 15.

70. Anna's wardrobe change recalls Joan Riviere's thoughts about masquerade in her 1929 essay "Womanliness as Masquerade." On the availability of this notion to a feminist reading, see also Mary Ann Doane, "Film and Masquerade: Theorizing the Female Spectator," in *Writing on the Body: Female Embodiment and Feminist Theory,* ed. Katie Conboy, Nadia Medina, and Sarah Stanbury (New York: Columbia University Press, 1997), 176–194. *La Sindrome di Stendhal* and the way it hinges on doubled or fractured female identity also recalls Alfred Hitchcock's *Vertigo.* That "Viterbo," Anna's home town, is also a virtual anagram of "Vertigo," may also sign Argento's homage to Hitchcock. I am grateful to Mark Chu for this observation.

71. Zagarrio remarks on Anna's rejection of "normal love" in her attitude toward Marco. See Zagarrio, "Perdere la testa (per Argento)," 22.

72. Without a tribe to come to abet her violence against heteronormativity, Anna is the subject caught in the jaws of phallocentrism. Even though she attempts a state of becoming not unlike the nomadic subject of Rosi Braidotti, her quest is individual and truncated, and her violence is punished by the state—quite literally—thus restoring law and order. It is worth remembering Braidotti's sober thoughts about nomadic violence that relies on tribal support. While nomadic violence is "opposed to state apparatus violence," at the same time "the *tribe* is the counterarmy. . . . Is this why nomads have always been persecuted as dangerous criminals by the state?" See Rosi Braidotti, *Nomadic Subjects: Embodiment and Sexual Difference in Contemporary Feminist Theory* (New York: Columbia University Press, 1994), 27 (my italics).

73. Mark Seltzer distinguishes between serial and multiple homicides: serial homicides are murders happening in similar circumstances at regular intervals; multiple homicides, on the other hand (like the term "spree," associated with fashion designer Gianni Versace's killer, Andrew Cunanan) lack the indication of a time interval. See Seltzer, *Serial Killers,* 9 and esp. 64–70.

74. Zagarrio, "Perdere la testa per Argento," 18–19.

75. Knee, "Gender, Genre, Argento," 226.

76. Reich's skepticism concerning the first two installments in Argento's Trilogy of the Mothers holds for the last film, *La terza madre,* where the subversive witches fare no better. Gracey would appear to agree, noting in his section of "trivia" about the film that Ferrini, Argento's cowriter, had proposed an ending that provided an escape for Anna: "Ferrini wanted the film to end with Anna imprisoned, her only source of consolation a print of one of Gainsborough's pastoral landscapes that she eventually escapes into." See Gracey, *Dario Argento,* 132.

77. Paul Smith, *Clint Eastwood: A Cultural Production* (Minneapolis: University of Minnesota Press,1993).

78. "*Il gioco di identificazione proposto allo spettatore non vuole ridursi ad una dicotomia, ma, sembra qui suggerire Argento, richiede un modello più sfumato e complesso.*" Deborah Toschi, "Attraverso lo specchio. *La Sindrome di Stendhal,*" in *Argento vivo: Il cinema di Dario Argento tra genere e autorialità,* ed. Vito Zagarrio (Venice: Marsilio, 2008), 316.

79. "*Tutti i miei film hanno avuto problemi con la censura.*" Quoted in Damien Granger, *Mad Movies* 77 (1999), quoted in Lucantonio, *Dario Argento,* 36.

80. See Giuseppe Colombo, "Produrre Dario Argento," in *Dario Argento*, ed. Luca Lardieri (Rome: Sovera Multimedia, 2007), 57. Colombo produces Argento's films. For an overview of the legal norms concerning censorship and cinema in Italy since Fascism, see Lillo Fiorello, *Cinema, regole, e censura* (Naples: Arte Tipografia Editrice, 2005). Alfredo Baldi's *Schermi proibiti: La censura in Italia dal 1947–1988* (Venice: Marsilio, 2002) offers details and useful background. For a general overview of censorship in contemporary Italy not limited to a cinematic context, see Vanessa Roghi, "Television and Censorship: Preliminary Research Notes" in *Culture, Censorship and the State in Twentieth-Century Italy*, ed. Guido Bonsaver and Robert Gordon (Oxford: Legenda Press, 2005), 150–157; Alan O'Leary, "Film and Anni di piombo: Representations of Politically-Motivated Violence in Recent Italian Cinema," in *Culture, Censorship and the State*, 168–178; and Alberto Abbruzzese, "Censorship in the Time of Berlusconi," *Culture, Censorship and the State*, 179–190.

81. "*Gesti volgari, comportamenti amorali, scene erotiche o di violenza, operazioni chirurgiche, fenomeni ipnotici o medianici, odio e vendetta, crimini o forme di suicidio che potrebbero causare emulazione.*" Rinaldo Censi, "Le forbici e il film bifronte," in *L'eccesso della visione. Il cinema di Dario Argento*, ed. Giulia Carluccio, Giacomo Manzoli, and Roy Menarini (Turin: Lindau, 2003), 204.

82. Fiorello, *Cinema, regole, e censura*, 76.

83. "*Gesti volgari, comportamenti amorali, scene erotiche o di violenza, operazioni chirurgiche, fenomeni ipnotici o medianici, odio e vendetta, crimini o forme di suicidio che potrebbero causare emulazione.*" Fiorello, *Cinema, regole, e censura*, 76.

84. Censi, "Le forbici e il film bifronte," 205.

85. "*Nei film, nei telefilm, senza capire che l'origine è sociale, non è colpa del cinema thriller, che viene visto da un certo tipo di pubblico, e non certo dai serial killer.*" Tentori, *Dario Argento*, 44.

86. Seltzer, 71. Scientific research supports the problems associated with the notion of "filling the subject from the outside in"; that is, with the concept that violence and aggression are imitative. Jonathan Freedman's *Media Violence and its Effect on Aggression: Assessing the Scientific Evidence* (Toronto: University of Toronto Press, 2002) reviews a range of experiments meant to measure aggressiveness and the presumed links to the visual display of violence, usually via television. The hypothesis that some causal link exists between the visual consumption of violence and the reproduction of violent behavior was repeatedly disproved.

87. See Christian Metz, *The Imaginary Signifier: Psychoanalysis and the Cinema* (Bloomington: Indiana University Press, 1982); Joan Copjec, "The Orthopsychic Subject: Film Theory and the Reception of Lacan," *October* 49 (Summer 1989): 53–71; Mary Ann Doane, *Femmes Fatales: Feminism, Film Theory, Psychoanalysis* (New York: Routledge, 1991); E. Ann Kaplan, "Freud, Film, and Culture," in *Freud: Conflict and Culture: Essays on His Life, Work, and Legacy*, ed. Michael Roth (New York: Knopf, 1998), 152–164; Barbara Creed, "Film and Psychoanalysis," in *The Oxford Guide to Film Studies*, ed. John Hill, Pamela Church Gibson, Richard Dyer, E. Ann Kaplan, and Paul Willemen (Oxford: Oxford University Press, 1998), 77–90; and Laura Mulvey, "Visual Pleasure and Narrative Cinema," in *Feminist Film Theory: A Reader*, ed. Sue Thornham (New York: New York University Press, 1999), 58–69.

88. See Dennis Howitt, *Crime, the Media, and the Law* (Chichester, England: John Wiley, 1998); W. James Potter, *On Media Violence* (Thousand Oaks, Calif.: Sage Publications, 1999); Gregory K. Moffatt, *Blind-Sided: Homicide Where It is Least Expected* (Westport, Conn.: Praeger, 2000); Martin Barker and Julian Petley, eds., *Ill Effects: The Media/Violence Debate* (London: Routledge, 2001); and Sheila Brown, *Crime and Law in Media Culture* (Buckingham: Open University Press, 2003).

89. See Rizzolatti, Fogassi, and Gallese, "Neuropsychological Mechanisms Underlying the Understanding and Imitation of Action"; Prinz, "An Ideomotor Approach to Imitation." If this view concerning imitation were to be accepted on a wider scale, it would have consequences of some moment for the film and advertising industries, which could perceive stronger government and social intervention in the conditions of display of their products and activities—in brief, greater censorship. For an excellent overview, see Hurley, "Imitation, Media Violence, and Freedom of Speech"; and Hurley and Chater, "Introduction: Why Imitation Matters."

90. Alessandri, *La leggenda del vampo*, 69.

91. "*Se ne sta ore incollato alla televisione: guarda di tutto, ma soprattutto i film pornografici e quelli del genere horror.*" Ibid., 68.

92. *Maniac*, William Lustig, 1980 (Grindhouse Releasing).

93. Alessandri, *La leggenda del Vampa*, 69.

94. "*A lungo aspetta quel film che l'ha tanto colpito, giunga a Firenze: ma invano.*" Ibid., 71.

95. Ibid., 380.

96. See Guins, "Blood and Black Gloves on Shiny Discs."

Part 2: Matricide and Fratricide

1. Julian Stallabrass, "Empowering Technology," in *Studying Culture: An Introductory Reader*, ed. Ann Gray and Jim McGuigan (London: Arnold Press, 1997), 357. This recalls Alan Turing's experimental "gender game," which consisted of "a man and a woman in separate rooms conversing only with written messages (who) try to convince each other that they are both women." See Turing "Computing Machinery and Intelligence," *Mind* 59 (1950): 433–460, available at http://loebner.net/Prizef/TuringArticle.html (accessed June 13, 2011).

2. After appearing on a RAI broadcast, the still was widely used in print and electronic media.

3. Although the face is still the sine qua non of identification in criminal investigation, increasingly, identity assigned by the state is based equally on a numeric system as on a photographic one, as in the form of the passport, for example, used for travel among differing sovereign states. Identity theft, for example, is based almost entirely on numerical identities (social security numbers, access codes, credit card numbers, etc.). For a more postmodern understanding of the ways in which faces may not convey identity, see also Lucy Grealy's *Autobiography of a Face* (Boston: Houghton Mifflin, 1994) and the coverage of Isabella Dinoire's face transplant in France in November 2005.

4. Jacques Lacan has commented fruitfully on this concept. See his *Freud's Papers on Technique*, 1953–1954, trans. and ed. by John Forrester (New York: Norton, 1988).

5. See Angela McRobbie, *Postmodernism and Popular Culture* (London: Routledge, 1994), 156.

6. This struggle bears obvious similarities to the struggle toward language and all that language acquisition subtends (entry into society, its laws and practices) that Jacques Lacan describes in his essay "The Mirror Stage" in *Écrits*, trans. Robert Sheridan (New York: W. W. Norton, 1977), 1–7.

4. Sono stati loro

1. Marco Imarisio, "Il fidanzato in cella: 'vorrei solo tornare indietro'," *Il Corriere della sera*, February 24, 2001. This and all translation mine unless otherwise indicated.

2. Fiorenza Sarzanini, "Io di te mi fiderò di ogni cosa," *Il Corriere della sera*, February 28, 2001.

3. Please see map 2.

4. Victims included Luciano Pavarotti's dietologist, whose Modena home was burgled (December 1999); Domenico Spartà, television quiz show host Pippo Baudo's physician, who was taken hostage in his villa and forced to open his safe (January 13, 2000); and the designer Mariella Burani and her family, who were surprised by intruders in their home in Emilia-Romagna (also on January 13). Finally, in the same period, three armed robbers shot and killed a man in a robbery outside Carpi, near Bologna.

5. Although Manuel Castells observed that cities would "be at the forefront of the waves of racism and xenophobia," the suburbs have emerged as another important proving ground, at least as witnessed in the violent upheaval in a three-week riot in 2005 in Seine-Saint-Denis, a suburb of Paris. See Manuel Castells, "European Cities, the Informational Society, and the Global Economy," in *Studying Culture: An Introductory Reader*, ed. Ann Gray and Jim McGuigan (London: Arnold Press, 1997), 324. On the 2005 riots in Paris's suburbs, see Marc Augé, "L'incendio di Parigi," *MicroMega* 7 (2005): 187–195.

6. Luigi Offreddu, "Lo sfogo del padre: 'maledetto il giorno che l'ha incontrata," *Il Corriere della sera*, February 25, 2011.

7. "Marocchini" literally means "Moroccans," but has been used as a catchall racist designation for black Africans, regardless of what their provenance is or whether they are legal immigrants. The racialized slippage between various African provenances returns in the Amanda Knox case explored in the epilogue.

8. The concept of moral panic is outlined in the introduction. Classic studies of "moral panics" include Stanley Cohen, *Folk Devils and Moral Panics: The Creation of the Mods and the Rockers* (Oxford: Basil Blackwell, 1972); and Stuart Hall, ed., *Policing the Crisis: Mugging, the State, and Law and Order* (London: MacMillan, 1978). See also Stanley Cohen and Jock Young, eds., *The Manufacture of the News: Deviance, Social Problems and the Mass Media* (London: Constable Press, 1973); and Sheila Brown, *Crime and Law in Media Culture* (Buckingham: Open Univer-

sity Press, 2003). For specific treatment of the "Slavic" contribution to moral panic in Italy, see Nicola Mai, "Myths and Moral Panics: Italian Identity and the Media Representation of Albanian Immigration," in *The Politics of Recognising Difference: Multiculturalism Italian Style*, ed. R. D. Grillo, and J. Pratt (Aldershot: Ashgate, 2002), 77–95.

9. The Novi Ligure double homicide was like a hot ember dropped in the already smoldering mass of anxiety created by the presence of Albanians in Italy, dating to the 1992 elections and the ouster of the Communists. Piero Vereni ably describes the representation of Italian xenophobia in the daily press in 1997, when rioting in Albania prompted an increased flow of Albanian immigrants to Italy. See Vereni's *Identità catodiche: Rappresentazioni mediatiche di appartenenze collettive* (Rome: Meltemi, 2008), 69–99. See also Ardian Vehbiu and Rando Devole, *La scoperta dell'Albania: gli albanesi secondo i mass media* (Milan: Paoline, 1996); Derek Duncan, "The Sight and Sound of Albanian Migration in Contemporary Italian Cinema," http://www.cardiff.ac.uk/euros/subsites/newreadings/volume8/abstracts/duncanabstract.html, accessed April 3, 2011; and Nicola Mai and Russell King, *Out of Albania: From Crisis Migration to Social Inclusion in Italy* (New York: Berghahn, 2008).

10. "*Ha ammesso che la richiesta di sicurezza risponde a una esigenza reale però . . . certi tg hanno esasperato i fatti di sangue in cui sono protagonisti gli stranieri.*" Maria Antonietta Calabrò, "Amato: no al clima d'intolleranza," *Il Corriere della sera*, February 24, 2001.

11. As the headline from the *Il Corriere della sera* of February 23 reads: "*An e Lega contro gli immigrati. Il Viminale: si indaga in tutte le direzioni.*"

12. "*Un immigrato in regola . . . avev(a) paura.*" Fiorenza Sarzanini, "Il superteste è un immigrato," *Il Corriere della sera*, March 2, 2001.

13. For the indistinct confluence of various regions in the rhetoric of the northern leagues, see Anna Cento Bull, "Challenging the Nation-State: Between Localism and Globalism," in *The Politics of Italian National Identity*, ed. Gino Bedani and Bruce Haddock (Cardiff: University of Wales Press, 2000), esp. 263.

14. See Benedict Anderson, *Imagined Communities: Reflections on the Origins and Spread of Nationalism* (London: Verso, 1991). On the vitality of regional identity in Italy as a category for analysis see Carl Levy, ed., *Italian Regionalism: History, Identity, Politics* (Oxford: Berg Press, 1996), esp. 1–80; John Dickie, "Imagined Italies," *Italian Cultural Studies*, ed. David Forgacs and Robert Lumley (Oxford: Oxford University Press, 1996), 19–33; Anna Cento Bull, *Social Identities and Political Cultures in Italy: Catholic, Communist, and Leghist Communities between Civicness and Localism* (New York: Berghahn Books, 2000); and, with Mark Gilbert, *The Lega Nord and the Northern Question in Italian Politics* (New York: Palgrave, 2001); Agnew, *Place and Politics in Modern Italy*; Albarosa Macrì Tronci, "Regionalismo, identità nazionale e vocazione europea: un prezioso sistema di forze," *Otto/Novecento* 26, no. 3 (2002): 129–144; and Jennifer Burns and Loredana Polezzi, eds., *Borderlines: Identità di confine nel Novecento* (Isernia, Italy: Cosmo Iannone, 2005).

15. *Il Fatto*, TG1, RAI 1, February 28, 2001.

16. "Ciampi: il nostro cinema non alimenta la violenza," *Il Corriere della sera*, February 27, 2001.

17. *"Nel nostro cinema raramente ha trovato alimento quella cultura di morte, quell'esaltazione della violenza anche estrema che può provocare danni gravi soprattutto nella formazione dei giovani."* La Repubblica, February 27, 2001. There may have been some concern that the Novi Ligure homicides would spawn copycat crimes: on March 4, *Il Corriere della sera* ran an article entitled *"Effetto Erika: ragazza accoltella la madre con il fidanzato."* Indeed, the March 5, 2001, dailies reported about three sets of parents (or their daughters) who, worried about guilt by association, applied for official permission to change their daughters' (or their) names from "Erika," with that idiosyncratic spelling.

18. See Forgacs, "The Mass Media and the Question of National Identity in Italy," in *The Politics of Italian National Identity,* ed. Gino Bedani and Bruce Haddock (Cardiff: University of Wales Press, 2000), 143.

19. Paolo Crepet, *Voi, noi. Sull'indifferenza di giovani e adulti* (Turin: Einaudi, 2003). When Erika and Omar attempted to eliminate the adults in Erika's life and "adopt" her younger brother—initially, Gianluca was not an intended target—they represented heteronormativity gone amok. For a representation of a non-heternormative adolescent couple that also becomes stronger in union than independently, see Elena Stancanelli's *Benzina* (Turin: Einaudi, 1998) and Monica Stambrini's 2001 film adaptation (*Benzina/Gasoline*). See also Charlotte Ross, "Queering the Habitus: Lesbian Identity in Stancanelli's *Benzina,*" in *Romance Studies* 22, no. 3 (2004): 237–250. I examine *Benzina* in chapter 5.

20. When they attended Cassini's and Gianluca De Nardo's funeral, Omar allegedly said to Erika that they were like "Bonnie and Clyde." See Marco Imarisio, "Così Erika ingannò e uccise il fratellino," *Il Corriere della sera,* February 13, 2002. See also Luigi Offreddu, "Ditemelo, vi prego: in che cosa ho sbagliato con lei," *Il Corriere della sera,* February 26, 2002; Cinzia Tani's study of homicidal couples, *Coppie assassine: Uccidere in due per odio o per amore, per denaro o perversione* (Milan: Mondadori, 1999); and Gordiano Lupi and Sabina Marchesi's *Coppie diaboliche* (Florence: Olimpia Editoriale), 2008.

21. Any society outside their own completely diminished for the teens during the course of their romance. Friends of the young couple attested to changes in attitudes and behaviors since the time they began dating: other friendships fell away, they spent each afternoon Monday–Saturday together, typically at the Fàvaro house where Omar's father was absent for work and his mother was perceived as less strict than Susy.

22. This is the bold, banner headline of *La Repubblica* from February 23, 2001.

23. *"Ha ricostruito l'accaduto con la precisione di una trentenne."* Ibid.

24. Quote from *TG2 Dossier,* RAI 2, March 24, 2001. See also Gaia Beretta and Santa Di Nuovo, "Devianza femminile: tra responsabilità e sanzione. Il 'caso Nove Ligure' attraverso i mass media," *Psicologia giuridica* 2, no. 2 (2001), http://www .psicologiagiuridica.com/index.php?sz=archivio&tp=art&r=7 (accessed June 14, 2011). The topic of the cool affect of a female accused of the murder of a family member returns in chapter 6, where I examine the trial of Annamaria Franzoni for the murder of her son, Samuele Lorenzi.

25. In fact, since Erika's and Omar's drug use was deemed habitual, the notion of a *raptus,* or drug-induced blackout, was not available as a defense.

26. For the Valentine's Day present, see Lidia Ravera, *Il freddo dentro* (Milan: Rizzoli, 2003), 147.

27. *"Quel bamboccio in tuta con la faccia rigata di pianto, il moccio a naso."* La *Repubblica,* February 26, 2001.

28. Paolo Crepet, *Non siamo capaci di ascoltarli: riflessioni sull'infanzia e adolescenza* (Turin: Einaudi, 2001).

29. I return to the cultural production of Niccolò Ammaniti in chapters 5 and 9. See Paolo Crepet, *I figli non crescono più* (Turin: Einaudi, 2005); Paolo Crepet and Giancarlo De Cataldo, *I giorni dell'ira. Storie di matricidi* (Milan: Feltrinelli, 2002); Giancarlo De Cataldo, *Teneri assassini* (Turin: Einaudi, 2000); Giancarlo De Cataldo, *Il padre e lo straniero* (Rome: Edizioni e/o, 2004); Aldo Busi, *Il manuale del perfetto papà (beati gli orfani)* (Milan: Mondadori, 2001); and Niccolò Ammaniti and Massimo Ammaniti, *Nel nome del padre: l'adolescenza raccontata da un padre e da un figlio* (Milan: Mondadori, 1995).

30. *"Se mamma sapesse"* literally means "if Mom should know" or "if Mom should find out." My translation of "should Mom suspect" observes the acronym (SMS) and maintains the sense of the turn of phrase.

31. *"Ogni altro tipo di ombelico elettronico."* Aldo Grasso, "Nello spot degli SMS tutta la distanza nelle famiglie," *Il corriere della sera,* February 25, 2001. See Heather Horst and Daniel Miller, *The Cell Phone: An Anthropology of Communication* (Oxford: Berg Publishers, 2006), esp. 84, where a Jamaican woman describes being linked to her child and other children who can help her run her errands. See also Leslie Haddon, *Information and Communication Technologies in Everyday Life* (Oxford: Berg Press, 2004), esp. 35–43; and Jarice Hanson, *24/7: How Cell Phones and the Internet Change the Way We Live* (Westport, Conn.: Praeger, 2007). At the time of the Erika and Omar case, the generation gap that emerged concerning cell phone use, especially texting, was particularly acute. See CENSIS-U.C.S.I., *Terzo rapporto sulla comunicazione: Media & Giovani* (Milan: Franco Angeli, 2004), 31–45 and 50–55. See also CENSIS-U.C.S.I., *Quarto rapporto sulla comunicazione in Italia. I media che vorrei* (Milan: Franco Angeli, 2005), 81; and Andrea Granelli, "Una scarsa cultura informatica fra i giovani: Come intervenire," in CENSIS-U.C.S.I., *Quarto rapporto,* 238–239.

32. CENSIS-U.C.S.I., *Terzo rapporto,* 54. CENSIS (Centro Studi Investimenti Sociali) is an independent research agency focused primarily on gathering data on socioeconomic issues in Italy.

33. *"Non si staccano mai"*; *"si mett(ono) sotto il cuscino quando dorm(ono)."* Ibid., 51.

34. Crepet, *Non siamo capaci,* esp. 25–27.

35. *"Il cellulare è diventato un prolungamento del corpo dei giovani."* CENSIS-U.C.S.I., *Terzo rapporto,* 55. See also Marshall McLuhan, *Understanding Media: The Extensions of Man,* ed. W. Terrence Gordon (Corte Madera, Calif.: Gingko Press, 2003), 17–36.

36. For the ways these types of affiliative processes are transformed in the Internet age, see Mattelart, *Networking the World,* esp. 75–96. Concerning the ease with which Italian youth used both the Internet and the cell phone between 2000 and 2005, see CENSIS-U.C.S.I., *Quarto rapporto,* esp. 71–89. See also William Mitchell,

E-Topia, 4; and Marcel Danesi, "Observations on the Supposed Influence of Cyber-language on Contemporary Italian," *Forum Italicum* 40, no. 2 (2006): 428–446.

37. Joshua Meyrowitz, "The Generalized Elsewhere," *Critical Studies in Mass Communication* 6, no. 3 (1989): 326–334. See also Haddon, *Information and Communication Technologies in Everyday Life,* 43–49.

38. See Don Slater, "Social Relationships and Identity On-Line and Off-Line," in *Handbook of New Media: Social Shaping and Consequences of ICTs,* ed. Leah Lievrouw and Sonia Livingstone (Thousand Oaks, Calif.: Sage Publications: 2002), 533–543; and David Morley, "Belongings: Place, Space and Identity in a Mediated World," *European Journal of Cultural Studies* 4, no. 4 (2001): 425–448.

39. Marco Imarisio and Luigi Offreddu, "Su Internet un sito dedicato a Erika," *Il corriere della sera,* March 6, 2001.

40. "*Erika, hai fatto bene, (v)orrei avere il tuo coraggio.*" Ibid.

41. "*Marilyn Manson, Puff Daddy, Erika e Omar? Non è un giudizio, ma vicende come queste mi suggeriscono quanto sia stupendamente diverso dal normale ciò che è universalmente ritenuto normale. Dio mio quanto sono difficili gli esseri umani.*" Comment of "Miao," in ibid.

42. "*Voi filosofeggiate e due innocenti sono stati massacrati.*" Comment of "Uno," in ibid.

43. RAI's multimedia catalogue discloses 131 "hits" representing coverage of Erika and Omar between February 27 and the end of December 2001. This does not mean that 131 separate programs aired. Records for broadcasts on privately held channels are not reliably available. Mediaset, for example, does not archive its broadcast materials. That the RAI should extensively archive its broadcasted programs owes to its position as the state-sponsored television network, something that establishes a very different relation with the viewing public than that of Mediaset or other private television networks. I am grateful to Prof. Patrizio Rossano for his assistance in this matter. In the year 2001, archived material for the RAI radio network shows 398 broadcasts concerning the Novi Ligure murders. This is also not to suggest that interest in the case ends with the calendar year 2001 or with Erika's and Omar's jail sentences. The Novi Ligure murders are used generally in February programming, marking the anniversary of the deaths of Susy and Gianluca. In addition, the events of Novi Ligure are invoked when exploring the topics of violent youth, domestic violence, youth "at risk," etc.

44. See Garofano, *Delitti imperfetti Atto I e Atto II* (Milan: Marco Tropea Editore, 2006), 13–40.

45. See Gianfranco Bettin, *Eredi: Da Pietro Maso a Erika e Omar* (Milan: Feltrinelli, 2007).

46. Gustavo P. Charmet, *I nuovi adolescenti: Padri e madri di fronte a una sfid*a (Milan: Raffaello Cortina, 2000), esp. 175–176.

47. The presentation of the Erika and Omar case illustrates the problematic inculpation of violence expressed in cultural practice, most particularly but not exclusively in cinema, an approach wherein the consumer of violence, like the viewer of pornography, is impelled to reenact that which she or he views, reads, or thumbs through. Please see chapter 3, where I discuss this. For a critique of pornography's cumbersome association with violence against women see Laura Kipnis, "(Male)

Desire and (Female) Disgust: Reading *Hustler*," in *Cultural Studies,* ed. Lawrence Grossberg, Cary Nelson, and Paula Treichler (New York: Routledge, 1992), 373–391. See also Slavoj Žižek's critique of this faulty reasoning in Slavoj Žižek, *Metastases of Enjoyment: Six Essays on Woman and Causality* (London: Verso, 1994), 73–75.

48. Giovanni Verga, *Tutte le novelle* (Milan: Mondadori, 1985), 325.

49. The judge to question Erika was Giovanni Garena, a forensic psychiatrist and the *giudice a latere,* who sits next to the presiding judge (*presidente*) at trial. It is not unusual for a judge to intervene in the proceedings.

50. See the lyrics to "The End" at http://www.elyrics.net/read/d/doors-lyrics/the-end-lyrics.html (accessed April 12, 2011).

51. See Consuelo Corradi, *Il nemico intimo: una lettura sociologica dei casi di Novi Ligure e Cogne* (Rome: Meltemi, 2005).

52. Judge: "*Ti ispiravano quelle parole? Condividete quella visione?*" Erika's response: "*i Doors le piacevano, ma niente di più, erano la passione di Omar.*" Marco Imarisio, "Erika, volevo morire, ho cercato di impiccarmi," *Il corriere della sera,* 29 November, 2001.

53. Lack of affect, so noteworthy in a juvenile offender such as Pietro Maso or in myriad pop-culture examples of serial killers, recalls Frederic Jameson's stylistic descriptions of postmodernism, which for Jameson is characterized by the "waning of affect" and the "emergence of a new kind of flatness or depthlessness, a new kind of superficiality in the most literal sense—perhaps the supreme formal feature of all postmodernisms." See Jameson, "Postmodernism, or the Cultural Logic of Late Capitalism," *New Left Review* 146 (July–August 1984): 60.

54. SeeAlessandri, *La leggenda del Vampa.*

55. Porporati is best known for the screenplay for *Lamerica* (1994), which he coauthored with that film's director, Gianni Amelio. Porporati's film, alternatively titled *Sole negli occhi,* tied with *Tornando a casa* (Going home) for the Gran Prix at the Annecy Italian Cinema Festival that year.The Italian National Syndicate of Film Journalists also nominated Gifuni for best male lead, Gianni Cavina for best supporting actor for his role as Marco's father, and Porporati for best new director.

On the representation of matricide in contemporary Italian literature, see Nicoletta Di Ciolla, "Crime and the Female Subject: Matricide, Filicide and the Law of the Father in Contemporary Italian Literature: The Case of Laura Grimaldi and Barbara Garlaschelli," in *Women's Writing in Western Europe: Gender, Generation and Legacy,* ed. Adalgisa Giorgio and Julia Waters (Newcastle upon Tyne, England: Cambridge Scholars, 2007), 200–215.

56. See Joanna Bourke, *An Intimate History of Killing: Face-to-face Killing in Twentieth-century Warfare* (New York: Granta, 1999).

57. Charmet, *I nuovi adolescenti,* 73–77. See also Vittorino Andreoli, *Giovani. Sfida, rivolta, speranza, futuro* (Milan: BUR Biblioteca Univ. Rizzoli, 1997); and V. L. Carminati and R. Ghidelli, *Adolescenza: sfida e risorsa della famiglia* (Milan: Vita e pensiero, 1993).

58. *La Stanza del figlio* (*The Son's Room*), 2001 (Miramax Home Entertainment).

59. Guido Bonsaver, "The Egocentric Cassandra of the Left: Representations of Politics in the Films of Nanni Moretti," *Italianist* 21–22 (2001–2002):158–183. See

also Fabio Vighi, "Unravelling Moretti's (Political) Unconscious: The Abyss of the Subject in *La Stanza del figlio*," *Journal of Romance Studies* 3, no. 2 (2003): 79–94.

60. *Io sono un autarchico* (*I Am Self Sufficient*), 1976 (Warner Home Video Italy); *Ecce bombo*, 1978 (Warner Home Video Italy); and *Aprile*, 1998 (Warner Home Video Italy).

61. "*Un microscosmo di una società rotta.*" Quote from *Gap: Generazioni alla prova!* RAI 3, July 23, 2004. It is worth noting that in 2003, the year *Il freddo dentro* was published and one year before Ravera's appearance on GAP, Italians were again confronted with the "secret" life of teenagers. Melissa P.'s incendiary *100 colpi di spazzola prima di andare a dormire* (*100 Strokes of the Brush before Bed*) (Rome: Fazi Editore, 2003) hinges on a Sicilian teenager's secret life, sexual experimentation, and coming of age. The autobiographical novel was revealed to have been written by Melissa Panarello. (The book was adapted for the screen by Barbara Alberti, Christiana Farina, and Luca Guadagnino in 2005, with Guadagnino directing.)

62. "*Ha costretto noi a costruire la figura del genitore.*" Quote from *Gap: Generazioni alla prova!* RAI 3, July 23, 2004.

63. Although this novel appears to have been largely passed over in criticism on Vassalli, it could be that *Archeologia del passato* is as "historical" a novel as some of the others in the author's oeuvre, something the term "archeology" might suggest. See for example Carla Giacobbe, "*La chimera* di Sebastiano Vassalli: note sulle fortune del romanzo in veste storica, ovvero alla ricerca del suono perduto," in *Piccole finzioni con importanza: Valori della narrativa italiana contemporanea,* ed. Nathalie Roelens and Inge Lanslots (Ravenna: Longo, 1993), 183–190. For a review of national identity that is consonant with the project for generational identity in Vassalli that I am describing, see Merial Tulante, "Italia Mia? National Identity in the Novels of Sebastiano Vassalli," *Forum for Modern Language Studies* 45, no. 3 (2009): 337–350. See also Zygmunt Baranski, "Sebastiano Vassalli: Literary Lives," in *The New Italian Novel,* ed. Zygmunt Baranski and Lino Pertile (Edinburgh: Edinburgh University Press, 1993), 239–257.

64. "*Forse Marlon le dirà qualcosa di nuovo,*" ha aggiunto il guidice. "*Forse le spiegherà perchè lui e Gigliola hanno decisio di sterminare la famiglia Ferrari. Chi ha avuto l'idea e chi ha sparato. A noi, il ragazzo continua a ripetere sempre la stessa storia . . . . Dice di aver agito in un raptus e che Gigliola, con la strage, non c'entra. Cerca di scagionare la sua compagna, che invece si comporta in modo opposto e non gli risparmia nessuna accusa, pur di tornare libera.*" Sebastiano Vassalli, *Archeologia del presente* (Turin: Einaudi, 2001), 165.

65. See Hannah Arendt, *Eichmann in Jerusalem: A Report on the Banality of Evil* (New York: Penguin Books, 1976).

66. "*I miei genitori adottivi si sono occupati di me soltanto perchè diventassi uguale a loro. Volevano un figlio fotocopia.*" Vassalli, *Archeologia del presente,* 166.

67. *I dreamers* (*The Dreamers*), Fox Searchlight Pictures, 2003.

68. "*A tutti quelli che in ogni epoca hanno speso le loro vite per far diventare il mondo perfetto, e a che prezzo di sofferenze e di enormi fatiche sono riusciti a portarlo dov'è adesso, cioè sull'orlo del baratro. Ho scosso la testa. Ho ripetuto: Che idioti.*" Vassalli, *Archeologia del presente,* 172.

5. The Raw and the Cooked

1. See chapter 4, where I position the De Nardo and Fàvaro case with regard to Graneris, Ferdinando Carretta's murder of his parents in 1989, and, two years later, Pietro Maso.

2. "*Singhiozzi lunghi, inarrestabili.*" " Marco Imarisio, "Condannate Erika a vent'anni e Omar a sedici," *Il Corriere della sera,* December 12, 2001. All translations are mine unless otherwise indicated.

3. "*Si è pietrificato.*" Ibid.

4. "*Ho ammazzato i miei genitori perché usavano un bagnoschiuma assurdo, Pure & Vegetal.*" Aldo Nove, *Superwoobinda* (Turin: Einaudi, 1998), 7.

5. See Marco Berisso, "Linguistic Levels and Stylistic Solutions in the New Italian Narrative (1991–8)," in *Italian Pulp Fiction: The New Narrative of the "Giovani Cannibali" Writers,* ed. and trans. Stefania Lucamante (Madison, N.J.: Fairleigh Dickinson University Press, 2001), 76–97.

6. Stefania Lucamante, "Introduction," in *Italian Pulp Fiction: The New Narrative of the "Giovani Cannibali" Writers,* ed. and trans. Stefania Lucamante (Madison, N.J.: Fairleigh Dickinson University Press, 2001), 30.

7. Daniele Brolli's edited collection *Gioventù cannibale: la prima antologia italiana dell'orrore estremo* (Turin: Einaudi, 1996) sold 30,000 copies in its first printing and was subsequently reprinted eight times. See Monica Jansen and Inge Lanslot, "Ten Years of *Gioventù cannibale:* Reflections on the Anthology as a Vehicle for Literary Change," in *Trends in Contemporary Italian Narrative, 1980–2007,* ed. Gillian Ania and Anna Hallamore Caesar (Newcastle upon Tyne, England: Cambridge Scholars, 2007), 115.

8. Distaste and disdain for the *"cannibali"* also appears in Renato Barilli's *È arrivata la terza ondata. Dalla neo alla neo-neoavanguardia* (Turin: Testo and Immagine, 2000); and Nanni Ballestrini and Renato Barilli, eds., *Narrative Invaders: Narratori di "Ricercare" 1993–1999* (Turin: Testo and Immagine, 2000).The literary offerings of the Young Cannibals fared no better in terms of critical reception than did the efforts of the Italian filmmakers engaged in "cannibal cinema." Liliana Cavani's 1969 *I cannibali* (*The Year of the Cannibals*) (American International Pictures), itself a remake of Sophocles' *Antigone,* is excluded from such efforts as Joe D'Amato's 1977 *Emanuelle e gli ultimi cannibali* (*Emanuelle and the Last Cannibals*) (Flora Film); Ruggero Deodato's 1977 *Ultimo mondo cannibale* (*Last Cannibal World*) (Video City Productions), or 1979 *Cannibal Holocaust* (Grindhouse Releasing); Umberto Lenzi's 1981 *Cannibal ferox* (*Make Them Die Slowly*) (Grindhouse Releasing); Mario Gariazzo's *Schiave bianche: Violenza in Amazzonia* (*Amazzonia: The Catherine Miles Story*) (Camp Motion Pictures), from 1985; *Nudo e selvaggio* (*Massacre in Dinosaur Valley*) (Media Blasters), directed by Michele Massimo Tarantini in 1985. The South American locations for these and other zombie films made in the Caribbean in the same period makes them part of the "Latsploitation" phenomenon. See Andrew Snyder, "'I Wonder Who the Real Cannibals Are': Latin America and Colonialism in European Exploitation Cinema," in *Latsploitation, Exploitation Cinemas, and Latin America,* ed. Victoria Ruétalo and Dolores Tierney (New York: Routledge, 2009), 70–84. One should add Marco Ferreri's 1988 *Come*

sono buoni i bianchi/Ya bon les blancs (How good white people are) to Snyder's list of Italian cannibal films in a colonial context. I am grateful to Marìa Ospina for her observations about the cannibal cinema of Latsploitation.

9. See Pierpaolo Antonello, "Cannibalizing the Avant-Garde," in *Italian Pulp Fiction: The New Narrative of the "Giovani Cannibali" Writers,* ed. and trans. Stefania Lucamante (Madison, N.J.: Fairleigh Dickinson University Press, 2001), 38–57. Antonello compares some of the Giovani Cannibali to the "old" cannibals, some avant-garde practitioners of the 1920s. He begins by comparing the Giovani Cannibali and Picabia's *Manifeste cannibale,* first declaimed in 1920 and published in the first edition of the magazine *Le cannibale* the following year, then describes comic-book author Andrea Pazienza's familiarity with the iconoclastic poet, essayist, and artist Tristan Tzara.

10. I refer to Luca Gervasutti's *Dannati e sognatori. Guida alla nuova narrativa italiana* (Paisan di Prato: Campanotto Editore, 1998); and the essays collected and edited by Raffaelle Cardone, Franco Galato, Fulvio Panzeri in *Altre storie: inventario della nuova narrativa fra anni '80 e '90* (Milan: Marcos y Marcos, 1996). Filippo La Porta's assemblage of material in *La nuova narrativa italiana: travestimenti e stili fine secolo* (Turin: Bollati Boringhieri, 1995) differs notably from the other two thematically organized collections and stretches beyond the received categories by establishing critical links between different groups of writers. For sales of anthologies, see Jansen and Lanlots, "Ten Years of *Gioventù cannibale,*" 122–123. See also Jennifer Burns, *Fragments of Impegno: Interpretations of Commitment in Contemporary Italian Narrative (1980–2000)* (Leeds: Northern University Press, 2001).

11. Fabio Giovannini and Antonio Tentori, eds., *Cuore di pulp: antologia di racconti italiani* (Rome: Stampa alternativa, 1997).

12. Some critics think the category of pulp should be limited to two collections of short stories: Niccolò Ammaniti's collection *Fango* (Milan: Mondadori, 1996); and Aldo Nove's *Woobinda e altre storie senza lieto fine* (Rome: Castelvecchi, 1996), revised as *Superwoobinda* and released by Einaudi in 1998. See Daniele Brolli, "Introduzione," in *Gioventù cannibale,* v–x.

13. "*Usciamo, all'imbrunire.*" Ammaniti, *Fango,* 139.

14. "*affamati. Affamati di fica. Affamati di fica ruvida.*" Ibid.

15. "*Veniteci a dire qualcosa. Forza. Tirateli fuori questi coglioni.*" Ibid.

16. See Stefano Magni, "Voci e punti di vista in *Fango* di Ammaniti," *Narrativa* 20–21 (2001): 305–319, esp. 309.

17. *Il Branco,* dir. Marco Risi (Cecchi Gori Editoria Elettronica, 1994).

18. See Maria Novella De Luca, "Parla Andrea Carraro, dal suo libro è nato il film *Il Branco,*" *La Repubblica,* November 6, 1994. It is less likely that the notorious events that took place at a villa in Circeo, to the southwest of Rome, on September 29, 1975, are the source of either Ammaniti's story or Carraro's novel. On that date three young men from Rome's wealthy Parioli neighborhood invited two young women to a party at the villa of one of the men near Circeo. The three men physically abused the women, killing one, while the second, feigning death, survived. Beyond the senseless violence against the women, socioeconomic class received a great deal of attention. Coverage of the case dwelled on the wealth and social

stature of the young men. Class as a defining characteristic of Ammaniti's savage collective is not an element worthy of note. Class plays a more prominent role in Carraro's novel, but it is the social underclass of the Roman hinterland, something that draws Risi's earlier films into proximity with the project of *Il branco*. The two films Risi had already made, *Mery per sempre* (1989) and *Ragazzi fuori* (1990), had each confronted the woes of a contemporary southern Italy that offered young men nothing but reform school and prison. With *Mery Per Sempre* and *Ragazzi fuori*, Risi attempted "to draw attention to the dangers for the country of failing to address the underemployment and exploitation of young southerners." See Wood, *Italian Cinema*, 144. See also Rodica Diaconescu-Blumenfeld, "Homme Fatal(e): The Expropriation of Gender in Marco Risi's *Mery per sempre*," *Romance Languages Annual* 10 (1998): 235–240. Risi's cinematic adaptation of *Il branco* may have moved north from the Palermitan and Neapolitan settings of his earlier films, but the desperate social situation of young Italian men, whether in south or central Italy, draws together all three films.

19. The collective consciousness and voice in Ammaniti's story distinguishes it from Enrico Brizzi's 1996 novel *Bastogne*, which, as it follows a group of violent young men in Nice, treads some of the same thematic territory as "Rispetto" but eschews the choral narrative voice.

20. Valerio Ferme, "Note su Niccolò Ammaniti e il fango di fine millennio," *Narrativa* 20–21 (2001): 332.

21. The fact that Ammaniti sets his later novels far from Rome, casting them throughout the peninsula, is a topic I take up in chapter 8.

22. See Filippo La Porta, "Postfazione," in Andrea Carraro, *Il Branco* (Rome: Gaffi Editore, 2005), 167.

23. Augusta Lagostena Bassi with Emanuela Moroli, *L'avvocato delle donne: dodici storie di ordinaria violenza* (Milan: Mondadori, 1991). The miniseries consisted of six episodes that aired in March and April 1997. Lagostena Bassi was a law professor and sometime representative of Forza Italia, Berlusconi's first political coalition, which formed in late 1993. (It evolved into Il Popolo della Libertà (The People of Freedom) in early 2009.) She was also a television personality; she hosted the Odeon channel's talk show *Tina-mite* and was Italy's version of Judge Judy when she acted as arbitrator for *Forum* on Rete 4 (Mediaset). She died in 2008.

24. La Porta, "The Horror Picture Show and the Very Real Horrors: About the Italian Pulp" in *Italian Pulp Fiction: The New Narrative of the "Giovani Cannibali" Writers*, ed. and trans. Stefania Lucamante (Madison, N.J.: Fairleigh Dickinson University Press, 2001), 69.

25. See Stefania Lucamante's "Intervista a Tiziano Scarpa," *Italica* 83, nos. 3–4 (2006): 693.

26. Lucamante, "Introduction," 36n9. *Italian Pulp Fiction* remains the only book-length treatment of this young group of writers that emerged in the 1990s. See Jansen and Lanslot, "Ten Years of *Gioventù cannibale*."

27. Michel Foucault, "Nietzsche, Genealogy, History," in *Language, Counter-Memory, Practice*, esp. 139.

28. Other writers mentioned in association with the Cannibals include Bret Easton Ellis, Raymond Carver, Grace Paley, John Fante, Lorrie Moore, Samuel

Beckett, F. Scott Fitzgerald, Hubert Selby, Louis-Ferdinand Céline, and Robert Musil.

29. See Gian Paolo Renello, "The Mediatic Body of the Cannibale Literature," in *Italian Pulp Fiction: The New Narrative of the "Giovani Cannibali" Writers,* ed. and trans. Stefania Lucamante (Madison, N.J.: Fairleigh Dickinson University Press, 2001), 139. Tiziano Scarpa's 2006 interview with Stefania Lucamante is useful for the way he interrogates literary groupings as well as for the detailed portrait of the 1994–1996 period. See "Intervista a Tiziano Scarpa di Stefania Lucamante," esp. 696. See also Lucamante, "Introduction," 35n2.

30. I discuss the notion of the *filone* and this hybrid genre in chapter 3.

31. Giovannini and Tentori, *Cuore di pulp,* 5.

32. Giusi Ferré, "Questi romanzi vietati ai maggiori," *L'Europeo,* February 8, 1995, 74–77. The reference is to the rating of film in Italy. See also Tommaso Pomilio, "Le narrative generazionali dagli anni ottanta agli anni novanta," in *Storia generale della letteratura italiana,* vol. 12: *Sperimentalismo e tradizione del nuovo,* ed. Nino Borsellino and Walter Pedullà (Milan: Federico Motta Editore, 1999).

33. See, among others, Alcide Paoline, "Tarantineide," *Messaggero Veneto,* June 29,1996; and the anonymous "I nipotini di Tarantino specchio di un'Italia 'cannibale,'" http://www.cyberlogic.it/abitare/Dic96/libri.htm#uno (accessed June 23, 2009). It is worth observing that affection for the name "cannibal" endured at least into 2001, when the director of short animated "zombie" films, Marco Bertoldo, described his collaboration with Niccolò Ammaniti as "uno scrittore che amo definire 'cannibale.'" See Francesca Romana Avesani, "Marco Bertoldo, un giovane sbarca in America," *Divertimento.it,* March 28, 2006, http://www.divertimento.it/ articolo/marco-bertoldo-un-giovane-sbarca-in-america/30952 (accessed September 15, 2009).

34. "*Le mie letture sono disordinatissime . . . come riferimenti culturali . . . sono molto più vicino a* Supertifo, Mountain Biking *che a* good ol' *Carlo Emilio Gadda.*" Quoted in Gervasutti, *Dannati e sognatori,* 55. Carlo Emilio Gadda (1893–1973) ranks as one of the most influential writers in the canon of twentieth-century Italian literary modernism.

35. Barilli, *È arrivata la terza ondata,* 94–95.

36. See Andy Bennett, *Popular Music and Youth Culture: Music, Identity, and Place* (London: Macmillan, 2000). For a reading of music specifically in Ammaniti's work, see Paolo Chirumbolo, "La funzione della musica, nella narrativa di Niccolò Ammaniti: da *Branchie* Io non ho paura," *Quaderni d'italianistica* 26, no. 1 (2005): 121–136.

37. "*Chi oggi ha meno di vent'anni ha conosciuto i* clip *di MTV e di Videomusic più che il vecchio rock monolitico dei grandi gruppi. Forse i* teenager *di oggi non hanno coordinate musicali molto chiare (la mercificazione elimina la prospettiva), ma anche se parliamo di* kids *che ascoltano veramente musica e non fans dei* Take That, *credo che la definizione 'rock' sia ormai troppo stretta; anche i due minuti dei* Sex Pistols, *da soli, non bastano più. Credo che l'immaginario della mia generazione, e dunque anche degli scrittori che ne fanno parte, sia colonizzato dal* crossover, *dal mescolarsi di suoni diversi coi fondamentali del punk. Considero dunque estremamente indicativo il fatto che tra le* band *più significative e influenti ci siano nomi*

come i Red Hot Chili Peppers, Green Day, *o i mai abbastanza esaltati* Primus." Enrico Brizzi, quoted in Gervasutti, *Dannati e sognatori,* 25.

38. See also Patrizia La Trecchia, "New Media (B)orders in Contemporary Neapolitan Music: Rethinking Aesthetic Experience in the Age of Globalization" in *Italian Cultural Studies, 2001: Selected Essays,* ed. Anthony Tamburri, Myriam Swennen, Graziella Parati, and Ben Lawton (Boca Raton, Fla.: Bordighera Press, 2004), 69–92.

39. *"La musica è un elemento mercuriale, che mette in relazione piani diversi . . . avvicina al pensiero senza le parole e i percorsi faticosi della filosofia."* Quoted in Elisabetta Rasy, "Scritti sul pentagramma," *Panorama,* September 12, 1996.

40. *"Mi proponevo di riprendere la struttura di quei dischi, elaborando capitoli brevi, come fossero pezzi di un album."* Quoted in Gervasutti, *Dannati e sognatori,* 24.

41. On rap and hip-hop in a global setting see André J. M. Prevos, "Communication through Popular Music in the Twenty-First Century? The Example of French Rap Music and Hip Hop Culture," in *Language and Communication in the New Century,* ed. Jesse Levitt, Leonard R. N. Ashley, and Wayne Finke (East Rockaway, N.Y.: Cummings and Hathaway, 1998), 137–148; William Perkins, "Youth's Global Village," in *Droppin' Science: Critical Essays on Rap Music and Hip Hop Culture,* ed. W. Perkins (Philadelphia, Pa.: Temple University Press, 1996), 257–273; and Tony Mitchell, "Doin' Damage in My Native Language: The Use of 'Resistance Vernaculars' in Hip Hop in France, Italy, and Aotearoa/New Zealand," *Popular Music and Society* 24, no. 3 (2000): 41–54.

For readings of rap and hip-hop specifically within an Italian social and cultural context, see Steve Wright, "A Love Born of Hate: Autonomous Rap in Italy," *Theory, Culture & Society* 17, no. 3 (2000): 117–135; and Marco Santoro and Marco Solari, "Authors and Rappers: Italian Hip Hop and the Shifting Boundaries of *Canzone d'Autore,*" *Popular Music* 26, no. 3 (2007): 463–488; which, while focused on hip-hop since the 1990s, nevertheless reviews its evolution in Italy.

42. See also Daniele Barbieri, *Il linguaggio del fumetto* (Milan: Bompiani, 1991).

43. *"A dire il vero . . . è abbastanza deludente, però dimostra una volta di più il desiderio di fondere la musica e la letteratura."* Gervasutti, *Dannati e sognatori,* 29.

44. Abbate is the author of *Oggi è un secolo* (1992), *Dopo l'estate* (1995), *La peste bis* (1997). For Abbate's recollection, see Gervasutti, esp. 40–45.

45. See "Vermicino," in Aldo Grasso ed., *Enciclopedia della Televisione* (Milan: Garzanti, 2002), 807.

46. Ibid.

47. Ibid.

48. This law, as Francesco Pinto observed, was deemed, "the end of an era . . . in a period of transition, the RAI was divided between an attempt at breaking with the old model and resistance against any kind of real transformation." See Pinto, *Il Modello Televisivo,* 178.

49. *"È una cosa importante. È forse la cosa più importante, avere qualcosa da ricordare come Vermicino."* Nove, *Superwoobinda,* 23.

50. *"C'è qualcosa di solido che rimane. Da raccontare ai tuoi nipotini. La storia."* Ibid.

51. *"Eravamo milioni di persone e lui giú, lí da solo."* Ibid. The experience of viewing something simultaneously contributes to the sense of a collective, though not exclusively a generational collective. The notion of "liveness" has been fundamental in television studies since Raymond Williams's exploration in the 1970s. See his *Television: Technology and Form* (Hanover, N.H.: Wesleyan University Press, 1974). For other examples of televised "events," including several in the Italian market, see Guido Barlozzetti, *Eventi e riti della televisione. Dalla Guerra del Golfo alle Twin Towers* (Milan: FrancoAngeli, 2002); and Federico Boni, *Etnografia dei media* (Rome-Bari: Laterza, 2004), 58–60. Cf. William Uricchio, "Storage, Simultaneity, and the media technologies of modernity," in *Allegories of Communication: Intermedial Concerns from Cinema to the Digital*, eds. Jan Olsson and John Fullerton, (Eastleigh: John Libbey, 2004), 123–138.

52. *"Momento neutro per mandare la pubblicità dei croccanti per il cane, come quando nelle partite la palla esce dal campo."* Nove, *Superwoobinda*, 24.

53. The shift from "Paleo-" to "Neotelevision" is discussed in chapter 1. In that chapter, see notes 22 and 23.

54. "Zapping," as rapid channel changing with the remote control is called, was thought to be a characteristic practice of viewers of the "new" television, or *neotelevisione*. See "neotelevisione," in Grasso, *Enciclopedia della televisione*, 472. See also Gius Gargiulo, "Una maleducazione televisiva: Gli scrittori cresciuti davanti alla television: Aldo Nove e Luca Doninelli," *Narrativa* 16 (1999), 183–203. For a reading of the the effect of cinema on the Italian novel in this period, see Gius Gargiulo, "Ciac. Si scrive! Alcune considerazioni sui codici narrativi degli sceneggiatori-romanzieri degli anni Settanta e Ottanta," in *Gli spazi della diversità II*, ed. Serge Vanvolsem, Franco Musarra, and Bart Van den Bossche (Rome: Bulzoni, 1995), 331–349. See also Lucamante, "Introduction," 34; and Alberto Piccini, "Telecommandos," *La Bestia* 1 (1997): 60–65.

55. Nove, *Superwoobinda*, 25.

56. Francesca Anania, "Italian Public Television in the 1970s: A Predictable Confusion," *Historical Journal of Film, Radio, and Television* 15, no. 3 (1995): 403. See also RAI, "Modificazioni nell'utenza televisiva, Radiotelevisione Italiana," in *Rapporto di Ricerca I* (1982), 23–24.

57. See chapter 4, notes 16 and 17.

58. *"Guardo parecchio la TV, per quanto maldicendomi, e ne traggo spunti per trasformarla, materiale grezzo da lavorare. . . . Io mi lascio trafiggere dalla TV e spero che ne nasca qualcosa."* Quoted in Gervasutti, *Dannati e sognatori*, 42.

59. RAI began broadcasting *Woobinda* in 1978. See "TV dei ragazzi," in Grasso, *Enciclopedia della Televisione*, 280.

60. A graduate of the Università di Bologna, Krismer was "discovered" by Pier Vincenzo Tondelli, the spiritual father of young Italian writers emerging in the late 1980s. My unpublished interview with Krismer in Bologna, June 1998.

61. In addition to Krismer, who has enjoyed much less critical attention, Alda Teodorani, Luisa Brancaccio, Isabella Santacroce, and perhaps even Silvia Ballestra are all engaged in this sort of minimalist literature that flirts with violence. Lucamante has used the *pulpistes'* use of pornography to locate a resistant mode of representation. See Stefania Lucamante, "Everyday Consumerism and Pornography above the Pulp Line," in *Italian Pulp Fiction*, 98–134.

62. *Mi sistemai comoda sul divano, lasciai che la magia dello schermo mi facesse prigioniera e la visione degli incubi telepatici vincesse il piccolo velo di sonno. Le due e venti.*
Avevo ancora a disposizione un'ora e mezzo di alterazioni cellulari strepitose, prima di raggiungere camera mia. Okay, mi dissi. Mettiamoci ancora più comode e cerchiamo di tenere gli occhi bene aperti. Il mio problema principale era prestare attenzione ai punti di snodo del racconto, far tesoro delle soluzioni narrative che consentivano il crescendo della suspense. Si poteva imparare parecchio da un maestro così.
Raffaella Krismer, *Il signore della carne* (Milan: Zelig, 1997), 13.

63. *"Effetti speciali . . . di un realismo agghiacciante."* Ibid.

64. *"Grandi demoni regionali e antiprogressisti."* Ibid., 134.

65. See Barbara Creed, *The Monstrous-Feminine: Film, Feminism, and Psychoanalysis* (London: Routledge, 1993).

66. See Kristeva, *The Powers of Horror: An Essay on Abjection,* trans. Leon Rouidiez (New York: Columbia University Press, 1982).

67. *Hellraiser* (1987) is the only film in the series directed by Clive Barker. Tony Randel directed *Hellraiser II:Hellbound* (1988); Anthony Hickox directed *Hellraiser III: Hell on Earth* (1992); Kevin Yagher and Alan Smithee collaborated on *Hellraiser: Bloodline* (1996); Scott Derrickson directed *Hellraiser: Inferno* (2000); and Rick Bota directed *Hellraiser: Hellseeker* (2002) and *Hellraiser: Hellworld* in 2005.

68. Krismer clearly nods to her Anglo-American influences at as early a point as the novel's epigraphs, one from Barker and the other from J. D. Salinger's short story "Laughing Man," collected in *Nine Stories* (New York: Little Brown, 1991).

69. See chapter 3, where I discuss the notion of the "final girl" in conjunction with Dario Argento's cinema. See Carol Clover, *Men, Women, and Chain Saws: Gender in the Modern Horror Film* (Princeton: Princeton University Press, 1992); and Carol Clover, "Her Body, Himself: Gender in the Slasher Film," in *The Dread of Difference: Gender and the Horror Film,* ed. Barry Keith Grant (Austin: University of Texas Press, 1996), 66–113.

70. See Stefania Lucamante, *A Multitude of Women: The Challenges of the Contemporary Novel* (Toronto: University of Toronto Press, 2008), 18–19.

71. "L'ultimo capodanno dell' umanità" was the lead story in *Fango,* followed by "Rispetto." In connection with Marco Risi's 1998 adaptation for the screen, the story was published under separate cover, *L'ultimo capodanno* (Milan: Mondadori, 1998).

72. See Gillian Ania, "Apocalypse and Dystopia in Contemporary Italian Writing," in *Trends in Contemporary Italian Narrative, 1980–2007,* ed. Gillian Ania and Ann Hallamore Caesar (Newcastle upon Tyne, England: Cambridge Scholars, 2007), 155–181.

73. For a reading of lesbian habitus in the novel, see Charlotte Ross, "Queering the Habitus: Llesbian Identity in Stancanelli's *Benzina," Romance Studies* 22, no. 3 (2004): 237–250; and Patrizia Sambuco, "Women, Relationships, and Space in Stancanelli's *Benzina* (1998)," *Romance Studies* 22, no. 2 (2004): 127–138.

74. Monica Lisa Stambrini's 2001 film adaptation, also entitled *Benzina* (Gasoline, Strand Releasing), significantly changes Stella's culpability. In the novel, Stella does not premeditate murdering Giovanna, but she does pick up the heavy wrench

nearby and hit her squarely on the head with it. This differs from what happens in Stambrini's film version, in which Stella (played by Maya Sansa) slaps the never-named Giovanna (played by Mariella Valentini) hard enough to cause the fall that results in her death.

75. See Claudia Pompei Karagoz, "Gazing Women: Elena Stancanelli's *Benzina*," *Italica* 83, nos. 3–4 (2006): 392, 402n4.

76. See Marianne Hirsch, *The Mother/Daughter Plot* (Bloomington: Indiana University Press, 1989). Other novels in the generation before the Cannibals that invite inquiry along these lines include Fabrizia Ramondino's *Althénopis* (1981) and Francesca Sanvitale's *Madre e figlia* (1980). Cf. Pompei Karagoz, "Gazing Women," 391.

77. Sambuco, "Women, Relationships, and Space in Stancanelli's *Benzina*," 130.

78. See Silverman, *The Acoustic Mirror*, viii and 42–50. Cf. Pompei Karagoz, "Gazing Women," 413n7.

Part 3: Filicide

1. See Roberto Pozzan, *Cogne: L'intervista* (Rome: Editori Riuniti, 2006), 33. In addition to Pozzan, other nonfiction accounts of the Cogne case include Elena Davoglio, *Il Caso Cogne* (Rome: Adnkronos Libri, 2003); Carmelo Lavorino's *Cogne: delitto infernale* (Naples: Tullio Pironti Editore, 2006); Maria Grazia Torri, *Cogne un enigma svelato* (Bologna: Giraldi, 2007); and Carlo Taormina, "La mia verita sul delitto di Cogne," *Il Giornale*, (April 2007).

2. See Pino Corrias, *Luoghi Comuni: Dal Vajont a Arcore, la geografia che ha cambiato l'Italia* (Milan: Rizzoli, 2006), 165–185.

3. "*Per la prima volta nella storia giudiziaria del nostro paese*" the conditions in which "*le indagini preliminari . . . sono state integralmente seguite in diretta dai mezzi di comunicazione.*" Enzo Tardino, "*Chi ha uccisio Samuele?: Il racconto dell'assassinio di Cogne*" (Ferrara: Gabriele Corbo, 2003), 7.

4. See Daniel Soulez-Larivière, *Il circo mediatico-giudiziario*, trans. Maria Giustozzi (Macerata: Liberilibri, 1994).

5. See Guy Debord, *The Society of the Spectacle*, trans. Donald Nicholson-Smith (New York: Zone Books, 1995), esp. 150–154; Brown, *Crime and Law in Media Culture;* and David Kidd-Hewitt and Richard Osborn, *Crime and the Media: The Postmodern Spectacle* (East Haven, Conn.: Pluto, 1995). Given its primacy over print journalism in terms of consumption, my chief focus will be on televised coverage. See Michela Bani, "La criminalità femminile nella rappresentazione mediatica," in *La televisione del crimine*, ed. Gabrio Forti and Marta Bertolino (Milan: Vita e pensiero, 2005), 589–618. For a summary of the treatment of the Cogne case in the dailies see also Corradi, *Il nemico intimo*, 129–168.

6. See Angela McRobbie and Sarah Thornton, "Rethinking Moral Panic for Multi-Mediated Social Worlds," *British Journal of Sociology* 46, no. 4 (1995), 559–574.

7. This actually hearkens back to a 1936 public address Mussolini made in Bologna and captures the essence of Italian Fascism's pronatalist intentions. Cited in Victoria De Grazia, *How Fascism Ruled Women: Italy, 1922–45* (Berkeley: University of California Press, 1992), 46. I am grateful to Erin Teske for reminding me of this locution.

8. *"Voglio pensare che sia innocente perchè se non lo è siamo di fronte ad un mostro di freddezza"* (*Porta a porta*, November 8, 2004). Later the same month, Franzoni's memoir was published, timed to coincide with the start of the appeals phase of her case. I return to this point below. Iva Zanicchi hosted *Il prezzo è giusto* (the Italian version of the game show *The Price Is Right*) from 1987 to 2000.

9. See Annalisa Cavallone, "La sindrome di Medea: cosa spinge una madre ad uccidere il proprio figlio," *Psychofenia* 11, no. 18 (2008): 124–172.

10. See Adriana Cavarero, *Horrorism: Naming Contemporary Violence,* trans. Brian Guaig (New York: Columbia University Press, 2009), 29–32. It is worth noting that Cavarero has said she was explicitly considering the Cogne case while she worked on the Medean aspects of horror. (Personal correspondence with author.) See also Gian Carlo Nivoli, *Medea tra noi: Le madri che uccidono il proprio figlio* (Rome: Carocci editore, 2002).

6. The Yellow and the Black

1. See also Gennaro De Stefano's novelized version, *L'Uomo di Cogne* (Rome: Aliberti editore, 2008). De Stefano, a writer for the weekly magazine *Gente,* Italy's version of *People,* also helped Annamaria Franzoni with her memoir, *La Verità* (Casale Monferrato: Piemme Books, 2006).

2. *"Quando sono entrata il bambino gemeva. Avevo davanti un bambino vivo."* See Ilaria Cavo, *La chiamavano bimba* (Milan: Mondadori, 2007), 120. I have drawn on the *sentenza* delivered by the Corte di Cassazione in May 2008 in my reconstruction of events. I am grateful to Ret. Col. Luciano Garofano for making it available. This and all translations are mine unless otherwise noted.

3. As Bianchi indicated in his testimony at trial and later in conversation with Ilaria Cavo, *"Per me, Samuele, al nostro arrivo, era già morto"* (To me, Samuele already seemed dead when we arrived). Cavo, *La chiamavano bimba,* 130. The conflicting reports made time of death uncertain, impeding the official reconstruction the events.

4. *"Sono sicuro che Samuele è morto lì in quell'istante, mentre lo stavo osservando."* Quoted in ibid., 138–139.

5. The GIP is a powerful figure in any investigation and is the member of the judiciary whose role is to oversee the gathering of all data pertaining to the crime under investigation as well as to establish its juridical parameters (e.g., designating whether it is a homicide (*omicidio volontario*) or manslaughter (*omicidio colposo*), establishing the term of sentence that will be sought and argued for, etc.) before submitting the case to the *pubblico ministero* (PM, or prosecutor), who will argue it before the trial judge (*giudice di primo grado*).

6. Curiously, author Maria Grazia Torri took up the aneurysm defense in her 2007 publication *Cogne un enigma svelato* (Bologna: Giraldi). Veering wide from her usual topics of art and cultural criticism, Torri argued that the medical examiners did not adequately investigate the possibility that aneurysm might have been the cause of death, which would have exonerated Franzoni of any wrongdoing. Perhaps it is only coincidental that the deus ex machina of an aneurysm appeared in both Veronesi's and Ammaniti's fiction, which I discuss in the chapters that follow.

7. Contemporary Italian feminist theory and philosophy, for example, has considered the designation of the prima facie "monstrosity" of women in general. With the elevation of the universal male neuter as the standard measure, Western philosophy's phallocentrism establishes women as the site of the lack. Adriana Cavarero covers the evolution of this concept but inverts it, designating phallocentric discourse itself as monstrous. She writes, "There is something monstrous, since the logic of absolutizing the finite pays for its daring with monstrosity: after all, the neutral (not yet sexed) or the hermaphrodite (already sexed both ways) have been monsters for a long time. But the true monster, revealed in logical processes, is the neutral male, an unrepresentable monster and yet so familiar to whomever says: 'Man is a rational animal,' 'Man is the Child of God,'" and so forth. Cavarero, "Toward a Theory of Sexual Difference," in *The Lonely Mirror: Italian Perspectives on Feminist Theory*, ed. Sandra Kemp and Paola Bono (New York: Routledge, 1993), 190.

8. See Frances Heidensohn, *Women and Crime* (London: MacMillan, 1986), 195. See also chapter 5, "House Arrest," in my *Prison Terms: Representing Confinement During and After Italian Fascism* (Toronto: University of Toronto Press, 2001), 137–175.

9. Reference to disciplinary institutions recalls explicitly the findings of Michel Foucault, most clearly articulated in part 3 of *Discipline and Punish: The Birth of the Prison*, trans. Alan Sheridan (New York: Vintage, 1979), 135–308.

10. Heidensohn, *Women and Crime*, 195.

11. Teresa de Lauretis considers the utility of considering "gender along the lines of Michel Foucault's theory of sexuality as a 'technology of sex' and to propose that gender, too, both as representation and self-representation, is the product of various social technologies, such as cinema, and of institutionalized discourses, epistemologies, and critical practices, as well as practices of daily life." Teresa de Lauretis, *Technologies of Gender: Essays on Theory, Film, and Fiction* (Bloomington: Indiana University Press, 1987), 2.

12. This is Althusser's formulation of the "interpellation" of the social subject "hailed" by ideology, a notion most clearly expressed in his *Lenin and Philosophy and Other Essays*, trans. Ben Brewster (New York: Monthly Review Press, 1971), esp. 164 and 175.

13. Quoted in Gillian Rose, *Feminism and Geography: The Limits of Geographical Knowledge* (London: Routledge, 1993), 4.

14. On maternity as represented in contemporary Italian literature, see Laura Benedetti, *The Tigress in the Snow* (Toronto: University of Toronto Press, 2007); Carol Lazzaro-Weiss, "The Concept of Difference in Italian Feminist Thought: Mothers, Daughters, Heretics," in *Italian Feminist Theory and Practice: Equality and Sexual Difference*, ed. Graziella Parati and Rebecca West (Madison, N.J..: Fairleigh Dickinson University Press, 2002), 31–49; Adalgisa Giorgio, "The Passion for the Mother: Conflicts and Idealisations in Contemporary Italian Narrative" in *Writing Mothers and Daughters: Renegotiating the Mother in Western European Narratives by Women*, ed. Adalgisa Giorgio (New York: Berghahn, 2002), 119–154; and Lucamante, *A Multitude of Women*. For a corresponding investigation of cinematic narrative, see Giovanna Grignaffini, *La scena madre: scritti sul cinema*

(Bologna: Bononia University Press, 2002); Colleen Ryan-Scheutz, *Sex, the Self, and the Sacred: Women in the Cinema of Pier Paolo Pasolini* (Toronto: University of Toronto Press, 2007); and Giuliana Bruno and Maria Nadotti, eds., *Off Screen: Women and Film in Italy* (London: Routledge, 1988). On the representation of infanticide in contemporary Italian literature, see Nicoletta Di Ciolla, "Crime and the Female Subject: Matricide, Filicide and the Law of the Father in Contemporary Italian Literature: The Case of Laura Grimaldi and Barbara Garlaschelli," in *Women's Writing in Western Europe: Gender, Generation and Legacy*, ed. Adalgisa Giorgio and Julia Waters (Newcastle upon Tyne, England: Cambridge Scholars, 2007), 200–215.

15. The United States, Italy, and the Democratic Republic of Congo are the three countries whose vital statistics data are analyzed in the *Population Bulletin* 63, no. 3 (2008): 4 and 5. These pages offer the highlights of the Population Reference Bureau's 2008 World Population Data Sheet; available at http://www.prb.org/Publications/Datasheets/2008/2008wpds.aspx (accessed March 11, 2011).

16. This actually hearkens back to a 1936 public address Mussolini made in Bologna and captures the essence of Italian Fascism's pronatalist intentions. Quoted in De Grazia, *How Fascism Ruled Women: Italy 1922–1945* (Berkeley: University of California Press, 1992), 46.

17. In the extensive bibliography of population studies in Italy, see Gianpiero Dalla Zuanna, Alessandra De Rose, and Filomena Racioppi, "Low Fertility and Limited Diffusion of Modern Contraception in Italy during the Second Half of the Twentieth century," *Journal of Population Research* 22, no. 1 (2005): 21–48; Gianpiero Dalla Zuanna and Giuseppe Micheli, eds., *Strong Family and Low Fertility: A Paradox? New Perspectives in Interpreting Contemporary Family and Reproductive Behavior*, ed. (Dordrecht, Netherlands: Kluwer Academic Publishers, 2004); Marzio Barbagli, Maria Castiglioni, and Gianpiero Dalla Zuanna, *Fare famiglia in Italia: Un secolo di cambiamenti* (Bologna: Il Mulino, 2003); Marzio Barbagli, ed., *Lo Stato delle famiglie in Italia* (Bologna: Il Mulino, 1997); and Anna Laura Fadiga Zanatta and Maria Luisa Mirabile, *Demografia, famiglia, e società: come cambiano le donne* (Rome: Ediesse, 1993).

18. The significance of this datum is largely beyond my scope in these pages, but we might speculate as to the delay of pregnancy relative to a woman's cohabitation with other female members of a family as well as the distance in time from a social space such as high school may occasion a perceived need to consult manuals with greater frequency.

19. For the company's history consult either www.Prénatal.com or http://www.prenatal.it/prenatal/it/home.html (accessed June 9, 2011).

20. Data concerning publishing and distribution was provided by Ettore Lazzarini, Prénatal's director of marketing. *La mia gravidanza* has also been translated into Spanish, Portuguese, Greek, and Russian. Since the company finds that the book's aim is for personal use, Prénatal's Centro Studi has no archived copies of expectant mothers' diaries.

21. "*Di bambini non si parlava. Una volta avevo tirato fuori l'argomenti davanti a lei. 'Lo faremo, certo. Ho trentatré anni, ho calcolato che ho ancora qualche anno: intendo usare al massimo il limite del periodo riproduttivo,' mi aveva risposto.*" Cristina Comencini, *L'illusione del bene* (Milan: Feltrinelli, 2007), 34.

22. *"Un'esperta di corredino . . . spiegava nei dettagli e con esempi pratici come scegliere e usare gli indumenti e gli oggetti necessari alle prime settimane di vita del neonato."* Ettore Lazzarini, correspondence with author, September 2008.

23. *"Future mamme e . . . papà . . . vivere serenemente e consapevolmente il periodo della gravidanza."* Ibid.

24. *"Un percorso che passa attraverso i sensi"; "cambiamenti emozionali e fisiologici, di bonding, di rilassamento musicale."* Ibid.

25. My review of Sandro Veronesi's *Caos calmo* in the following chapter clarifies this point.

26. *"'Il bambino-risorsa,' cioè, il bambino mero oggetto e strumento di gratificazione per l'adulto e per il mondo degli adulti."*Alfredo Carlo Moro, "Solo bambini violati, solo bambini violati," in *La televisione del crimine,* ed. Gabrio Forti and Marta Bertolino (Milan: Vita e pensiero, 2005), 263.

27. I examine the interrelationships of murder and the body and the consequent uncoupling of the body and critical theory in the introduction.

28. In the Italian justice system, women who are pregnant or have children under the age of three cannot be placed under *custodia cautelare* (taken into custody) except in extreme cases.

29. *"Mi aiuti a fare un altro?"* Lacking the properly placed pronoun *ne*, this question—widely reported on and repeated—is notable for its lack of grammatical coherence as well as its equivocality. The question should read *"Mi aiuti a far̲n̲e̲ un altro?"* Even in the context that was attributed, that is, Franzoni's alleged stated wish for another child, I note that the use of the indefinite pronoun—*"u̲n̲ altro"*—could mean anything

30. *"Se questo è il metro di misura, anch'io posso aver ucciso mio nipote. Anch'io ho passato notte insonni, notti agitate a sognare Samuele. Al mattino non sapevo più dove fossi, se fosse stato tutto un incubo o la realtà. Anch'io sono stato preso dall'ansia. Non si possono giudicare le reazioni di mia nuora dopo il delitto perchè sono inevitabilmente influenzate dal trauma che ha subìto."* Quoted in Cavo, *La chiamavano bimba,* 23.

31. David Kidd-Hewitt and Richard Osborne, *Crime and the Media: The Postmodern Spectacle* (East Haven, Conn.: Pluto, 1995), 29.

32. *"Non c'è un bruto che va a colpire i bambini, e neppure un serial killer in libertà."* Quoted in Cavo, *La chiamavano bimba,* 168.

33. We might say that a foreign murderess, such as Amanda Knox, for example, captures interest even more effectively.

34. Robert Reiner, "Media Made Criminality," in *The Oxford Handbook of Criminology,* ed. M. Maguire, R. Morgan, and R. Reiner (Oxford, UK: Oxford University Press, 2007), 302–337. See also Gemma Marotta, *Donne, criminalità e carcere* (Rome: Euroma La Goliardica, 1989), 84–92.

35. Meda Chesney-Lind and Lisa Pasko, *The Female Offender: Girls, Women, and Crime* (Thousand Oaks, Calif.: Sage Publications, 2004), 98.

36. Cavo, *La chiamavano bimba,* 171.

37. Freud described his observations of the child playing the game of disappearance and return in "Beyond the Pleasure Principle." Sigmund Freud, "Beyond the Pleasure Principle" (1920), in *The Standard Edition of the Complete Psychological*

Works of Sigmund Freud, vol. 18, ed. James Strachey (London: Hogarth, 1957), 14–15. The classic "trio" reading Poe's "The Purloined Letter" for what it reveals about repetition compulsion and trauma are Jacques Lacan, *Écrits* (Lacan reading Poe); Jacques Derrida, "The Purveyor of Truth," *Yale French Studies* 53 (1975) (Derrida reading Lacan reading Poe); and Barbara Johnson, "The Frame of Reference: Poe, Lacan, Derrida," *Yale French Studies* 55/56 (1977): 457–505 (Johnson reading everyone and everything).

38. This is akin to Antonio Gramsci's theories of the social articulation of hegemony in a variety of discursive forms. See Ernesto Laclau and Chantal Mouffe, *Hegemony and Socialist Strategy: Towards a Radical Democratic Politics* (London: Verso, 1985), esp. 134–137.

39. See Mary Ann Doane, "The Close-Up: Scale and Detail in the Cinema," *differences* 14, no. 3 (2003): 89–111.

40. See Kaja Silverman, *The Acoustic Mirror: The Female Voice in Psychoanalysis and Cinema* (Bloomington: Indiana University Press, 1988), esp. 42–50.

41. *"Una madre che continua a singhiozzare, ha le lacrime agli occhi." Porta a porta,* March 11, 2002.

42. Annamaria Franzoni with Gennaro De Stefano, *La Verità,* (Casale Monferrato: Piemme Books, 2006), 65.

43. Ibid.

44. *"Mezzo addormentato . . . disperato perchè non aveva trovato Davide a suo fianco."* Ibid., 67.

45. *"Il mio odore sul cuscino."* Ibid.

46. *"Sicuramente Samuele mi sentirebbe."* Ibid., 68. On Franzoni's use of the present tense (in this instance in the conditional mood) in her text, see note 49 below.

47. Cavo, *La chiamavano bimba,* 145.

48. Carlo Taormina, *La mia verita sul delitto di Cogne* (*Il Giornale,* April 2007).

49. *"Mi sfilo le scarpe che lascio per terra e mi infilo le ciabbate."* Franzoni, *La verità,* 7. Franzoni frequently uses the present tense in her memoir, particularly at the beginning, which is set on the day of the crime and is meant as prelude to her account of the criminal investigation and trials. She also uses it to dramatize events and capture her state of mind. It is as though Franzoni, writing with *Gente* columnist Gennaro De Stefano, believes that the present will obviate history, which will at any moment change, negating or otherwise altering the fact of Samuele's death.

50. Ibid., 14.

51. Cavo, *La chiamavano bimba,* 115–117.

52. *"L'importante è che abbia fatto in modo di non lasciare nessuna traccia. . . . Questo gesto non poteva essere automatico. Abbiamo valutato che fosse necessariamente voluto, cosciente."* Cavo, *La chiamavano bimba,* 325.

53. *"Mi è sembrato di avergli tolto qualcosa di suo."* Ibid., 175.

54. See Julia Kristeva, *The Powers of Horror: An Essay on Abjection,* trans. Leon Roudiez (New York: Columbia University Press, 1982); Barbara Creed, *The Monstrous-Feminine: Film, Psychoanalysis, and Feminism* (London: Routledge, 1993); and Elizabeth Grosz, *Sexual Subversions: Three French Feminists* (Sydney: Allen & Unwin, 1989.)

55. See the text of the introduction in this volume and note 55 there.

56. Sigmund Freud, "On the Sexual Theories of Children," in *The Standard Edition of the Complete Psychological Works of Sigmund Freud*, 18:220, quoted in Creed, *The Monstrous-Feminine*, 18.

57. See Linda Williams, "Film Bodies: Gender, Genre, and Excess," *Film Quarterly* 44:4 (1991).

58. "*Immagini impressionanti, quasi inguardabili.*" Cavo, *La chiamavano bimba*, 172.

59. "*Ha prevalso la mia coscienza . . . la pena umana nei confronti di una madre su cui non riuscivo a infierire.*" Quoted in ibid., 173 (my emphasis) .

60. "*Se lo avessi fatto forse il processo sarebbe andato diversamente e non saremmo andati avanti a parlare di giallo per tutti questi anni. Forse, così, avrebbe potuto avere una reazione significativa, chiara.*" Quoted in ibid.

61. "*Parlare, raccontare e rispondere alle domande mi aiuta.*" Franzoni, *La Verità*, 137.

62. "*Dover dimostrare tutte le volte che non sono pazza e non ho dimenticato nulla.*" Ibid.

63. "*Colloqui, test ed esami i periti del giudice scriveranno che sono sana di mente.*" Ibid.

64. See also Dana Becker, *Through the Looking Glass: Women and Borderline Personality Disorder* (Boulder, Colo.: Westview, 1997); and Janet Wirth-Cauchon, *Women and Borderline Personality Disorder* (New Brunswick, N.J.: Rutgers University Press, 2000), both of which discuss the politics of gender in the diagnosis of borderline personality disorder.

65. Arguing for the gendered equality of perpetrators—that is, identifying and accepting female perpetrators as part of a feminist practice—stands at some distance from Carol Gilligan's clarion call in her 1982 study *In a Different Voice: Psychological Theory and Women's Development* for an acknowledgment of women's unique sense of justice based on experiences deriving from activities such as mothering, caring, and nurturing. See also Orit Kamir, *Framed: Women in Law and Film* (Durham, N.C.: Duke University Press, 2006), 12 and 217–242.

66. "*Se consideriamo le statistiche ufficiali delle condannate, in particolare dagli anni Settanta in poi, durante i quali è aumentato il grado d'istruzione e di partecipazione alla vita lavorativa, ci appare chiaro che non solo non vi è aumentato del numero delle condannate ma che si è registrato un graduale decremento.*" Michela Bani, "La criminalità femminile nella rappresentazione mediatica," in *La televisione del crimine*, ed. Gabrio Forti and Marta Bertolino (Milan: Vita e pensiero, 2005), 608–609n46.

67. See Bronwyn Naylor, "The 'Bad Mother' in Media and Legal Texts," *Social Semiotics* 11, no. 2 (2001): 156.

68. "*Mi spiace molto anche perché a me dell'aspetto politico (Grosso di sinistra, Taormina di destra), non interessa nulla.*" Franzoni, *La verità*, 144.

69. See Marco Catino, *Sociologia di un delitto: Media, giustizia, e opinione pubblica nel caso Marta Russo* (Rome: Luca Sossella editore, 2001).

70. "*Ho perso molto ad accettare il mandato di questa causa: sia al livello di immagine sia per il tempo che ho dovuto sottrarre alla mia attività professionale.*" Cavo, *La chiamavano bimba*, 269.

71. Taormina, *La mia verità*.

72. "*Ha avuto tutto il tempo occorrente a uccidere, a togliersi gli indumenti usati per l'azione delittuosa, a lavarsi e a nuovamente riprendere freddezza e razionalità, sí da potersi rendere conto che, commesso il fatto, la priorità era costituita dal non consentire che venisse accertata la propria penale responsabilità.*" Quoted in Roberto Pozzan, *Cogne: L'Intervista* (Rome: Editori Riuniti, 2006), 104.

73. See R. Emerson Dobash, Russell Dobash, and Lesley Noakes, *Gender and Crime* (Cardiff: University of Wales Press, 1995), 207.

74. "*Non si accontentano di ottenere un parere tecnico sull'esistenza di una condizione di infermità capace di incidere sull'imputabilità dell'autore del reato; sentono la necessità di 'capire', di 'comprendere' come si sia potuto realizzare un simile atto, cercano spiegazioni psicologiche che rendano ragione all'accaduto.*" Roberto Cattanesi and Carlo Troccoli, "La madre omicida. Aspetti criminologici," *Rassegna italiana di criminologia* 5 (1994): 167.

75. "*Le aspettative di infermità fossero talmente forti da non far accettare agevolmente a nessuna delle parti, neppure al pubblico ministero, relazioni che concludessero per la mancanze di vizio di mente.*" Ibid., 173.

76. "*Le cassette saranno presto acquisite, compresa quella del famoso fuori onda in cui Annamaria si domanda a voce alta: 'Non avrò mica pianto troppo?'*" "Cogne esame sulle interviste tv," *La Repubblica*, December 12, 2005.

77. "*I giudici hanno sbagliato: per una perizia psichiatrica non si può usare materiale di questo genere.*" Quoted in "Cogne, esame sulle interviste tv La Franzoni: 'No alla perizia,'" *La Repubblica*, December 15, 2005.

7. Spectacular Grief and Public Mourning

1. See Peppino Ortoleva, *Mediastoria: Comunicazione e cambiamento sociale nel mondo contemporaneo* (Parma: Nuova Pratiche Editrice, 1995), esp. 143–156. Joshua Meyrowitz anticipated Ortoleva's thoughts in his discussion of the public sense of loss and mourning over "media friends"—largely characters in TV series—in his 1985 study *No Sense of Place: The Impact of Electronic Media on Social Behavior* (Oxford: Oxford University Press, 1985), 118–122. See also James Curran and Tamar Liebes, eds., *Media, Ritual, and Identity* (London: Routledge, 1998). Criminological scholarship demonstrates that female deviance is reported with greater frequency in a televised medium than in the press. See Philip Schlesinger and Howard Tumber, *Reporting Crime: The Media Politics of Criminal Justice* (Oxford: Oxford University Press, 1994), esp. 88; and Robert Reiner, "Media Made Criminality. The Representation of Crime in the Mass Media," in *The Oxford Handbook of Criminology*, ed. M. Maguire, R. Morgan, and R. Reiner (Oxford: Oxford University Press, 2007), 302–337. For confirmation of this tendency in the Italian market, see Michela Bani, "La criminalità femminile nella rappresentazione mediatica," in *La televisione del crimine*, ed. Gabrio Forti and Marta Bertolino (Milan: Vita e pensiero, 2005), 589–618.

2. "*Fredda, anaffettiva, cinica, bugiarda, falsa.*" Franzoni with De Stefano, *La Verità*, 19. This an all other translations mine unless otherwise indicated.

3. "*Con lucidità, cinismo, e spietata freddezza*"; "*notevole e anomala freddezza.*" Ibid., 19 and 17. Gramola's announcement is available, among other places, in Pozzan, *Cogne*. Franzoni was described as "cold" by the press too many times to count.

4. Coverage of the Cogne case revealed fixed ideas about mourning and its elaboration that substantially adhere to the formulation Freud laid out early in the twentieth century. The Freudian project insists on the subject passing from mourning to pathological mourning and from there to melancholia, the phase in which loss detaches from a specific object. See Freud, "Mourning and Melancholia" (1921), in *The Standard Edition of the Complete Psychological Works of Sigmund Freud* (1957), 14:243–248. See also Jacques Derrida, *The Work of Mourning*, ed. Pascale-Ann Brault and Michael Naas (Chicago: University of Chicago Press, 2001).

5. For a discussion of the superimposition of the mythical Ariadne onto the character of Arianna, see Fabio Vighi, "Unravelling Moretti's (Political) Unconscious: The Abyss of the Subject in *La Stanza del figlio*," *Journal of Romance Studies* 3:2 (2003).

6. "*Un caso di reazione atipica al dolore. . . . Il protagonista del romanzo è sereno, diventa un padre più amorevole, un genitore esemplare. . . . A volte . . . si siede ad aspettare che succeda qualcosa. Ma no: la bomba del dolore non esplode mai.*" Maria Grazia Torri, *Cogne un enigma svelato*, (Bologna: Giraldi, 2007), 128.

7. In *Un enigma svelato*, Torri sought to publicize the possibility that Samuele had died of natural causes (an aneurysm) and that Franzoni's statement during her 118 call that her son's head "had exploded" was truthful and merited greater investigation. *Caos calmo* is only briefly mentioned for its portrayal of the decorum and expectations surrounding public grief. For Torri's reaction to Veronesi's lack of response, see Maria Grazia Torri, "Letter aperta alla Franzoni" (Open Letter to Franzoni), *Parliamo fra noi*, June 7, 2008, http://parliamofranoi.blogspot.com/2008/06/lettera-aperta-alla-franzoni-di-maria.html (accessed March 11, 2011). Torri was critical of many commentators and cultural critics, including several touched on in this book (Andrea Pinketts, Carlo Lucarelli, Tiziano Scarpa, Maurizio Costanzo, Bruno Vespa). Nor did I escape her criticism for keeping a healthy distance from her project.

8. As Vighi has detailed in his Lacanian reading of Moretti's film, this links to "*ex-timité*," or extimacy (a neologism by Jacques-Alain Miller). Regarding Moretti's film and the "threat" that Giovanni and Paola's family perceives from the "outside" event of Andrea's death, Vighi notes that "the traumatic event which strikes at the heart of the symbolic field *was always at the heart of such field*, coinciding with the very void around which any symbolic order, from family to social contract, is structured " (italics in original). See Vighi, "Unravelling Moretti's (Political) Unconscious," 81.

9. "*(Ha più) sconvolto l'opinione pubblica negli ultimi vent'anni.*" Gennaro De Stefano, *L'uomo di Cogne* (Rome: Aliberti Editore, 2008), inside cover. De Stefano assisted Franzoni in writing her memoir, *La Verità*.

10. See Consuelo Corradi, *Il nemico intimo: una lettura sociologica dei casi di Novi Ligure e Cogne* (Rome: Meltemi, 2005). Clearly, the "*nemico intimo*" relates also to the concept of extimacy.

11. Interview with Sandro Veronesi, included in the extra material on the DVD *Caos calmo (Calm Chaos)* (01 Distribuzione, 2008).

12. William Uricchio and Susanne Kinnebrock, "Introduction," in *Media Cultures*, ed. William Uricchio and Susanne Kinnebrock (Heidelberg: Universitätsverlag Winter, 2006), 3–4.

13. Both Veronesi and Moretti emphasize the importance of the public space of the park, the former for the way it demarcates the space of the *schiavitù*, or slavery, of mourning that the Pietro character will eventually breach and overcome, the latter for the way it became part of his own habitus as an actor in the making of the film. Both interviews are contained in the extra material on the DVD of *Caos calmo*.

14. "*Come se tutti qui dessero per scontato che non potrò occuparmi di mia figlia.*" Sandro Veronesi, *Caos calmo* (Milan: Bompiani, 2005), 30. Veronesi's novel is available in English as *Quiet Chaos: A Novel,* trans. Michael Moore (New York: Ecco Books, 2011).

15. Recent Italian narrative does not lack for representations of contemporary paternity. It is present, for example, in fiction of Ugo Pirro, Giorgio van Straten, Enrico Palandri, Romolo Bugaro, among others, all of whom lack the hilarity of Aldo Busi in his *Manuale del perfetto papà*. See also Lorenza Rocco Carbone, "*La forza del passato,*" *Silarus* 41 (2001): 75–78. I examine Niccolò Ammaniti's portrayal of single fatherhood in chapter 8.

16. *Le chiavi di casa* (*Keys to the House*), dir. Gianni Amelio, 2004 (Lions Gate Home Entertainment, 2005).

17. "*Svegliare Claudia, fare colazione insieme a lei, portarla a scuola e restare qui davanti ad aspettarla come tutti i giorni mi è sembrato d'un tratto l'Eden perduto.*" Veronesi, *Caos calmo,* 233.

18. In her review of the novel, Antonella Cilento maintains that Pietro's grief for Lara arrives in the middle of the evening meeting, the break from his previous behavior signaled by his loss of consciousness when he faints. This is true only in part, for Pietro spends the remainder of the novel dancing away from the full realization of Lara's death and turns to face it fully only at novel's end. See Antonella Cilento, "La recensione de L'Indice," n.d.,*Indice dei Libri,* http://www.ibs.it/code/9788845234897/veronesi-sandro/caos-calmo.html, accessed April 15, 2011.

19. "*Un computer che cancella i files, ma non definitivamente: li accantona in un cestino da cui, con appositi commandi, è possibile recuperarli.*" Cavo, *La chiamavano Bimba,* 178.

20. "*È reversibile: uno mica può restare lì sempre, no?*" Veronesi, *Caos calmo,* 445.

21. "*Claudia sembra seguire me: frastornata, stupita, ma ancora lontana dal dolore vero. In quel turbinio siamo stati sempre insieme . . . e abbiamo fatto molte cose anche banali. . . . Ogni volta io pensavo che fosse l'ultima. . . . Ma ogni volta, con mia grande sorpresa, ne uscivamo indenni.*" Ibid., 28.

22. "*Serena. Come se non fosse mai successo nulla.*" Ibid., 335.

23. "*La sua reazione è un mistero, e io non mi sono ancora azzardato ad affrontarlo.*" Ibid., 198.

24. "*Sta imitando solo te. Vede che tu non soffri, e non soffre nemmeno lei.*" Ibid.

25. "*Lara muore e voi due non siete tristi: bella roba.*" Ibid., 102.

26. "*Distruggerò quella posta, distruggerò tutto, e non ripeterò l'errore di prima. . . . È semplice: Modifica. Selezione tutto. 4332 elementi selezionati. Elimina. Zot, eliminati, senza nemmeno passare per il cestino. La posta elettronica di Lara non c'è più. Non c'è mai stata.*" Ibid., 138 (emphasis in original). We could say that Pietro remembers to forget; see Viktor Mayer-Schönberger, *Delete: The Virtue of Forgetting in the Digital Age* (Princeton, N.J.: Princeton University Press, 2009), 92–127.

27. *"Noi non soffriamo ancora, l'abbiamo presa così, per adesso, anzi direi che non l'abbiamo ancora presa."* Veronesi, *Caos calmo*, 112.

28. *"Mi piacerebbe che lei desse un'occhiata fuori della finestra e mi vedesse. Mi piacerebbe accorgermene, voglio dire."* Ibid., 40.

29. This is discussed in chapter 4 in relation to the Novi Ligure case. Crepet, *Non siamo capaci di ascoltarli*, esp. 25–27. See also CENSIS and U. C. S. I., *Terzo rapporto sulla comunicazione in Italia: Giovani & Media* (Milan: FrancoAngeli, 2004), esp. 45–47 and 162–165.

30. *"Sono venuti qui da me a scaricarmi addosso il loro dolore, ciecamente, accanitamente, davanti a questa scuola."* Veronesi, *Caos calmo*, 79.

31. *"Capire che devo proteggermi. Devo difendermi, se non voglio ritrovarmi, mentre ancora riesco a evitare il mio dolore, a sprofondare nottetempo in quello altrui. . . . È importante tenere a mente che io non sono loro."* Ibid., 146 (emphasis in original).

32. *"Tu sei l'unica persona di cui mi fido."* Ibid., 89.

33. Ibid., 302.

34. *"Come se non fosse mai successo nulla."* Ibid., 335.

35. For Veronesi's thoughts on contemporary (and nonfictional) corporate mergers and their psychological consequences, see *Il corriere della sera*, September 4, 2006, *Economia* insert.

36. *"Laggiù si parla più di me che della fusione e che comunque i due argomenti sono considerati strettamente legati."* Veronesi, *Caos calmo*, 376.

37. *"No alla fusione! Questo è successo. Questo è stato il nostro patto."* Ibid., 71.

38. *"Molto popolare, da quando sei piazzato qui. Da come mi hanno tempestato di domande direi che l'alta borghesia di questa città ti segue appassionatamente."* Ibid., 188.

39. Antonello Grimaldi's direction of the film *Caos calmo*, which starred Nanni Moretti and was released in February 2008, captures neither the design nor the subtlety of the sodomy scene with Eleonora, although official Vatican censure ensured its success, both at the box office and on YouTube, where pirated downloads were available just as the film was released.

40. *"Aveva bisogno di incularsele, prima una e poi l'altra."* Veronesi, *Caos calmo*, 361.

41. *"Per ragioni . . . storiche e indiscutibili, la sodomia era l'unico strumento in grado di rendere un rapporto veramente solido e duraturo, andando a costruire quell'unicum inespugnabile che lui chiamava 'sodalizio simbiotico.'"* Veronesi, *Caos calmo*, 361 (my emphasis).

42. *"Quel che ci è successo due mesi fa ti ha risvegliato qualcosa di rimosso e inconfessabile come ha fatto con me."* Ibid., 364.

43. *"Gli ebrei ricchi l'Olocausto è stato Olocausto due volte, perchè ha annientato le persone e le sostanze."* Ibid., 409 (emphasis in original).

44. *"Invulnerabile, perché stavo lavorando . . . per i morti."* Ibid.

45. *"Come se fosse mai nulla successo"*; *"mai avvenuto."* Ibid., 411.

46. *"Gerarchico e immutabile."* Ibid., 268.

47. *"Elastico and complesso."* Ibid.

48. *"Rigido, pesante, totalmente privo dei dispositivi di amortizzazione messi a punto dal cristianesimo, che non a caso è più recente, più moderno."* Ibid., 429.

49. "*Neutra, astratta, senza poteri, che se ne sta lì, ininfluente e tuttavia necessa-ria, a far da garante del rapporto tra le altre due.*" Ibid., 430.

50. Like the fossil or the teapot in *La stanza del figlio*, the Peugeot in *Caos calmo* symbolizes mishap and a threat to the integrity of the family. But while Ariadne, like the mythically ordained guide she is named for, can assist the family in Moret-ti's film out of their maze of grief, no such guide exists for Pietro in *Caos calmo*.

51. Veronesi, *Caos calmo*, 96.

52. Franzoni, *La Verità*, 138 passim.

8. Unspeakable Crimes

1. "*Io te lo avevo detto che andavo al pulmino da solo . . . se te stavi con Samuele non sarebbe successo nulla.*" Annamaria Franzoni with Gennaro De Stefano, *La Verità*, (Casale Monferrato: Hemme, 2006) 91–92. This and all other translations mine unless otherwise indicated.

2. "*Indicano Davide come possibile autore dell'omicidio.*" Ibid.,139. This greatly resembles some of the chatter in a similar case, the December 1996 murder of Jon-Benét Ramsey in Boulder, Colorado. See Joyce Carol Oates's 2008 novelization of this possible version of the events, *My Sister, My Love,* which takes the form of the narcoticized ramblings of an older brother whose sister was murdered in circum-stances remarkably like those of the Ramsey case.

3. "*Gli faccio cenno di stare in silenzio.*" Franzoni, *La Verità*, 68. Franzoni uses the present tense in her narrative of the events. See chapter 6 notes 46 and 49.

4. As detailed in chapter 4, the description of cell phones as a virtual umbilical cord was used by the press to describe Erika De Nardo's generation of "wired" teen-agers and their parents. See Aldo Grasso, "Negli spot degli SMS tutta la distanza delle famiglie," *Il corriere della sera*, February 25, 2001. See also Heather Horst and Daniel Miller, *The Cell Phone: An Anthropology of Communication* (Oxford: Berg Publishers, 2006).

5. Silence about the victim of murder is in fact an ethical problem in any narra-tion of the crime, as Michelle Boulous Walker has explored with regard to Hélène Rythmann, who was found strangled to death on the floor of the École Normale Superieure rooms she shared with philosopher Louis Althusser, her husband. After the "silencing" of his psychiatric treatment, Althusser's voice returns in the narra-tive he wrote of the events, *L'avenir dure longtemps suivi de "Les Faits,"* published first in 1992. It was published in English as *The Future Lasts a Long Time and The Facts,* ed. Olivier Corpet and Yann Moulier Boutang, trans. Richard Veasey (Lon-don: Chatto and Windus, 1993). Boulous Walker's point is that while Althusser' s voice may have been "restored," Rythmann will always be silent. See Michelle Bou-lous Walker, *Philosophy and the Maternal Body: Reading Silence* (London: Rout-ledge, 1998), 46.

6. My interest in Tamaro's text is sympathetic to, yet differs from, that of Ni-coletta Di Ciolla MacGowan in "Anima Parvuli: A Child's Destiny according to Susanna Tamaro," *Forum Italicum* 33, no. 2 (1999): 459–484. Di Ciolla MacGowan valuably traces the geneaology of violence in Tamaro's oeuvre, thematically linking *Per voce sola* to Tamaro's other novels. My interest in these particular stories is in

the way they show the transformation of children from victims of crime to perpe-trators and how at least one of the stories gives expression to anxieties about natal-ity, conception, and demographics in contemporary Italy.

7. *"Adesso a sei anni sanno già tutto."* Susanna Tamaro, *Per voce sola* (Venice: Marsilio, 1991), 63. Tamaro's novel is available in English as *For Solo Voice*, trans. Sharon Wood (Manchester: Carcanet Press, 1995).

8. See Laura Rorato, "Childhood Prisons, Denied Dreams and Denied Realities: The Ritualization of Pain in the Novels of Susanna Tamaro," *Romance Studies* 28 (1996): 61–78.

9. Researchers in the interrelated fields of neuroscience, social psychology, and cognitive psychology have demonstrated increasingly strong evidence of the "hard wiring" of the human brain as concerns imitative behavior. This is a point dis-cussed in chapter 3.

10. See chapter 6, note 17 for the literature on Italy's low fertility rate. For a read-ing of the cinematic "absence" of children see Paul Sutton, "The Missing Child of Contemporary Italian Cinema," *Screen* 46, no. 3 (2005): 353–359.

11. *"Dal momento in cui la nostra impossibilità di avere figli era stata accertata non avevamo desiderato altro."* Tamaro, *Per voce sola*, 12.

12. *"Sostiene che è il momento di tirare fuori storie terrificanti . . . mostri, streghe, giganti con la bava, patrigni terribili e carnivori."* Ibid.

13. *"La sua è proprio una storia a lieto fine. Una vera fiaba."* Ibid., 19.

14. *"Mi ha offerto ripetutamente quelle che aveva staccato dalla bambola. Allora le ho detto che se voleva, dopo aver finito il pullover ne avrei fatto uno uguale identico per la sua bambola. Mi ha teso le manine e se l'è fatto infilare."* Ibid., 20.

15. *"Come sempre vorrà sentire Barbablù o Pollicino."* Ibid., 13.

16. It is worth noting that both Roberto Saviano's 2006 book *Gomorra* and Mat-teo Garrone's adaptation (*Gomorrah*, 2008, The Criterion Collection), explicitly link children with refuse. Saviano's belief that Naples is the dumping ground of Italy could not be more clear. When Franco (Toni Servillo) replaces the unionized truck drivers with baby gangsters so small they cannot reach the trucks' cabs, he further underscores how at risk children are in that environment. *Certi bambini*, Diego De Silva's 2001 novel, offers similar representations. Although De Silva never names the Italian metropolis that Rosario and his buddies navigate, the 2004 film adaptation is set in very recognizable Neapolitan slums; *Certi bambini* (*A Chil-dren's Story*), codirected by Antonio Frazzi and Andrea Frazzi, cowritten by Diego De Silva and Marcello Fois (Filmfreak Distributie, 2004).

17. *"La bambina è magra, disattenta, sembra deperita. Non è la prima volta che succede. Ho ripetuto a questa maestra quel che ho detto alle altre: non si sa da chi sia venuta al mondo, le prime ore le ha trascorse tra i detriti, nel disagio più totale."* Tamaro, *Per voce sola*, 16.

18. *"L'aveva sollevata con le sue braccia forti, la faceva piroettare in aria, quando cadeva la raccoglieva a terra e la lanciava un'altra volta."* Ibid., 21.

19. *"Non ce l'ha fatta ad alzarsi . . . ha voluto lo stesso che le mettessi il completo da ballo."* Ibid., 22.

20. *"Si è sporcata; si è fatta tutto addosso come quando era piccola. Poi ha vomi-tato la colazione sul jabot di pizzo."* Ibid.

21. *"Era ormai troppo tardi. Stavo lì dentro già grande, non si poteva più snidarmi."* Ibid., 68.

22. *"Sotto la crosta dura la terra ha un cuore di fuoco e molle. Sta tutto là sotto chiuso, compresso ma se qualcosa si rompe (. . .) il cuore molle viene su, sale e sale fin dentro i rubinetti e un giorno esce al posto dell'acqua e uccide tutti."* Ibid., 71.

23. Ibid., 90.

24. Marco Risi's 1989 film *Mery per sempre,* released two years before publication of *Per voce sola,* also helped distribute cultural knowledge about same-sex relations in a boy's reformatory. Another key cinematic example of a treatment of the institutionalization of children that features a subtext of sexual exploitation is Gianni Amelio's 1992 *Ladro di bambini.* See also Nazzareno Zambotti, *Perché non sono diventato un serial killer: Autobiografia di un uomo solo* (Turin: Einaudi, 2003).

25. *"Per i primi mesi me l'hanno fatto e poi ho cominciato a farlo anch'io agli altri."* Tamaro, *Per voce sola,* 90.

26. Such an act of cannibalism would appear to offer qualification enough to admit Tamaro to the annals of the "Giovani Cannibali," the Young Cannibals discussed in chapter 5, but she is never associated with that school, if such it may be called. See Stefania Lucamante, "Introduction," in *Italian Pulp Fiction: The New Narrative of the "Giovani Cannibali" Writers,* ed. and trans. Stefania Lucamante (Madison, N.J.: Fairleigh Dickinson University Press, 2001), 36n9.

27. Simona Vinci, *Dei bambini non si sa niente* (Turin: Einaudi, 1997). Vinci's novel is available in English as Simona Vinci, *A Game We Play,* trans. Minna Proctor (London: Chatto & Windus, 1999).

28. Filippo La Porta has also briefly noted the similarities between *Per voce sola* and *Dei bambini non si sa niente.* See La Porta, "The Horror Picture Show and the Very Real Horrors," in *Italian Pulp Fiction: The New Narrative of the "Giovani Cannibali" Writers,* ed. and trans. Stefania Lucamante (Madison, N.J.: Fairleigh Dickinson University Press, 2001), 64.

29. Julia Kristeva, *The Powers of Horror: An Essay on Abjection,* trans. Leon Roudiez (New York: Columbia University Press, 1982), 1 (emphasis in original).

30. Ibid., 2.

31. Calling Vinci's first novel *"un passo falso"* in her career as a writer, Renato Barilli criticizes the author for her exaggeration of the "evil" actions of her protagonists, which he attributes to her stance outside the children's world rather than within it. See Renato Barilli's *È arrivata la terza ondata. Dalla neo alla neoneoavanguardia* (Turin: Testo and Immagine, 2000), 147. Stefania Lucamante's examination of Vinci and other contemporary women writers in Italy might be considered a corrective to Barilli. For her thoughts on Vinci's *"cattivismo,"* her nastiness, see Lucamante, *A Multitude of Women: The Challenges of the Contemporary Italian Novel* (Toronto: University of Toronto Press, 2008), 234–236.

32. *"Il culo della macchina"; "come se fossero la stessa cosa: immondizia, robe rotte, da buttare."* Vinci, *Dei bambini,* 152 (my emphasis).

33. *"Ci ha adeguatamente istruito, avvisandoci che esso non è certo il regno dell'innocenza."* Barilli, *È arrivata la terza ondata,* 147. Indeed, it would appear that Barilli, first, is subject to the very criticism he levels at Vinci, and, second, has not

strayed too far from an undiluted Freudian understanding of the configuration of juvenile sexual desire.

34. *Dei bambini non si sa niente* shares some characteristics with the later short story "Fotografie." The story's first-person narrator, Tommaso, a dwarf, is chiefly concerned with Sara's photographic voyeurism, of which he is the unknowing subject. Photography is a "way to preserve the truth. . . . She needs to document an understanding she can no longer achieve or organize by way of her sense alone," Tommaso says. Simona Vinci, "Fotografie," in Vinci, *In tutti i sensi amore* (1999), 52–53. See also Barilli, *È arrivata la terza ondata,* 149.

35. As stipulated by articles 5 and 6 of Legge 15 febbraio 1996 n. 66, available as a PDF document at it.missingkids.com/it_IT/PDF/LEGGE_66_-_15_febbraio_1996 .pdf (accessed April 2, 2011). The issue of consent particularly with regard to anal sex is also the issue of the culminating scene in the first part of *Caos calmo,* detailed in the preceding chapter.

36. "*Attori che fanno finta di essere morti, oppure sono morti davvero, ma sono solo immagini che passano veloci su uno schermo piatto.*" Vinci, *Dei bambini,* 148 (my emphasis).

37. Ibid., 44.

38. "'*Gang bang,' (in) caratteri grandi e rossi.*" Ibid., 86.

39. The designation "body genre" is Linda Williams's. See her "Body Genres," in *The Oxford Guide to Film Studies.*

40. "*Alternavano i giochi della rivista*"; "*guardavano riviste sempre diverse e provavano le posizioni.*" Vinci, *Dei bambini,* 91.

41. "*Avevano fatto un rumore rapido e violento, come lo schiocco di una frustata.*" Ibid., 118.

42. "*La loro presenza si sentiva, erano lí, tutt'intorno, animali in agguato, con gli artigli già piantati dentro la carne delle vittime.*" Ibid., 120.

43. Ibid., 94.

44. "*Quella zona minuscola e strana era diventata il centro degli esperimenti.*" Ibid., 137.

45. "*Continuava a piangere ma in modo sommesso, appena percettibile . . . e lei non diceva niente.*" Ibid., 141.

46. "*Era bastato un movimento di Greta, che . . . tentava di sollevarsi e di strappare via con la mano lo scotch.*" Ibid., 144.

47. "*Ti nascondi, puoi stare zitto, come se fossi da solo, e nessuno ci fa caso.*" Ibid., 27.

48. *Le relazioni . . . erano definite eppure fluide. . . . Quello che rendeva le cose meno nette era che nel momento preciso in cui erano nudi, gli uni davanti agli altri diventavano uguali. I corpi si assomigliavano, femmine e maschi erano diversi, sí, ma per un unico dettaglio. Tutti avevano il torace piatto e liscio e i fianchi stretti. Avevano la pelle liscia e tesa, senza ombre, grinze o peli.*" Ibid., 56.

49. "*Anche i maschi avevano permesso alle dita delle bambine di intrufolarsi in quei posti e avevano scoperto e erano piú o meno tutti uguali, lí. Tutte le differenze si annullavano in quella zona minima dei corpi.*" Ibid., 137–138.

50. "*Del gemellaggio era una fissa . . . non faceva che ripeterlo, una specie di ossessione.*" Ibid. 33.

51. Gayle Rubin, "The Traffic in Women: Notes on the 'Political Economy' of Sex," in *Toward an Anthropology of Women*, ed. Rayna Reiter (New York: Monthly Review Press, 1975), 157–210.

52. "*Magari ci andiamo da sole qualche volta.*" Vinci, *Dei bambini*, 147.

53. "*Le sembrava di parlare e invece non diceva niente.*" Ibid.

54. "*Perché Greta fosse al centro di questa scena. Era una cavia e sembrava accettarlo. Nessuno di loro in realtà sapeva esattamente perché lei e non Martina, o Luca o Matteo. Era accaduto così.*" Ibid., 142.

55. "*Un brivido conosciuto guizzava tra le sue cosce, un brivido che sentiva già da tanto tempo.*" Ibid., 43.

56. "*Una finestra molto alta con una luce strana che entrava.*" Ibid., 40.

57. "*Guardava fuori e fuori era un dentro.*" Ibid.

58. "*Questa cosa diversa, questa cosa che erano loro insieme*, senza sguardi interni." Ibid., 47 (my emphasis).

59. "*Era una cosa sconosciuta e allo stesso tempo familiare. Come se fosse una cosa che sapeva, che aveva già conosicuto, ma di cui chissà perché si era dimenticata.*" Ibid., 64.

60. Ibid., 52.

61. Ibid.

62. By screen memory I refer to Freud's conceptualization of an early memory used as a screen onto which contemporary feelings are projected for examination. Freud's editor, James Strachey, defines it as "problems concerning the operation of memory and its distortions, the importance and *raison d'être* of phantasies, the amnesia covering our early years, and, behind all this, infantile sexuality." "Screen Memories" (1899), in *The Standard Edition of the Complete Psychological Works of Sigmund Freud*, (1962), 3:301.

63. "*Anche lui aveva pensato che era strano e poi che assomigliava a qualcosa che sapeva già.*" Vinci, *Dei bambini*, 65.

64. "*Un posto a parte, diverso, con proprie leggi.*" Ibid., 55.

65. "*Dritto per cinque minuti dentro i campi, poi ancora dritto, seguendo il fosso, tra le ortiche, i fiori gialli e viola, gli insetti. Dentro il fosso con le rane, sempre dritto, fino in fondo. Col granturco che si muove appena sotto il vento, altissimo. Ancora qualche settimana, forse qualche giorno, poi lo taglieranno tutto.*" Ibid., 11.

66. Marco Risi's *L'ultimo capodanno* (Istituto Luce, 1998), based on the long first story of *Fango*, was released in 1998. I discuss both the film and the collection in chapter 5. Gabriele Salvatores adapted for the screen both *Io non ho paura* (*I'm Not Scared*) (Medusa Distribuzione, 2003), and *Come Dio comanda* (*As God Commands*) (01 Distribuzione, 2008).

67. I discuss Foucault's thoughts on the utility of "parchments" as a methodological approach in the introduction. See Michel Foucault, "Nietzsche, Genealogy, History," in *Language, Counter-Memory, Practice: Selected Essays and Interviews*, ed. Donald Bouchard, trans. Donald Bouchard and Sherry Simon (Ithaca: Cornell University Press, 1977), 139.

68. Translations of Ammaniti's texts include *I'm Not Scared*, trans. Jonathan Hunt (Edinburgh: Canongate, 2003); *Steal You Away*, trans. Jonathan Hunt (Ed-

inburgh: Canongate, 2006); and *As God Commands,* trans. Jonathan Hunt (New York: Black Cat Press, 2009).

69. *"Gli faceva venire delle strane voglie. Voglie violente."* Niccolò Ammaniti, *Ti prendo e ti porto via* (Milan: Mondadori, 1999), 96.

70. *"Non reagisci. Sei timido. . . . Non hai spina dorsale. Ti hanno bocciato perchè permetti agli altri di farti fare una cosa che non vuoi fare."* Ibid, 412.

71. *"Un maledetto attimo capace di cambiarti la vita."* Ibid., 413.

72. *"Lo tempestò di pugni in faccia, sul collo, sulle spalle, emettendo degli strani versi rauchi. E se non ci fosse stato Pierini . . . chissà che gli avrebbe fatto."* Ibid., 441.

73. *"Lo guardò negli occhi. E lo disse. 'Lo so. L'ho ammazzata io.'"* Ibid.

74. Alberto Bianchi, "L'autenticità dell'immagine: Lo specchio catodico di Niccolò Ammaniti," *Narrativa* 20–21 (2001): 341.

75. *Ti prendo e ti porto via,* 451.

76. *"P.S. Preparati, perchè quando passo da Bologna ti prendo e ti porto via."* Ibid., 452. For the "perfect" endings characteristic of Ammaniti's prose narrative until the publication of *Io non ho paura,* see Giuliana Adamo, "Riflessioni sulle opere di due scrittori italiani contemporanei: Niccolò Ammaniti e Diego De Silva," *Italianist* 27, no. 1 (2007): 171.

77. Paul Sutton sees Filippo's kidnapping as emblematic of the anxiety over the "disappearing" child, or, as he calls it, the *"bambino negato,"* in contemporary Italian cinema. For a reading of the cinematic "absence" of children see Sutton, "The Missing Child of Contemporary Italian Cinema."

78. See also Anthony Cristiano, "'I'm Not Scared' . . . I'm Marketable," *Belphagor* 5, no. 1 (2005), http://etc.dal.ca/belphegor/vol5_no1/articles/05_01_cristiano_iamnot_fr.html (accessed April 15, 2011).

79. Ammaniti's oeuvre is relentlessly contemporary, *Io non ho paura* no less so: the "present" of Michele the narrator is located at the earliest in the mid-1990s, but may be coeval with the 2001 publication date. Such historical location would position Ammaniti toward the front of the line of practitioners seeking to re-evaluate the events of the 1970s and specifically the events of 1978. I am referring to Giancarlo De Cataldo, *Romanzo criminale* (2002); Marco Tullio Giordana, *La meglio gioventù* (2003); Marco Bellocchio, *Buongiorno, notte* (2003); Guido Chiesa, *Lavorare con lentezza* (2004); and Michele Placido's film adaptation of *Romanzo criminale* (2004). All of these narratives are set in a historical past. The diachronic interplay between 1978 and a date sometime after that in the novel *Io non ho paura* suggests meditation on the past and relation between the two historical moments, which aligns it more with something like Marco Baliani's performance piece about the Moro affair, *Corpo di Stato,* which debuted on the RAI in May 1998 and offers sustained meditation on the two decades that had passed. By stripping away a contemporary toehold, Salvatores's version of *Io non ho paura* obviates any need to invoke the adult Michele. See *Body of State: The Moro Affair, a Nation Divided,* trans. Nicoletta Marini-Maio, Ellen Nerenberg, and Thomas Simpson, intro. Nicoletta Marini-Maio and Ellen Nerenberg (Madison, N.J.: Fairleigh Dickinson University Press, forthcoming 2012).

80. Niccolò Ammaniti, *Io non ho paura* (Turin: Mondadori, 2001), 16.

81. Ibid., 219.

82. *"Se ne stava steso, rinsecchito."* Ibid., 43.

83. *"Incominciava a scuoterlo come una bambola e Lazzaro alla fine si alzava e gli azzanava la gola."* Ibid..

84. See Ian Thompson, "When an Italian Slob Tries an Italian Job," *Observer* (London), January 4, 2009, http://www.guardian.co.uk/books/2009/jan/04/review-crossroads-niccolo-ammaniti (accessed March 13, 2010).

85. Niccolò Ammaniti, *Come Dio comanda* (Milan: Mondadori, 2006), 41.

86. *"Dovresti capire cosa vuol dire soffrire ed essere compassionevole. Lo sai che cos'é la compassione?"* Ibid., 476.

87. *"Imbrattato di sangue senza provare nessuna pena . . . senza sentire vergogna . . . senza nessun rimorso."* Ibid., 491.

88. Ibid., 495.

89. Ibid.

90. *"Mio padre era un uomo cattivo. Ha violentato e ammazzato una ragazzina innocente. Merita di finire all'inferno. E io con lui per averlo aiutato. Io non so perché lo ho aiutato. Giuro che non lo so. Mio padre era un ubriacone, un violento, un buono a nulla. Menava tutti. Mio padre mi ha insegnato ad usare la pistola, mio padre mi ha aiutato a riempire di botte uno a cui avevo tagliato la sella della moto. Mio padre mi è sempre stato vicino dal giorno che sono nato. Mia madre è scappata e lui mi ha tirato su. Mio padre mi portava a pescare. Mio padre era un nazista ma era buono. Credeva in Dio e non bestemmiava. Mi voleva bene e voleva bene a Quattro Formaggi e Danilo. Mio padre sapeva quello che era giusto e quello che era sbagliato. Mio padre non ha ucciso Fabiana. Io lo so."* Ibid.

91. *"Lui senza Cristiano non era più niente."* Ibid., 95.

92. *"tenere alta la guardia."* Ibid., 42.

93. *"Nessuno ti deve picchiare. Mai più. . . . Tu non sei un finocchio che si fa menare dal primo stronzo che gli si mette davanti. Io vorrei, non sai quanto vorrei aiutarti, ma non posso. Sei tu che devi sbrigarti i tuoi casini. E per questo esiste solo un modo: devi diventare cattivo. . . . Tu sei troppo buono. Sei molliccio. Non sei abbastanza incazzato. Sei fatto di roba morbida. Dove stanno i coglioni?"* Ibid., 160–161.

94. Trecca exhibits many more traits of the maternal father—the *"mammo"*— than either Rino or Signor Ponticelli, Fabiana's father, as we see below. See Simona Argentieri, *Il padre materno da San Giuseppe ai nuovi mammi* (Rome: Meltemi, 1999). It is significant that Argentieri begins her exploration with San Giuseppe, for it is the strong and vengeful father figure who has the final say in *Come Dio comanda,* a novel wherein the representation of God is far more Old Testament than New Testament.

95. It is worth noting the structural similarities *Come Dio comanda* bears to Raymond Carver's collection of intersecting stories, *Short Cuts* (published in 1993 and made into a film by Robert Altman the same year): a driver hits a pedestrian who appears to suffer no injury and walks away, the body of a young woman is found floating in a waterway, a man generally not given to violence attacks a woman in an isolated forest setting by bashing her head in with a stone. Ammaniti's novel shares much more with Carver than, for example, with J. G. Ballard, as Ian Thompson believes. See Thompson, "When an Italian Slob Tries an Italian Job."

96. *Migliaia di pupazzetti raccolti nei cassoni della spazzatura, trovati nella discarica o dimenticati dai bambini ai giardini comunali.*

Sopra la montagna più alta di tutte c'era una stalla con il Bambin Gesù, Maria, Giuseppe e il bue e l'asinello. Quelli glieli aveva regalati suor Margherita per Natale, quando aveva dieci anni. Quattro Formaggi, muovendosi con una insospettabile grazia, attraversò il presepe senza far cadere niente e sistemò meglio il ponte su cui avanzava una fila di Puffi blu capitanata da un Pokémon.

Ammaniti, *Come Dio comanda,* 36–37.

97. "*Aveva trovato un pupazzo di King Kong senza un braccio per il presepe quando aveva visto arrivare la biondina con un ragazzo su una moto.*" Ibid., 66.

98. "*Si accorgeva di quanto tutto fosse sbagliato.*" Ibid., 375.

99. "*E metterlo nel presepe. Era per questo che l'aveva uccisa. E Dio lo avrebbe aiutato.*" Ibid.

100. "*Dai soldatini, dai pastori, dalle macchinine. Sui piccoli seni, ragni e iguane e pecore. Sui capezzoli scuri, piccoli coccodrilli verdi. Tra i peli della fica dinosauri e soldatini.*" Ibid.

101. "*C'era chi sollevava i telefonini per fotografarli e fare video*"; "*li fecero sedere in prima fila accanto al sindaco, a un sacco di personaggi importanti e ai poliziotti in divisa.*" Ibid., 487.

102. "*Prese in braccio il figlio mentre le telecamere delle televisioni zoomavano in un primo piano.*" Ibid.

103. "*Le indagini preliminari . . . sono state integralmente seguite in diretta dai mezzi di comunicazione.*" Enzo Tardino, *"Chi ha uccisio Samuele?" Il racconto dell'assassinio di Cogne* (Ferrara: Gabriele Corbo, 2003), 7.

Epilogue

1. "Missingplec1" is the signature of a reader who commented on "A Long Way from Home: 48 Hours Investigates the U.S. Student Jailed in Italy for Her Roommate's Murder," the blog entry linked to CBS's April 12, 2008, episode of *48 Hours,* which explored the murder and Amanda Knox's detention. See http://www.cbsnews.com/stories/2008/04/10/48hours/main4005725_page8.shtml?tag=contentMain;contentBody#comments (accessed September 21, 2009). This remark by missingplec1 is on the fifth page of comments.

2. "lin" is the signature of a reader who posted a comment in response to Phoebe Natanson's online *ABC News* story "Mental State of Amanda Knox Co-Defendant Raffaele Sollecito Worries Lawyer," December 10, 2009. The comment was posted on April 19, 2010. The story and the comment are at http://abcnews.go.com/International/AmandaKnox/amanda-knox-codefendant-raffaele-sollecito-mental-problems/comments?type=story&id=9300723 (accessed April 30, 2010).

3. *"Tanti perugini che abitavano in centro hanno preso casa in periferia e con il vecchio appartamento è come se avessero un buono stipendio in più."* (Many Perugians who used to live in the city center have found houses on the edge of town and with the old apartment it is as if they had an extra salary). Jenner Meletti, "Perugia

si ribella. Basta show in TV," *La Repubblica,* November18, 2007. This and all translations mine unless otherwise indicated.

4. I discuss the way this links to Gilles Deleuze and Félix Guattari's notions of deterritorialization in chapter 3.

5. See Barbie Latza Nadeau, *Angel Face: The True Story of Student Killer Amanda Knox* (New York: Beast Books, 2010), 72–75.

6. Ibid., 38.

7. See "Perugia, Guede catturato in Germania: Lumumba scarcerato: 'Mancanza di indizi,'" *La Repubblica,* November 20, 2007.

8. Douglas Preston, author of *The Monster of Florence,* has criticized Mignini's assignment to the Kercher murder. Preston points to the official reprimand for misconduct Mignini received for collaborating with Michele Giuttari of the Florence police and their investigation of the theory that a Satanic sect based in Umbria was involved in the serial murders attributed to the "Monster" of Florence. See Douglas Preston with Mario Spezi, *The Monster of Florence* (New York: Grand Central Publishing, 2008), 267–268. For Preston's reaction to Mignini's appointment to the investigation and trial of Amanda Knox, see "American Girl, Italian Nightmare," *CBS News,* April 14, 2009, http://www.cbsnews.com/video/watch/?id=4937069n (accessed September 15, 2009). See also Timothy Egan, "An American Abroad," *New York Times,* June 10, 2009, http://egan.blogs.nytimes.com/2009/06/10/an-innocent-abroad/ (accessed July 15, 2009). For Mignini and Giutarri's sentences, see chapter 1, note 53.

9. The judges in the case, Giancarlo Massei and Beatrice Cristiani, wrote that "the motive for the killing was a 'crescendo . . . (of) erotic sexual violence.'" See "Italian Judges Say Knox Did Not Plan Kercher Murder," *Reuters,* March 4, 2010, http://www.reuters.com/article/idUSTRE6233W320100304, accessed April 15, 2011.

10. See Richard Owen and Chris Ayres, "Amanda Knox and Raffaele Sollecito Keep Hopes High over Appeal," *Sunday Times* (London), December 7, 2009, http://www.timesonline.co.uk/tol/news/world/europe/article6946496.ece, accessed April 4, 2011. Knox's libel conviction was not overturned, and she was released for time already served. As the book goes to press in October 2011, various legal processes are still being played out. The judge presiding over the appeal, Claudio Pratillo Hellman, will issue the cart's ruling within a 90-day period. Parties have 45 days after this ruling to appeal to Cazzione, the third and final level of the Italian justice system.

11. Giovanni Maria Bellu, "Perugia incredula e sotto choc. Quegli assassini erano tra noi," *La Repubblica,* November 7, 2007.

12. See Letizia Paoli, "Crime, Italian Style," *Daedalus* 130, no. 3 (2001): 158; Marzio Barbagli, "Lost Primacy: Crime in Italy at the End of the Twentieth Century," *Journal of Modern Italian Studies* 9, no. 2 (2004): 148; Marzio Barbagli and Laura Sartori, "Law Enforcement Activities in Italy," *Journal of Modern Italian Studies* 9, no. 2 (2004): 161–185; and *Il rapporto sulla sicurezza,* 2006, a 500-page document available as a PDF for downloading at http://www.interno.it/mininterno/export/sites/default/it/sezioni/sala_stampa/notizie/sicurezza/0993_20_06_2007_Rapporto_Sicurezza_2006.html (accessed April 5, 2011).

13. I am grateful to Nicoletta Marini-Maio for highlighting this linguistic particularity.

14. As Nadeau remarks, the headlines for the dailies that day read "One Black for Another." See Nadeau, *Angel Face,* 73.

15. This is Nadeau's theory of the crime. Knox and Sollecito, with Guede, killed Kercher and sought to cover their tracks. The memory lapses, Nadeau allows, could be genuine. See ibid., 162–168.

16. A considerable bibliography exists on the subject of racial profiling in the United States, in terms of both analysis of criminological data and critical analysis of the representation of such data in the media. The putative black male criminal was crucial to the development of concept of moral panic in the 1970s in the classic text *Policing the Crisis,* especially concerning the perception of Afro-Caribbean men "as threats" in urban centers in the United Kingdom. See Stuart Hall, *Policing the Crisis: Mugging, the State, and Law and Order,* ed. Stuart Hall (London: MacMillan, 1978). The notion of a social underclass of "super-predators" enters into the public discourse of racial profiling and crime in the United States in the mid-1990s with works by John Dilulio and former secretary of education William Bennett that foretold the coming crime wave. See John J. Dilulio Jr., "The Coming of the Super-Predators," *Weekly Standard,* November 27, 1995, http://www.weeklystandard.com/Content/Protected/Articles/000/000/007/011vsbrv.asp (accessed 21 April, 2010); and William Bennett, John Dilulio, Jr., and John Walters, *Body Count: Moral Poverty—and How to Win America's War against Crime and Drugs* (New York: Simon and Schuster, 1996).

Sources that pay explicit attention to the role played by the media in the circulation of information necessary to the start of moral panic include Robert Entman, "Blacks in the News: Television, Modern Racism, and Cultural Change," *Journalism Quarterly* 69, no. 34 (1992): 1–36; Robert Entman, "Representation and Reality in the Portrayal of Blacks on Network Television News," *Journalism Quarterly* 71 (1994): 509–520; Schlesinger and Tumber, *Reporting Crime;* Franklin Gilliam, Shanto Iyengar, Adam Simon, and Oliver Wright, "Crime in Black and White: The Violent, Scary World of Local News," *Harvard International Journal of Press Politics* 1, no. 3 (1994): 6–23; Travis Dixon and Daniel Linz, "Overrepresentation and Underrepresentation of African Americans and Latinos as Lawbreakers on Television News," *Journal of Communication* 50 (2000): 131–154; Travis Dixon and Daniel Linz, "Race and the Misrepresentation of Victimization on Local Television News," *Communication Research* 27, no. 5 (2000): 547–573; and Travis Dixon, Christina Azocar, and Michael Casas, "The Portrayal of Race and Crime on Network News," *Journal of Broadcasting and Electronic Media* 47, no. 4 (2003): 495–520. I am indebted to Ruth Glynn for her thoughts on this subject.

17. See Colin Fernandez and Beth Hale, "Foxy Knoxy: Inside the Twisted World of Flatmate Suspected of Meredith's Murder," *Mail Online,* November 6, 2007, http://www.mailonsunday.co.uk/news/article-492092/Foxy-Knoxy-Inside-twisted-world-flatmate-suspected-Merediths-murder.html (accessed September 20, 2009).

18. See "Hershey's History" at http://www.thehersheycompany.com/about-hershey/our-story/hersheys-history.aspx (accessed March 15, 2011); and "La storia" from the pulldown menu "tutto su baci" at http://www.baciperugina.it/ita/world.asp?mondo=amore accessed March 15, 2011).

19. *Filone*, as outlined first in chapter 3, means a large strand of braided elements, and is a term used to describe the hybrid cinematic genre of the slasher-noir-*giallo*-horror film. See note 3 in chapter 3.

20. The film adaptation of *Kiss Me Deadly* (1955) follows Mike Hammer (Ralph Meeker) as he tries to piece together the circumstances that led to the torture death of Christine (Cloris Leachman), the mysterious hitchhiker he picked up. Christine's death leads Hammer to Lily (Gaby Rodgers), who is trailing an attaché case that carries a mysterious hot substance that sets Lily aflame when she opens it at the film's climax. This may (or may not) have suggested to Tarantino the device of the suitcase of glowing contents (which is never shown to the viewer) that Vincent (John Travolta) and Jules (Samuel L. Jackson) haul across Greater Los Angeles in *Pulp Fiction*. The suitcase is itself a suturing narrative device that links the discrete stories that make up the prize-winning screenplay.

21. I am indebted to Julia Heim for her thoughts on the semiosis of Knox's courtroom appearances. Heim pays particular attention to the media coverage of Knox's wardrobe and observes that in addition to her role as the femme fatale, Knox appeared in the media as a star of another cinematic genre: the horror film.

22. See Clifford Geertz, "Description: Toward and Interpretive Theory of Culture," in Geertz, *The Interpretation of Cultures: Selected Essays* (New York: Basic Books, 1973), 3–30. See introduction to this volume, note 3.

23. Knox's trial for the murder of Meredith Kercher compares to the trials I examine in the way that my foci in *Murder Made in Italy* compare to Karen Pinkus's treatment of the 1953 Wilma Montesi scandal. The Montesi scandal and trial marked a point in the development of mass media in the middle of the twentieth century well before the homicides and murders that I contemplate here, which offered radically different "mediascapes." The increased rapidity of the relay between news reporting and its delivery, in addition to ramped-up use of such social networking sites as Youtube, Twitter, MySpace, and Facebook, has created a still different mediascape from those characterizing the mechanisms in place for coverage of even the most recent of cases I am interested in, against Annamaria Franzoni, which began in 2003. (The trial phase concluded in July 2004, the first appeal ran from November 2005 until April 2007, and the final decision confirming her sentence was handed down by Italy's Corte di Cassazione in May 2008). See Karen Pinkus, *The Montesi Scandal: The Death of Wilma Montesi and the Birth of the Paparazzi in Fellini's Rome* (Chicago: University of Chicago Press, 2003); and Daniel Soulez-Larivière, *Il circo mediatico-giudiziario*, trans. Maria Giustozzi (Macerata: Liberilibri, 1994).

24. See the introduction to this volume, note 13.

25. "Injustice in Perguia," a Web site that favors Knox's acquittal and proclaims her innocence, lists evidenciary problems, jury bias, the prosecutor's alleged abuse of office, and police procedure. See http://www.injusticeinperugia.org (accessed March 22, 2010). Since the day before the verdict was delivered (December 4, 2009), 116 Facebook blogs have denounced the Italian justice system and the verdict.

26. See Nadeau, *Angel Face*, 93 and 193.

27. Sarah Annunziato in "The Amanda Knox Case: The Representation of Italy in American Media Coverage," *Historical Journal of Film, Radio, and Television* 31,

no. 1 (2011): 61–78, is interested in a question inverse to my own. She offers a very thorough assessment of the ways Italy was covered in the period in question, and the table (68) charting frequency and type of media coverage during the investigation and trial is valuable.

28. See Anne Bremner, "Supporters of Amanda Knox Want You to Know . . . ," at http://annebremner.com/Amanda%20Knox.htm (accessed September 21, 2009); and "Milano, emergenzi stupri," http://video.corriere.it/?vxSiteId=404a0ad6–6216–4e10–abfe-f4f6959487fd&vxChannel=Dall%20Italia&vxClipId=2524_ea936ac6–9ec8–11dd-b7ca-00144f02aabc&vxBitrate=300 (accessed September 21, 2009).

29. See the comments of "stedmondo" in response to "A Long Way from Home: 48 Hours Investigates the U.S. Student Jailed in Italy for Her Roommate's Murder," at http://www.cbsnews.com/stories/2008/04/10/48hours/main4005725.shtml#comments (accessed September 21, 2009). They appear on page 6 of the comments section.

30. See Daniel Boffey, "Amanda Knox 'a Victim of Anti-American Trial' as Campaigners Urge Hillary Clinton to Launch Investigation," *Mail Online* (London), December 5, 2009, at http://www.dailymail.co.uk/news/article-1233539/Amanda-Knox-victim-anti-American-trial-campaigners-urge-Hillary-Clinton-launch-investigation.html#ixzz0iT05Yeu4 (accessed March 20, 2011).

31. Nadeau, who believes in Knox's guilt, judiciously reviews these problems. See Nadeau 50–52 and 153–156. For their colorful treatment of the case, *Darkness Descending: The Murder of Meredith Kercher* (London: Simon and Schuster, 2010), Paul Russell and Graham Johnson hired Col. Luciano Garofano (retired), formerly of the forensic team of the carabinieri, to assess the evidence. In Garofano's estimation, the ERT had made a series of mistakes collecting evidence. Some, like the handling of the alleged murder weapon, a kitchen knife, as well as the use of Luminol to illuminate trace blood, were more problematic than others. See Russell and Johnson, 365–388.

32. See Richard Owen, "Hillary Clinton Drawn into Row over Conviction of Amanda Knox," *Sunday Times* (London), December 7, 2009, http://www.timesonline.co.uk/tol/news/world/europe/article6947549.ece?token=null&offset=0&page=1 (accessed December 28, 2009). The translations in this article were done by *Times* staff.

33. See "National News Briefs; Pilot Out of Prison in Ski Gondola Case," *New York Times,* October 13, 1999, http://www.nytimes.com/1999/10/13/us/national-news-briefs-pilot-out-of-prison-in-ski-gondola-case.html (accessed April 15, 2011).

34. Ibid. Criticisms of the Italian justice system and calls for the court to set aside the verdict ran counter to the insistence that Americans should be able to adjudicate in crimes that take place on sovereign U.S. soil. Italians remembered the case of Silvia Baraldini, an Italian citizen active in the Black Power movement in the United States in the 1970s. Baraldini was incarcerated in a U.S. federal penitentiary after her 1983 conviction for racketeering and conspiracy to commit armed robbery but was allowed to return to Italy in 1999 to serve the remainder of her sentence. See Owen, "Hillary Clinton Drawn into Row over Conviction of Amanda Knox."

35. Among other works, see *Italian Colonialism*, ed. Ruth Ben-Ghiat and Mia Fuller (New York: Palgrave MacMillan, 2008); Graziella Parati, *Migration Italy: The*

Art of Talking Back in a Destination Culture (Toronto: Toronto University Press, 2005), esp. 10–16 and 23–53; Derek Duncan, "Italy's Postcolonial Cinema and Its Histories of Representation," *Italian Studies* 62, no. 2 (2008): 195–211; and Aine O'Healy, "'Non è una somala: Deconstructing African Femininity in Italian Film," *Italianist* 29, no. 2 (2009): 175–198.

36. See Massimo Malpica, "Un capello e un prof svizzero diranno se Lumumba è innocente," *La Repubblica*, November 12, 2007. See also "Il DNA scoperto sul corpo di Mez (e non i testimoni) scagionano Patrick," *La Repubblica*, December 6, 2007. "Mez" was Meredith Kercher's nickname.

37. Lumumba appeared on *Matrix*, broadcast on the Mediaset network, as well as other talk shows. "Lumumba in TV. Sono stato umiliato ma non picchiato," *La Repubblica*, November 27, 2007.

38. "*Perugia è una città che vanta una lunga e consolidata tradizione di cultura, civiltà e accoglienza. . . . Le sue strade, le sue piazze e i suoi locali riecheggiano del vociare libero, allegro e multirazziale di una moltitudine di studenti di tutte le età e di ogni provenienza che frequentano le sue due celebri università.*" Meo Ponte, "Meredith uccisa da aguzzini senza pieta," *La Repubblica*, December 6, 2007.

39. Meo Ponte, "Lumumba era nel suo locale," *La Repubblica*, November 12, 2007.

40. "*Sono contento di tornare a casa. . . . Ringrazio Dio e tutti i miei amici perugini che mi hanno difeso.*" "Perugia, Guede catturato in Germania; Lumumba scarcerato: 'Mancanza di indizi,'"*La Repubblica*, November 20, 2007.

41. The situation wherein the content of what is an outrage (or outrageous) has not been revealed, but what "must have been said" nevertheless appears to be somehow patent, is reminiscent of the reception of Salman Rushdie's 1988 novel, *The Satanic Verses*, in the United Kingdom. Notwithstanding a general lack of familiarity with Rushdie's novel (or the style with which the subject of apostasy was represented), the religious faithful worldwide acknowledged Ayatollah Ruhollah Khomeini's call for a *fatwa* against the novelist for blasphemy. See Arjun Appadurai, *Modernity at Large: Cultural Dimensions of Globalization* (Minneapolis: University of Minnesota Press, 1996).

42. For coverage in the *Guardian*, see Matt Scott, "Materazzi Joins Zidane as Target of Fifa Inquiry," *Guardian*, July 12, 2006. For reference to *Globo*, see Alessandro Bocci, "Tutto è nato da un insulto alla sorella," *Il corriere della sera*, July 11, 2006.

43. As James Richardson has written, "The popular theory in Italy is that he (Materazzi) said: 'Out of contract? Why not come join Inter?', at which point the French skipper understandably lost his rag. It's highly plausible." James Richardson, "After the World Cup Was Won," *Guardian*, July 12, 2006.

44. The British tabloid *Daily Star* seemed to sensationalize both the racist and the sexist aspects. For example, the paper's headlines included the following: "What Made ZZ Blow His Top—'Your Mum's a Terrorist Whore'" and "Zid's Vicious over Whore Slur on Mum—The Cruel Taunt That Made Legend Lose It." See Chris Tryhorn, "Zidane Headbutt Victim Wins Star Apology," *Guardian*, April 7, 2008, http://www.guardian.co.uk/media/2008/apr/07/pressandpublishing.medialaw (accessed April 13, 2011).

45. See Aldo Grasso, "Il caso ora è chiuso (Se si danno la mano)," *Il corriere della sera*, July 13, 2006.

46. Ibid.

47. See John Foot, *Calcio: A History of Italian Football* (London: HarperCollins, 2007), 531, where he reviews the various claims. This version tallies with what *Globo's* lip-readers had determined from watching the film. Zidane has neither confirmed nor denied that this constituted the exchange between him and Materazzi, though the latter has confirmed it in his book *Che cosa ho detto veramente a Zidane* (Milan: Mondadori, 2006). See also Aldo Grasso, "Niente razzismo, termini da campo di calcio," *Il corriere della sera*, August 19, 2007.

48. The 2006 World Cup Final head-butting incident recalls the 1997 incident in which Latrell Sprewell, a player for the Golden State Warriors, choked his coach, P. J. Carlesimo. The content of Carlesimo's comments to Sprewell was not made public, but it was assumed that Carlesimo had directed a specific racial epithet at Sprewell. Like Zidane, who initially walked away from Materazzi, Sprewell also walked away, only to quickly turn around and attack Carlesimo. A review of this well-known incident is available at http://espn.go.com/classic/s/add_sprewell_latrell.html (accessed March 15, 2011).

49. Materazzi said to the press: "*Gli avrei detto terrorista? Ma dai, io sono ignorante*" (I called him a terrorist? Come on, I'm a dummy.) "Chirac a Zidane: 'Sei un genio': ma la Francia si divide," *La Repubblica,* July 10, 2006, http://www.republica.it/2006/07/speciale/mondiali/servizi/zidane-domenech/polemiche/polemiche.html?ref=search (accessed April 12, 2011). Materazzi's self-defense seems to be his own stupidity, as if he were not smart or worldly enough to invoke such a context.

50. See Aldo Grasso, "Il caso ora è chiuso (se si danno la mano)," *Corriere della Sera*, July 13, 2006, http://archiviostorico.corriere.it/2006/luglio/13/Caso_ora_Chiuso_Danno_Mano_co_9_060713006.shtml (accessed March 15, 2011).

51. See Alice Mauri, "Caso Zidane Materazzi: il sessismo è meno grave del razzismo?" *Il Paese della donna,* August 22, 2007, http://www.womenews.net/spip3/spip.php?article833 (accessed April 12, 2011). See also Fadwa El Guindi, *Veil: Modesty, Privacy and Resistance* (Oxford: Berg, 1999); and Lila Abu-Lughod, ed., *Remaking Women: Feminism and Modernity in the Middle East* (Princeton, N.J.: Princeton University Press, 1998).

52. A similar accident of fate is the way that another chocolate manufacturer—Pernigotti—hovers at the edges of the Novi Ligure double homicide. Francesco De Nardo (Erika's father) is a manager there.

53. See, for example, "Boycott Italy!," http://www.facebook.com/board.php?uid=18268784389&status=512 (accessed April 26, 2010).

54. See IEE Network, "Study Abroad: Leading Destinations," 2009, http://www.iie.org/en/Research-and-Publications/Open-Doors/Data/US-Study-Abroad/Leading-Destinations/2007-09 (accessed April 4, 2011). Italy is second only to the UK as a destination chosen by U.S. undergraduates for study abroad. Countries where Spanish is spoken were disaggregated from the survey.

55. Sophie Egan, "Junior Fear Abroad," *New York Times*, December 5, 2007, http://www.nytimes.com/2007/12/05/opinion/05egan.html (accessed April 4, 2011).

56. *Blu Notte*, RAI 3, 16 February 2003.

57. Nadeau, *Angel Face*, 125.

58. See Frank Rich, "Nobody Knows the Lynchings He's Seen," *New York Times*, October 7, 2007, http://www.nytimes.com/2007/10/07/opinion/07rich.html (accessed April 4, 2011).

59. The program *Il Graffio* on the Telenorba channel aired footage showing Kercher's abject corpse and other forensic elements. See Fiorenza Sarzanini, "Film choc su Meredith, è lite. I tre sospetti restano in carcere," *Il Corriere della sera*, April 1, 2008.

60. Knox's social networking sites were deactivated in late 2007 but are valuably chronicled in Nadeau, *Angel Face*. For the way social networking sites function also as panopticons, never allowing their creators to know when their Web pages are being scrutinzed, see Mayer-Schönberger, *Delete*, 1–15 and esp. 109.

61. See, for example, "Amanda Knox," *Eyes for Lies* (blog), November 9, 2007, http://www.eyesforlies.blogspot.com/2007/11/amanda-knox.html (April 1, 2011).

62. See Colin Fernandez and Beth Hale, "Foxy Knoxy: Inside the Twisted World of Flatmate Suspected of Meredith's Murder," http://www.mailonsunday.co.uk/news/article-492092/Foxy-Knoxy-Inside-twisted-world-flatmate-suspected-Merediths-murder.html (accessed April 15, 2011).

63. With increased reliance on Internet sources for news and the subsequent falling of readership for the dailies, newspapers have begun imitating Internet structures. For the Italian aspect of this see Felice Froio, *L'informazione spettacolo: giornali e giornalisti oggi* (Rome: Riuniti, 2000).

64. See "A Long Way from Home."

65. Meo Ponte, "Raffaele: Nessuno di noi c'entra," *La Repubblica*, December 9, 2007.

66. Silvio Pellico, *My Prisons* (Boston: Roberts Brothers, 1889), xix. See also Charles Klopp, *Sentences: The Memoirs and Letters of Italian Political Prisoners from Benvenuto Cellini to Aldo Moro* (Toronto: Toronto University Press, 1999).

67. Nadeau, *Angel Face*, 97.

68. "*Mi hanno descritto come una mangiatrice di uomini, hanno detto che ho avuto una lista di amanti lunga così, ma io qui in Italia ne ho avuti solo due.*" Quoted in Alessandro Capponi, "Amanda in aula sbuffa e canta," *Il Corriere della Sera*, September 17, 2008.

69. Nadeau, *Angel Face*, 27–28.

70. Indeed, Barbie Latza Nadeau notes that Perugia is considered to be a less expensive and viable option for study in Italy than, for example, Florence. See Nadeau, *Angel Face*, 3. Nadeau's book was released April 6, 2010. Other journalistic treatments of the Kercher murder and the Knox trial include Gary King, *The Murder of Meredith Kercher* (London: John Blake Publishing, 2010); Candace Dempsey, *Murder in Italy: The Shocking Slaying of a British Student, the Accused American Girl, and an International Scandal* (New York: Penguin Books, 2010); Russell and Johnson, *Darkness Descending*. See also Nina Burleigh, *The Fatal Gift of Beauty: The Trials of Amanda Knox* (New York: Broadway, 2011). Burleigh's book was published in August 2011, as Knox's case entered its appeals phase.

71. See my *Prison Terms*, esp. chapter 4, "Love for Sale or That's Amore: Brothels, Prison, Revision," 105–136.

72. Nadeau, *Angel Face*, 141.

73. *"Tre diari . . . sembrano già pronti per la trasposizione in una fiction televisiva mentre il giallo di Perugia a più di un mese dalla scoperta del cadavere della studentessa inglese appare ancora tutto da scrivere."* Meo Ponte, "Raffaele: Nessuno di noi c'entra," *La Repubblica,* December 9, 2007.

74. On Thursday, March 24, Knox appeared in a Perugia court to lodge a complaint against the Lifetime Movie Network (LMN). "I am distressed by this invasion into my life and the way my life is," Knox told the civil judge. "I consider this the culmination of repeated violations by the media of my personality and my story. These are all things that don't correspond to the truth." Cited in Barbie Latza Nadeau, "Could a Homeless Man Free Amanda Knox?" in http://www.the daily-beast
.com/articles/2011/3/28/amanda-knox-appeal-homeless-mans-contradictory-testimony. html, accessed October 11, 2011.

BIBLIOGRAPHY

Abbate, Fulvio. *Oggi è un secolo*. Rome: Theoria, 1992.

———. *Dopo l'estate*. Milan: Bompiani, 1995.

———. *La peste bis*. Milan: Bompiani, 1997.

Abu-Lughod, Lila, ed. *Remaking Women: Feminism and Modernity in the Middle East*. Princeton, N.J.: Princeton University Press, 1998.

Adamo, Giuliana. "Riflessioni sulle opere di due scrittori italiani contemporanei: Niccolò Ammaniti e Diego De Silva." *Italianist* 27, no. 1 (2007): 166–84.

Agamben, Giorgio. *Means without End: Notes on Politics*. Trans. Vincenzo Binetti and Cesare Casarino. Minneapolis: University of Minnesota Press, 2000.

———. *State of Exception*. Trans. Kevin Attell. Chicago: University of Chicago Press, 2005.

Agnew, John. *Place and Politics in Modern Italy*. Chicago: University of Chicago Press, 2002.

Aldrich, Robert, dir. *Kiss Me Deadly*. 1955.

Alessandri, Giuseppe. *La leggenda del Vampa: La storia del Mostro di Firenze?* Florence: Loggia de Lanzi, 1995.

Allen, Beverly. *Rape Warfare: The Hidden Genocide in Bosnia-Herzegovina and Croatia*. Minneapolis: University of Minnesota Press, 1996.

Allen, Beverly, and Mary Russo, eds. *Revisioning Italy: National Identity and Global Culture*. Minneapolis: University of Minnesota Press, 1998

Althusser, Louis. *The Future Lasts a Long Time and The Facts*. Ed. Olivier Corpet and Yann Moulier Boutang, trans. Richard Veasey. London: Chatto and Windus, 1993.

———. *Lenin and Philosophy and Other Essays*. Trans. Ben Brewster. New York: Monthly Review, 1971.

Altman, Robert, dir. *Short Cuts*. 1993.

Amelio, Gianni, dir. *Ladro di bambini*. 1992.

———. *Le chiavi di casa*. 2004.

Ammaniti, Niccolò. *Come Dio comanda*. Milan: Mondadori, 2006.

———. *Fango*. Milan: Mondadori, 1996.

———. *Io non ho paura*. Milan: Mondadori, 2001.

———. *L'utimo capodanno dell'umanità*. Milan: Mondadori, 1998.

———. *Ti prendo e ti porto via*. Milan: Mondadori, 1999.

Ammaniti, Niccolò, and Massimo Ammaniti. *Nel nome del padre: l'adolescenza raccontata da un padre e da un figlio.* Milan: Mondadori, 1995.

Anania, Francesca. "Italian Public Television in the 1970s: A Predictable Confusion." *Historical Journal of Film, Radio, and Television* 15, no. 3 (1995).

Anderson, Benedict. *Imagined Communities: Reflections on the Origins and Spread of Nationalism.* London: Verso, 1991.

Andreoli, Vittorino. *Giovani. Sfida, rivolta, speranze, futuro.* Milan: BUR Biblioteca Univ. Rizzoli, 1997.

Ania, Gillian. "Apocalypse and Dystopia in Contemporary Italian Writing." In *Trends in Contemporary Italian Narrative, 1980–2007,* ed. Gillian Ania and Ann Hallamore Caesar, 155–181. Newcastle: Cambridge Scholars, 2007.

Annunziato, Sarah. "The Amanda Knox Case: The Representation of Italy in American Media Coverage." *Historical Journal of Film, Radio, and Television* 31, no. 1 (2011): 61–78.

Antonello, Pierpaolo, and Alan O'Leary, eds. *Imagining Terrorism: The Rhetoric and Representation of Political Violence.* Leeds: Legenda, 2009.

Antonioni, Michelangelo, dir. *Blow-up.* 1968.

Appadurai, Arjun. *Modernity at Large: Cultural Dimensions of Globalization.* Minneapolis: University of Minnesota Press, 1996.

Arendt, Hannah. *Eichmann in Jerusalem: A Report on the Banality of Evil.* New York: Penguin Books, 1976.

Argentieri, Simona. *Il padre materno da San Giuseppe ai nuovi mammi.* Rome: Meltemi, 1999.

Argento, Dario, dir. *Due occhi diabolici.* 1990.

———. *Il cartaio.* 2004.

———. *Il fantasma dell'opera.* 1998.

———. *Inferno.* 1980.

———. *La Sindrome di Stendhal.* 1996.

———. *La Terza Madre.* 2007.

———. *L'uccello dalle piume di cristallo.* 1970.

———. *Non ho sonno.* 2001.

———. *Opera.* 1987.

———. *Profondo rosso.* 1975.

———. *Quattro mosche di velutto grigio.* 1971.

———. *Suspiria.* 1977.

———. *Tenebre.* 1982.

———. *Trauma.* 1993.

Arkin, Alan, dir. *Little Murders.* 1971.

Augé, Marc. "L'incendio di Parigi." *MicroMega* 7 (2005): 187–195.

———. *Non-Places: Introduction to an Anthropology of Supermodernity.* Trans. John Howe. London: Verso: 1995.

"Au revoir les enfants. RAI: i bambini e la rappresentazione del dolore in TV. 8 Luglio 2002. Sintesi 2. Il caso di Cogne: dalla cronaca al *giallo.*" www.censis.it, accessed August 29, 2009.

Barker, Clive, dir. *Hellraiser.* 1987.

Barker, Martin, and Julian Petley, eds. *Ill Effects: The Media/Violence Debate.* London: Routledge, 2001.

Baldi, Alfredo. *Schermi proibiti: La censura in Italia dal 1947–1988.* Venice: Marsilio, 2002.

Baldini, Eraldo. *Bambine.* Rome: Ritmi Theoria, 1995.

Baliani, Marco. *Body of State: The Moro Affair. A Nation Divided.* Trans. Nicoletta Marini-Maio, Ellen Nerenberg, and Thomas Simpson. Madison, N.J.: Fairleigh-Dickinson University Press, 2012.

Balmain, Colette. "Female Subjectivity and the Politics of 'Becoming Other,'" *Kinoeye: New Perspectives on European Film* 2, no. 12 (2002). http://www .kinoeye.org/02/12/balmain12.php.

Ballestrini, Nanni, and Renato Barilli, eds. *Narrative Invaders: Narratori di "Ricercare" 1993–1999.* Turin: Testo and Immagine, 2000.

Baranski, Zymunt, and Robert Lumley, eds. *Culture and Conflict in Postwar Italy: Essays on Mass and Popular Culture.* New York: St. Martin's Press, 1990.

Barbagli, Marzio. "Lost Primacy: Crime in Italy at the End of the Twentieth Century." *Journal of Modern Italian Studies* 9, no. 2 (2004): 131–160.

———. ed. *Lo Stato delle famiglie in Italia.* Bologna: Il Mulino, 1997.

Barbagli, Marzio, Maria Castiglioni, and Gianpiero Dalla Zuanna. *Fare famiglia in Italia: Un secolo di cambiamenti.* Bologna: Il Mulino, 2003.

Barbagli, Marzio, and Laura Sartori. "Law Enforcement Activities in Italy." *Journal of Modern Italian Studies* 9, no. 2 (2004): 161–185.

Barbieri, Daniele. *Il linguaggio del fumetto.* Milan: Bompiani, 1991.

Barilli, Renato. *È arrivata la terza ondata. Dalla neo alla neo-neoavanguardia.* Turin: Testo & Immagine, 2000.

Barlozzetti, Guido. *Eventi e riti della televisione. Dalla Guerra del Golfo alle Twin Towers.* Milan: FrancoAngeli, 2002.

Bauman, Zygmunt. *Postmodernity and Its Discontents.* New York: New York University Press, 1999.

Becker, Dana. *Through the Looking Glass: Women and Borderline Personality Disorder.* Boulder, Colo.: Westview, 1997.

Bellocchio, Marco, dir. *Buongiorno notte.* 2003.

Benedetti, Laura. *The Tigress in the Snow.* Toronto: University of Toronto Press, 2007.

Ben-Ghiat, Ruth, and Mia Fuller, ed. *Italian Colonialism.* New York: Palgrave MacMillan, 2008.

Bennett, William, John Dilulio Jr., and John Walters. *Body Count: Moral Poverty— and How to Win America's War against Crime and Drugs.* New York: Simon and Schuster, 1996.

Benigni, Roberto, dir. *Il Mostro.* 1994.

———. *Johnny Stecchino.* 1991.

———. *La tigre e la neve.* 2005.

———. *La vita è bella.* 1998.

———. *Pinocchio.* 2002.

Bennett, Andy. *Popular Music and Youth Culture: Music, Identity, and Place.* London: Macmillan, 2000.

Bennett, Tony, Lawrence Grossberg, and Meaghan Morris, eds. *New Keywords: A Revised Vocabulary of Culture and Society.* Malden, Mass.: Blackwell Publications, 2005.

Bennett, William, John Dilulio Jr., and John Walters. *Body Count: Moral Poverty—and How to Win America's War against Crime and Drugs.* New York: Simon and Schuster, 1996.

Bennington, Geoffrey. *Interrupting Derrida.* London: Routledge, 2000.

Berenstein, Rhona. *Attack of the Leading Ladies: Gender, Sexuality, and Spectatorship in Classic Horror Cinema.* New York: Columbia University Press, 1996.

Beretta, Gaia, and Santa Di Nuovo. "Devianza femminile: tra responsabilità e sanzione. Il 'caso Nove Ligure' attraverso i mass media." *Psicologia giuridica* 2, no. 2 (2001). http://www.psicologiagiuridica.com/index.php?sz=archivioandtp=artandr=7.

Bersani, Leo. "Is the Rectum a Grave." *October* 43 (1987): 197–222.

Bertolucci, Bernardo, dir. *I Dreamers.* 2003.

Bettin, Gianfranco. *Eredi: Da Pietro Maso a Erika e Omar.* Milan: Feltrinelli, 2007.

Bettini, F., and R. Di Marco. *Terza ondata: Il Nuovo Movimento della Scrittura in Italia.* Bologna: ES/Synergon, 1993.

———, eds. *Gruppo 93: La recente avventura del dibattito teorico letterario in Italia.* Lecce: Manni, 1990.

Bianchi, Alberto. "L'autenticità dell'immagine: Lo specchio catodico di Niccolò Ammaniti." *Narrativa* 20–21 (2001): 337–348.

Blu Notte. RAI 3. February 16 and 23, 2003. http://www.carlolucarelli.net/blunotte.htm, accessed August 26, 2009.

Boni, Federico. *Etnografia dei media.* Rome-Bari: Laterza, 2004.

Bonsaver, Guido. "The Egocentric Cassandra of the Left: Representations of Politics in the Films of Nanni Moretti." *Italianist* 21–22 (2001–2002): 158–183.

Bonsaver, Guido, and Robert Gordon, eds. *Culture, Censorship and the State in Twentieth-Century Italy.* Oxford: Legenda Press, 2005.

Bota, Rick, dir. *Hellraiser: Hellseeker.* 2002.

———. *Hellraiser: Hellworld.* 2005.

Boulous Walker, Michelle. *Philosophy and the Maternal Body: Reading Silence.* London: Routledge, 1998.

Bourke, Joanna. *An Intimate History of Killing: Face-to-face Killing in Twentieth-Century Warfare.* New York: Granta, 1999.

Braidotti, Rosi. *Nomadic Subjects: Embodiment and Sexual Difference in Contemporary Feminist Theory.* New York: Columbia University Press, 1994.

Brizzi, Enrico. *Bastogne.* Milan: Baldini & Castoldi, 1996.

———. *Jack Frusciante è uscito dal gruppo.* Ancona: Transeuropa, 1994.

Brolli, Daniele, ed. *Gioventù cannibale: la prima antologia italiana dell'orrore estremo.* Turin: Einaudi, 1996.

Brooks, Peter. "Narrative Transactions—Does the Law Need a Narratology?" http://www.law.virginia.edu/pdf/workshops/0405/pbrooks.pdf, accessed August 29, 2009.

Brooks, Peter, and Paul Gewirtz, eds. *Law's Stories: Narrative and Rhetoric in the Law.* New Haven, Conn.: Yale University Press, 1996.

Browder, Laura. "Dystopian Romance: True Crime and the Female Reader." *Journal of Popular Culture* 39, no. 6 (2006): 928–953.

Brown, Sheila. *Crime and Law in Media Culture.* Buckingham: Open University Press, 2003.

Brunetta, Gian Piero. *Storia del cinema italiano*. Vol. 4. Rome: Riuniti, 1998.

Bruno, Giuliana, and Maria Nadotti, eds. *Off Screen: Women and Film in Italy*. London: Routledge, 1988.

Bucarelli, Alessandro. *Criminalità e giustizia penale nella Sardegna del periodo Sabaudo*. Cagliari: Scuola Sarda, 1998.

Bufacchi, Vittorio, and Simon Burgess. *Italy since 1989: Events and Interpretations*. London: MacMillan, 1998.

Burkert, Walter, René Girard, and Jonathan Z. Smith. *Violent Origins*. Stanford, Calif.: Stanford University Press, 1989.

Burleigh, Nina. *The Fatal Gift of Beauty: The Trials of Amanda Knox* (New York: Broadway, 2011).

Burns, Jennifer. *Fragments of Impegno: Interpretations of Commitment in Contemporary Italian Narrative (1980–2000)*. Leeds: Northern University Press, 2001.

Burns, Jennifer, and Loredana Polezzi, eds. *Borderlines: Identità di confine nel Novecento*. Isernia, Italy: Cosmo Iannone, 2005.

Busi, Aldo. *Il manuale del perfetto papà (beati gli orfani)*. Milan: Mondadori, 2001.

Butler, Judith. *Undoing Gender*. New York: Routledge, 2004.

Camaiti Hostert, Anna. *Passing: Dissolvere le identità, superare le differenze*. Rome: Castelvecchi, 1996.

Caprettini, Gianpaolo. *La scatola parlante, L'evoluzione del linguaggio televisivo*. Rome: Editori Riuniti, 1996.

Caputi, Jane. *The Age of Sex Crime*. Bowling Green, Ohio: Bowling Green State University Popular Press, 1987.

Cardone, Raffaele, Franco Galato, and Fulvio Panzeri, eds. *Altre storie: inventario della nuova narrativa italiana fra anni '80–'90*. Milan: Marcos y Marcos, 1996.

Carloni, Massimo. "La geografia metropolitana del *giallo* italiano contemporaneo: Roma e Milano." *Letteratura italiana contemporana* 2 (1984): 247–252.

———. *L'Italia in giallo: Geografia e storia del giallo italiano contemporaneo*. Reggio Emilia: Diabasis, 1994.

Carlson, David Gray, Drucilla Cornell, and Michel Rosenfeld, eds. *Deconstruction and the Possibility of Justice*. New York: Routledge, 1992.

Carluccio, Giulia, Giacomo Manzoli, and Roy Menarini, eds. *L'eccesso della visione: Il cinema di Dario Argento*. Turin: Lindau, 2003.

Carminati, V. L., and R. Ghidelli, eds. *Adolescenza: sfida e risorsa della famiglia*. Milan: Vita e pensiero, 1993.

Carofiglio, Gianrico. *Testimone inconsapevole*. Palermo: Sellerio, 2002.

Carpenter, John, dir. *Halloween*. 1978.

Carraro, Andrea. *Il Branco*. Rome: Gaffi Editore, 2005.

Carver, Raymond, and Robert Altman. *Short Cuts*. New York: Vintage, 1993.

Casalinuovo, Aldo. "Un nuovo capitolo nella storia del diritto italiano: Le norme penali della legge Merlin." *Rivista penale* 38 (1958): 553–572.

Castells, Manuel. "European Cities, the Informational Society, and the Global Economy." In *Studying Culture: An Introductory Reader,* ed. Ann Gray and Jim McGuigan, 319–332. London: Arnold Press, 1997.

Catanesi, Roberto, and Carlo Troccoli. "La madre omicida: aspetti criminologici." *Rassegna italiana di criminologia* 5 (1994): 167–193.

Catino, Marco. *Sociologia di un delitto: Media, giustizia, e opinione pubblica nel caso Marta Russo.* Rome: Luca Sossella editore, 2001.

Cavallone, Annalisa. "La sindrome di Medea: cosa spinge una madre ad uccidere il proprio figlio." *Psychofenia* 11, no. 18 (2008): 124–72.

Cavani, Liliana, dir. *I cannibali.* 1969.

Cavarero, Adriana. *Horrorism: Naming Contemporary Violence.* Trans. Brian Mc-Guaig. New York: Columbia University Press, 2009.

———. "Toward a Theory of Sexual Difference." In *The Lonely Mirror: Italian Perspectives on Feminist Theory,* ed. Sandra Kemp and Paola Bono. New York: Routledge, 1993.

Cavo, Ilaria. *La chiamavano bimba.* Milan: Mondadori, 2007.

Cento Bull, Anna. "Challenging the Nation-State: Between Localism and Globalism." In *The Politics of Italian National Identity,* ed. Gino Bedani and Bruce Haddock, 259–276. Cardiff: University of Wales Press, 2000.

———. *Social Identities and Political Cultures in Italy: Catholic, Communist, and "Leghist" Communities between Civicness and Localism.* New York: Berghahn Books, 2000.

Chang, Elaine. "Spaghetti Eastern: Mutating Mass Culture, Transforming Ethnicity." In *Revisioning Italy: National Identity and Global Culture,* ed. Beverly Allen and Mary Russo, 292–313. Minneapolis: University of Minnesota Press, 1998.

Charmet, Gustavo P. *I nuovi adolescenti: Padri e madri di fronte a una sfida.* Milan: Raffaello Cortina, 2000.

Chesney-Lind, Meda, and Lisa Pasko. *The Female Offender: Girls, Women, and Crime.* Thousand Oaks, Calif.: Sage Publications, 2004.

Chiappetta-Miller, Concetta. "Projections: Monster and Diva from Vision to Voice." New York University, 2005.

Chiesa, Guido, dir. *Lavorare con lentezza.* 2004.

Chirumbolo, Paolo. "La funzione della musica, nella narrativa di Niccolò Ammaniti: da *Branchie* a *Io non ho paura.*" *Quaderni d'italianistica* 26, no. 1 (2005): 121–136.

Clark, Martin. "Sardinia: Cheese and Modernization." In *Italian Regionalism: History, identity, and Politics,* ed. Carl Levy, 81–106. Oxford: Berg Press, 1996.

Clover, Carol. "Her Body, Himself: Gender in the Slasher Film." *Representations* 20 (1987):187–228.

———. "Law and the Order of Popular Culture." In *Law in the Domains of Culture,* ed. Austin Sarat and Thomas Kearns, 97–119. Ann Arbor: University of Michigan Press, 1999.

———. *Men, Women, and Chainsaws: Gender in the Modern Horror Film.* Princeton, N.J.: Princeton University Press, 1992.

Cohen, Stanley. *Folk Devils and Moral Panics: The Creation of the Mods and the Rockers.* Oxford: Basil Blackwell, 1972.

Cohen, Stanley, and Jock Young, eds. *The Manufacture of the News: Deviance, Social Problems and the Mass Media.* London: Constable Press, 1973.

Comencini, Cristina. *L'illusione del bene.* Milan: Feltrinelli, 2007.

Comitato di Solidarietà con il Proletariato Prigioniero Sardo Deportato. *Colonizzazione, auto-determinazione, "criminalità" in Sardegna: l'altra storia del banditismo.* Guasila: Editziones de su Arkiviu Bibrioteka, 1993.

Contini, Gianfranco. *La letteratura italiana*. Florence-Milan: Sansoni-Accademia, 1974.

Cooper, Dennis. *Frisk: A Novel*. New York: Grove/Atlantic, 2011.

Copjec, Joan. "The Orthopsychic Subject: Film Theory and the Reception of Lacan." *October* 49 (Summer 1989): 53–71.

Corradi, Consuelo. *Il nemico intimo: una lettura sociologica dei casi di Novi Ligure e Cogne*. Rome: Meltemi, 2005.

Corrias, Pino. *Luoghi Comuni: Dal Vajont a Arcore, la geografia che ha cambiato l'Italia*. Milan: Rizzoli, 2006.

Costantini, Daniele, and Francesco Dal Bosco. *Nuovo cinema Inferno: L'opera di Dario Argento*. Milan: Pratiche, 1997.

Covacich, Mauro. *Colpo di Lama*. Vicenza: Neri Pozza, 1995.

Craven, Wes, dir. *Scream*. 1996.

Creed, Barbara. *The Monstrous-Feminine: Film, Psychoanalysis, and Feminism*. London: Routledge, 1993.

Crepet, Paolo. *I figli non crescono più*. Turin: Einaudi, 2005.

———. *Non siamo capaci di ascoltarli: rflessioni sull'infanzia e adolescenza*. Turin: Einaudi, 2001.

———. *Voi, noi. Sull'indifferenza di giovani e adulti*. Turin: Einaudi, 2003.

Crepet, Paolo, and Giancarlo De Cataldo. *I giorni dell'ira. Storie di matricidi*. Milan: Feltrinelli, 2002.

Cristiano, Anthony. "'I'm Not Scared' . . . I'm marketable." *Belphagor* 5, no. 1 (2005): n.p.

Criminal Statistics, England and Wales 1997. London: Home Office, 1998.

Crutchfield, Susan. "Touching Scenes and Finishing Touches: Blindness in the Slasher Film." In *Mythologies of Violence in Postmodern Media*, ed. Christopher Sharrett, 275–299. Detroit: Wayne State University Press, 1999.

Curran, James, and Tamar Liebes, eds. *Media, Ritual, and Identity*. London: Routledge, 1998.

Currie, Mark. *Transitions: Postmodern Narrative Theory*. New York: St. Martin's Press, 1996.

Dagrada, Elena. "Television and Its Critics." In *Italian Cultural Studies: An Introduction*, ed. David Forgacs and Robert Lumley, 233–247. Oxford: Oxford University Press, 1996.

Dalla Zuanna, Gianpiero, Alessandra De Rose, and Filomena Racioppi. "Low Fertility and Limited Diffusion of Modern Contraception in Italy during the Second Half of the Twentieth Century." *Journal of Population Research* 22, no. 1 (2005): 21–48.

Dalla Zuanna, Gianpiero, and Giuseppe Micheli, eds. *Strong Family and Low Fertility: A Paradox? New Perspectives in Interpreting Contemporary Family and Reproductive Behavior*. Dordrecht, Netherlands: Fluwer Academic Publishers, 2004.

D'Amato, Joe, dir. *Emanuelle e gli ultimi cannibali*. 1977.

Danesi, Marcel. "Observations on the Supposed Influence of Cyberlanguage on Contemporary Italian." *Forum Italicum* 40, no. 2 (2006): 428–446.

Davis, John. *Conflict and Control: Law and Order in 19th Century Italy*. London: MacMillan, 1998.

Davoglio, Elena. *Il Caso Cogne*. Rome: Adnkronos Libri, 2003.

Debord, Guy. *The Society of Spectacle*. Trans. Donald Nicholson Smith. New York: Zone Books, 1995.

De Bernardinis, Flavio. *Nanni Moretti*. Milan: Il Castoro, 2001.

De Cataldo, Giancarlo. *Il padre e lo straniero*. Rome: Edizioni e/o, 2004.

———. *Romanzo criminale*. Turin: Einaudi, 2002.

———. *Teneri assassini*. Turin: Einaudi, 2000.

De Certeau, Michel. *The Practice of Everyday Life*. Trans. Steven Rendall. Berkeley: University of California Press, 1988.

De Grazia, Victoria. *How Fascism Ruled Women: Italy 1922–45*. Berkeley: University of California Press, 1992.

De Lauretis, Teresa. *Technologies of Gender: Essays on Theory, Film, and Fiction*. Bloomington: Indiana University Press, 1987.

Deleuze, Gilles, and Félix Guattari. *Anti-Oedipus. Capitalism and Schizophrenia*. Trans. Robert Hurley, Mark Seem, and Helen Lane. Minneapolis: University of Minnesota Press, 1983.

———. *Kafka: Toward Minor Literature*. Trans. Dana Polan. Minneapolis: University of Minnesota Press, 1986.

———. *A Thousand Plateaus: Capitalism and Schizophrenia*. Trans. Brian Massumi. Minneapolis: University of Minnesota Press, 1987.

Della Porta, Donatella. *Lo scambio occulto: Casi di corruzione politica in Italia*. Bologna: Il Mulino, 1992.

DeMarr, Mary Jean. "True Crime Books: Socio-Psycho-Babble or Socially Redeeming Voyeurism." *Clues: A Journal of Detection* 17, no. 2 (1996): 1–18.

De Mauro, Tullio. *Storia linguistica dell'Italia unita*. Bari, Italy: Laterza, 1963.

Demme, Jonathan, dir. *The Silence of the Lambs*. 1991.

Dempsey, Candace. *Murder in Italy: The Shocking Slaying of a British Student, the Accused American Girl, and an International Scandal*. New York: Penguin Books, 2010.

Denicolai, Lorenzo. "L'oralità tecnologica e la sua religione: il caso della televisione e le sue declinazioni." *Turin D@MS Review*, May 26, 2008. http://www.turindamsreview.unito.it/sezione.php?idart=410.

Deodato, Ruggero, dir. *Cannibal Holocaust*. 1979.

———. *Ultimo mondo cannibale*. 1977.

De Palma, Brian, dir. *Carrie*. 1976.

De Pasquali, Paolo. *Serial Killer in Italia: Un'analisi psicologica, criminologica, e psichiatrico-forense*. Milan: FrancoAngeli, 2001.

Derrickson, Scott, dir. *Hellraiser: Inferno*. 2000.

Derrida, Jacques. "Force of Law." Trans. Mary Quaintance. In *Deconstruction and the Possibility of Justice*, ed. Drucilla Cornell, Michael Rosenfeld, and David Gray Carlson, 3–67.. New York: Routledge, 1992.

———. "The Purveyor of Truth." *Yale French Studies* 53 (1975): 31–113.

———. *The Work of Mourning*. Ed. Pascale-Ann Brault and Michael Naas. Chicago: University of Chicago Press, 2001.

De Stefano, Gennaro. *L'Uomo di Cogne*. Rome: Aliberti editore, 2008.

Diaconescu-Blumenfeld, Rodica. "Homme Fatal(e): The Expropriation of Gender in Marco Risi's *Mery per sempre*." *Romance Languages Annual* 10 (1998): 235–240.

Di Ciolla MacGowan, Nicoletta. "Anima Parvuli: A Child's Destiny according to Susanna Tamaro." *Forum Italicum* 33, no. 2 (1999): 459–484.

———. "Crime and the Female Subject: Matricide, Filicide and the Law of the Father in Contemporary Italian Literature: The Case of Laura Grimaldi and Barbara Garlaschelli." In *Women's Writing in Western Europe: Gender, Generation and Legacy*, ed. Adalgisa Giorgio and Julia Waters, 200–215. Newcastle upon Tyne, England: Cambridge Scholars, 2007.

———. "The Eternal City as Dystopia: Or Perfect Imperfection." *Romance Studies* 25, no. 4 (2007) 297–307.

———. "Perfecting Females/Pursuing Truths: Texts, Subtexts and Postmodern Genre-Crossing in Salvatori's Noir, *Sublime anima di donna*." In *Trends in Contemporary Italian Narrative, 1980–2007*, ed. Gillian Ania and Ann Hallamore Caesar, 29–49. Newcastle upon Tyne, England: Cambridge Scholars, 2007.

———. "Relative Values: Resisting Desire and Individuation in Barbara Garlaschelli's *Alice nell'ombra* and *Sorelle*." *Rivista di Studi Italiani* 21, no. 1 (2003): 119–133.

Di Ciolla MacGowan, Nicoletta, and Mirna Cicioni, eds. *Differences, Deceits, and Desires: Murder and Mayhem in Italian Crime Fiction*. Dover: University of Delaware Press, 2008.

Dickie, John. "Imagined Italies." In *Italian Cultural Studies*, ed. David Forgacs and Robert Lumley, 19–33. Oxford: Oxford University Press, 1996.

Dilulio, John J., Jr. "The Coming of the Super-Predators." *The Weekly Standard*, November 27, 1995. http://www.mcsm.org/predator.html.

Dimock, Wai Chee. *Residues of Justice: Literature, Law, Philosophy*. Berkeley: University of California Press, 1997.

Dixon, Travis, Christina Azocar, and Michael Casas. "The Portrayal of Race and Crime on Network News." *Journal of Broadcasting and Electronic Media* 47 (2003): 495–520.

Dixon, Travis, and Daniel Linz. "Overrepresentation and Underrepresentation of African Americans and Latinos as Lawbreakers on Television News." *Journal of Communication* 50 (2000): 131–154.

———. "Race and the Misrepresentation of Victimization on Local Television News" *Communication Research* 27, no. 5 (2000): 547–573.

Doane, Mary Ann. "The Close-Up: Scale and Detail in the Cinema." *differences* 14, no. 3 (2003): 89–111.

———. *Femmes Fatales: Feminism, Film Theory, Psychoanalysis*. New York: Routledge, 1991.

———. "Film and Masquerade: Theorizing the Female Spectator." In *Writing on the Body: Female Embodiment and Feminist Theory*, ed. Katie Conboy, Nadia Medina, and Sarah Stanbury, 176–194. New York: Columbia University Press, 1997.

———. "Technology's Body: Cinematic Vision in Modernity." *differences: A Journal of Feminist Cultural Studies* 5, no. 2 (1993): 1–21.

Dobash, R. Emerson, Russell Dobash, and Lesley Noakes. *Gender and Crime*. Cardiff: University of Wales Press, 1995.

Dobraszczk, Paul. "'Monstrous Sewers': Experiencing London's Main Drainage System." In *Monsters and the Monstrous: Myths and Metaphors of Enduring Evil*, ed. Niall Scott, 9–32. Amsterdam: Rodopi, 2007.

Douglas, Mary. *Natural Symbols: Explorations in Cosmology.* London: Pantheon, Penguin, 1970.

———. *Purity and Danger: An Analysis of Conceptions of Pollution and Taboo.* London: Routledge and Kegan Paul, 1966.

Drake, Richard. *The Aldo Moro Murder Case.* Cambridge, Mass.: Harvard University Press, 1995.

Duncan, Derek. "Italy's Postcolonial Cinema and Its Histories of Representation." *Italian Studies* 62:2 (2008): 195–211.

———. "The Sight and Sound of Albanian Migration in Contemporary Italian Cinema," http://www.cardiff.ac.uk/euros/subsites/newreadings/volume8/abstracts/duncanabstract.html.

Eco, Umberto. *Opera aperta: forma e indeterminazione nelle poetiche contemporanee.* Milan: Bompiani, 1969.

———. *Sette anni di desiderio.* Milan: Bompiani, 1983.

Egger, Steve. *The Killers among Us: An Examination of Serial Killers.* Upper Saddle River, N.J.: Prentice Hall, 1997.

El Guindi, Fadwa. *Veil: Modesty, Privacy and Resistance.* Oxford: Berg, 1999.

Entman, Robert. "Blacks in the News: Television, Modern Racism, and Cultural Change." *Journalism Quarterly* 69, no. 34 (1992): 1–36.

———. "Representation and Reality in the Portrayal of Blacks on Network Television News." *Journalism Quarterly* 71 (1994): 509–520.

Fadiga Zanatta, Anna Laura, and Maria Luisa Mirabile. *Demografia, famiglia, e società: come cambiano le donne.* Rome: Ediesse, 1993.

Feenberg, Andrew, and Maria Bakardjieva. "Consumers or Citizens? The Online Community Debate." In *Community in the Digital Age: Philosophy and Practice,* ed. Andrew Feenberg and Maria Bakardjieva, 1–28. Lanham, Md.: Rowman and Littlefield, 2004.

Ferite d'Italia. (TV show.) RAI 2.

Ferme, Valerio. "Note su Niccolò Ammaniti e il fango di fine millennio." *Narrativa* 20–21 (2001): 321–335.

Ferrario, Cesare, dir. *Il mostro di Firenze.* 1986.

Ferreri, Marco, dir. *Chiedo asilo.* 1979.

———. *Come sono buoni i bianchi/Ya bon les blancs.* 1988.

Ferri, Francesco. *Il caso Pacciani: Storia di una colonna infame?* Florence: Edizioni Pananti, 1997.

Ferroni, Giulio. *Per un'ecologia letteraria.* Torino: Einaudi, 1996.

Fiorello, Lillo. *Cinema, regole, e censura.* Naples: Arte Tipografia Editrice, 2005.

Foot, John. *Calcio: A History of Italian Football.* London: HarperCollins, 2007.

———. *Milan since the Miracle: City, Culture, and Identity.* Oxford: Berg, 2001.

Forgacs, David. *Italian Culture in the Industrial Era.* Manchester: Manchester University Press, 1990.

———. "The Mass Media and the Question of National Identity in Italy." In *The Politics of Italian National Identity,* ed. Gino Bedani and Bruce Haddock, 142–62. Cardiff: University of Wales Press, 2000.

Forgacs, David, and Stephen Gundle. *Mass Culture and Italian Society from Fascism to the Cold War.* Bloomington: Indiana University Press, 2007.

Forgacs, David, and Robert Lumley, eds. *Italian Cultural Studies: An Introduction.* New York: Oxford University Press, 1996.

Forti, Gabrio, and Marta Bertolino, eds. *La televisione del crimine.* Milan: Vita e pensiero, 2005.

Foucault, Michel. "The Confession of the Flesh." In *Power/Knowledge,* 194–228. Ed. Colin Gordon. New York: Pantheon Books, 1980.

———. *Discipline and Punish: The Birth of the Prison.* Trans. Alan Sheridan. New York: Vintage, 1979.

———. *Language, Counter-Memory, Practice: Selected Essays and Interviews.* Ed. Donald Bouchard, trans. Donald Bouchard and Sherry Simon. Ithaca, N.Y.: Cornell University Press, 1977.

Fourny, Jean-François. "Fashion, Bodies, and Objects." *Studies in Twentieth-Century Literature* 20, no. 2 (1996): 393–404.

Franzoni, Annamaria, with Gennaro De Stefano. *La Verità.* Casale Monferrato: Piemme Books, 2006.

Frazzi, Antonio, and Andrea Frazzi, dir. *Certi bambini.* 2004.

Freccero, Carla. "Historical Violence, Censorship, and the Serial Killer: The Case of *American Psycho*." *Diacritics* 27, no. 2 (1997): 44–58.

Freedman, Jonathan. *Media Violence and Its Effect on Aggression: Assessing the Scientific Evidence.* Toronto: University of Toronto Press, 2002.

Freud, Sigmund. *Sexuality and the Psychology of Love.* New York: Collier, 1963.

———. *The Standard Edition of the Complete Psychological Works of Sigmund Freud.* Gen. ed. James Strachey. London: Hogarth, 1953–1974.

Frizzi, Adria. "Performance, or Getting a Piece of the Other, or In the Name of the Father, or The Dark Continent of Femininity, or Just Like a Woman: Anna Maria Ortese's *L'iguana*." *Italica* 79, no. 3 (2002): 379–390.

Froio, Felice. *L'informazione spettacolo: giornali e giornalisti oggi.* Rome: Riuniti, 2000.

Fuss, Diana. "Fashion and the Homospectatorial Look." *Critical Inquiry* 18, no. 4 (1992): 713–737.

Gallant, Chris. "Threatening Glances, Voyeurism, Eye Violation: From *Peeping Tom* to *Opera*." In *Art of Darkness: The Cinema of Dario Argento,* ed. Chris Gallant, 11–21. Godalming, UK: Fab Press, 2001.

Garbesi, Marina. *I serial killers.* Rome: Edizioni Theoria, 1996.

Gargiulo, Gius. "Ciac. Si scrive! Alcune considerazioni sui codici narrativi degli sceneggiatori-romanzieri degli anni Settanta e Ottanta." In *Gli spazi della diversità II,* ed. Serge Vanvolsem, Franco Musarra, and Bart Van den Bossche, 331–349. Rome: Bulzoni and Leuven: Leuven University Press, 1995.

———. "Una maleducazione sentimentale televisiva; Gli scrittori cresciuti davanti al video: Aldo Nove e Luca Doninelli." *Narrativa* 16 (1999): 183–203.

Gariazzo, Mario, dir. *Schiave bianche: Violenza in Amazzonia.* 1985.

Garofano, Luciano. *Delitti Imperfetti, Atto I e Atto II.* Milan: Marco Tropea Editore, 2006.

Garrone, Matteo, dir. *Gomorra.* 2008.

———. *L'imbalsamatore.* 2002.

Geertz, Clifford. *The Interpretation of Culture.* New York: Basic Books, 1977.

Genna, Giuseppe. *Dies irae*. Milan: Rizzoli, 2006.

Gervasutti, Luca. *Dannati e sognatori. Guida alla nuova narrativa italiana*. Paisan di Prato: Campanotto Editore, 1998.

Ghezzo, Flora Maria. "Paesaggi del desiderio, ovvero *devenir femme* tra terra e acqua." In *". . . e c'e di mezzo il mare": lingua, letteratura e civiltà marina,* ed. Art van den Bossche, Michael Bastiansen, and Corinna Salvadori Lonergan, 265–278. Florence: Franco Cesati Editore, 2002.

Giallo 1. Mediaset.

Giannangelo, Stephen. *The Psychopathology of Serial Murder: A Theory of Violence.* Westport, Conn.: Praeger Press, 1997.

Gilbert, Mark. *The Lega Nord and the Northern Question in Italian Politics.* New York: Palgrave, 2001.

Gilliam, Franklin, Shanto Iyengar, Adam Simon, and Oliver Wright. "Crime in Black and White: The Violent, Scary World of Local News." *Harvard International Journal of Press/Politics* 1, no. 3 (1994): 6–23.

Gilligan, Carol. *In a Different Voice: Psychological Theory and Women's Development.* Cambridge, Mass.: Harvard University Press, 1993.

Ginsborg, Paul. *Italy and its Discontents: Family: Civil Society, State 1890–2001.* New York: Palgrave MacMillan, 2003.

———. *Silvio Berlusconi: Television, Power and Patrimony.* London: Verso, 2004.

———. *Stato dell'Italia.* Milan: Il Saggiatore, 1994.

Ginsburg, Faye, Lila-Abu-Lughod, and Brian Larkin, eds. *Media Worlds: Anthropology on a New Terrain.* Berkeley: University of California Press, 2002.

Giorgio, Adalgisa. "The Passion for the Mother: Conflicts and Idealisations in Contemporary Italian Narrative." In *Writing Mothers and Daughters: Renegotiating the Mother in Western European Narratives by Women,* ed. Adalgisa Giorgio, 119–154. New York: Berghahn, 2002.

Giovannini, Fabio, and Antonio Tentori, eds. *Cuore di pulp: antologia di racconti italiani.* Rome: Stampa alternativa, n.d.

Girard, René. *Violence and the Sacred.* Trans. Patrick Gregory. Baltimore: Johns Hopkins University Press, 1977.

Giuttari, Michele. *Il mostro: anatomia di un'indagine.* Milan: Rizzoli, 2006.

Giuttari, Michele, and Carlo Lucarelli. *Compagni di sangue.* Florence: Le Lettere, 1998.

Glynn, Ruth, and Giancarlo Lombardi, eds. *Remembering Moro: Historiographical and Cultural Representations of the Moro Affair.* Oxford: Legenda, 2012.

Gordon, Robert. "Pasolini's Murder: Interpretation, Event Narratives, and Postmodern *Impegno*." In *Assassinations and Murder in Modern Italy,* ed. Stephen Gundle and Lucia Rinaldi, 153–165. New York: Palgrave, 2007.

Gracey, James. *Dario Argento.* Harpenden, Herts, England: Kamera Books, 2010.

Grasso, Aldo, ed. *Enciclopedia della Televisione.* Milan: Garzanti, 2002.

———. *Storia della televisione italiana.* Milan: Garzanti, 2004.

Grealy, Lucy. *Autobiography of a Face.* Boston: Houghton Mifflin, 1994.

Grignaffini, Giovanna. *La scena madre: scritti sul cinema.* Bologna: Bononia University Press, 2002.

Grimaldi, Antonello, dir. *Caos calmo.* 2008.

Grosz, Elizabeth. *Sexual Subversions: Three French Feminists.* Sydney: Allen & Unwin, 1989.

———. *Space, Time and Perversion.* London: Routledge, 1995.

Guarnieri, Carlo. *Magistratura e politica: pesi senza contrappesi.* Bologna: Il Mulino, 1993.

Guins, Raiford. "Blood and Black Gloves on Shiny Discs: New Media, Old Taste, and the Remediation of Italian Horror Films in the United States." In *Horror International,* ed. Stephen Schneider and Tony Williams, 15–32. Detroit: Wayne State University Press, 2005.

Gundle, Stephen. "RAI and Fininvest in the Year of Berlusconi." In *Italian Politics: The Year of the Tycoon,* ed. Richard Katz and Piero Ignazi, 195–218. Bologna: Istituto Cattaneo, 1996.

Gundle, Stephen, and Noëlleanne O'Sullivan. "The Mass Media and the Political Crisis." In *The New Italian Republic: From the Fall of the Berlin Wall to Berlusconi,* ed. Stephen Gundle and Simon Parker, 206–220. London: Routledge, 1996.

Gundle, Stephen, and Lucia Rinaldi, eds. *Assassinations and Murder in Modern Italy, Transformations in Society and Culture.* New York: Palgrave, 2007.

Haddon, Leslie. *Information and Communication Technologies in Everyday Life.* Oxford: Berg Press, 2004.

Halberstam, Judith. "Skinflick: Posthuman Gender in Jonathan Demme's *The Silence of the Lambs.*" *Camera Obscura* 27 (September 1991): 37–53.

Hall, Stuart, ed. *Policing the Crisis: Mugging, the State, and Law and Order.* London: MacMillan, 1978.

Hanson, Jarice. *24/7: How Cell Phones and the Internet Change the Way We Live.* Westport, Conn.: Praeger, 2007.

Harper, Glen. "The Other Carlo Lucarelli." *International Noir Fiction* (Weblog). July 8, 2008. http://internationalnoir.blogspot.com/2008/07/other-carlo-lucarelli.html.

Harrowitz, Nancy. "Primo Levi and Holocaust Tourism." In *Primo Levi: The Austere Humanist,* ed. Joseph Farrell, 203–214. Oxford: Peter Lang, 2004.

Heidensohn, Frances. *Women and Crime.* London: MacMillan, 1986.

Hickox, Anthony, dir. *Hellraiser III: Hell on Earth.* 1992.

Hirsch, Marianne. *The Mother/Daughter Plot.* Bloomington: Indiana University Press, 1989.

Hitchcock, Alfred, dir. *The Birds.* 1966.

Hooper, Tobe, dir. *The Texas Chainsaw Massacre.* 1974.

Horst, Heather, and Daniel Miller. *The Cell Phone: An Anthropology of Communication.* Oxford: Berg Publishers, 2006.

Howitt, Dennis. *Crime, the Media, and the Law.* Chichester, England: John Wiley, 1998.

Hurley, Susan. "Imitation, Media Violence, and Freedom of Speech." *Philosophical Studies: An International Journal for Philosophy in the Analytic Tradition* 117 (2004): 165–218.

Hurley, Susan, and Nick Chater. "Introduction: Why Imitation Matters." In *Perspectives on Imitation: From Neuroscience to Social Science,* ed. Susan Hurley and N. Chater, 2:1–52. Cambridge, Mass.: MIT Press, 2005.

Incerti, Stefano, dir. *La vita come viene*. 2003.

Ingebretsen, Edward. "The Monster in the Home: True Crime and the Traffic in Body Parts." *Journal of American Culture* 21, no. 1 (1998): 27–34.

Infascelli, Alex, dir. *Almost Blue*. 2000.

Irigaray, Luce. "Women, the Sacred, and Money. *Paragraph: A Journal of Modern Critical Theory* 8 (1986): 6–17.

Isaac, Allan Punzalen. *American Tropics: Articulating Filipino America*. Minneapolis: University of Minnesota Press, 2006.

Jaggar, Alison. "Introduction: Living with Contradictions." In *Living with Contradictions: Controversies in Feminist Social Ethics,* ed. Alison Jaggar, 1–12. Boulder, Colo.: Westview Press, 1994.

James, Bill. *Popular Crime: Reflections on the Celebration of Violence*. New York: Scribner, 2011.

Jameson, Frederic. "Postmodernism, or the Cultural Logic of Late Capitalism," *New Left Review* 146 (July–August 1984): 53–92.

Jansen, Monica, and Inge Lanslot, "Ten Years of *Gioventù cannibale:* Reflections on the Anthology as a Vehicle for Literary Change." In *Trends in Contemporary Italian Narrative, 1980–2007,* ed. Gillian Ania and Anna Hallamore Caesar, 114–135. Newcastle upon Tyne, England: Cambridge Scholars, 2007.

Jenkins, Philip. *Using Murder: The Social Construction of Serial Homicide*. New York: Aldine de Gruyter, 1994.

Jewell, Keala, ed. *Monsters in the Italian Literary Imagination*. Detroit: Wayne State University Press, 2001

Johnson, Barbara. "The Frame of Reference: Poe, Lacan, Derrida." *Yale French Studies* 55/56 (1977): 457–505.

Jones, Tobias. *Dark Heart of Italy*. New York: Farrar, Strauss, Giroux, 2003.

Kamir, Orit. *Framed: Women in Law and Film*. Durham, N.C.: Duke University Press, 2006.

Kaplan, Ann. "Freud, Film, and Culture." In *Freud: Conflict and Culture: Essays on His Life, Work, and Legacy,* ed. Michael Roth, 152–164. New York: Knopf, 1998.

———. *Trauma Culture: The Politics of Terror and Loss in Media and Literature*. New Brunswick, N.J.: Rutgers University Press, 2005.

Kaufman, Philip, dir. *Invasion of the Body Snatchers*. 1978.

Kawana, Sari. *Murder Most Modern: Detective Fiction and Japanese Culture*. Minneapolis: University of Minnesota Press, 2008.

Kidd-Hewitt, David, and Richard Osborne. *Crime and the Media: The Postmodern Spectacle*. East Haven, Conn.: Pluto, 1995.

King, Gary. *The Murder of Meredith Kercher*. London: John Blake Publishing, 2010.

Kipnis, Laura. "(Male) Desire and (Female) Disgust: Reading *Hustler*." In *Cultural Studies,* ed. Lawrence Grossberg, Cary Nelson, and Paula Treichler, 373–391. New York: Routledge, 1992.

Klopp, Charles. *Sentences: The Memoirs and Letters of Italian Political Prisoners from Benvenuto Cellini to Aldo Moro*. Toronto: Toronto University Press, 1999.

Knee, Adam. "Gender, Genre, Argento." In *The Dread of Difference,* ed. Barry Grant, 213–230. Austin: University of Texas Press, 1996.

Koven, Mikel. *La Dolce Morte: Vernacular Cinema and the Italian Giallo Film*. Lanham, Md.: Scarecrow Press, 2006.

Krismer, Raffaella. *Il signore della carne*. Milan: Zelig, 1997.

Kristeva, Julia. *The Powers of Horror: An Essay on Abjection*. Trans. Leon Roudiez. New York: Columbia University Press, 1982.

Lacan, Jacques. *Écrits*. Trans. Robert Sheridan. New York: W. W. Norton, 1977.

———. *Freud's Papers on Technique, 1953–1954*. Trans. and ed. John Forrester. New York: Norton, 1988.

La Cecla, Franco. *Surrogati di presenza, Media e vita quotidiana*. Milan: Bruno Mondadori, 2006.

Laclau, Ernesto, and Chantal Mouffe. *Hegemony and Socialist Strategy: Towards a Radical Democratic Politics*. London: Verso, 1985.

Lagostena Bassi, Augusta, with Emanuela Moroli. *L'avvocato delle donne: dodici storie di ordinaria violenza*. Milan: Mondadori, 1991.

Landy, Marcia. *Italian Film*. Cambridge: Cambridge University Press, 2000.

Lane, John Francis. "The Monster," *Screen International* 982 (1994): 41.

La Porta, Filippo. *La nuova narrativa italiana: travestimenti e stili di fine secolo*. Turin: Bollati Boringhieri, 1995.

Lardieri, Luca, ed. *Dario Argento*. Rome: Sovera Multimedia, 2007.

La Trecchia, Patrizia. "New Media (B)orders in Contemporary Neapolitan Music: Rethinking Aesthetic Experience in the Age of Globalization." In *Italian Cultural Studies, 2001: Selected Essays,* ed. Anthony Tamburri, Myriam Swennen, Graziella Parati, and Ben Lawton, 69–92. Boca Raton, Fla.: Bordighera Press, 2004.

Latza Nadeau, Barbie. *Angel Face: The True Story of Student Killer Amanda Knox*. New York: Beast Books, 2010.

Lavorino, Carmelo. *Cogne: delitto infernale*. Naples: Tullio Pironti Editore, 2006.

Lazzaro-Weiss, Carol. "The Concept of Difference in Italian Feminist Thought: Mothers, Daughters, Heretics." In *Italian Feminist Theory and Practice: Equality and Sexual Difference,* ed. Graziella Parati and Rebecca West, 31–49. Madison, N.J.: Fairleigh Dickinson University Press, 2002.

Leitch, Vincent. "Costly Compensations: Postmodern Fashion, Politics, Identity." *Modern Fiction Studies* 42:1 (1996): 111–128.

Lenzi, Umberto. *Cannibal ferox*. 1981.

Lepre, Aurelio. *Storia della prima repubblica. L'Italia dal 1943 al 2003*. Bologna: Il Mulino, 2004.

Lepschy, Anna Laura, and Arturo Tosi, eds. *Languages and Italy: Histories and Dictionaries*. Ravenna: Longo Editore, 2007.

Lepschy, Giulio. *Mother Tongues and Other Reflections on the Italian Language*. Toronto: University of Toronto Press, 2002.

Levy, Carl, ed. *Italian Regionalism: History, Identity, Politics*. Oxford: Berg Press, 1996.

Lewandoski, Mark. "Tourist Season at Auschwitz." *Gettysburg Review* 12, no. 2 (1999): 293–302.

Lombardi, Giancarlo. "I misteri d'Italia nella fiction TV." In *Strane storie: Il cinema e i misteri d'Italia,* ed. Christian Uva, 182–195. Rome: Rubbettino, 2011.

Losito, Gianni. *Il potere dei media*. Rome: Carocci, 1994.

Lucamante, Stefania. "Intervista a Tiziano Scarpa di Stefania Lucamante." *Italica* 83, no. 3–4 (2006): 691–706.

————. *A Multitude of Women: The Challenges of the Contemporary Novel.* Toronto: University of Toronto Press, 2008.

Lucamante, Stefania, ed. and trans. *Italian Pulp Fiction: The New Narrative of the Giovani Cannibali Writers.* Madison, N.J.: Fairleigh Dickinson University Press, 2001.

Lucantonio, Gabrielle, ed. *Dario Argento.* Rome: Dino Audino Editore, 2001.

Lucarelli, Carlo. *Almost Blue.* Turin: Einaudi, 1997.

————. *Carta bianca.* Palermo: Sellerio, 1990.

————. *L'estate torbida.* Palermo: Sellerio, 1991.

————. *Lupo mannaro.* Rome: Edizioni Theoria, 1994.

————. *Misteri d'Italia: i casi di Blu Notte.* Turin: Einaudi, 2002.

————. *Mistero in blue.* Turin: Einaudi, 1999.

————. *Nuovi misteri d'Italia: i casi di Blu Notte.* Turin: Einaudi, 2004.

————. *Via delle Oche.* Palermo: Sellerio, 1996.

Lucarelli, Carlo, and Massimo Picozzi. *Scena del crimine: Storie di delitti efferati e di investigazioni scientifiche.* Milan: Mondadori, 2005.

————. *Serial Killers: Storie di ossessione omicida.* Milan: Mondadori, 2003.

Lucchetti, Daniele, dir. *Mio fratello è figlio unico.* 2007.

Luperini, Romano, and P. Cataldo. *La scrittura e l'interpretazione* III: *Dal naturalismo al postmoderno.* Palermo: Palumbo, 1999.

Lupi, Gordiano, and Sabina Marchesi. *Coppie diaboliche.* Florence: Olimpia Editoriale, 2008.

Lustig, William, dir. *Maniac.* 1980.

Lyotard, Jean-François. *The Postmodern Condition: A Report on Knowledge.* Trans. Geoff Bennington and Brian Massumi. Minneapolis: University of Minnesota Press, 1984.

MacNeil, William. *Lex Populi: The Jurisprudence of Popular Culture.* Stanford, Calif.: Stanford University Press, 2007.

Maeder, Costantino. "Italian Crime Novels." In *Investigating Identities: Questions of Identity in Contemporary International Crime Fiction,* ed. Marieke Krajenbrink and Kate Quinn, 261–276. Amsterdam: Rodopi Press, 2009.

Magherini, Graziella. *La Sindrome di Stendhal.* Florence: Ponte alle Grazie, 1989.

Magni, Stefano. "Voci e punti di vista in *Fango* di Ammaniti." *Narrativa* 20–21 (2001): 305–319.

Mai, Nicola. "Myths and Moral Panics: Italian Identity and the Media Representation of Albanian Immigration." In *The Politics of Recognising Difference: Multiculturalism Italian Style,* ed. R. D. Grillo, and J. Pratt, 77–95. Aldershot: Ashgate, 2002.

Mai, Nicola, and Russell King. *Out of Albania: From Crisis Migration to Social Inclusion in Italy.* New York: Berghahn, 2008.

Maiello, Fabio. *L'occhio che uccide.* Naples: Edizioni Scientifiche, 1996.

Malaparte, Curzio. *The Skin.* Trans. David Moore. Marlboro, Vt.: Marlboro Press, 1952.

Malcolm, Janet. *Iphigenia in Forest Hills: Anatomy of a Murder Trial.* New Haven, Conn.: Yale University Press, 2011.

————. *The Journalist and the Murderer.* New York: Vintage Books, 1990.

Marotta, Gemma. *Donne, criminalità e carcere.* Rome: Euroma La Goliardica, 1989.

Marshall, George, dir. *The Blue Dahlia.* 1946.

Materazzi, Marco. *Che cosa ho detto veramente a Zidane.* Milan: Mondadori, 2006.

Mattelart, Armand. *The Invention of Communication.* Trans. Susan Emanuel. Minneapolis: University of Minnesota Press, 1996.

———. *Networking the World: 1794–2000.* Trans. Liz Carey-Librecht and James Cohen. Minneapolis: University of Minnesota Press, 2000.

Maurizio Costanzo Show. Canale 5.

Mayer-Schönberger, Viktor. *Delete: The Virtue of Forgetting in the Digital Age.* Princeton, N.J.: Princeton University Press, 2009.

McDonagh, Maitland. *Broken Mirrors/Broken Minds: The Dark Dreams of Dario Argento.* New York: Citadel, 1994.

McLuhan, Marshall. *Understanding Media: The Extensions of Man.* Ed. W. Terrence Gordon. Corte Madera, Calif.: Gingko Press, 2003.

McRobbie, Angela. *Postmodernism and Popular Culture.* London: Routledge, 1994.

McRobbie, Angela, and Sarah Thornton. "Rethinking Moral Panic for Multi-mediated Social Worlds." *British Journal of Sociology* 46, no. 4 (1995): 559–574.

Merlin, Lina, and Carla Barberis, eds. *Lettere dalla casa chiuse.* Milan-Rome: Edizioni Avanti!, 1955.

Metz, Christian. *The Imaginary Signifier: Psychoanalysis and the Cinema.* Bloomington: Indiana University Press, 1982.

Meyrowitz, Joshua. "The Generalized Elsewhere." *Critical Studies in Mass Communication* 6, no. 3 (1989): 326–334.

———. *No Sense of Place: The Impact of Electronic Media on Social Behavior.* Oxford: Oxford University Press, 1985.

Miccichè, Lino. *Cinema italiano: gli anni '60 e oltre.* Venice: Marsilio, 2002.

Mikula, Maja. "Displacement and Shifting Geographies in the Noir Fiction of Cesare Battisti." In *Exile Cultures, Misplaced Identities,* ed. Paul Allatson and Jo McCormack, 209–223. Amsterdam: Rodopi Press, 2008.

Minella Maurizio, Fantoni. *Non riconciliati. Politica e società nel cinema italiano dal neorealismo a oggi.* Turin: UTET, 2004.

Mitchell, Tony. "Doin' Damage in My Native Language: The Use of 'Resistance Vernaculars' in Hip Hop in France, Italy, and Aotearoa/New Zealand." *Popular Music and Society* 24:3 (2000): 41–54.

Mitchell, William. *E-topia: "Urban Life, Jim—But Not as We Know It."* Cambridge, Mass.: MIT Press, 1999.

Moffatt, Gregory K. *Blind-Sided: Homicide Where It Is Least Expected.* Westport, Conn.: Praeger, 2000.

Montale, Eugenio. *Tutte le poesie.* Milan: Mondadori, 1977.

Monteleone, Franco. *Storia della Radio e della Televisione in Italia.* Venice: Marsilio, 1992.

Mora, Teo. *Storia del cinema dell'orrore.* Vol. 1, *Dal 1957 al 1966.* Rome: Fanucci, 2002.

———. *Storia del cinema dell'orrore.* Vol. 2, *Dal 1966 al 1978.* Rome: Fanucci, 2003.

Moretti, Franco. *Signs Taken for Wonders: Essays in the Sociology of Literary Forms.* Trans. Susan Fischer, David Forgacs, and David Miller. London: Verso, 1993.

Moretti, Nanni, dir. *Aprile,* 1998.

———. *Caro diario,* 1993.

———. *Ecce bombo,* 1978.

———. *Io sono un autarchico!* 1978.

———. *La stanza del figlio,* 2001.

Morley, David. "Belongings: Place, Space and Identity in a Mediated World." *European Journal of Cultural Studies* 4, no. 4 (2001): 425–448.

Mulvey, Laura. "Visual Pleasure and Narrative Cinema." In *Feminist Film Theory: A Reader,* ed. Sue Thornham, 58–69. New York: New York University Press, 1999.

Nadeau, Barbie Latza. *Angel Face: The True Story of Student Killer Amanda Knox.* New York: Beast Books, 2010.

Naylor, Bronwyn. "The 'Bad Mother' in Media and Legal Texts." *Social Semiotics* 11, no. 2 (2001): 155–176.

Nelken, David. "A Legal Revolution? The Judges and *Tangentopoli.*" In *The New Italian Republic: From the Fall of the Berlin Wall to Berlusconi,* ed. Stephen Gundle and Simon Parker, 191–205. London: Routledge, 1996.

Nerenberg, Ellen. *Prison Terms: Representing Confinement during and after Italian Fascism.* Toronto: University of Toronto Press, 2001.

Newitz, Annalee. "Serial Killers, True Crime, and Economic Performance Anxiety." In *Mythologies of Violence in Postmodern Media,* ed. Christopher Sharrett, 65–83. Detroit: Wayne State University Press, 1999.

Nivoli, Gian Carlo. *Medea tra noi: Le madri che uccidono il proprio figlio.* Rome: Carocci editore, 2002.

Nove, Aldo. *Superwoobinda.* Turin: Einaudi, 1998.

———. *Woobinda e altre storie senza lieto fine.* Rome: Castelvecchi, 1996.

Oates, Joyce Carol. *My Sister, My Love: The Intimate Story of Skyler Rampike.* New York: Ecco Press, 2008.

O'Healy, Àine. "'Non è una somala: Deconstructing African Femininity in Italian Film." *Italianist* 29, no. 2 (2009): 175–198.

O'Leary, Alan. "Dead Man Walking: The Aldo Moro Kidnap and Palimpsest History in Buongiorno Note." *New Cinemas: Journal of Contemporary Film* 6, no. 1 (2008): 33–45.

Orengo, Nico. *Una lieve impressione.* Milan: Garzanti, 1991.

Ortoleva, Peppino. *Mediastoria: Comunicazione e cambiamento sociale nel mondo contemporaneo.* Parma: Nuova Pratiche Editrice, 1995.

Ortu, Leopoldo. *La questione sarda tra Ottocento e Novecento: aspetti e problemi.* Cagliari: CUEC, 2005.

P., Melissa. *100 colpi di spazzola prima di andare a dormire.* Rome: Fazi Editore, 2003.

Paoli, Letizia. "Crime, Italian Style." *Daedalus* 130, no. 3 (2001): 157–185.

Parati, Graziella. *Migration Italy: The Art of Talking Back in a Destination Culture.* Toronto: Toronto University Press, 2005.

Past, Elena. "Lucarelli's *Guernica,* or the Predicament of Postmodern Impegno." *Italica* 84, no. 2 (2007): 290–308.

Pellico, Silvio. *My Prisons.* Boston: Roberts Brothers, 1889.

Perkins, William, ed. *Droppin' Science: Critical Essays on Rap Music and Hip hop Culture.* Philadelphia: Temple University Press, 1996.

Perugini, Ruggero. *Un uomo abbastanza normale: la caccia al mostro di Firenze.* Milan: Mondadori, 1995.

Petri, Elio, dir. *Indagine su un cittadino al di sopra di ogni sospetto.* 1970.

Piccini, Alberto. "Telecommandos." *La Bestia* 1 (1997): 60–65.

Pieri, Giuliana. "Crime and the City in the Detective Fiction of Giorgio Scerbanenco." In *Italian Cityscapes: Culture and Urban Change in Contemporary Italy,* ed. Robert Lumley and John Foot, 144–155. Exeter: University of Exeter Press, 2004.

———. "Milano nera: Representing and Imagining Milan in Italian Noir and Crime Fiction." *Romance Studies* 25, no. 2 (2007): 123–135.

Pinketts, Andrea. *Il senso della frase.* Milan: Feltrinelli, 1995.

———. *Il vizio dell'agnello.* Milan: Feltrinelli, 1994.

———. *Lazzaro, Vieni Fuori.* Milan: Feltrinelli, 1992.

Pinkus, Karen. *The Montesi Scandal: The Death of Wilma Montesi and the Birth of the Paparazzi in Fellini's Rome.* Chicago: University of Chicago Press, 2003.

Pinto, Francesco. *Il Modello Televisivo: professionalità e politica da Bernabei alla terza rete.* Milan: Feltrinelli, 1980.

Pistelli, Maurizio and Norberto Cacciaglia, eds., *Perugia in giallo: indagine sul poliziesco italiano.* Rome: Donzelli, 2009.

Pizzato, Mark. "Jeffrey Dahmer and Media Cannibalism: The Lure and Failure of Sacrifice." In *Mythologies of Violence in Postmodern Media,* ed. Christopher Sharrett, 85–118. Detroit: Wayne State University Press, 1999.

Placido, Michele, dir. *Romanzo criminale.* 2005.

Pomilio, Tommaso. "Le narrative generazionali dagli anni ottanta agli anni novanta." In *Storia generale della letteratura italiana,* vol. 12: *Sperimentalismo e tradizione del nuovo,* ed. Nino Borsellino and Walter Pedullà. Milan: Federico Motta Editore, 1999.

Pompei Karagoz, Claudia. "Gazing Women: Elena Stancanelli's *Benzina.*" *Italica* 83, no. 3–4 (2006): 391–417.

Potter, W. James. *On Media Violence.* Thousand Oaks, Calif.: Sage Publications, 1999.

Porporati, Andrea, dir. *Luce negli occhi.* 2001.

Powell, Anna. *Deleuze and the Horror Film.* Edinburgh: Edinburgh University Press, 2005.

Porta a porta. RAI 1.

Pozzan, Roberto. *Cogne: L'intervista.* Rome: Editori Riuniti, 2006.

Preston, Douglas, with Mario Spezi. *The Monster of Florence.* New York: Grand Central Publishing, 2008.

Prevos, André J. M. "Communication through Popular Music in the Twenty-First Century? The Example of French Rap Music and Hip Hop Culture." In *Language and Communication in the New Century,* ed. Jesse Levitt, Leonard R. N. Ashley, and Wayne Finke, 137–148. East Rockaway, N.Y.: Cummings and Hathaway, 1998.

Prinz, Wolfgang. "An Ideomotor Approach to imitation." In *Perspectives on Imitation: From Neuroscience to Social Science,* ed. Susan Hurley and Nick Chater, 1:141–156. Cambridge, Mass.: MIT Press, 2005.

Pugliese, Roberto. *Dario Argento.* Milan: Il Castoro, 1996.

Quan-Haase, Anabel, and Barry Wellman, with James Witte and Keith Hampton. "Capitalizing on the Net: Social Contact, Civic Engagement, and Sense of Community." In *The Internet in Everyday Life,* ed. Barry Wellman and Caroline Haythornthwaite, 291–324. Oxford: Blackwell, 2002.

Quarto rapporto sulla comunicazione in Italia: i media che vorrei. CENSIS-U.C.S.I. Milan: Franco Angeli, 2005.

Radice, Emilio. "Si fa presto a dire Serial Killer." *La Repubblica,* August 11, 1987.

Randel, Tony, dir. *Hellraiser II: Hellbound.* 1988.

Reiner, Robert. "Media Made Criminality." In *The Oxford Handbook of Criminology,* ed. M. Maguire, R. Morgan, and R. Reiner, 302–337. Oxford: Oxford University Press, 2007.

Risi, Marco, dir. *Il Branco.* 1994.

———. *L'ultimo capodanno.* 1998.

———. *Mery per Sempre.* 1989.

———. *Ragazzi fuori.* 1990.

Rizzolatti, Giacomo, Leonardo Fogassi, and Vittorio Gallese. "Neuropsychological Mechanisms Underlying the Understanding and Imitation of Action. *Nature Reviews: Neuroscience* 2 (September 2001): 661–670.

Romero, George, dir. *Dawn of the Dead.* 1978.

———. *Night of the Living Dead.* 1968.

Rorato, Laura. "Childhood Prisons, Denied Dreams and Denied Realities: The Ritualization of Pain in the Novels of Susanna Tamaro." *Romance Studies* 28 (1996): 61–78.

Rose, Gillian. *Feminism and Geography: The Limits of Geographical Knowledge.* London: Routledge, 1993.

Ross, Charlotte. "Creating the Ideal Posthuman Body? Cyborg Sex and Gender in the Work of Buzzati, Vacca, and Ammaniti." *Italica* 82, no. 2 (2005): 222–247.

———."Queering the Habitus: Lesbian Identity in Stancanelli's *Benzina.*" *Romance Studies* 22, no. 3 (2004): 237–250.

Ross, Silvia. *Tuscan Spaces: Literary Construction of Place.* Toronto: University of Toronto Press, 2010.

Rothenberg, Molly, and Joseph Valente. "Fashionable Theory and Fashion-Able Women: Returning Fuss's Homospectatorial Look." *Critical Inquiry* 22, no. 2 (1996): 372–382.

Rubin, Gayle. "Thinking Sex: Notes for a Radical Theory of the Politics of Sexuality." In *Pleasure and Danger,* ed. Carole Vance, 267–319. London: Routledge and Kegan Paul, 1984.

———. "The Traffic in Women: Notes on the 'Political Economy' of Sex." In *Toward an Anthropology of Women,* ed. Rayna Reiter, 157–210. New York: Monthly Review Press, 1975.

Rushdie, Salman. *The Satanic Verses.* New York: Picador, 1988.

Russell, Paul, and Graham Johnson. *Darkness Descending: The Murder of Meredith Kercher.* London: Simon and Schuster UK, 2010.

Ryan, Marie-Laure, ed. *Narrative across Media: The Languages of Storytelling.* Lincoln: University of Nebraska Press, 2004.

Ryan-Scheutz, Colleen. *Sex, the Self, and the Sacred: Women in the Cinema of Pier Paolo Pasolini.* Toronto: University of Toronto Press, 2007.

Salinger, J. D. *Nine Stories*. New York: Little Brown, 1991.

Salvatores, Gabriele, dir. *Come Dio comanda*. 2008.

———. *Io non ho paura*. 2003.

———. *Quo vadis, baby?* 2005.

Sambuco, Patrizia. "Women, Relationships, and Space in Stancanelli's Benzina (1998)." *Romance Studies* 22, no. 2 (2004): 127–138.

Santoro, Marco, and Marco Solari. "Authors and Rappers: Italian Hip Hop and the Shifting Boundaries of *Canzone d'Autore*." *Popular Music* 26, no. 3 (2007): 463–488.

Saviano, Roberto. *Gomorra*. Milan: Mondadori, 2006.

Schlesinger, Philip, and Howard Tumber. *Reporting Crime: The Media Politics of Criminal Justice*. Oxford: Oxford University Press, 1994.

Schmid, David. "Imagining Safe Urban Space: The Contribution of Detective Fiction to Radical Geography." *Antipode* 27 (1995): 242–269.

Sciascia, Leonardo. *L'Affaire Moro*. Palermo: Sellerio Editore, 1978.

Seltzer, Mark. *Serial Killers: Death and Life in America's Wound Culture*. New York: Routledge, 1998.

———. "Serial Killers (II): The Pathological Public Sphere," *Critical Inquiry* 22, no. 1 (1995): 122–149.

———. *True Crime: Observations on Violence and Modernity*. New York and London: Routlege, 2006.

Sereni, Clara. *Manicomio primaverile*. Florence: Giunti Editore, 1997.

Serra, Tonino. *Violenza, criminalità e giustizia in Sardegna dal 1500 al 1871*. Sestu: Zonza, 2007.

Shapiro, Ann-Louise. *Breaking the Codes: Female Criminality in fin-de-siècle Paris*. Stanford, Calif.: Stanford University Press, 1996.

Sherwin, Richard. *When the Law Goes Pop: The Vanishing Line between Law and Popular Culture*. Chicago: University of Chicago Press, 2000.

Siegel, Don, dir. *Invasion of the Body Snatchers*. 1956.

Silverman, Kaja. *The Acoustic Mirror: The Female Voice in Psychoanalysis and Cinema*. Bloomington: Indiana University Press, 1988.

Simpson, Thomas. *Murder and Media in the New Rome: The Fadda Affair*. New York: Palgrave MacMillan, 2010.

Slater, Don. "Social Relationships and Identity On-Line and Off-Line." In *Handbook of New Media: Social Shaping and Consequences of ICTs*, ed. Leah Lievrouw and Sonia Livingston, 533–543. Thousand Oaks, Calif.: Sage Publications, 2002.

Smith, Paul. *Clint Eastwood: A Cultural Production*. Minneapolis: University of Minnesota Press, 1993.

Snyder, Andrew. "'I Wonder Who the Real Cannibals Are': Latin America and Colonialism in European Exploitation Cinema." In *Latsploitation, Exploitation Cinemas, and Latin America*, ed. Victoria Ruétalo and Dolores Tierney, 70–84. New York: Routledge, 2009. Sobchak, Vivian. *The Address of the Eye: A Phenomenology of Film Experience*. Princeton, N.J.: Princeton University Press, 1992.

Somigli, Luca. "The Realism of Detective Fiction: Augusto De Angelis. Theorist of the Italian *giallo*." *Symposium* 59 (2005): 70–83.

Soulez-Larivière, Daniel. *Il circo mediatico-giudiziario.* Trans. Maria Giustozzi. Macerata: Liberilibri, 1994.

Spillane, Mickey. *Kiss Me Deadly.* New York: Signet Books, 1960.

Stallabrass, Julian. "Empowering Technology." In *Studying Culture: An Introductory Reader,* ed. Ann Gray and Jim McGuigan, 346–364. London: Arnold Press, 1997.

Stancanelli, Elena. *Benzina.* Turin: Einaudi, 1998.

Stille, Alexander. *Excellent Cadavers.* New York: Vintage, 1996.

Stone, Oliver, dir. *The Doors.* 1991.

Sunstein, Cass. *Republic.Com.* Princeton, N.J.: Princeton University Press, 2001.

Sutton, Paul. "The Missing Child of Contemporary Italian Cinema." *Screen* 46, no. 3 (2005): 353–359.

Tamaro, Susanna. *Anima mundi.* Milan: Baldini and Castoldo, 1997.

———. *Per voce sola.* Venice: Marsilio, 1991.

Tani, Cinzia. *Coppie assassine: Uccidere in due per odio o per amore, per denaro o perversione.* Milan: Mondadori, 1999.

Taormina, Carlo. "La mia verita sul delitto di Cogne." *Il Giornale,* April 2007.

Tarantini, Michele Massimo, dir. *Nudo e selvaggio.* 1985.

Tarantino, Quentin, dir. *Pulp Fiction.* 1994.

Tardino, Enzo."Chi ha uccisio Samuele?": Il racconto dell'assassinio di Cogne.* Ferrara: Gabriele Corbo, 2003.

Tatar, Helen. *Lustmord: Sexual Murder in Weimar Germany.* Princeton, N.J.: Princeton University Press, 1995.

Tentori, Antonio. *Dario Argento: Dario Argento: sensualità dell'omicidio.* Alessandria: Edizioni Falsopiano, 1997.

Terzo rapporto sulla comunicazione: Media and Giovani. CENSIS-U.C.S.I. Milan: Franco Angeli, 2004.

Teti, Camillo, dir. *Firenze: L'assassino è ancora tra di noi.* 1986.

Theweleit, Klaus. *Male Fantasies.* Vol. 1, *Women, Floods, Bodies, History.* Trans. Steven Conway. Minneapolis: University of Minnesota Press, 1987.

Tithecott, Richard. *Of Men and Monsters: Jeffrey Dahmer and the Construction of the Serial Killer.* Madison: University of Wisconsin Press, 1997.

Torri, Maria Grazia. *Cogne un enigma svelato.* Bologna: Giraldi, 2007.

Trillin, Calvin. *Killings.* New York: Ticknor and Fields, 1984.

Tronci, Albarosa Macrì. "Regionalismo, identità nazionale e vocazione europea: un prezioso sistema di forze." *Otto/Novecento* 26, no. 3 (2002): 129–144.

Tulante, Merial. "Italia Mia? National Identity in the Novels of Sebastiano Vassalli." *Forum for Modern Language Studies* 45, no. 3 (2009): 337–350.

Tullio Giordana, Marco, dir. *La meglio gioventù.* 2003.

Tuttle, Frank, dir. *This Gun for Hire.* 1942.

Turing, Alan. "Computing Machinery and Intelligence." *Mind* 59 (1950): 433–460. http://loebner.net/Prizef/TuringArticle.html, accessed June 13, 2011.

Uricchio, William. "Storage, Simultaneity, and the Media Technologies of Modernity." In *Allegories of Communication: Intermedial Concerns from Cinema to the Digital,* ed. Jan Olsson and John Fullerton, 123–138. Eastleigh, UK: John Libbey, 2004.

Uricchio, William, and Susanne Kinnebrock, eds. *Media Cultures*. Heidelberg: Universitätsverlag Winter, 2006.

Vassalli, Sebastiano. *Archeologia del presente*. Turin: Einaudi, 2001.

Vehbiu, Ardian, and Rando Devole. *La scoperta dell'Albania: gli albanesi second i mass media*. Milan: Paoline, 1996.

Verasani, Grazia. *Quo vadis, baby?* Milan: A. Mondadori, 2004.

Vereni, Piero. *Identità catodiche: Rappresentazioni mediatiche di appartenenze collettive*. Rome: Meltemi, 2008.

Verga, Giovanni. *Tutte le novelle*. Milan: Mondadori, 1985.

Vermandere, Dieter, Monica Jansen, and Inge Lanslots, eds., *Noir de noir: un'indagine pluridisciplinare*. Bruxelles and New York: Peter Lang, 2010.

Vernant, Jean-Pierre, and Marcel Detienne. *Cuisine of Sacrifice among the Greeks*. Trans. Paula Wissing. Chicago: University of Chicago Press, 1989.

Veronesi, Sandro. *Caos calmo*. Milan: Bompiani, 2005.

———. *La forza del passato*. Milan: Bompiani, 2000.

Vighi, Fabio. "Unravelling Moretti's (Political) Unconscious: The Abyss of the Subject in *La Stanza del figlio*." *Journal of Romance Studies* 3, no. 2 (2003): 79–94.

Vinci, Simona. *Dei bambini non si sa niente*. Turin: Einaudi, 1997.

———. *In tutti i sensi amore*. Turin: Einaudi, 1999.

Virilio, Paul. *La bomba informatica*. Milan: Cortina, 2000.

Wagner-Pacifici, Robin. *The Aldo Moro Morality Play: Terrorism as Social Drama*. Chicago: University of Chicago Press, 1986.

Walkowitz, Judith. *The City of Dreadful Delight: Narratives of Sexual Danger in Late-Victorian London*. Chicago: University of Chicago Press, 1992.

Watney, Simon. *Policing Desire: Pornography, AIDS, and the Media*. London: Methuen Press, 1987.

West, Robin. *Narrative, Authority and the Law*. Ann Arbor: University of Michigan Press, 1993.

Williams, Linda. "Body Genres." In *The Oxford Guide to Film Studies*, ed. John Hill, Pamela Gibson, Richard Dyer, E. Ann Kaplan, and Paul Willemen, 339–341. New York: Oxford University Press, 1998.

———. "An Eye for an Eye." *Sight and Sound* 4, no. 4 (1994): 4–16.

———. "Film Bodies: Gender, Genre, and Excess." *Film Quarterly* 44, no. 4 (1991): 2–13.

———. "When the Woman Looks." In *The Dread of Difference*, ed. Barry Grant, 15–34. Austin: University of Texas Press, 1996.

Williams, Patricia. "On Being the Object of Property." In *Theorizing Feminism: Parallel Trends in the Humanities and Social Sciences*, ed. Anne C. Herrmann and Abigail J. Stewart, 198–213. Boulder, Colo.: Westview Press, 1994.

Williams, Raymond. *Television: Technology and Form*. Hanover, N.H.: Wesleyan University Press, 1974.

Wirth-Cauchon, Janet. *Women and Borderline Personality Disorder*. New Brunswick, N.J.: Rutgers University Press, 2000.

Wood, Mary. *Italian Cinema*. New York: Berg, 2005.

Wright, Steve. "A Love Born of Hate: Autonomous Rap in Italy." *Theory, Culture & Society* 17, no. 3 (2000): 117–135.

"Wu Ming Audiotheque." http://www.wumingfoundation.com/suoni/audiotheque
.htm, accessed June 15, 2009.

Yagher, Kevin, and Alan Smithee, dir. *Hellrasier: Bloodline*. 1996.

Young, Elizabeth. "*The Silence of the Lambs* and the Flaying of Feminist Theory."
Camera Obscura 27 (1991): 5–35.

Zabala, Santiago. "'Weak Thought' and the Reduction of Violence: A Dialogue with
Gianni Vattimo," trans. Yaakov Mascetti. *Common Knowledge* 8, no. 3 (2002):
452–463.

Zagarrio, Vito, ed. *Argento vivo: Il cinema di Dario Argento tra genere e autorialità*.
Venice: Marsilio, 2008.

Zambotti, Nazzareno. *Perché non sono diventato un serial killer: Autobiografia di
un uomo solo*. Turin: Einaudi, 2003.

Žižek, Slavoj. *Metastases of Enjoyment: Six Essays on Woman and Causality*. London: Verso, 1994.

INDEX

ELLEN NERENBERG is Professor of Italian Studies and Feminist, Gender, and Sexuality Studies at Wesleyan University. Her book *Prison Terms: Representing Confinement during and after Italian Fascism* was awarded the Howard R. Marraro Prize by the Modern Language Association for the best publication on an Italian subject in the field of either Italian Studies or Comparative Literature in 2002. She has published on the cinema of Vittorio De Sica, Gianni Amelio, and Dario Argento.